SHAKESPEARE JAHRBUCH

BAND 157

DEUTSCHE SHAKESPEARE-GESELLSCHAFT

SHAKESPEARE JAHRBUCH

herausgegeben von

SABINE SCHÜLTING

in Verbindung mit

NORBERT GREINER, STEPHAN LAQUÉ,
FELIX SPRANG und LENA STEVEKER

Band 157/2021

ALFRED KRÖNER VERLAG STUTTGART

Wissenschaftlicher Beirat

LUKAS ERNE (Université de Genève)
EWAN FERNIE (Shakespeare Institute, University of Birmingham)
MARTA GIBIŃSKA (Uniwersytet Jagielloński, Kraków)
DIANA HENDERSON (Massachusetts Institute of Technology)
TON HOENSELAARS (Universiteit Utrecht)
VERENA LOBSIEN (Humboldt-Universität zu Berlin)
ANDREAS MAHLER (Freie Universität Berlin)
ÁNGEL-LUIS PUJANTE (Universidad de Murcia)
HANNA SCOLNICOV (Tel-Aviv University)
JYOTSNA G. SINGH (Michigan State University)
NATHALIE VIENNE-GUERRIN (Université Paul Valéry Montpellier 3)

Mitglieder der Deutschen Shakespeare-Gesellschaft erhalten das Jahrbuch unentgeltlich. Anmeldungen zur Mitgliedschaft bei der Geschäftsstelle der Deutschen Shakespeare-Gesellschaft, Windischenstraße 4–6, 99423 Weimar.

GESAMTREDAKTION des Jahrbuchs: Prof. Dr. Sabine Schülting, Institut für Englische Philologie, Freie Universität Berlin, Habelschwerdter Allee 45, 14195 Berlin (sabine.schuelting@fu-berlin.de). Redaktionsassistenz: Dr. Kareen Seidler (Berlin).

Wir danken für die Förderung durch die Freie Universität Berlin.

Shakespeare Jahrbuch Band 157/2021
herausgegeben von Sabine Schülting in Verbindung mit
Norbert Greiner, Stephan Laqué, Felix Sprang und Lena Steveker
Stuttgart: Kröner 2021
ISSN: 1430-2527
ISBN: 978-3-520-95002-4

© 2021 by Alfred Kröner Verlag Stuttgart
Printed in Germany · Alle Rechte vorbehalten
Gesamtherstellung: Friedrich Pustet Regensburg

Tanz

Es entbehrt nicht einer gewissen Ironie, dass 'Shakespeare und Tanz' just in dem Jahr auf dem Programm der Jahrestagung der Shakespeare-Gesellschaft hätte stehen sollen, in dem das öffentliche Tanzen fast durchgängig verboten war und auch (Tanz)Theater-Inszenierungen abgesagt werden mussten. Aufgrund der Corona-Pandemie konnten unsere Tagungen nicht vor Ort stattfinden, und die Frühjahrstagung musste ganz ausfallen. So ist es umso erfreulicher, dass viele der Wissenschaftler*innen, die im Frühjahr gewissermaßen zum Tanz hätten bitten und vortragen wollen, ihre Aufsätze für das *Jahrbuch* eingereicht haben; hinzu kommen weitere Beiträge, die auf den Call for Papers reagiert haben. Gemeinsam zeigen sie mit großem Nachdruck, dass 'Shakespeare und Tanz' derzeit ein außerordentlich dynamisches Forschungsfeld ist, das einen zentralen, aber häufig vernachlässigten Aspekt des frühneuzeitlichen Dramas und Theaters in den Blick rückt. Die Aufsätze betrachten faszinierende Adaptionen der Stücke in Tanztraditionen und -genres aus verschiedenen historischen und kulturellen Kontexten, vom Ritus über das klassische Ballett bis zum modernen Tanztheater. Darüber hinaus arbeiten sie die kulturellen und politischen Funktionen und Implikationen des Tanzes sowie der tänzerischen und choreographischen Bearbeitungen der Shakespeare-Stücke heraus. Die Auseinandersetzung mit dem Tanz erschließt überraschende neue Facetten und Bedeutungsvarianten der Dramen und lotet das mediale Spannungsfeld zwischen Sprache, Musik und Bewegung aus.

Sabine Schülting

Call for Papers

Der 159. Band des *Jahrbuchs* (2023) wird dem Rahmenthema "Shakespeares Odysseen" gewidmet sein. Beiträge sollten bis zum 30. April 2022 an die Herausgeberin (sabine.schuelting@fu-berlin.de) geschickt werden. Weitere Informationen finden Sie auf der Website der Shakespeare-Gesellschaft.

Vorstand der Deutschen Shakespeare-Gesellschaft

Ehrenpräsident: SIR KENNETH BRANAGH

Präsidentin: PROF. DR. CLAUDIA OLK (München)
Vizepräsident: PROF. DR. ROLAND WEIDLE (Bochum)
Schatzmeister: HARTMUT KRUSE (Erfurt)

PROF. DR. WERNER BRÖNNIMANN (St. Gallen)
PROF. DR. MARIA EISENMANN (Würzburg)
PROF. DR. ANNE ENDERWITZ (Berlin)
DR. DIETER FUCHS (Wien)
KARL-MATTHIAS KLAUSE (Washington/Berlin)
DR. VANESSA SCHORMANN (München)
PROF. DR. FELIX SPRANG (Siegen)

Ex officio
DR. BETTINA BOECKER (Stellvertretende Leiterin der Shakespeare-Forschungs-Bibliothek München)
DIETMAR DIECKMANN (Kulturdezernent der Stadt Bochum)
DR. REINHARD LAUBE (Direktor der Herzogin Anna Amalia Bibliothek Weimar)
JULIA MIEHE (Stadtkulturdirektorin der Stadt Weimar)
JOHAN SIMONS (Intendant des Schauspielhauses Bochum)
PROF. DR. SABINE SCHÜLTING (Herausgeberin des *Shakespeare Jahrbuchs*)
HASKO WEBER (Generalintendant des Deutschen Nationaltheaters Weimar)

Die Adresse der Deutschen Shakespeare-Gesellschaft:
Windischenstraße 4–6
99423 Weimar
Telefon/Fax (0 36 43) 90 40 76

Website der Deutschen Shakespeare-Gesellschaft:
http://www.shakespeare-gesellschaft.de

Inhaltsverzeichnis

AUFSÄTZE: TANZ

Shakespeare and Dance
  (BARBARA RAVELHOFER) 13
Wondrous Motion: Recovering Dance from *The Tempest*
  (LYNSEY MCCULLOCH) 31
Licence to Speak: Gender and Masking in Shakespearean Dance Scenes
  (EMILY WINEROCK) 46
Romeo und Julia: die Tragödie als Ballett (IRIS JULIA BÜHRLE) 65
Dance of Death: Hitler and the Morris Men (RICHARD WILSON) 85
Macbeth Dances in the Zār Ritual:
  The Significance of Dancing in an Iranian Adaptation of *Macbeth*
  (MOHAMMADREZA HASSANZADEH JAVANIAN) 110
Performing *Macbeth* in India's Endangered Sanskrit Theatre Art
  of *Kutiyattam* (THEA BUCKLEY) 124
Movement, Music and Silence in Cheek by Jowl's *Measure for Measure*,
  The Winter's Tale and *Périclès, Prince de Tyr* (LINDA MCJANNET) 141
"Like an old tale": *The Winter's Tale* on the Balletic Stage
  (JONAS KELLERMANN)... 162
Von Shakespeare zum Ballett und zurück – Der intermediale Blick
  auf eine polydirektionale Shakespeare-Adaption:
  Christopher Wheeldons *The Winter's Tale*
  (MARIA MARCSEK-FUCHS) 180

THEATERSCHAU
Shakespeare auf deutschsprachigen Bühnen 2019/2020
(Gesamtredaktion: Norbert Greiner und Felix Sprang)

Spektakel und Drastik: Shakespeare im Norden (UTE BERNS) 201
Kann das Theater nach Hause kommen? *Romeo und Julia* im Chat,
  Hamlet kurz vor dem Lockdown, Berliner Shakespeare *on demand*
  und Stimmen aus leeren Theatern (LUKAS LAMMERS) 203
"Das ist keine Komödie mehr!" Theater in NRW erteilen Absage
  an die unerträgliche Leichtigkeit des Scheins (SARAH BRIEST,
  JAN MOSCH, SARA TUCKWELL, ROLAND WEIDLE und JAN WILLING) .. 208
Menschliche und familiäre Abgründe an der Corona-Kante:
  Lady Macbeth von Mzensk und *Otello* an der Oper Frankfurt
  (FELIX SPRANG) 219
Künstlerglück und Künstlerpech: Theaterschau Österreich 2019/2020
  (LUDWIG SCHNAUDER) 227
Kritische Rücksprache mit Shakespeare: "Zwei wuchtig lahme Stunden"
  in Bern und ein "Shakespeare-Abend der Sonderklasse" in Zürich
  (NORBERT GREINER) 232
Verzeichnis der Shakespeare-Inszenierungen der Spielzeit 2019/2020
  (BETTINA BOECKER und MARIETTA WENNING) 238

BÜCHERSCHAU
(Gesamtredaktion: Stephan Laqué und Lena Steveker)

Andy Amato, *The Ethical Imagination in Shakespeare and Heidegger*
  (CHRISTOPHER CROSBIE) 247
Thomas Cartelli, *Reenacting Shakespeare in the Shakespeare Aftermath:*
  The Intermedial Turn and Turn to Embodiment (RUDOLPH GLITZ) 248
Claude Fretz, *Dreams, Sleep, and Shakespeare's Genres*
  (JOACHIM FRENK) 250
Marta Gibińska, Małgorzata Grzegorzewska,
  Jacek Fabiszak and Agnieszka Żukowska eds,
  This Treasure of Theatre. Essays in Honour of Professor Jerzy Limon
  (SABINE SCHÜLTING) 252
Julián Jiménez Heffernan, *Limited Shakespeare: The Reason of Finitude*
  (CHRISTIAN KRUG) 255

Katherine Hennessey and Margaret Litvin eds,
  Shakespeare & the Arab World (MARCUS HARTNER) 256
Rory Loughnane and Edel Semple eds, *Staged Normality*
  in Shakespeare's England (ANNE ENDERWITZ) 258
Eric S. Mallin, *Reading Shakespeare in the Movies:*
  Non-Adaptations and Their Meaning (ELISABETH BRONFEN) 262
Lindsay Ann Reid, *Shakespeare's Ovid and the Spectre of the Medieval*
  (WOLFRAM KELLER) 263
James Shapiro, *Shakespeare in a Divided America* (DORIS FELDMANN) ... 266
Tiffany Stern ed., *Rethinking Theatrical Documents*
  in Shakespeare's England (LENA STEVEKER) 267

BERICHTE

Tätigkeitsbericht der Präsidentin (Frühjahr 2020) (CLAUDIA OLK) 273
"*Romeo und Julia*": Online Herbsttagung, 20. – 22. November 2020
  (JONAS KELLERMANN) 277

NACHRUFE

Zum Gedenken an den Shakespeare-Übersetzer
  Frank Günther (1947–2020) 281
Catherine Belsey (1940–2021) 286

Register 287

Über die Autorinnen und Autoren 297

Martin-Lehnert-Preis 301

Aufsätze:
Tanz

Shakespeare and Dance

BARBARA RAVELHOFER

> First my fear, then my curtsy, last my speech.
> (2H4, Epil., 1)[1]

Shakespeare was a deeply musical writer. A pulse beats in his lines, from the lyricism of his blank verse in *Richard II* to the versatile rhythmic patternings of his romances. When Lear exclaims "Never, never, never, never, never" (5.3.284),[2] pointed stresses on syllables that should go unmarked in iambic pentameter voice a railing against fate. The plodding start of a line in Sonnet 50 echoes a sullen horse's movements and the foul mood of its rider. Rhythm ticks its progress as Sonnet 12 begins "When I do count the clock that tells the time", and in Sonnet 128, fingers are dancing with the leaping jacks on the virginal. It should come as no surprise that Shakespeare was so drawn to dance: as a medium that shows rhythm in movement, it complements the speaking voice. To readers of this article I propose an experiment: assume the role of any Shakespearean character, and speak a set of lines while attempting not to make the slightest movement whatsoever. Do you find the experience counterintuitive? To underline what you say by a gesture, a movement of the head, or some other physical expression, be it ever so small, is a common, natural human impulse. From an anthropological point of view,

> dancing exercises a fundamental sensory creativity whose nuance and range distinguishes humans from other living organisms. This creativity is one that finds expression in an ability to notice and recreate patterns of movement and so nurture mutually life-enabling relationships with whomever or whatever sustains our ongoing human living.[3]

---

1   William Shakespeare, *King Henry IV Part 2*, ed. by James C. Bulman. The Arden Shakespeare, Third Series (London: Bloomsbury Arden, 2016).
2   Folio text. If not indicated otherwise, all quotations are from William Shakespeare, *The Complete Works*, ed. by Stanley Wells and Gary Taylor. The Oxford Shakespeare, 2nd ed. (Oxford: Clarendon Press, 2005).
3   Kimerer LaMothe, *Why We Dance: A Philosophy of Bodily Becoming* (New York: Columbia University Press, 2015), 3.

It is fit that the actor delivering the epilogue of *2 Henry IV*, combating stage fright, addresses the audience with a gesture even *before* beginning to speak. "If my tongue cannot entreat you to acquit me, will you command me to use my legs? And yet that were but light payment, to dance out of your debt" (16–18), the actor offers, falling into a jig, a lively dance that customarily concluded plays in the commercial theatres of Shakespeare's time. Shakespeare's work throbs with the excitement of dance rhythms, even where it is least expected. As Caius Martius Coriolanus glumly appears at the house of Aufidius to offer his service to his arch-enemy, the latter gushes,

> *Aufidius*: I loved the maid I married; never man
> Sighed truer breath. But that I see thee here,
> Thou noble thing, more dances my rapt heart
> Than when I first my wedded mistress saw
> Bestride my threshold.
> (*Cor*, 4.5.115–119)

Fulsome welcome indeed for the hammer of the Volscians. Aufidius's martial epithalamion recalls lines spoken earlier by Martius to his general Cominius in the heat of battle:

> O, let me clip ye
> In arms as sound as when I wooed, in heart
> As merry as when our nuptial day was done,
> And tapers burnt to bedward!
> (1.7.29–32)

Cominius greets this hearty assertion of loyalty, akin to the most solemn vows that can be offered in Roman society, with overwhelmed relief ("flower of warriors!", 1.7.33). Act 4 sees a giddy reversal, with the roles of speaker and addressee curiously inverted. Now the general woos in erotic language the soldier who has, in crossing the threshold to Aufidius's home, broken his former symbolic marriage vow to Rome. Coriolanus has come again as a conqueror, taking in Aufidius's "rapt" heart, or so Aufidius says, and possibilities are racing – dancing? – in the mind of the Volscian leader whose language is at once calculating and overly cordial. Addressing the guest as a "noble thing" smacks of coldness, at odds with the hyperbolic register of loving courtship, and gestures forward to the way in which Aufidius will go on to instrumentalize and ultimately destroy Coriolanus.

In *Coriolanus*, dancing as a metaphor reveals the undercurrents of relationships. In other plays, the names of particular dance genres conjure up mental worlds: a "canary" is a wine from the Canary islands (to which Falstaff is partial) but also a sprightly dance, *canario*, with a characteristic step sequence (a small slide forward and a small slide backwards, followed by a stamp, all executed with the same foot), which enables Shakespeare to pun on Mediterranean flair and *joie de vivre*.[4] In *All's Well That Ends Well*, Lafeu promises to the ailing king

> a medicine
> That's able to breathe life into a stone,
> Quicken a rock, and make you dance canary
> With sprightly fire and motion
>
> (2.1.71–74);

and indeed, the patient's interest is sufficiently piqued to allow Lafeu to introduce the healer Helena.

Dances mentioned – and performed – in Shakespeare's work comprise genres that must have been specially choreographed for the stage, such as those for *The Tempest*'s wedding masque. Others would have resonated with audiences from their own practice, for the plays also refer to many social dances fashionable in early modern England, such as canarios, galliards (*cinquepace*), voltas and corantos, as well as particular steps or formations, such as slides or rounds.[5] My discussion will first turn to early dance in historical context, and then to actual performance practice and its implications for editors of Shakespeare's plays.

---

4   The Host "will to my honest knight Falstaff, and drink canary with him", upon which Ford mutters aside, "I think I shall drink in pipe-wine first with him: I'll make him dance." (*The Merry Wives of Windsor*, ed. by G. Melchiori. The Arden Shakespeare, Third Series [London: Thomson, 2000], 3.2.78–81).

5   For the most recent comprehensive assessment of historical dance practice, see especially the excellent contributions by Nona Monahin, Emily Winerock, Roger Clegg, Jennifer Nevile and Anne Daye in Lyndsey McCulloch and Brandon Shaw (eds), *The Oxford Handbook of Shakespeare and Dance* (Oxford: Oxford University Press, 2019).

Dance Cultures in Early Modern Europe

Figure 1. *Volta* danced by Stefan Haberl and Doris Von der Aue, *The Sacred and the Profane*, Durham, 9 July 2016.[6] Photo: Lee Dobson. Copyright B. Ravelhofer.

Famously, Queen Elizabeth I learnt "to dance high" "in the Italian manner", and allegedly exercised herself in the morning with[6] galliards.[7] She also had an Italian instructor, Jasper Gaffoyne. In her youth, the French ambassador De Maisse reported, the queen

> danced very well, and composed measures and music, and had played them herself and danced them [...] without doubt she is a mistress of the art, having learnt in the Italian manner to dance high [...] they called her "the Florentine".[8]

---

6 For a video recording of the show, see https://www.youtube.com/watch?time_continue=210 6&v=GHxZ8Su6yLQ&feature=emb_logo; for the full volta, from 33:20, last access 1 August 2020.

7 John Stanhope's letter to Lord Talbot (1589) alludes to "six or seven galliards in a morning"; qtd. in Alan Brissenden, *Shakespeare and the Dance* (London: Macmillan, 1981), 5.

8 André Hurault, Sieur de Maisse, *A Journal* [...] *Anno Domini 1597*, ed. by G. B. Harrison and R. A. Jones (Bloomsbury: Nonesuch, 1931), 95.

De Maisse's extraordinary observation claims the queen even composed music *and* choreographies (one meaning of 'measure' at the time) herself.[9] The athletic Italian style remained in fashion under the early Stuarts; in 1604, Henry Prince of Wales impressed onlookers with sprightly yet decorous "caprioles", i.e. jumps with nimble foot movements in mid-air, possibly inspired by Italian masters such as Cesare Negri and Fabritio Caroso, who were celebrated beyond the Italian-speaking sphere.[10] The ability to compose choreographies or perform elaborate capers suggests both extensive instruction and stamina. Good dancing was certainly considered an important accomplishment for elite self-presentation; yet dancing schools were widely available to teach "lavoltas high and swift corantos" (*Henry V*, 3.6.33).[11] Shakespeare's works reflect a wide spectrum of social situations and levels of attainment across all levels of society, including the children of local townspeople in *The Merry Wives of Windsor*. This in turn mirrors a world with a deep kinetic grammar, derived from a rich dance repertory and its associated vocabulary.

And so, Beatrice in *Much Ado About Nothing* compares humanity's progress from courtship to the married state in terms of dancing:

> [...] wooing, wedding and repenting is as a Scotch jig, a measure and a cinque-pace. The first suit is hot and hasty, like a Scotch jig, and full as fantastical; the wedding mannerly-modest as a measure, full of state and ancientry; and then comes Repentance, and with his bad legs falls into the cinque-pace faster and faster, till he sink into his grave. (2.1.64–70)[12]

Often, seventeenth-century dance suites will begin more slowly and, after forms of mixed tempo, end with a rapid, short bravura piece. Beatrice has sternly redirected the flow, thus indicating that the endgame of marriage may surprise

---

9   Barbara Ravelhofer, "Dancing at the Court of Queen Elizabeth", in Christa Jansohn (ed.), *Queen Elizabeth I: Past and Present* (Münster: LIT, 2004), 101–115, at 104.

10 Judy Smith and Ian Gatiss, "What Did Prince Henry Do with His Feet on Sunday 19 August 1604?", *Early Music*, 14:2 (1986), 198–207. The authors propose that Henry may have perused Cesare Negri's *Nuove inventioni di balli* (1604) and Fabritio Caroso's *Nobiltà di dame* (1600). Copies derived from the Royal Library are mentioned in seventeenth-century catalogues of the British Library. The hypothesis requires that they were indeed available to Henry, and that Henry did use them for dancing rather than acquiring them as a bibliophile.

11 William Shakespeare, *King Henry V*, ed. by Andrew Gurr. The New Cambridge Shakespeare (Cambridge: Cambridge University Press, 1992).

12 William Shakespeare, *Much Ado About Nothing*, ed. by Claire McEachern. The Arden Shakespeare, Third Series (London: Bloomsbury, 2016).

expectations. The cinquepace (*cinque passi, cinq pas*) was synonymously used for galliard, in which a dancer improvised on a basic five-step sequence over six beats: lower, introductory jumps in beats one, two and three; a vigorous leap over beats four and five; landing on the feet in beat six; and beginning again, starting with the other foot. Galliard variations survive in Renaissance choreographies for both men and women. As the Florentine master Lutio Compasso, active in the mid-sixteenth century, asserted, "the Gagliarda is extremely fashionable and there is neither lady nor gentlewoman who doesn't enjoy it or who doesn't dance it".[13] The most exhaustive known compendium of the galliard-heavy Italianate style which de Maisse had seen is the *Mastro da Ballo* (1614) by Ercole Santucci, a dancing master from Perugia who catered for patrons in the papal state.[14] 214 rules explain individual steps and comportment – how to greet each other, how to manage sword and cape while dancing, and so on – before the author moves on to actual step sequences. Altogether 360 longer variations follow on the *cinque passi*, and 267 examples of how to dance one *tempo* (the six-beat measure) of *gagliarda*.[15] Here is a short instruction for a lady's *cinque passi*:

> Havendo il Piè sinistro indietro in Passo naturale, farà con esso un passo naturale inanzi, voltando un poco il fianco sinistro inanzi, poi col destro darà un sottopiede paro al sinistro, et inalborando il sinistro inanzi, farà un passo in aria, et inalborando il destro inanzi farà una Cadenza, e cosi potrà fare per contrario.
>
> [Starting from a natural standing position with the left foot behind, with more weight on the right foot, she will step forward with the left foot, moving a little her left side forward, then she will undercut the left foot with the right foot, and placing the left foot, which is in front, firmly on the ground, she will jump in the air, and then, placing the right foot firmly on the ground, she will do a cadenza, and then do the same in this manner to the contrary (i.e. starting with the right foot).][16]

---

13 "So che la maggior parte delli intretenimenti che si fanno il ballar, de la Gagliarda si costuma assai, ne signora: ò gentil' donna che sia è chi non sen' diletti, ò non balli." (Lutio Compasso, *Ballo della Gagliarda* [1560], intr. by Barbara Sparti [Freiburg: fa-gisis, 1995], sig. Aij^v–Aiij^r, Sparti's trans., 15.)

14 Ercole Santucci, *Mastro da Ballo*, Carina Ari Library, Stockholm, no shelfmark. Dated 1614 by the scribe.

15 Ercole Santucci Perugino, *Mastro da Ballo (Dancing-Master) 1614*, ed. by Barbara Sparti (Hildesheim: Olms, 2004), 65.

16 "Regola Prima" in Perugino (2004), 385, silently expanded, u/v spelling normalized; my liberal trans. Thanks to Lieven Baert for a discussion of the passage.

Santucci's work represents an extreme case in the surviving body of Italian dance manuals. Yet even if dancers did not attempt the highest levels of technical sophistication, a galliard was always a physical challenge. If imprudent individuals overexerted themselves, the ostentatious display might either peter out in a single slow step, *passo grave*, or indeed the "grave", as captured in Beatrice's double entendre. The Arden 3 editor thinks actual dance might accompany Beatrice's remarks about marriage: she might skip a few steps of Scotch jig, measure or *cinquepace* to illustrate her words.[17] In theory this is possible but would require some physical effort especially for the *cinquepace* elements. For a modern audience, it might help to see the lines fortified with some pantomime; Clément Poirée's 2012 production at London's Globe Theatre did. In Shakespeare's time, there might have been the risk of over-egging the pun with redundant movement, treating clued-up spectators as if they were slow on the uptake. The case for an actual demonstration of galliard variations seems stronger for *Twelfth Night*, where Sir Andrew Aguecheek is relentlessly teased by Sir Toby to prove that his leg has indeed been "formed under the star of a galliard" (1.3.127–128).

Social dances required different levels of mastery. Some of the examples surviving in Renaissance Europe attest to remarkable capacity on the part of the performer, as demanded by Santucci's most challenging variations. Others are easier. English 'measures' gravitate towards the sedate end of the spectrum. Shakespeare makes prominent use of them, in both a performative and figurative sense. In dancing theory, 'measure' emerged in fifteenth-century Italian dance treatises as *misura*, meaning 'mode' (such as tempo), 'dance' or 'sense of proportion'.[18] In evolving musical practice over the sixteenth and seventeenth centuries, *misura* was about keeping time, and thus related to French *mésure*, Italian *battuta/tatto* and English *beat*. The language of early modern musical theory sustained a sense of physical motion: beating with the hand, lowering the hand or foot, or the beating of the heart all indicated tempo and rhythm, which implied that keeping time comes natural to the human body.[19] As proportion is a correlative to decorum, *misura* was from the start not only quantitative but also qualitative, corresponding to ideals of moderation as endorsed in Renaissance rhetoric and

---

17 Claire McEachern, "Introduction", in Shakespeare (2016), 81.
18 Domenico da Piacenza, *De arte saltandi*, Paris, BN f. Ital.972, transcribed in A. William Smith (ed.), *Fifteenth-Century Dance and Music: Twelve Transcribed Italian Treatises and Collection in the Tradition of Domenico da Piacenza*. Vol. 1 (Stuyvesant: Pendragon Press, 1995), 17.
19 "Measure", in Graham Strahle, *An Early Music Dictionary: Musical Terms from British Sources, 1500–1740* (Cambridge: Cambridge University Press, 1995); Roger Grant, *Beating Time and Measuring Music in the Early Modern Era* (Oxford: Oxford University Press, 2014), 16.

ethics; after all, Latin *mens* (mind, character, conscience, memory, reason) was etymologically related, and this sense is especially palpable in later developments of the term. In Shakespeare's time, the meanings of the English noun 'measure' comprised, among others: (self-)control and balance; behaviour appropriate to the situation; and cadence and rhythm in poetry, music and dance. Furthermore, 'measure' conjured up slower, simpler processional dances of a dignified nature – but could also, confusingly, mean "any dance".[20] In sword-fighting onstage, the distance between opponents was "measured" by a fencer's reach when lunging.[21] This bewildering range of meanings offered many opportunities to Shakespeare for extended punning.

> *King*: Say to her, we have measured many miles
> To tread a measure with her on this grass.
> *Boyet*: They say that they have measured many a mile
> To tread a measure with you on this grass.
> *Rosaline*: It is not so. Ask them how many inches
> Is in one mile? If they have measured many,
> The measure then of one is easily told.
> *Boyet*: If to come hither you have measured miles,
> And many miles, the Princess bids you tell
> How many inches doth fill up one mile.
> *Berowne*: Tell her we measure them by weary steps.
> *Boyet*: She hears herself.
> *Rosaline*: How many weary steps,
> Of many weary miles you have o'ergone,
> Are numbered in the travel of one mile?
> *Berowne*: We number nothing that we spend for you.
> (*LLL*, 5.2.184–198)[22]

The exchange in relatively regular iambic pentameter is beautifully dance-like: two lines are parried with another two; three with three. Each couple of speak-

---

20 Robert Mullally, "*Measure* as a Choreographic Term in the Stuart Masque", *Dance Research* 16:1 (1998), 67–73.
21 "Measure", in Alan Dessen, *A Dictionary of Stage Directions in English Drama, 1580–1642* (Cambridge: Cambridge University Press, 1999).
22 William Shakespeare, *Love's Labour's Lost*, ed. by H. R. Woudhuysen. The Arden Shakespeare, Third Series (London: Nelson, 1998); see also Woudhuysen's introduction to this edition, 28–29.

ers delivers verbally what an early modern courtly choreography might have required as a standard: mirroring a partner's figure by repeating it, or mirroring a step sequence started with the left foot by another started with the right. The king and his men adopt the rhetoric of *polyptoton* – a word's root redeployed with different endings – which encourages the polysemy of 'measure' as (a) reckoning the miles in one's travel, or (b) stately dance in a masque. As Charles Forker observes about *anthimeria*, a technique of converting nouns into verbs, the device "energizes the verse in notable ways", which "can convey impatience".[23] This surely applies to the Muscovite masquers who have come to court their ladies, only to find a cold reception. The play's Arden editor finds that its men are fascinated by numbers, which almost assume the importance of minor characters; numbers in themselves are, of course, "the stuff of poetry, which is made out of metrical numbers and feet".[24] Winding through the exchange, the word 'measure' is such a significant performer, charged with extra kinetic force. By wilfully ignoring the lords' effort at wit, Rosaline takes their numerical obsession at its most literal, cutting the high-flown rhetoric of courtship down to inch size and exposing its silliness. Perhaps Berowne learns from this, for his riposte foreshadows Antony's "there's beggary in the love that can be reckoned" (*AC*, 1.1.15).[25] The scene turns out to be an object lesson in 'measure': integrity of character shows in keeping due proportion, which requires more than verbal ostentation or the ability to count.

'Measure' as a linch-pin of interpersonal capacity occurs also in the history plays, and Shakespeare makes intriguing use of it to chart Hal's development. Warwick expresses his faith in Hal as follows:

> The Prince will in the perfectness of time
> Cast off his followers, and their memory
> Shall as a pattern or a measure live,
> By which his grace must mete the lives of other,
> Turning past evils to advantages.
> (*2H4*, 4.3.74–78)[26]

---

23   William Shakespeare, *King Richard II*, ed. by Charles Forker. The Arden Shakespeare, Third Series (London: Bloomsbury, 2002), 89.
24   Woudhuysen, "Introduction", in Shakespeare (1998), 28–30.
25   Antony here replies to Cleopatra's question, "if it be love indeed, tell me how much" (1.1.14).
26   Shakespeare, ed. Bulman (2016).

This transformation to a solid pattern of measured maturity is redolent of dance movement – casting off, turning, meeting – as befits a character who is one of Shakespeare's most self-conscious performers. So how is Princess Catherine of France to understand King Henry's proposal?

> *King*: Marry, if you would put me to verses, or to dance for your sake, Kate, why, you undid me. For the one I have neither words nor measure, and for the other I have no strength in measure, yet a reasonable measure in strength. If I could win a lady at leapfrog, or by vaulting into my saddle with my armour on my back, under the correction of bragging be it spoken I should quickly leap into a wife.
>
> (*H5*, 5.2.127–133)

Neither as prince nor as king does Henry ever grace his audience with a soliloquy that might elucidate his heartfelt motivations. Here he already assumes the familiar "Kate" rather than a more formal address acknowledging her rank. Henry is either the honest plain-dealer, speaking to an individual rather than the role she inhabits, or pulls rank with condescension. An ability to dance (too) well is often associated with effeminacy or cowardice – Richard III's sneer at courtiers who have exchanged soldierly marches for nimble capers (1.1.8–12) comes to mind – and Henry here makes a remarkable effort to emphasize his manliness: vaulting onto a horse becomes the all-too-close prequel to the crude leaping 'into' a wife. Henry resorts to chiasmus, a figure of balance ("strength in measure" / "measure in strength"), which belies his assertion "I have neither words nor measure" for poetic diction. Henry's prose is at once clever and coarse, deliberately displaying art *and* artlessness. Through the *Henry IV* plays, Andrew Gurr observes, "Henry the actor […] learns the impossibility of establishing an honest relationship with anyone". When Henry woos Kate, Gurr views his "I love thee cruelly" (5.2.185) as "a neatly ambiguous sentiment for a 'plain soldier' who sees love as besieging maiden cities".[27] It depends very much on the actor whether the character will pull off these difficult lines or trip up.

---

27 Gurr, "Introduction", in Shakespeare (1992), 12, 16.

The English 'Measures'

As dances, English 'measures' survive in eight manuscripts of the mid-sixteenth to mid-seventeenth centuries. These include pieces such as *La Chemise, Spanioletta, The Measures of Heaven and Earth*, or the *French Levolto*, as well as a set of 'old measures', which generally comprises: the *Quadran Pavan, Turkeyloney*, the *Earl of Essex Measure, Tinternell*, the *Old Almain*, the *Queen's Almain, Cecilia Almain* (also known as *Madam Sicilia Pavan*) and the *Black Almain* (with time some of these evolved while others dropped out of the repertoire).[28] The manuscripts are often connected with London's Inns of Court; whether the 'measures' therefore reflect specific practice at the lawyers' revels or social repertory taught more widely in dancing schools remains a point of debate. In Britain, choreographic evidence before John Playford's *The English Dancing Master* (printed from 1651 onwards) is rare. No other group of step instructions survives in as many English manuscripts before the mid-seventeenth century. In manuscript circulation, the 'measures' also reached the English provinces, and they survived in variants in several early witnesses. These factors suggest a lasting practice in wider social circles. This would also be continuous with Beatrice's allusion to "measure full of state and ancientry".

Four of the 'measures' manuscripts are dated close to Shakespeare's time – the Dulwich MS (c. 1590s), the Willoughby MS (1594), John Ramsey's "Practise for Dauncinge", which formed part of a conduct book (1609), and a miscellany compiled by John Stow sometime between 1611 and 1621.[29] The *Black Almain* is a good example for a processional dance of couples, mentioned (with variations) in all but one of the above sources; in addition, a music score survives.[30] A fairly representative instruction was noted down by John Willoughby in 1594:

---

28 Robert Mullally, "More about the Measures", *Early Music* 22:3 (1994), 417–438.
29 Anne Daye and Jennifer Thorp, "English Measures Old and New: Dulwich College MS. XCIV/f.28", *Historical Dance* 4:3 (2018), 27–40; Willoughby MS, Taunton, Somerset Record Office, DD/O 55/7, item 36, transcribed in James Stokes and Ingrid Brainard, "'The Olde Measures' in the West Country: John Willoughby's Manuscript", *Records of Early English Drama* 17:2 (1992), 1–10; Ramsey, Bodleian Library MS Douce 280, fols 66a^v–66b^v; Stow, British Library MS Harl. 367, fols 178^r–179^v. See also D. R. Wilson, "Dancing in the Inns of Court", *Historical Dance* 2:5 (1986–87), 3–16; John Ward, "The English Measure", *Early Music* 14:1 (1986), 15–21; "Newly Devis'd Measures for Jacobean Masques", *Acta Musicologica* 60:2 (1988), 111–142; and "Apropos 'The Olde Measures'", *Records of Early English Drama* 18:1 (1993), 2–21.
30 Transcription in Wilson (1986–87), Stokes and Brainard (1992) and Daye and Thorp (2018). Score in London Royal College of Music, MS 1119, fol. 24^r; transcribed and ed. by Ian Payne,

> ffower doubles forwarde, parte handes, a double back one from an other, a double meetinge againe, a double on your lefte hande & an other on your righte, take both handes & goe A double round & traverse: 4: on your lefte hande, A double rounde & traverse fower on your righte[31]

John Ramsey's version keeps to the same scheme, at the end of which it tells the partners (who are looking at each other at this point) to "slyde downe" four steps.[32] Another manuscript of uncertain date instructs them to "hold hands and dance Snicke a pace once round about the hearth";[33] this could be interpreted as a 'slip' (as later in Playford's *The English Dancing Master*), *chassé à côté* or a gallop sideways – basically any step to the side, chased with the next step.[34]

The *Black Almain* is a simple dance that can be learnt within a very short time. As an experiment conducted in Durham Castle in 2018 proved, amateurs of average ability, many of them without any prior experience of early dance, were able to perform it after about ten minutes of rehearsal.[35] The *Black Almain* was also performed in 2016 by a different set of fully costumed amateurs who had received several weeks of instruction.[36] Both performances are documented in films and available online. They show that a dance of this technical level allows for much informal interaction, including conversation. Such modern productions cannot capture the behaviour of dancers in Shakespeare's London. What they demonstrate, however, is the *potential* for communication: if modern amateurs are able to talk during the *Black Almain*, then a better-trained early modern society would, in principle, have been capable of chatting or joking during a 'measure'. Renaissance antitheatricalists from John Stubbes to William Prynne regularly fulminated against especially mixed dancing as a form of indecent physical and moral exposure. Such vituperation makes particular sense if social dancing offered women an opportunity to meet, touch and (if the steps weren't too difficult) converse with men whom they would otherwise not have been able to approach, and vice versa.

The Almain in Britain, c. 1549–1675: A Dance Manual from Manuscript Sources (Aldershot: Ashgate, 2003), 201.
31 Stokes and Brainard (1992), 6–7.
32 Oxford, Bodleian Library MS Douce 280, fol. 66a[v], transcribed in Wilson (1986–87), 7.
33 London, Royal College of Music MS 1119, fol. 1[v], transcribed in Wilson (1986–87), 13.
34 My thanks to Lieven Baert for the discussion of "slides", French and otherwise.
35 Documentary *Souls of the North*, 10 November 2018, http://community.dur.ac.uk/reed.ne/?page_id=3961, see from 41:25, last access 1 August 2020.
36 *The Sacred and the Profane*, 10 July 2016, http://community.dur.ac.uk/reed.ne/?page_id=27, see from 35:00, last access 1 August 2020.

Some manuscript evidence underscores the sociable, improvisational nature of English repertory of the early seventeenth century. The *Pattricke Manuscript* records country dances which often allow for changes depending on the participants' preferences. *The Goddesses* is a dance "for 10 or more"; in another, a man may, when turning, salute his lady "if he likes her". *An Old Man with a Bed Full of Bones* invites a raise of the lady's arm ("if you please yo^u may turne her arme over her head"), and *Good Your Worship* provides "if you please you may prolong every one his part, like as in leading to the bottome". In *Step Stately*, the dancers form, unusually, a half moon, which can only work if the dancers communicate by watching, instructing, or adjusting to each other.[37] "As You Like It" seems to be the motto of many of these more informal dances. A relatively controlled choreography saw to a modicum of decorum while accommodating informal improvisation, and easy rules helped distracted dancers find back into the scheme. The *Pattricke Manuscript* gives us therefore an important clue for some unscripted dimensions of social dancing. This has implications for editors who attempt to script dance back into a playtext.

Editing Dance

The few and fragmentary choreographic witnesses, combined with the often improvisational nature of performance, make it very difficult to determine what exactly happens when characters are dancing in Shakespeare's plays. One scene from *Much Ado About Nothing* – the masque in Act 2 – illustrates the challenges for directors and editors. Claire McEachern's Arden 3 edition makes interventions in stage directions transparent where other editors silently implement them. Square brackets highlight McEachern's idea of the entry:

> *Enter Don Pedro, Claudio, Benedick, Balthasar*[, *masked, with a Drum, Margaret and Ursula,*] *and Don John*[, *Borachio and others. Music and dancing begin*].
>
> Don Pedro [*to Hero*]: Lady, will you walk a bout with your friend?
> Hero: So you walk softly, and look sweetly, and say nothing, I am yours for the walk; and especially when I walk away.

---

37 Pattricke Manuscript, also known as Lovelace Manuscript, Houghton Library, Harvard, MS Eng 1356, fols. 7^v, 9^v, 12^r, 19^r, 32^v. See also Carol Marsh, "The Lovelace Manuscript: A Preliminary Study", in Uwe Schlottermüller and Maria Richter (eds), *Morgenröte des Barock: Tanz im 17. Jahrhundert* (Freiburg: fa-gisis, 2004), 81–90.

Don Pedro:	With me in your company?
Hero:	I may say so, when I please.
Don Pedro:	And when please you to say so?
Hero:	When I like your favour – for God defend the lute should be like the case!
Don Pedro:	My visor is Philemon's roof: within the house is Jove.
Hero:	Why then, your visor should be thatched.
Don Pedro:	Speak low if you speak love. [*They move aside; Balthasar and Margaret come forward.*]
Balthasar:	Well, I would you did like me.
Margaret:	So would not I, for your own sake, for I have many ill qualities.
Balthasar:	Which is one?
Margaret:	I say my prayers aloud.
Balthasar:	I love you the better; the hearers may cry amen!
Margaret:	God match me with a good dancer!
Balthasar:	Amen!
Margaret:	And God keep him out of my sight when the dance is done! Answer, clerk.
Balthasar:	No more words; the clerk is answered. [*They move aside; Ursula and Antonio come forward.*]
Ursula:	I know you well enough; you are Signor Antonio.
Antonio:	At a word, I am not.
Ursula:	I know you by the waggling of your head.
Antonio:	To tell you true, I counterfeit him.
Ursula:	You could never do him so ill-well, unless you were the very man. Here's his dry hand up and down. You are he, you are he!
Antonio:	At a word, I am not.
Ursula:	Come, come, do you think I do not know you by your excellent wit? Can virtue hide itself? Go to, mum; you are he; graces will appear, and there's an end. [*They move aside; Benedick and Beatrice come forward.*]
Beatrice:	Will you not tell me who told you so?
Benedick:	No, you shall pardon me.
Beatrice:	Nor will you not tell me who you are?
Benedick:	Not now.
Beatrice:	That I was disdainful, and that I had my good wit out of *The Hundred Merry Tales*! Well, this was Signor Benedick that said so.
Benedick:	What's he?
Beatrice:	I am sure you know him well enough.
Benedick:	Not I, believe me.

Beatrice:	Did he never make you laugh?
Benedick:	I pray you, what is he?
Beatrice:	Why he is the prince's jester, a very dull fool; only his gift is in devising impossible slanders. None but libertines delight in him, and the commendation is not in his wit but in his villainy, for he both pleases men and angers them, and then they laugh at him and beat him. I am sure he is in the fleet; I would he had boarded me.
Benedick:	When I know the gentleman, I'll tell him what you say.
Beatrice:	Do, do. He'll but break a comparison or two on me, which, peradventure not marked, or not laughed at, strikes him into melancholy, and then there's a partridge wing saved, for the fool will eat no supper that night. We must follow the leaders.
Benedick:	In every good thing.
Beatrice:	Nay, if they lead to any ill I will leave them at the next turning.

Dance. Exeunt [all but Don John, Borachio and Claudio].

(2.1.76–140)

Are the speakers walking and having a chat, or are they dancing? The earliest witnesses of the scene leave this question open. The Folio (1623) has "*Maskers with a Drum*" among the characters entering at line 76. Neither the First Quarto (1600) nor the Folio offer any stage direction for dancing during these lines. Q1 gives "*Dance*" only once, *after* Beatrice's "I will leave them at the next turning" (sig. C^r); F provides "*Exeunt. Musicke for the dance*" at this point (105). Editors (and directors) have two possibilities:

1. The early witnesses are treated as authoritative, which means the couples are slowly advancing towards the position they will take in a subsequent dance.
2. Editors decide that the stage directions are not in line with what is actually happening on stage; in which case the couples may already be engaged in some form of dancing.

Recent editions incline to the latter solution. F. H. Mares (New Cambridge Shakespeare) inserts the explicit stage direction "*the dance begins*" as the couples enter the stage (2.1.61).[38] From a bibliographical point of view, the decision is viable because mismatched stage directions are not unusual in printing practice

---

38 William Shakespeare, *Much Ado About Nothing*, ed. by F. H. Mares. The New Cambridge Shakespeare, updated ed. (Cambridge: Cambridge University Press, 2003).

of the period.³⁹ Yet editors appear to be less interested in compositors; they base their rationale on *dance* rather than *text*, following Alan Brissenden's influential interpretation of the scene. The invitation to "walk a bout" may certainly be interpreted as a "round" or "turn" in a dance. As Brissenden goes on to argue, what follows is a pavan, "for in that elegant perambulation the couples can be side by side with hands linked at arm's length and the steps involve turns back and forth, retreats and advances, so that it is ideal for highlighting dramatic conversation". His suggestion is accepted to the letter in Arden 3.⁴⁰ Brissenden divides the above dialogue into four units, one per couple, with four exchanges of line per partner and a concluding sentence. These lines "are spoken as the dancers move"; for instance, Hero walks away as she says she does, and Don Pedro answers "with me in your company" when they come together again. Brissenden proposes a version of *Madam Sicilia Pavan* as particularly suitable because the dance in the scene must be "relatively slow, in duple time and with four or eight figures. A pavan is the obvious choice for the dance Shakespeare had in mind." Beatrice and Benedick have more lines than the previous couples, which might indicate that they have perhaps stopped dancing and are just bickering; "if there were a dance on the stage at this point, it could be a galliard".⁴¹ Arden 3 follows a similar line in the commentary: here, Beatrice's "we must follow the leaders" might count as implicit stage direction: they have fallen out of step, and hence need to "regain their place in the dance pattern".⁴²

In principle the idea of having the characters perform a dance during their dialogue is compelling. Rather than having four couples trooping across the stage, an early production may well have included some sort of slower, relatively simple dance with figures. This could have added variety to the stage dynamics, setting Beatrice and Benedick apart from the other dancing couples, and accentuating what is being said without descending into overexplicit pantomime. During performance, certain early modern dance genres can demonstrably accommodate verbal exchanges of the kind found in *Much Ado About Nothing* – jokes about Don Pedro's mask without a wig (the roof without a thatch), Antonio's doddering gait, religious fervour expressed in loud prayer, or the melancholy man's inability to eat even something as inconsequential as a partridge's wing. Beyond that, there is only speculation: pavans, almains or other sorts of 'measures' might all

---

39 As illustrated with detailed examples in Alan Dessen, *Recovering Shakespeare's Theatrical Vocabulary* (Cambridge: Cambridge University Press, 1995).
40 Brissenden (1981), 49; cited in McEachern (2016), 221, note to line 76.
41 Brissenden (1981), 49–50.
42 McEachern (2016), 225, note to line 137.

have been possible options. Given the heterogeneity of the lines spoken – which include iambic pentameter, trimeter and prose – rhythm would have made no difference. A skilled choreographer would have been equally able to cast the dialogue in a duple-time pavan or in, say, the triple-time *Black Almain*. The opportunities are infinite. Indeed, modern productions have taken great liberties with this scene. At the Globe Theatre, London, Jeremy Herrin's 2011 production saw a lively duple-time dance, with the four couples stepping out towards the front of the stage, some of them forgetting to dance as the argument became more animated; one year later, Poirée's masquers turned in a languid triple-time valse.

Renaissance choreographers understood dance as quasi-verbal communication. As Fabritio Caroso commented on his dance *Laura Suave*, an elegant composition for couples, partners' feet partook in a dialogue:

> just as we say that when two people converse they are engaging in a dialogue, so here, when the gentleman dances one group of steps (or one variation) with his feet, and the lady answers the same way, this foot conversation leads me to term it "pedalogue".[43]

The idea of dance as pedalogue – both physical and verbal – might fruitfully apply to Shakespeare's drama. Dialogue can be whimsical, unpredictable, reaching beyond scripted instruction. It runs like quicksilver between speakers who playfully attend to, and depart from, the decorum of patterned lines, which makes a performance – spoken or danced – alluring in the first place. As editors seek to tame elusive movements into prescriptive stage directions, speculation is valuable and even necessary, especially when specific choreographies for specific scenes are impossible to determine. The extent of such speculation might yet be more rigorously reflected and signposted in current editions. For certain, dance added deep colour to Shakespeare's work. Dance brought out latent dimensions of characters, elucidated unspoken relationships and tested what was said against what was shown. The finest scholarship on Shakespeare's plays will be attuned to such dramatic conversations by leg and voice, and declare where imagination has rendered mute dialogue audible.

---

43 "Si come due persone che discorrono insieme, si dice che parlano in Dialogo: cosi, facendo il Cavaliere nel Ballo un Tempo di Moti, overo una Mutanza con gli piedi; & rispondendogli il medesimo la Dama, per questa corrispondenza che fanno con gli piedi, gli hò dato questo nome di Pedalogo" (Fabritio Caroso, *Nobiltà di dame* [Venice: Il Muschio, 1600], 115; translation in *Nobiltà di dame*, ed. by Julia Sutton and F. Marian Walker [New York: Dover, 1995], 164).

Zusammenfassung

Shakespeares Sprache ist zutiefst musikalisch. Dies äußert sich nicht nur im Versmaß und Rhythmus seiner Stücke und Sonette, sondern auch in seinen Sprachbildern. Dieser Beitrag zeigt, dass Tanz in den Dramen eine große Rolle spielt, sowohl in Metaphern und Wortspielen – z. B. in *Coriolanus* oder *Henry IV, Teil 1* und *2* – als auch bei Tänzen auf der Bühne. Die zu Shakespeares Zeiten bekannten Tänze werden vorgestellt und die noch erhaltenen Tanzanleitungen analysiert. Am Beispiel von *Much Ado About Nothing* wird schließlich erläutert, dass Tanz und Konversation auf der Shakespearebühne miteinander verwoben werden konnten – auch wenn die Szenenanweisungen der Originaltexte nicht explizit darauf hinweisen – und dass sich somit auch für heutige Textausgaben und Inszenierungen interessante Interpretationsmöglichkeiten bieten.

Wondrous Motion:
Recovering Dance from *The Tempest*

LYNSEY MCCULLOCH

The Tempest narrates processes of recovery. It is a tale of shipwreck and of salvage. Of rescued human cargo and of memories retrieved. Of families reunited and of power restored. But the play's internal focus on recovery and the depth from which people and things might be reclaimed – "Full fathom five thy father lies" (1.2.396)[1] – conflicts with external approaches to the text's status and significance. These surface readings present the play as one of Shakespeare's most straightforward works. After all, *The Tempest*'s textual history is – relative to its dramatist's back catalogue of adapted source material, multi-authored dramas and competing print editions – uncomplicated. *The Tempest* has no obvious, single source. It is single-authored. And it appears for the first time in print in the 1623 Folio. Alan Brissenden remarks that "[t]he First Folio text of *The Tempest* is accepted as being exceptionally good, one of the most carefully prepared in the whole volume".[2] That it appears as the opening play in the First Folio only cements its status as Shakespeare's touchstone, a work that is reliably uncontroversial. For many Shakespeareans, the play's performance history is similarly stable. It was performed twice, both times at court – in 1611 before James I on 'Hallowmas nyght',[3] and in 1613 as part of the nuptial celebrations of the King's daughter, Elizabeth, to Elector Palatine. Given the play's courtly pedigree and its seeming debt to the masque genre, the identification of *The Tempest* with private, rather than public, performance appears sound. But, to use a well-worn phrase, absence of evidence is not evidence of absence. Stephen Orgel has warned against the "inferences" made on the basis of these historical facts, ones that have "conditioned views of the play"[4] and diminished its capacity for subversion.

---

1 William Shakespeare, *The Tempest*, ed. by David Lindley (Cambridge: Cambridge University Press, 2013). All subsequent references are to this edition unless otherwise stated.
2 Alan Brissenden, *Shakespeare and the Dance* (Alton: Dance Books, 1981), 96–97.
3 E. K. Chambers, *William Shakespeare: A Study of Facts and Problems*. Vol. 2 (Oxford: Clarendon Press, 1930), 342.
4 Stephen Orgel, "Introduction" to William Shakespeare, *The Tempest*, ed. by Stephen Orgel (Oxford: Oxford University Press, 1987), 1.

And, although subsequent postcolonial readings have dug 'deeper' to access the play's geopolitical significance, its textual and performance histories remain incomplete. This article considers a specific absence from these histories: dance. In examining *The Tempest*'s "excellent dumb discourse" (3.3.39), I employ the play's own reclamation techniques to recover a danced history all but invisible on the surface of the text.

Dance within *The Tempest* has received little attention from the play's recent editors. The Arden 3 editors, Virginia Mason Vaughan and Alden T. Vaughan, describe the play as a "theatrical wonder cabinet",[5] a drama imbued with the spirit of discovery and rediscovery. And yet their own rediscovery of the play's more wondrous elements is restricted to its music. Dance is not indexed in their edition and plays no part in their discussion of *The Tempest*'s stagecraft, despite its relationship to the soundscape of the play and its centrality to the court masques replicated in it. Several editions of the play, including Stephen Orgel's 1987 text for Oxford University Press and David Lindley's 2002 text for Cambridge University Press, contain appendices on the play's music but, again, little to no treatment of dance. The centrality of music to *The Tempest* is not in dispute but, given the ubiquity of dance in the drama of the early modern period and its close relationship with music, these are significant omissions. More widely, dance, as an integral element of theatrical display in the English Renaissance, has been under-researched.

The close association, in Shakespeare's late plays, of dancing with the masque may provide one explanation for the neglect of dance as a subject within early modern literary criticism. Shakespeare's reputation with the public has long surpassed that of Ben Jonson but scholars remain susceptible to Jonson's apparent distaste both for the tragicomic genre and the masque from which the tragicomedy took so many of its effects. Jonson's Prologue to his 1616 printing of *Every Man in His Humour* satirizes the special effects required for tragicomedy, including the type of sound technology used in *The Tempest*. The playwright guarantees the absence of such elements in his own comic work, no "nimble squib" nor

>rolled bullet heard
>To say, it thunders; nor tempestuous drum
>Rumbles, to tell you when the storm doth come;
>(Prologue, 17–20)[6]

---

5   Virginia Mason Vaughan and Alden T. Vaughan, "Introduction" to William Shakespeare, *The Tempest*, ed. by Virginia Mason Vaughan and Alden T. Vaughan (London: Bloomsbury, 2011), 3.
6   Ben Jonson, *Every Man in His Humour*, ed. by Robert N. Watson (London: Methuen, 1998).

Jonson's close involvement in court performance did not prevent him from identifying its shortcomings, in particular its investment in bland spectacle. In one of the many pot-shots aimed at his long-term collaborator, the designer and architect Inigo Jones, Jonson wrote that "[p]ainting and carpentry are the soul of masque".[7] Music, also associated with the masque genre, can be preserved with notation but dance, as an apparently ephemeral art that exists only in the moment of performance, takes its place amongst the perishable costumes and temporary set designs produced for the masque genre. Notwithstanding the complexity of Jonson's relationship with theatricality[8] or indeed the scholarly efforts made in recent years to disassociate dance and ephemerality,[9] dance as a feature of early modern stagecraft remains overlooked – categorized as a tangential, poorly-inscribed and unsalvageable art.

Dance historians, including both those who write about early dance and those who reconstruct it as a research method, have done much to inform Shakespeareans of the depth and diversity of movement practice in the sixteenth and seventeenth centuries. They have researched the influences of French and Italian dance on the English tradition. They have outlined the variety of early modern dance – from folk dance to courtly performance – alongside the varied locations in which dancing took place. They have, crucially, understood the social and political dimensions of dance. And several have worked tirelessly on Shakespeare's corpus to extract the dance within it.[10] Knowledge of the history of dance is, I

---

7   Ben Jonson, "An Expostulation with Inigo Jones", in William Gifford (ed.), *The Works of Ben Jonson*. Vol. 8 (London: W. Bulmer and Co., 1816), 116–120, quote 118.

8   Barbara Ravelhofer has questioned assumptions regarding Jonson's attitude to the stage and imaginatively reads the print layouts, typography and marginalia of his works as "dynamic" textual demonstrations of his theatricality, his "frontstage focus"; Jonson's texts may not describe dance but they invoke it. The growth of Sound Studies has also encouraged a re-evaluation of Jonson's appreciation for acoustic effects. Emergent here is a Jonson much more attuned to the extra-textual qualities of the theatre. See Barbara Ravelhofer, *The Early Stuart Masque: Dance, Costume, and Music* (Oxford: Oxford University Press, 2006), 206; Laura Jayne Wright, "'Red silence': Ben Jonson and the Breath of Sound", *Ben Jonson Journal* 26:1 (2019), 40–61.

9   Like Ravelhofer, André Lepecki complicates the oppositional relationship of dance and text, recognizing the possibilities of embodied language and a body that can be inscribed upon. Repositioning ephemerality within dance, he writes that "it's precisely dance's self-depiction as a lamentably ephemeral art form [...] that generates systems and performances of high reproducibility" (Lepecki, *Exhausting Dance: Performance and the Politics of Movement* [London: Routledge, 2006], 126).

10 See works by Margaret M. McGowan, Anne Daye, Jennifer Nevile, Emily Winerock and Nona Monahin, amongst others.

would suggest, a prerequisite for understanding it as a dramatic device. But a fuller understanding of the public theatre during Shakespeare's lifetime is also key. The finales of several Shakespearean plays involve music and/or dancing of some kind, often to mark the weddings that concluded comedies or their tragic counterparts, funerals; note *Much Ado About Nothing*'s "let's have a dance ere we are married, that we may lighten our own hearts, and our wives' heels" (5.4.111–112).[11] But, in addition to staged dancing within the frame of a play, dance interludes also occurred outside the main drama but as part of the overall theatrical event. These included dances preceding the performing of a play, inter-act entertainment and, most famously, the post-play jig, defined by Roger Clegg as "a short, usually comic, often bawdy, dramatic afterpiece sung and danced to popular tunes of the day".[12] In other words, dance was ubiquitous in the early modern English theatre.

This ubiquity is not always apparent, however. The pre-performance, post-performance and inter-act dancing so vital to an early modern audience's experience of the theatre is typically absent from printed play-texts. Moreover, the dance contained within plays was not always recorded in the published work. The English theatre had no accepted method of dance notation and, even if it had, publishers favoured the written text over more performative aspects of stage performance, leaving many theatrical collaborators – not only dancers and choreographers but also composers and designers – absent from the printed work. Missing from *The Tempest*, and indeed Shakespeare's other plays, are the dancing bodies of early modern stagecraft. Dance can occasionally be located within stage directions but, given the complex textual history of Shakespeare's work, these are not always reliable or indeed even present. Dance, often invisible on the surface of the text, demands reconstruction. For tips on salvaging aspects of the Shakespearean subtext, we should first emulate the dramatist's postcolonial readers. Susan Bennett writes that "[w]e can best salvage the Shakespearean text when we savage it, when we plunder it for its gaps and blind spots".[13] Prompted by the identification of Caliban in the dramatis personae of the First Folio as "a salvage and deformed slave" – with "salvage" as an obso-

---

11   William Shakespeare, *Much Ado About Nothing*, ed. by F. H. Mares, 3rd ed. (Cambridge: Cambridge University Press, 2018).
12   Roger Clegg, "'When the play is done, you shall have a jig or dance of all treads': Danced Endings of Shakespeare's Stage", in Lynsey McCulloch and Brandon Shaw (eds), *The Oxford Handbook of Shakespeare and Dance* (Oxford: Oxford University Press, 2019), 83–106, quote 84.
13   Susan Bennett, *Performing Nostalgia: Shifting Shakespeare and the Contemporary Past* (New York: Routledge, 1996), 149.

lete term for "savage" – Bennett recognizes the anti-colonial potential of *The Tempest*. This is a potential reliant on processes of adaptation, translation and over-reading, all of these acts of savagery – one could argue – towards the text. Just as postcolonial critics have scoured the text of *The Tempest* for evidence of colonial discourse, scholars in the field of literature and dance look for signs of movement.

Alan Brissenden, acknowledging the importance of music in *The Tempest*, identifies "three occasions [in which] the music is related to dance".[14] The first is in a song, sung by Ariel to Ferdinand in Act 1, scene 2. The second occasion takes the form of a short masque, or anti-masque, for Prospero's enemies in Act 3, scene 3. And the last, another "trick" (4.1.37) involving music and dance, occurs late in the play as a spectacle conceived for Miranda and Ferdinand. The latter two examples, via the use of stage directions and verbal cues, indicate staged dance and explicitly recall the court masques of Jacobean tradition. For the dance scholar, however, the two scenes are characterized by interruptions to the dancing. In Act 3, scene 3, the dancing, alongside a banquet laid on for the shipwrecked nobles, is interrupted by the appearance of Ariel as a harpy, castigating the lords for their crimes against Prospero:

> *Thunder and Lightning. Enter Ariel (like a Harpy) claps his wings upon the Table, and with a quaint device the Banquet vanishes.* (3.3.52 SD)[15]

The dancers return briefly after Ariel's speech but soon exit the scene once more: "*Enter the shapes again, and dance (with mocks and mows) and carrying out the Table.*" (3.3.82 SD) Similarly, in Act 4, scene 1, the dancing of the betrothal masque is rudely interrupted by Prospero's remembrance of Caliban's plot against him:

> *Enter certain Reapers (properly habited:) they join with the Nymphs, in a graceful dance, towards the end where-of,* Prospero *starts suddenly and speaks, after which to a strange hollow and confused noise, they heavily vanish.* (4.1.138 SD)

These interruptions, and the truncated choreographies on display, may diminish the amount of dancing within the play but they also point to dance's function as

---

14 Brissenden (1981), 96.
15 This and the following extract from *The Tempest* have been reproduced, as closely as possible, from the First Folio, with spelling modernized but capitalization and punctuation retained. Line numbering follows the Cambridge Shakespeare.

a narrative technique. Dance is not a spectacle or interlude but a dramatic device, integral to the plot.

Dance is also, I would argue, central to the play's political and philosophical discourse. If we look more closely at Act 3, scene 3, we see the shipwrecked Neapolitans and Milanese roaming the island – hungry, lost and apparently bereaved. Prospero, as part of his revenge plot for the loss of his dukedom, arranges an interlude for them. The stage directions are, in this instance, substantive and immediately indicative of a dance set to music:

> Solemn and strange Music: and Prospero on the top (invisible:) Enter several strange shapes, bringing in a Banquet; and dance about it with gentle actions of salutations, and inviting the King, etc. to eat, they depart. (3.3.17 SD)

The spirits who dance about the banquet performing "gentle actions of salutations" evoke the diplomacy of Jacobean monarchical culture and its embodiment in the dances of the masque. Martin Butler remarks upon the masque genre's "stupendous images of sovereignty"[16] and Prospero's appearance here "on the top", at "the highest point possible on the Jacobean stage",[17] produces just such an image. He may be invisible to his enemies at this stage of the revenge plot but he assumes majesty in the eyes of the spectators. But, more importantly for our purposes, Prospero's assumption of the monarch's role – here in the presence of the King of Naples in addition to Prospero's successor, Antonio, usurping Duke of Milan – is predicated on his ability to choreograph such a show of noble gentility. Dancing plays its part in political relations and cannot be underestimated as mere entertainment in this context. The "power of dance theatre as a political tool",[18] to use Anne Daye's phrase, is keenly felt in *The Tempest*. The combination of music and dance – "[s]uch shapes, such gesture, and such sound" (3.3.37) – seduces and perplexes the shipwrecked men, weakening them and rendering them vulnerable to Prospero's machinations: "They now are in my power" (3.3.90). These "high charms" (3.3.88), as Prospero puts it, have a direct political function.

---

16 Martin Butler, "Courtly Negotiations", in David Bevington and Peter Holbrook (eds), *The Politics of the Stuart Court Masque* (Cambridge: Cambridge University Press, 1998), 20–40, quote 20.
17 Orgel (1987), 164n.
18 Anne Daye, "'The power of his commanding trident': Tethys Festival as Royal Policy", *Historical Dance* 4:2 (2012), 19–28, quote 21.

But the play's setting, on an unidentified island, also offers Shakespeare an opportunity to comment on the relationship between the dance of the masque genre and English colonial practices. The strange shapes that dance do so as an act of welcome to the visitors. Gonzalo commends them for their nobility, despite their strange appearance.

> For certes, these are people of the island –
> Who though they are of monstrous shape, yet note
> Their manners are more gentle, kind, than of
> Our human generation you shall find
> Many, nay almost any.
>
> (3.3.30–34)

Gonzalo assumes that the moving shapes are indigenous to the island. What salvages these strange and "monstrous" foreigners is their grace, encapsulated in their dancing. While Gonzalo's description of kind and gentle manners might suggest to modern readers a polite and generous behaviour on the part of the dancers, editors have been quick to recognize Shakespeare's use of "gentle, kind" as an indication of nobility rather than humanity. But they rarely note his employment of "manners" to suggest, not socially accepted behaviour, but rather bodily gesture and deportment.[19] Gonzalo is not remarking upon the dancers' hospitality but rather their physical attributes and dancing ability – surpassing here the aristocratic dancers of the European court masque. The dancers' suitability for masquing performance aligns, in many ways, with Trinculo and Stephano's plan to make money from Caliban in Europe as a curiosity. Stephano cites England as the most lucrative market for such prodigies:

> A strange fish. Were I in England now – as once I was – and had but this fish painted, not a holiday-fool there but would give a piece of silver. There would this monster make a man; any strange beast there makes a man. When they will not give a doit to relieve a lame beggar, they will lay out ten to see a dead Indian. (2.2.25–30)

Shakespeare's baiting of his spectators and their lack of charity aside, the servants' scheme reflects the European market for curious attractions and exotica from

---

19 Stephen Orgel glosses "gentle, kind" as "either having the graciousness of nobility or noble-mannered". See Orgel (1987), 165n. See also the *OED*: "manner, n. 5.a. Outward bearing, deportment; a person's characteristic style of attitude, gesture, or speech" (*OED Online*, Oxford University Press, 2020, www.oed.com).

the New World.[20] Stephano later imagines Caliban as a profitable "present for any emperor" (2.2.63), recalling not only the displays of otherness at royal courts, in which non-European peoples were exhibited by foreign visitors and English travellers alike, but the incorporation of the exotic within masque performance.

Indeed, several high-profile English court masques, including Ben Jonson and Inigo Jones's *Masque of Blackness* (1605) and its sequel, the *Masque of Beauty* (1608), represented nationalities and ethnicities unfamiliar to most Britons, in this case Africans. These figures were not "monstrous" additions to the anti-masque but the daughters of Niger, represented in black makeup by Anne of Denmark, Queen consort to James I, and her ladies. For Clare McManus, this representation was less about race and more about gender: "royal female difference was reinscribed in motifs of sea voyages and blackness and through female performance itself".[21] But Shakespeare's dramatic alignment of racial otherness and dancing ability suggests a clear geopolitical agenda. While Gonzalo may see dance as an indicator of universal humanity, his recognition of dancing ability in the spirits could equally act as confirmation that "every savage can dance".[22] This is dance not as an equalizer but as the lowest form of art, one that anyone can artlessly master. However, I prefer to view dance in this scene as suggestive of agency. Sebastian describes the scene as a "living drollery" (3.3.21), indicating a puppet show or a picture that has come to life. Although the castaways are not sure who the dancers are, their response is one of awe and they recognize the movement of the spirits as magically given – art infused with life. But the dance, alongside Ariel's appearance as an avenging harpy, represents more than an artificial spectacle. Dance brings about an awakening in both the performer and the beholder. The display of motion, in a play in which Prospero regularly puts people to sleep in order to control them, identifies dance – not simply as movement – but as agency. Shakespeare theorizes dance as an embodied practice, one that confers self-determination on all, regardless of background.

In addition to using dance as a means of understanding colonial relations, Shakespeare also theorizes the vexed relationship of text and movement. Alonso's response to the spirits' dance hints at the perceived failure of language to express bodily motion:

---

20 Alden T. Vaughan, "Trinculo's Indian: American Natives in Shakespeare's England", in Peter Hulme and William H. Sherman (eds), *'The Tempest' and Its Travels* (London: Reaktion, 2000), 49–59.
21 Clare McManus, *Women on the Renaissance Stage: Anna of Denmark and Female Masquing in the Stuart Court (1590–1619)* (Manchester: Manchester University Press, 2002), 90.
22 Jane Austen, *Pride and Prejudice* (San Francisco: Ignatius Press, 2008), 26.

> I cannot too much muse,
> Such shapes, such gesture, and such sound, expressing –
> Although they want the use of tongue – a kind
> Of excellent dumb discourse.
>
> (3.3.36–39)

Alonso is here dependent on vocal tropes for capturing dance. Movement is characterized by the absence of speech, as Alonso struggles to verbalize the spirits' performance. The play itself shows no such illiteracy in its representation of the moving body, and dance scholars – like their postcolonial counterparts – use the play's somatic reality to challenge narrowly textual readings. Susan Bennett, discussing the play's "performing bodies", describes how their "spectacularity registers the bodily elements of Shakespeare's play as a corrective to the authority of the spoken text".[23] Bennett celebrates the play's physicality and that of its adaptations – manifested in the punished but dissident body of Caliban – as a counter to the authority of language. Given the play's imposition of a European language on the colonized Caliban, this is significant. It is also no coincidence, I would add, that Caliban is often considered the play's most dancerly character, at least in adaptation. In *Prospero's Books*, Peter Greenaway's 1992 film adaptation of Shakespeare's play, Caliban is played, not by an actor, but by the dancer Michael Clark. Prospero, played by John Gielgud, voices all the other characters in the play. This requires their actors to lip-sync but, in the case of Caliban, Clark simply dances to Gielgud's voiceover and to Michael Nyman's music. As a means of illustrating Prospero's dominance over the play and its characters, Gielgud's narration works incredibly well, especially if we accept that Prospero is an analogue for Shakespeare. But the conceit also offers Caliban the opportunity to communicate in another language – that of movement, thereby granting him a freedom of expression denied the other characters in the film.[24]

Dance adaptations of the play, such as Cathy Marston's 2004 *before the tempest…after the storm* for the Royal Ballet, also seem to pay particular attention to Caliban. Marston's ballet contains a central duet for Caliban and his mother Sycorax.[25] Directors and choreographers seem fascinated by this role and its physicality. But is our interest in Caliban as a dancerly figure problematic? Does it, to

---

23 Bennett (1996), 150.
24 Peter Greenaway, *Prospero's Books* (Miramax Films, 1991).
25 Cathy Marston, *before the tempest…after the storm* (Royal Ballet, 2004).

use Stephen Greenblatt's phrase, reinforce Miranda's view of him as "a savage who had no speech"?[26]

> I pitied thee,
> Took pains to make thee speak, taught thee each hour
> One thing or other. When thou didst not, savage,
> Know thine own meaning, but wouldst gabble like
> A thing most brutish, I endowed thy purposes
> With words that made them known.
> (1.2.353–358)

When we celebrate Caliban's physicality and perhaps also his ability to communicate in methods other than the traditionally textual, does this rush to silence him not echo Prospero and Miranda's misunderstanding of his language and interpretation of it as gabble? In other words, the "salvage and deformed slave" recuperated by a recognition of his non-verbal qualities could be made mute and more ineffectual in dance. The focus on Caliban's physicality may also distract from his own remarkable rhetoric. However, the emergence of Caliban, in the afterlife of Shakespeare's play, as a dancer is only problematic if we accept that dance has neither the complexity nor the diversity of language. And yet, as I hope we have already seen, early modern dance offered a range of connotative options to dramatists. The critical depiction of dance as a mere "symbol of harmony and concord"[27] falls short of the reality of somatic practices within Shakespeare's plays and their subsequent adaptations.

Recovering dance from *The Tempest* remains challenging, however, and reliant on the often derided practice of over-reading. The first example of dance identified by Alan Brissenden within the play, Ariel's song, is instructive here. It is perhaps the most ambivalent example of dance that Brissenden cites, chiefly because it is not clear whether staged dancing takes place. Brissenden does not engage with its possible staging and simply describes dance as the "subject"[28] of the song. Its interest in the relationship between music and dance is therefore salutary. And the textual debates it has given rise to amongst editors of the play are also instructive in this context. The song is sung by an invisible Ariel, ac-

---

26 Stephen Greenblatt, *Learning to Curse: Essays in Early Modern Culture* (New York: Routledge, 1990), 23.
27 Brissenden (1981), 3.
28 Ibid., 96.

companying himself, perhaps on a lute,[29] to a newly shipwrecked and isolated Ferdinand, son of the King of Naples. It functions as an invocation to the island's spirits, inviting them to sing and dance on the seashore:

> Enter Ferdinand and Ariel, invisible playing and singing.
> Ariel Song.   Come unto these yellow sands,
>   and then take hands:
>   Curtsied when you have, and kissed
>   the wild waves whist:
> Foot it featly here, and there, and sweet sprites bear
>   the burden.   Burden dispersedly.
> Hark, hark, bow wow: the watch-dogs bark,
>   bow-wow.
> Ar. Hark, hark, I hear, the strain of strutting Chanticleer
>   cry cock-a-diddle-dow.
>   (1.2.375–386)[30]

The song draws repeated attention to the physical movement implicit within music and the corresponding musicality of dance. Music and dance are here codependent. Ferdinand, later explaining the calming of the ocean with Ariel's arrival, describes how the

> music crept by me upon the waters,
> Allaying both their fury and my passion
> With its sweet air.
>   (1.2.391–393)

The personification of music as a figure passing Ferdinand on the waves reiterates Ariel's juxtaposition of song and moving bodies. In his song, Chanticleer, the cock heralding the arrival of morning, struts to his own musical strain. The spirits, whilst singing, are also encouraged to dance lightly, in addition to curtsying and kissing as part of the dance's honour or obeisance. Music does not exist here without dance. And Shakespeare's selection of musical terms is predicated on their relevance to physical activity. "Burden", "burthen" in the First Folio, refers to a chorus or, similarly, to the base note or low undersong that accompanies a

---

29   Lindley suggests the lute as the most fitting instrument for Ariel's song. See Lindley (2013), 138n.
30   Reproduced from the First Folio.

leading melody. Shakespeare, using it to denote the spirits' echoing of the song's refrains, makes full use of the word's better-known meaning as suggestive of load and physical labour: "sweet sprites bear the burden" (1.2.380).[31] Once again, the music is physicalized, or embodied, within the text.

Moreover, this heavy burden borne by the spirits is the same "sweet air" (1.2.393) or tune remarked upon by Ferdinand. Reflecting on this relationship between lightness and load, Ferdinand wonders also whether the music is "[i]'th'air, or th'earth" (1.2.387). The musical sense of "burden" as a heavier undersong carried by the lighter air and as a chorus representative of a song's core meaning hints at a reversal of the values typically attributed to lightness and load, with the hefty physicality of the latter bearing the semantic weight of the song. The exit of Caliban, the play's beast of burden, immediately before Ariel's song, also points towards the text's fascination with weight and its significance to the relationship of music and dance, pitting the musical discourse and "airy charm[s]" (5.1.54) of Ariel against the heft and earthy physicality of Caliban, a physicality that would much later attract choreographers to Prospero's rebellious servant. The play shows little favouritism but rather demonstrates the ways in which music is implicated in dance, and vice versa. Caliban's lowly status and physical prowess is, after all, no barrier to his musicality: "the isle is full of noises, / Sounds, and sweet airs, that give delight and hurt not" (3.2.127–128).

The significance of the word "burden", not only to the play's musical discourse but to its dancing practice, is made more obvious when one looks at Shakespeare's use of the term elsewhere. In several examples, "burden" conjures both music and dance. In *The Taming of the Shrew*, the mercenary Petruchio, after referring to courtship as a "maze" (1.2.52) or dancing pattern, describes his bride-to-be Katherina's wealth as its musical accompaniment, the "burden of my wooing dance" (1.2.65).[32] In another comedy, *Much Ado About Nothing*, Margaret looks to cheer Beatrice with a popular song and dance: "Clap's into *Light o'Love*: that goes without a burden: do you sing it and I'll dance it." (3.4.33–34) In addition to identifying the term "burden" with both song and dance, the play's bawdy banter focuses on the dichotomy of lightness and heaviness apparent also in *The Tempest*.

---

31 Editors of the play have routinely adjusted this phrase to read as "sweet sprites the burden bear", to rhyme with the earlier "there".
32 William Shakespeare, *The Taming of the Shrew*, ed. by Ann Thompson (Cambridge: Cambridge University Press, 1984). See also Michael West, "The Folk Background of Petruchio's Wooing Dance: Male Supremacy in *The Taming of the Shrew*", *Shakespeare Studies* 7 (1974), 65–73.

More problematic for dance scholars in recovering dance from Ariel's song in Act 1, scene 2, are the song's one-sided stage directions. The performers representing the spirits are said to "burden dispersedly", in other words, they sing the refrain at different times and possibly from different areas of the theatre, but there is little guidance on whether the dancing in Ariel's song is performed or simply described. The song appears to invite the spirits onto the stage and then instruct them to pay compliments to one another before commencing a dance. But there is no stage direction to indicate the performers' entrance onto the stage; only Ferdinand and Ariel are said to enter before the commencement of the song. Elsewhere in the play, as we have seen, stage directions are explicit in stating both the entrance of the dancers and the initiation of a dance. Not surprisingly perhaps, scholars of the play have been reluctant to imagine dance as an integral part of this musical interlude. David Lindley suggests that the singing spirits "probably echoed words from Ariel's song, either moving about the curtained music-room, or else positioned above, behind and possibly below the stage to give a stereophonic effect".[33] Whichever option of Lindley's one chooses results in the spirits being audible but not visible to the audience. In other words, there is no dance. Alan Brissenden also avoids any discussion of staged dancing to Ariel's song and instead suggests that dance within the lyric may be a metaphorical addition, not a genuine invitation to the spirits to dance but a figurative enticement of Ferdinand towards Miranda.[34] And yet, despite the lack of helpful stage directions, there are hints here that an audience would see a dance. Just as Ariel commands the spirits to "bear the burden" and sing, which they subsequently do, he instructs them in the particulars and order of his dance. To "foot it featly" is to dance nimbly and lightly. If the spirits are required to sing from different locations, then their dancing might also be dispersed across the stage and indeed the theatre. To "foot it featly *here, and there*" (my italics) suggests as much. These spirits seem to be, like Ariel, invisible to Ferdinand. Therefore, Ferdinand's responses to the music he can hear – he makes no mention of dancing – does not preclude the staging of a dance for the benefit of the audience. Stage directions are often key to our understanding of dance within *The Tempest* but they are not infallible and they do not, in my opinion, prohibit a staged dance at this point of the play.[35]

---

33   Lindley (2013), 139n.
34   Brissenden (1981), 96–99.
35   John Jowett has suggested that some of the stage directions in *The Tempest* were produced by Ralph Crane rather than by Shakespeare, based on Crane's memory of seeing the play in performance. The "quaint device" by which the banquet is removed at 3.3.52 certainly feels more like the description of a spectator – unaware of the stage tricks available to the theatrical pro-

The area of dancing custom within this scene that is of interest to editors takes the form of a textual crux, concerning this particular section of the song:

> Ariel Song.　　　*Come unto these yellow sands,*
> *and then take hands:*
> *Curtsied when you have, and kissed*
> *the wild waves whist:*

The punctuation, or lack of punctuation, in this section has been the subject of much debate. From the eighteenth century, with William Warburton's 1747 edition of Shakespeare's works, editors have typically inserted a comma after "kissed". These editors, unhappy with the Folio's suggestion that the spirits kiss the waves into silence or kiss until the waves become silent – Frank Kermode went so far as to call this notion "grotesque"[36] – have favoured an emendation that places the "wild waves whist" in parenthesis. As a result, the spirits can be said to curtsy and kiss as standard dance practice but their kissing does not affect the ocean or assist Ariel in his efforts to calm it. Much of this editorial debate hangs on whether kissing was a feature of the courtesies that accompanied dancing in the period. For Brissenden, and subsequently Orgel, the Folio is correct and a comma is inappropriate. Brissenden maintains that there is "no evidence that kissing was a usual part of the honour ('curtsy', 'bow', 'reverence') which preceded a dance".[37] He does, however, concede that embracing of various kinds could form part of a dance, even if it did not feature in the pre-dance routine. David Lindley, conversely, takes advice from dance specialists Barbara Ravelhofer and Lieven Baert, concluding that – at least in French and Italian traditions – kissing could be an element of the reverence.[38] But the research undertaken by editors into early dance practice does not inform our practical understanding of the logistics of dance in this scene or even its metaphorical or narrative import. Rather, it serves to solve a textual conundrum. Considered from another perspective, the

---

　　　ducer – than of the author of the work. Crane was a professional scribe working for the King's Men and responsible for producing transcripts of its plays. It is accepted that several of his transcripts, including *The Tempest*, were used as the printer's copy for the First Folio in 1623, the earliest publication in which *The Tempest* appears. Shakespeare may have produced stage directions for *The Tempest* but some may have been overwritten by Crane. See John Jowett, "New Created Creatures: Ralph Crane and the Stage Directions in *The Tempest*", *Shakespeare Survey* 36 (1983), 107–120.

36　William Shakespeare, *The Tempest*, ed. by Frank Kermode, rev. ed. (London: Methuen, 1962), 34.
37　Brissenden (1981), 97.
38　Lindley (2013), 139n.

common insertion of a comma at this point undercuts the image of a potentially powerful dance capable of quelling Prospero's storm. Scholars may dismiss the agency of dance in favour of music's hypnotic powers – John H. Long states confidently that "music calms the storm"[39] – but the language of containment used to describe Ariel's control of the tempest suggests the employment of both music and dance. To be "whist" is to be free from both noise and movement; the calmed waters are not only silenced but stilled.[40] To return to the song's textual crux, it is, in fact, not necessary to choose between the song's kiss as a pre-dance courtesy or an act of magic. If dance is accepted as a legitimate form and an art capable of influence and persuasion, it can be both.

The Tempest's synaesthetic approach to music and dance tells us much about the interaction, and effective cooperation, of the two mediums in the early modern period. The relationship between movement and language may be antagonistic, a lesser-known *paragone* if you like, but literature's debt to dance and its employment of choreographies (both real and imagined) point to dance's expressive qualities – qualities which have not yet been sufficiently explored in early modern criticism. The Tempest offers, not one, but multiple definitions of dance. Dance appears within the play as diplomacy, as agency and as an alternative to the dominance of language and the text. It is both a flexible dramatic device and the basis for figurative tropes. It provides the solution to textual difficulties and the inspiration for the play's translation into other genres. The play's "dumb discourse" (3.3.39) is indeed "excellent".

Zusammenfassung

In ihrer Auseinandersetzung mit Tanz und den Tänzen in *The Tempest* geht Lynsey McCulloch von der Überlegung aus, dass sich die tanzenden Körper auf der frühneuzeitlichen Bühne weder in diesem Stück noch in den anderen Dramen Shakespeares finden. Die Bühnenanweisungen in den erhaltenen Texten sind eher spärlich gesät und möglicherweise unzuverlässig, so dass die Tänze der frühneuzeitlichen Aufführungen schwer greifbar und für Leser*innen häufig nicht sichtbar sind. Vor diesem Hintergrund versucht der Aufsatz, Bewegungen im Shakespeare'schen Text zu rekonstruieren und Tanz als ein vielschichtiges und flexibles dramatisches Instrument zu begreifen.

---

39 John H. Long, *Shakespeare's Use of Music: The Final Comedies* (Gainesville: University of Florida Press, 1961), 99.
40 "whist, adj. 1.a. Silent, quiet, still, hushed; making no sound; free from noise or disturbance" (*OED Online*, 2020).

Licence to Speak: Gender and Masking in Shakespearean Dance Scenes

EMILY WINEROCK

> Masquers do therfore cover their faces,
> that they may open their affections.
> (John Lyly, *Euphues and his England*, 1605)

Dancing was a common yet controversial activity in England and Europe in the sixteenth and seventeenth centuries.[1] It was a popular and socially acceptable means of meeting and courting potential spouses, but it was also acknowledged as an activity that could lead to illicit or ill-advised sexual encounters. Life-cycle celebrations such as weddings, religious festivals like Whitsuntide and seasonal holidays such as May Day and Midsummer were often marked by dancing, but whether this was a good thing was disputed. Advocates argued that dancing embodied the harmonious union of love and facilitated "good neighbourliness" by bringing the community together. Critics complained that dancing at festivals was irreverent and encouraged antisocial behaviours such as drunkenness and fighting, as well as sins such as lust, fornication and adultery. Protestant reformers opposed dancing on Sundays and holy days, whereas Catholics and traditionalists permitted it, provided one attended church services beforehand.

Even the courtly dances of the nobility were controversial. Proponents believed dancing was essential for displaying noble grace and virtues and argued that choreographed dances best conveyed the orderly harmoniousness of the state and the cosmos. Opponents, however, saw courtly dancing as a vain and frivolous waste of time at best, at worst, the epitome of all that was wrong with contemporary court life.[2] These contradictory associations make it challenging to assess the significance of any one moment of dancing, but their diversity and

---

1   See also my "'The heaven's true figure' or an 'introit to all kind of lewdness'? Competing Conceptions of Dancing in Shakespeare's England", in Lynsey McCulloch and Brandon Shaw (eds), *The Oxford Handbook of Shakespeare and Dance* (Oxford: Oxford University Press, 2019), 21–47.
2   Alessandro Arcangeli, "Dance under Trial: The Moral Debate 1200–1600", *Dance Research* 12:2 (1994), 127–155.

contingency of meaning was also what made dancing a useful tool for meaning-makers, for authors and playwrights such as Shakespeare.

Whereas attitudes towards dancing can be gleaned from many historical sources, dance instruction manuals are the only surviving sources that document choreographies, describe their component steps and discuss the nuances of styling and dance floor etiquette. Mostly authored by dancing instructors to the nobility, these manuals explain, in varying degrees of clarity, how dances like the *galliard*, *pavane*, *coranto*, *canary*, *branle*, *volta* and other court dances were performed, and they enable us to reconstruct these dances in the present with some degree of accuracy.[3]

The manuals' choreographies and notes on etiquette also indicate that the Renaissance dance floor was a site of relative gender equality. Men and women performed the same steps and patterns and had most of the same freedoms: both could ask someone to dance, could lead a dance and could add embellishments and improvise solo combinations.[4] There were some gendered differences in styling – smoothness was prized more for women, fancy footwork for men. Similarly, dancing in an unsuitable style for one's rank was judged more harshly for men, while immodest motions were judged more harshly for women. However, these distinctions were lessened by the fact that men and women usually danced together. In single-sex group dances and solos, dancers might have utilized distinctly gendered styling, but most of the time men and women would have moved similarly on the dance floor and behaved similarly towards current and prospective partners.

The majority of the extant manuals are by Italian dancing masters, with a few by French and Spanish authors.[5] This is likely why the manuals contain numerous and detailed descriptions of dances like the galliard that were danced throughout Europe but do not mention those native to Britain such as the old measures and the jig. There are no English-authored dancing manuals between the so-called Gresley manuscript (c. 1500) and John Playford's *The English Danc-*

---

3   See Appendix 1: Choreographic Sources for Dances Mentioned in Shakespeare's Plays, 78–79, in Nona Monahin, "Decoding Dance in Shakespeare's *Much Ado About Nothing* and *Twelfth Night*", in McCulloch and Shaw (2019), 49–82.
4   Emily Winerock, "'Performing' Gender and Status on the Dance Floor in Early Modern England", in Kim Kippen and Lori Woods (eds), *Worth and Repute: Valuing Gender in Late Medieval and Early Modern Europe* (Toronto: Centre for Reformation and Renaissance Studies, 2011), 449–472.
5   Jennifer Nevile, "Dance in Europe 1250–1750", in Jennifer Nevile (ed.), *Dance, Spectacle, and the Body Politick, 1250–1750* (Bloomington: Indiana University Press, 2008), 7–64.

ing Master (1650).⁶ For the old measures, a set of processional dances, we can tentatively match step instructions from continental manuals to a dozen or so choreographic notes that survive in manuscript.⁷ For the jig, we do not have a single choreographic description, only scattered references to a fast, whirling dance associated variously with the Scots, the Irish and Will Kemp.⁸ The 'jig' that concludes contemporary performances at Shakespeare's Globe in London may be dramatically effective and an audience-pleaser, but choreographically it is, at best, historically inspired, not historically accurate.⁹

Despite the absence of surviving English dancing manuals from Shakespeare's time, dancing is certainly present in his plays. At least thirteen Shakespeare plays include staged dancing, and almost all the plays contain textual references to dance. The staged dances function variously, to illustrate character or highlight contrasts between characters, to advance the plot, to set the scene – especially to convey celebration or festivity, to entertain on- and offstage audiences and to confirm a happy ending or juxtapose a tragic one.¹⁰ Textual dance references occasionally describe dancing directly, but most often they employ dancing as a metaphor. Whereas all staged dances are in some sense positive or celebratory (at least from the perspective of the dancers), textual references may have negative connotations, such as in *The Winter's Tale*, when Leontes, considering his wife's possible infidelity, exclaims, "My heart dances, but not for joy, not joy" (1.2.141–142).¹¹

Of the thirteen plays with staged dancing, eight include dancers in disguise, and five feature masked dancers performing for an onstage audience and then

---

6   David Fallows, "The Gresley Dance Collection, c. 1500", *Royal Musical Association Research Chronicle* 29 (1996), 1–20. Two French dancing masters employed by George Villiers, the future Duke of Buckingham, presented him with dancing manuals in 1619 and 1623. However, their manuals were written in French and described French innovations and styling, not English practices. See Barthélemy de Montagut, *Louange de la Danse* (1619), ed. by Barbara Ravelhofer (Cambridge: RTM Publications, 2000).
7   Ian Payne, *The Almain in Britain, c. 1549 – c. 1675: A Dance Manual from Manuscript Sources* (Aldershot: Ashgate, 2003).
8   Emily Winerock, *Reformation and Revelry: The Practices and Politics of Dancing in Early Modern England, c. 1550 – c. 1640* (PhD diss., University of Toronto, 2012), 77–78.
9   Roger Clegg, "'When the play is done, you shall have a jig or dance of all treads': Danced Endings on Shakespeare's Stage", in McCulloch and Shaw (2019), 83–106.
10 For studies on Shakespeare and dance, see Alan Brissenden, *Shakespeare and the Dance* (Atlantic Highlands, NJ: Humanities Press, 1981); the "Shakespeare and Dance" special issue of *Borrowers and Lenders* 10:2 (2017), ed. by Elizabeth Klett; and McCulloch and Shaw (2019).
11 Unless otherwise specified, Shakespeare quotations are from *The Folger Shakespeare*, ed. by Barbara Mowat, Paul Werstine, Michael Poston and Rebecca Niles, last access 1 August 2020.

dancing (or expecting to dance) with the spectators. Act 4, scene 1 of *The Tempest* shows the influence of the early Stuart court masques, but the vast majority of Shakespeare's masked dance scenes draw on early Tudor and Italian masking practices.[12] This essay examines the masked dance scenes in *Much Ado About Nothing*, *Love's Labour's Lost* and *Timon of Athens*, with particular attention to the impact of mask-wearing on gender dynamics and perceptions of virtue.

Masks and Masking

Given the diversity of activities involving mask-wearing and the diversity of terms used to refer to masked activities in Shakespearean England, some discussion of terminology is warranted to clarify and delineate terms like *mumming*, *disguising*, *masquerade*, *mask*, *masque*, *common* and *vizard*.[13] In England prior to the 1580s, the term *mask* referred to an activity, not to an item worn. Face coverings were called *visers* (also *visars*, *visors*, *viziers*) or, increasingly in the sixteenth century, *vizards*. Other terms in use included *larva* (originally meaning 'malevolent ghost'), *face* and *head* (especially for whole-head coverings that rested on the shoulders).[14] Even once *mask* came into use for face coverings, stage directions reveal that it primarily indicated face coverings for women; men's face coverings continued to be called *vizards*.[15] Another potential source of confu-

---

12 James Knowles, "Insubstantial Pageants: *The Tempest* and Masquing Culture", in Jennifer Richards and James Knowles (eds), *Shakespeare's Late Plays: New Readings* (Edinburgh: Edinburgh University Press, 1999), 108–125.
13 In this section, I rely heavily on two works: Janette Dillon, "From Revels to Revelation: Shakespeare and the Mask", *Shakespeare Survey* 60 (2007), 58–71; and Meg Twycross and Sarah Carpenter, *Masks and Masking in Medieval and Early Tudor England* (Aldershot: Ashgate, 2002; repr. Abingdon: Routledge, 2016). Twycross and Carpenter's study builds on and corrects foundational works such as Enid Welsford, *The Court Masque: A Study in the Relationship between Poetry & the Revels* (Cambridge: Russell & Russell, 1927; repr. 1962); E. K. Chambers, *The Elizabethan Stage*, 4 vols. (Oxford: Clarendon Press, 1923); and Paul Reyher, *Les masques anglais: Étude sur les ballets et la vie de cour en Angleterre (1512–1640)* (New York: Blom, 1909; repr. 1964). It also provides essential background for understanding the Stuart court masque, complementing dance-focused studies like Barbara Ravelhofer, *The Early Stuart Masque: Dance, Costume, and Music* (Oxford: Oxford University Press, 2006); and Anne Daye, *The Jacobean Antimasque within the Masque Context: a Dance Perspective* (PhD diss., Roehampton University, 2008).
14 Twycross and Carpenter (2002), 328–336.
15 Alan Dessen and Leslie Thomson, *A Dictionary of Stage Directions in English Drama, 1580–1642* (Cambridge: Cambridge University Press, 1999), 140–141, 244.

Figure 1. The Daventry mask, sixteenth century. Velvet, silk and paper, with glass mouth-bead. Northamptonshire Archaeological Resource Centre: NARC–151A67. Creative commons license.

Figure 2. A man with a turban leading a woman wearing peacock feathers. From *The Masquerades*, after Jacques de Gheyn II (c. 1595). National Gallery of Art. Open access image.

sion is that modern scholars have tended to distinguish the earlier medieval and Tudor masked recreations from the later Stuart court spectacles by calling the former *masks* and the latter *masques*. Original sources, however, make no such distinctions and use these spellings interchangeably and indiscriminately.

Changing terminology combined with the chance survival of artifacts have also caused confusion among scholars and commentators. In Shakespeare's time, the most popular mask for women was the black, velvet and silk, full-face mask, which was held on by ribbons or with a mouth-bead, a bead attached to the mask that the woman held in her mouth.[16] The only surviving mask from sixteenth-century England, the Daventry mask, is of this type (see Figure 1). A mouth-bead

---

16 Special thanks go to M. Laura Martinez, Sarah Bendall, Allison Skewes, Linda J. Phillips and Christoph Heyl for generously sharing their knowledge of masks and early modern attire through personal correspondence when libraries were closed due to the coronavirus global pandemic.

GENDER AND MASKING IN SHAKESPEAREAN DANCE SCENES · 51

Figure 3. Elegant lady with peacock. Gillis van Breen, after anonymous (c. 1595 – c. 1610). Rijksmuseum. Public domain.

Figure 4. A veiled lady and two masked musicians. After Jacques de Gheyn II (c. 1595). Rijksmuseum. Public domain.

made a mask much easier to take on and off than masks that were tied or pinned on, but it was literally silencing. Primarily worn outdoors to protect a woman's face from sun exposure, it could also be worn for masking (see Figure 2). However, women also wore half-masks (see Figure 3).

While they provided less anonymity than a full-face mask, half-masks allowed for speech without unmasking. It seems likely that for scenes where female characters speak or sing while masked, the actors would have worn half-masks. Certainly, this seems more plausible than claims that actors would not have worn masks and vizards because they would have prevented speech.[17] Indeed, half-mask vizards were standard for musicians accompanying maskers in illustrations (see Figure 4).

---

17   Mattieu A. Chapman, "The Appearance of Blacks on the Early Modern Stage: *Love's Labour's Lost*'s African Connections to Court", *Early Theatre* 17:2 (2014), 77–94, quote 86; Virginia Mason Vaughan, *Performing Blackness on English Stages, 1500–1800* (Cambridge: Cambridge University Press, 2005), 10.

The masked dance scenes staged by Shakespeare draw on both English and continental masking traditions. Mumming was an English, mostly urban, Christmastime tradition dating back at least to the Middle Ages. Mummers would dress up in strange or fantastical clothes and visit other people's houses where they challenged the host to a game of dice. Mummers always concealed their faces, sometimes with visors, sometimes by blackening or whitening their faces. Another convention was that mummers could not speak, only gesture or mumble to communicate.[18] In the sixteenth century, a variant emerged that Meg Twycross and Sarah Carpenter term *courtly mumming*.[19] Disguised visitors brought a herald or interpreter to translate for them, and they gave gifts to their host instead of playing dice. Costumes were coordinated and thematic, with the visitors presenting themselves as ambassadors from foreign countries or ancient civilizations.[20]

Disguising was an English court tradition where the emphasis was on dressing up in "a strange *guise* (fashion)" rather than on necessarily obscuring one's identity.[21] Disguisers (male or female courtiers) would process into a hall, sometimes on pageant vehicles, and then perform "dyvers and many daunces".[22] Accounts emphasize the cost and extravagance of the matching costumes, which were fashioned for the event.[23] By the sixteenth century, masks were a standard component of disguising attire, with references to fantastical visors, simple caul or netted masks and realistic or neutral "well-favoured" full-face masks, although alternatively disguisers might blacken their faces, necks and arms with makeup or gauze.[24] Dancing took up the majority of a disguising, but the most exciting moment was the unmasking. The young Henry VIII was a particularly avid disguiser, and dramatic unmaskings at the end of the dancing became his trademark.[25]

Another influence on Henry VIII and his court were Italian masking traditions, especially the street masquerading of the carnival season, which extended

---

18 Twycross and Carpenter (2002), 83, 88, 92–93.
19 Ibid., 151.
20 Ibid., 160–161.
21 Ibid., 129.
22 Ibid., 136, 144; Dillon (2007), 61.
23 Twycross and Carpenter (2002), 133. Edward III favoured sets of 13 or 14, while Henry VIII preferred sets of six in coordinating colours.
24 Vaughan (2005), 11–12, 133, 137; Twycross and Carpenter (2002), 137–139, 142; Andrea Ria Stevens, *Inventions of the Skin: The Painted Body in Early English Drama* (Edinburgh: Edinburgh University Press, 2013), 91–92.
25 Twycross and Carpenter (2002), 149–150; Dillon (2007), 61–62.

from Christmas to Ash Wednesday, the period between the Advent and Lent fasts.[26] Sometimes the maskers serenaded women from the street; sometimes they threw eggs; sometimes the women threw eggs at them.[27] Street maskers were usually young men, although there are accounts of women masking, sometimes cross-dressed.[28] Street maskers ranged widely in rank and profession: carnival masquerading was both a popular and an elite practice. There was also a more exclusively elite version that Twycross and Carpenter have termed the "amorous masquerade".[29] This variant featured a group of (usually young, male) maskers who made surprise nocturnal visits to the houses of their peers rumoured to be hosting feasting and dancing. Masked and disguised, they would dance and flirt with the young women at the party who were not usually masked and whose fathers and husbands were obligated by the laws of hospitality to tolerate the visitors. Although originating in Italy, by the sixteenth century, amorous masquerading had been enthusiastically adopted across Europe, with Henry VIII reportedly introducing it in England.[30] Interestingly, while Henry VIII encouraged this "courtly version of Italian masking",[31] he tried to suppress some of the more traditional English masking practices. The "Acte against disguysed persons and Wearing of Visours" of 1511 outlawed street masquerades and selling masks.

During the sixteenth century, Tudor monarchs and their courtiers drew on all of these mask games and recreations – mumming, disguising and masquerading – mixing and repurposing them as they saw fit.[32] Of particular interest is the variant that sixteenth-century chronicler Edward Hall termed a *mask*, and that modern scholars have termed the *Tudor mask*.[33] A group of young people, masked and disguised, arrive unexpectedly at a party. They ask the (unmasked) members of the opposite sex to dance with them and 'common' together (chatting, flirting etc.). Then they either unmask or leave.

Shakespeare stages versions of the Tudor mask in *Romeo and Juliet* and in *Henry VIII*, as well as in the three plays discussed subsequently: *Much Ado About Nothing*, *Love's Labour's Lost* and *Timon of Athens*. In *Romeo and Juliet* and in

---

26 Twycross and Carpenter (2002), 52.
27 Ibid., 58.
28 Ibid., 65.
29 Ibid., 170.
30 Sydney Anglo, "The Evolution of the Early Tudor Disguising, Pageant, and Mask", *Renaissance Drama* 1 (1968), 3–44, quote 4; Twycross and Carpenter (2002), 170–174.
31 Dillon (2007), 62.
32 Ibid., 59.
33 Anglo (1968), 4–8; Dillon (2007), 59–60.

Much Ado About Nothing, the masking is essentially an amorous masquerade, while the masking in *Henry VIII*, *Love's Labour's Lost* and *Timon of Athens* incorporates elements of courtly mumming and disguising, such as the maskers communicating through an interpreter and presenting themselves as a delegation of foreign ambassadors or ancient warriors. Shakespeare also upends certain expectations, most notably by making the maskers in *Timon of Athens* women, but also by having the ladies visited by the maskers in *Love's Labour's Lost* also wear masks.

Much Ado About Nothing

Much Ado About Nothing was first performed around 1598 by the Lord Chamberlain's Men and was also performed at the English court in 1613. For most of the play, the two female leads are presented as opposites. Hero is sweet, reserved and obedient, while Beatrice is salty, sassy and anti-authoritarian. However, in the dance scene in Act 2, Hero exchanges remarks with the Prince that resemble Beatrice's mocking wit more than Hero's usual demure murmurings. When the Prince asks, "Lady, will you walk about with your friend?", Hero responds, "So you walk softly, and look sweetly, and say nothing, I am yours for the walk, and especially when I walk away", which she likely then does (2.1.84–88). Hero's attendants, Margaret and Ursula, as well as Beatrice herself, have similar feisty exchanges with other gentlemen at the party. The women can safely mock and flirt with the revellers because the men are masked, and Renaissance masking conventions extend the protection and licence of the mask to those who dance and converse with mask-wearers.[34]

Act 2 begins with Beatrice, Hero and Leonato, among others, on the way to the evening's entertainment.[35] Then 'revellers' enter: the Prince, Claudio and Benedick, among others, in disguise. Twycross and Carpenter categorize this scene as "a traditional amorous mask" where "masked men of the court choose unmasked dancing partners from among the women".[36] The plot and dialogue support this reading that the revellers are masked and the women are not. The Prince has agreed to woo Hero on behalf of Claudio, and upon entering, the Prince approaches Hero directly: there is no indication that he has to determine which

---

34   Twycross and Carpenter (2002), 172–179.
35   Nona Monahin offers detailed analysis and staging suggestions for Beatrice's dance-filled tirade against marriage in the opening of this scene; cf. Monahin (2019), 51–59.
36   Twycross and Carpenter (2002), 186.

lady she is, as he would if she were masked. Conversely, both the Prince and Hero refer to his visor (2.1.95–96). However, in modern productions of *Much Ado About Nothing*, whether the women wear masks has become a directorial choice.

Kenneth Branagh's 1993 film starring Emma Thompson as Beatrice and Branagh as Benedick is one of the most well-known versions of *Much Ado About Nothing*. The scene begins with a dramatic and almost medieval entrance for the revellers, whose disguises genuinely obscure their identities. Hero and Beatrice, along with many others at the party, also wear masks, but these are half-masks that do not really disguise their identities. The Prince gives his first line and takes Hero by the hand, but Hero responds with only a squeal of delight as they join the dancing. After some shots of masked dancers and musicians, the camera cuts to Beatrice and Benedick's exchange. The other three couple's exchanges in Shakespeare's text, including Hero and the Prince's, are eliminated. We then get more wonderfully evocative shots of masked dancers, before we see (as Claudio does), Hero in earnest conversation with the Prince in the distance, her mask in her hand. Indeed, Beatrice and Hero might as well not have masks, they wear them so rarely. While Kate Beckinsale's Hero has an appealing innocence and sweetness, Branagh's decision to cut all of her lines in this scene takes away her liveliest moments in the play.[37]

Joss Whedon's 2012 film version has a very different mood and aesthetic from Branagh's, especially in this scene, but Whedon makes some surprisingly similar staging choices and text cuts. He eliminates Ursula and Antonio's exchange entirely, simplifies and shortens Margaret and Borachio's exchange and cuts all of Hero's lines and all but one of the Prince's. At the same time, he lengthens their exchange – but we see it from a distance rather than hearing it. Like Claudio, we are relegated to observers. Both revellers and ladies are masked, but as with Branagh, the Prince's mask is a full-face mask that genuinely conceals his identity, while Hero's half-mask does not. Hero wears her mask throughout this scene, but it does little to hide her identity or expressions, and Beatrice hardly wears hers at all. Jillian Morgese's Hero is sophisticated and even wry at times, but because Whedon cuts her lines, we do not see Hero's quick wit.[38]

Two much-lauded productions of *Much Ado* graced London stages the year before. The Shakespeare's Globe 2011 production was directed by Jeremy Herrin, with Sian Williams as choreographer. The Shakespeare-era production famously starred Eve Best as Beatrice and Charles Edwards as Benedick. Ony Uhiara

---

37 This scene can be viewed at https://youtu.be/i8vRoPaPdb8, last access 1 August 2020.
38 This scene can be viewed at https://youtu.be/dYjp3fkcyMw, last access 1 August 2020.

played Hero. The dance scene began with a raucous fire-lighting and a few moments of dancing to establish the context. Then Hero and the Prince had their exchange downstage, while the dancing continued quietly behind them. Afterwards, they rejoined the dancing upstage while Margaret and Borachio took their places downstage for their exchange.

In this production, only the men wore masks; the women were unmasked, their identities known. This ought to have worked in performance, but Uhiara's energetic movement style, amplified by the way the Prince literally jerked her around, seemed out of character. Had Hero's identity been hidden by a mask, peasant-like motions could have been interpreted as an intentional and clever component of a disguise. However, because Hero's identity was known, we expected her to move with the smooth gracefulness of a noblewoman, an expectation enhanced by the historical costumes and period setting. In this production, Hero's exchange with the Prince indicated that she had more spirit and wit than was at first apparent, but the awkward and energetic movement style was unrealistic and inappropriate for the context: an unmasked noblewoman would not have acted or moved in a manner that called either her nobility and grace or her virtue into question.[39]

The Wyndham Theatre also did *Much Ado About Nothing* in 2011, starring Catherine Tate as Beatrice and David Tennant as Benedick. Directed by Josie Rourke, the dance scene in this modern-era production had a lot of festive energy and an element of decadence although it lacked the elegance of Whedon's masquerade ball. Sara Macrae's Hero retained her lines and wore a mask in Act 2, scene 1 of this production, but Macrae overdid the flirtation. Her body language was sexy and seductive with neither Morgese's reserve nor Beckinsale's sweetness. Perhaps this choice was supposed to reflect the production's modern setting – Macrae's Hero is faithful, just not virginal. The problem was that, by having Hero be seductive rather than simply saucy, it became too easy to believe Don John's assertions later in the play that she had been unfaithful to Claudio.[40] Hero's seductiveness lessened the distinctions, emphasized by Shakespeare, among the female characters: Margaret is outgoing and promiscuous, Hero is demure and virginal, Beatrice is outspoken but chaste. The production may have been trying to argue that sexy women can be faithful, but portraying Hero as worldly and seductive weakens the impact of Shakespeare's warning that a man inclined towards jealousy will believe outrageous lies about the woman he loves, even when

---

39   This scene can be viewed at https://youtu.be/QkJWAzUvCPg, last access 1 August 2020.
40   This scene can be viewed at https://youtu.be/M9tGZORbg2c, last access 1 August 2020.

those lies contradict his own experiences, her character, her past actions and her own words.

In *Much Ado About Nothing*, the masked dance scene highlights both the freedom afforded by masking and the downsides of that freedom. The audience knows that Hero is entirely innocent, but her sauciness in the dance scene helps us understand how Claudio, the Prince and even her own father could imagine Hero as anything other than a spotless virgin. Similar situations occur in *The Winter's Tale* and *Othello*, where a woman's entirely innocent gestures of friendship, when seen through a husband's jealous eyes, become evidence of her infidelity. Thus, we find Shakespeare repeatedly suggesting that modest women *ought* to be able to be friendly and even flirtatious without endangering their reputations while also acknowledging that there was always a danger that even innocent interactions could be misconstrued, sometimes with disastrous consequences.

Nevertheless, the Renaissance dance floor was a site where women equalled, and often reigned over, men. Thus, it should not be surprising that female speech on the dance floor conveys a confidence and authority, even audacity, that women were less likely to possess or express elsewhere. The licence afforded maskers and their partners extended this freedom of expression even further. It is ironic and unfortunate that so many modern productions that revel in Beatrice's independence and intelligence simultaneously silence Hero – eliminating the lines that show that she, too, has spirit and wit, not just virtue.

Love's Labour's Lost

Whereas productions of *Much Ado About Nothing* often cut Hero and her female attendants' lines, productions of Shakespeare's *Love's Labour's Lost* tend to retain the quips of all the female characters, not just those of Lady Rosaline, the play's female wit and counterpart to the male wit, Lord Berowne. First performed at court for Queen Elizabeth in 1597, the play explores the consequences when the King of Navarre and three of his courtiers take an oath that they will devote themselves to study and foreswear the company of women for three years. Shortly thereafter, the Princess of France and three of her ladies arrive as ambassadors from the French King. The men do not want to break their oath, but they are eager to see the visiting ladies, so they find a loophole. They will meet and talk with the visitors, but they will not formally welcome them. They house the women in a field instead of in the castle and otherwise withhold the hospitality due to a visiting princess and her entourage. Against their wills, they also fall in love with the ladies, although their oath makes them loathe to acknowledge this. Instead, they devise a device: they will disguise themselves, entertain the ladies with a masked entry and dancing and try to determine whether their love is returned.

However, the women get wind of this plot and resolve to undermine it, wanting to punish the men for their inhospitality. Explains the Princess to her ladies:

> There's no such sport as sport by sport o'erthrown,
> To make theirs ours and ours none but our own.
> So shall we stay, mocking intended game,
> And they, well mocked, depart away with shame.
> (5.2.160–163)

The women don masks, trade favours given to them by the lords and when the maskers arrive, they refuse to dance with them. However, the women do not simply decline the men's invitation to dance. Instead, they draw on Renaissance bowing etiquette to tease and mock their suitors.

A shortened version of this scene that I choreographed for *The Bard's Galliard, or How to Party like an Elizabethan* in 1999 highlights how the women use bowing conventions to confuse and confound the men.[41] The men bow upon entering the room, the men and women bow and curtsy to each other in asking and accepting the offer to dance and together they perform the opening *révérence* of a dance, all very correct for the time period. However, Rosaline, playing the part of the Princess, then stops the music and halts the dancing, the women turning their backs on their partners and literally leaving them 'off balance'. The men are understandably confused, and the King and Rosaline have a witty exchange where he tries to convince her that the women should resume their dancing. She seemingly agrees, saying that they should "take hands", but instead of dancing, she and the other ladies skip to the *conge*, or end-of-dance bow, and leave the dance floor: "Curtsy, sweethearts – and so the measure ends." (5.2.235) While directors tend to cut bows in modern productions, the audience's laughter demonstrates that even though bowing is no longer a familiar practice, the insult that the ladies give to the lords in this scene through their curtsies is perfectly clear in performance.

---

41   This version of Act 5, scene 2 cuts some of the speeches and repartee and shifts the timing of the ladies turning their backs but not the intended message. Archival footage of the 22 April 1999 performance at Princeton University is available at https://youtu.be/yxgAaYlUw4s?t=153, last access 1 August 2020.

In this scene, the women perform the correct bows to begin and end a dance, but they skip the dancing that ought to go in between; their dance is literally nothing but empty courtesies. In so doing, the women point to the emptiness of the men trying to 'honour them' on the dance floor, when they have not treated them honourably off of it. Likewise, they mimic the men's use of masks to disguise their true identities and true intentions, giving the men a taste of their own medicine. While the women's curtsies are intentionally misleading, their discourtesy is motivated by their desire to show the King of Navarre and his courtiers just how dishonourable the men's behaviour has been. Masks protect the women, somewhat, from repercussions, while simultaneously hiding and revealing the men's oath-breaking and disingenuousness.

In *Love's Labour's Lost*, the agenda of the male maskers might be dishonourable, but that of the masked female characters is virtuous and corrective, however playful its conveyance. In *Timon of Athens*, on the other hand, the motivations of the female masked dancers are suspect. Indeed, disguised intentions and their eventual unmasking is one of the play's main themes.

Timon of Athens

Timon of Athens is sometimes considered one of Shakespeare's "problem plays".[42] The play has few sympathetic characters, and the only text, from the 1623 First Folio, may be incomplete. Originally attributed just to Shakespeare, it is now widely acknowledged as one of his co-authored plays, most likely with Thomas Middleton.[43] While John Jowett argues for a composition date of 1606, and Andrew Hadfield suggests it was written (and possibly performed) in 1608, the first documented performance of the First Folio text was in 1761, almost 150 years after Shakespeare's death.[44] Today, it remains one of the least frequently performed of Shakespeare's plays.

---

42 See, for example, Francelia Butler, *The Strange Critical Fortunes of Shakespeare's Timon of Athens* (Iowa City: Iowa State University Press, 1966); and E. L. Risen, *Shakespeare and the Problem Play: Complex Forms, Crossed Genres, and Moral Quandaries* (Jefferson, NC: McFarland, 2012).

43 Eilidh Kane, "Shakespeare and Middleton's Co-Authorship of *Timon of Athens*", *Journal of Early Modern Studies* 5 (2016), 217–235.

44 Andrew Hadfield, "*Timon of Athens* and Jacobean Politics", *Shakespeare Survey* 56 (2003), 215–226, quote 218; John Jowett, "Introduction", in William Shakespeare, *Timon of Athens*, ed. by John Jowett. The Oxford Shakespeare (Oxford: Oxford University Press, 2004), 3.

Female maskers dressed as Amazon warriors appear in Act 2, scene 1 at one of Timon's famous banquets.[45] Their entrance is preceded by a trumpet fanfare and a messenger, Cupid, who announces that "certain ladies" desire admittance to the party (1.2.120). Timon welcomes them in, and the stage directions specify: "*Enter the masque of Ladies [as] Amazons, with lutes in their hands, dancing and playing*" (1.2.134 SD).

That the ladies are described as a "masque" likely indicates that they wear masks as well as costumes. That they hold lutes instead of weapons emphasizes their femininity and has choreographic implications: these Amazons would not be dancing the galliard or a sword dance. Lutes are instruments of love not war, implying, Anne Daye argues, "that the performance is transgressional, rather than martial".[46]

While the Amazons dance or just after, the play's misanthrope, Apemantus, complains: "What a sweep of vanity comes this way. / They dance? They are madwomen", and then, after some comments about flatterers and fools, he prophesizes, "I should fear those that dance before me now / Would one day stamp upon me." (1.2.136–137, 147–148) Interestingly, the Amazons do not appear again in the play after this scene, but the lords at the party do, and they certainly "stamp" on Timon later, so the comment can be understood as generalized to the whole assembly rather than being directed primarily at the dancers.

Following Apemantus's aside, the stage directions state: "*The Lords rise from table, with much adoring of Timon, and to show their loves each single out an Amazon, and all dance, men with women, a lofty strain or two to the hautboys, and cease*" (1.2.149 SD). Timon then thanks and compliments the dancers and invites them to partake of the banquet in the next room. The ladies happily accept the invitation and exit, presumably to the banquet hall.

Thus, there are two dances in this scene: a single-gender dance that brings the women onto the stage, and perhaps provides some pleasing entertainment, and a

---

45 This is one of the scenes generally attributed to Middleton; cf. Jowett (2004), 2. Dressing up as an Amazon or female warrior was popular throughout this period. Elizabethan Revels accounts for 1578/1579 include the purchase of silk to make "heares" (wigs) for Amazons; in January 1604, Anna of Denmark chose to portray Pallas Athena, goddess of war, in the masque *The Vision of the Twelve Goddesses*; and Penthesiliea, Queen of the Amazons, is one of the queens in the 1608 *Masque of Queens*; cf. Twycross and Carpenter (2002), 323; Clare McManus, *Women on the Renaissance Stage: Anna of Denmark and Female Masquing in the Stuart Court 1590–1619* (Manchester: Manchester University Press, 2002).

46 Anne Daye, "'The revellers are entering': Shakespeare and Masquing Practice in Tudor and Stuart England", in McCulloch and Shaw (2019), 105–131, quote 114.

mixed-gender dance of the Amazons with the lords at the party. This is a typical pairing of entry dance and social dancing, another amorous mask, as Twycross and Carpenter have termed it. However, in this example, it is women who enter as maskers and offer a single-gender dance, and then it is the spectators, not the performers, who choose their partners for the social dancing. Still, in *Timon of Athens*, the gender inversion does not feel controversial. The women are identified as Amazons in the stage directions, in other words, women associated with masculine skills and characteristics, so it feels fitting that they would also appropriate male masquerading practices. Moreover, the lords choose them for the social dancing, rather than the other way around, even though this was not uncommon.

Scholars have tended to emphasize the women's passivity and peripheral role in this scene: "The ladies in the masque are showgirls whose roles are confined to dancing. Their spokesperson is a male Cupid; they themselves say nothing."[47] While it is true that dancing is inherently expressive, communicating meaning through "a kind of mute rhetoric" that playgoers were perfectly capable of interpreting, this reading goes too far; female agency is still very much in evidence in the banquet scene.[48] Not only do the maskers invoke associations with female power by portraying Amazons and co-opt the male practice of masquerade, but they also appear to be the devisers as well as the performers of this entertainment. As Peter Davidson and Jane Stevenson contend, "devisership" is an important but often overlooked category of women's cultural production.[49] An entertainment's deviser was its mastermind, its artistic director and visionary, who might also be the author of the text, the composer of the music or the choreographer of the dances.

Despite abandoning the theme of Amazons, the ladies' mask in the 1999 production of *Timon of Athens* by the Seattle Shakespeare in the Park Company also conveyed a sense of female autonomy and authority. Directed by Ken Holmes and choreographed by Anna Maria Gutierrez, the women did not wear masks, but they entered veiled, invoking the mysteriousness of Renaissance masking,

---

47 Jowett (2004), 37.
48 Thoinot Arbeau, *Orchesography* [*Orchésographie*, 1589], trans. by Mary S. Evans, ed. by Julia Sutton (New York: Dover, 1967), 16. See also Bella Mirabella, "'In the sight of all': Queen Elizabeth and the Dance of Diplomacy", *Early Theatre* 15:1 (2012), 65–89.
49 Peter Davidson and Jane Stevenson, "Elizabeth I's Reception at Bisham (1592): Elite Women as Writers and Devisers", in Jayne Elisabeth Archer, Elizabeth Goldring and Sarah Knight (eds), *The Progresses, Pageants, & Entertainments of Queen Elizabeth I* (Oxford: Oxford University Press, 2007), 205–226, especially 209.

however briefly. The scene also preserved the two dances in the text. The women performed as a group initially, and then danced with the lords. The women's dancing, reminiscent of Egyptian *raqs sharqi* or 'belly dancing', was sensuous and provocative, but throughout the scene, and especially when dancing with the men, the women were clearly in control.[50]

Conclusion

In his widely read and influential discussion of court life and etiquette, *Il Cortegiano*, or *The Book of the Courtier*, Baldassare Castiglione explains that "to be in a maske bringeth with it a certaine libertie and lycence".[51] A mask obscured identity and thus afforded the wearer unusual freedom and even impunity. Moreover, the conventions of Renaissance masking extended this licence to those who danced and conversed with mask-wearers. One could not be held accountable for things said to someone whose identity was unknowable. Indeed, one could argue that because women's behaviour was more circumscribed than men's in the Renaissance, they benefited even more from the social loophole of the mask. At the same time, wearing a mask attracted unusual attention: observers scrutinized a mask-wearer's words and actions as they searched for clues to the masker's identity.

While mask-wearing was a customary practice in the Renaissance, playwrights used masks onstage to direct attention to what was hidden, misconstrued or misrepresented. Shakespeare's masked dance scenes feature onstage spectators whose reactions to, and interactions with, the maskers encourage us to ask, not just 'Who is truthful, honest, pure and well-intentioned?' but also, 'Who can recognize these characteristics in others?' and 'Who misinterprets what they see or is easily misled?' Shakespeare's masked dance scenes thus highlight the difference between being honest and virtuous and being perceived as such. They provide opportunities for agency and self-expression, especially for women, but they also show the fine line between wit and wantonness and the dangers for those who crossed, or were thought to have crossed, that line.

In *Much Ado About Nothing* and *Love's Labour's Lost*, the dancing and surrounding dialogue highlight female characters' wit and playfulness. In *Much Ado About Nothing*, the women take advantage of the licence afforded not just to

---

50 This scene can be viewed at https://youtu.be/BbeydWVobrI, last access 1 August 2020.
51 Baldesar Castiglione, *The Courtyer of Count Baldessar Castilio*, trans. by Sir Thomas Hoby (London, 1561), Book II, sig. M3.

those who wear masks, but to those who converse with them. In *Love's Labour's Lost*, the women use their obscured identities to trick the men, but they do so for the men's own good – to spotlight and correct the men's poor behaviour. Having female maskers in *Timon of Athens* upends many of the masquerade's gendered associations, even if having the Amazons carry lutes instead of weapons, and having the male spectators choose them instead of the other way around for social dancing, somewhat lessens the subversiveness of the role reversal. Moreover, in *Timon of Athens*, it is suggested that one or more of the women are the mask's devisers, even if a man wrote, as well as presents, Cupid's speech. Female devisership, or creative directorship, of entertainments offers another example of female agency that has been mostly overlooked within Shakespeare's plays. In *Love's Labour's Lost*, the women hijack the devisership of the mask, much to the men's surprise and discomfort. *The Merry Wives of Windsor* offers another example of virtuous, clever women devising a masked performance to punish and correct male misbehaviour.

Masked dance scenes show women in control of themselves, and sometimes others, and highlight their wit and intelligence as well as their beauty, virtue and grace. In most of these scenes, we also get to share in the women's spectatorship, with the male maskers as the objects on display, strutting their stuff literally and figuratively in their processional dance. Reversing the usual gender roles, it is the women who behold, and the men who are beheld. And yet this inversion of power is incomplete as well as short-lived. In all of these scenes, it is always the men who get to choose their partners for the partner dancing, even when the women are the maskers, as in the case of *Timon of Athens*. Nevertheless, masked dances give us enticing glimpses of female wit and wisdom, not just for characters like Beatrice and Rosaline, whose quick wits and silver tongues are emphasized throughout *Much Ado About Nothing* and *Love's Labour's Lost*, but also, importantly, for Hero and the Princess of France and her ladies, who are otherwise presented as models of modesty and decorum. Shakespeare's use of female masking in these plays thus functions similarly to female cross-dressing in plays like *Twelfth Night*, *Merchant of Venice* and *As You Like It*. In all of these plays, Shakespeare utilizes masks and disguises to reveal the lively personalities of women who otherwise conform to social expectations of silence and reserve to convey their honesty and virtue.

Directors of modern-day Shakespeare productions often feel that they must 'read between the lines' or 'read against the grain' to find and convey female characters' agency. Masked dance scenes offer an often-overlooked opportunity to highlight female characters' agency and authority and to do so in ways that are not just appropriate for the time period but are already in the play. Indeed, I would argue, to cut women's lines in these scenes is to rob them of the agency that Shakespeare granted them and squander the anonymizing protection of the mask that enabled them to express it.

Zusammenfassung

In der Renaissance gewährten Masken eine gewisse Freiheit, und zwar nicht nur denjenigen, die die Maske trugen, sondern auch jenen, die mit ihnen tanzten oder sich mit ihnen unterhielten. Die Maske erlaubte es Frauen, frei zu sprechen und ihren Wortwitz spielen zu lassen, ohne dabei ihren Ruf zu gefährden. Masken wurden jedoch auch mit Unaufrichtigkeit und Täuschung assoziiert. Der Aufsatz analysiert Tanzszenen in drei Shakespeare-Stücken – *Much Ado About Nothing*, *Love's Labour's Lost* und *Timon of Athens* –, in denen das Tragen von Masken beträchtliche Auswirkungen auf die Gender-Dynamik, den weiblichen Handlungsspielraum und die Wahrnehmung weiblicher Tugend hat. Der Artikel erörtert schließlich auch die Chancen und Herausforderungen, die solche Szenen für moderne Inszenierungen mit sich bringen.

Romeo und Julia: die Tragödie als Ballett

IRIS JULIA BÜHRLE

Jean-Georges Noverre, der bekannteste Theoretiker der Ballettreform des 18. Jahrhunderts, schrieb in seinen 1760 veröffentlichten *Briefen über die Tanzkunst:*

> Es ist recht erstaunlich, dass man bis heute kaum verstanden hat, dass das tragische Genre für den tänzerischen Ausdruck am besten geeignet ist; es bietet großartige Tableaus, edle Situationen und gelungene spektakuläre Wendungen; da die Leidenschaften überdies bei Helden stärker und entschiedener sind als bei gewöhnlichen Menschen, wird deren Darstellung einfacher und die Handlung der Pantomime wärmer, wahrhaftiger und verständlicher.[1]

Noverre gehörte zu den ersten Ballettmeistern, die versuchten, vollständige literarische Werke in Tanz umzusetzen. Es ging unter anderem darum, das Ballett, bis dahin meist ein handlungsarmes Divertissement innerhalb von Opern, als vollgültige imitative Kunstform zu etablieren. Die Umsetzung von Tragödien, dem damals angesehensten literarischen Genre, trug zur Legitimierung der neuen Kunstform bei, die unter dem Namen *ballet d'action* bekannt wurde. Ballette sollten Noverre zufolge wie Dramen aus "exposition", "noeud" (Verstrickung) und "dénouement" (Auflösung) bestehen. Das Ballett sollte die Leidenschaften darstellen und der Zuschauer sollte wie in einer Tragödie ergriffen werden.[2] So

---

1   Jean Georges Noverre, *Lettres sur la danse, et sur les ballets, par M. Noverre, maître des ballets de son Altesse sérénissime Monseigneur le duc de Wurtemberg, & ci-devant des théatres de Paris, Lyon, Marseille, Londres, &c.* (Lyon: Aimé Delaroche, 1760), Lettre III, 30–31: "Il est bien singulier, que l'on ait comme ignoré jusqu'à présent que le genre le plus propre à l'expression de la Danse est le genre tragique; il fournit de grands Tableaux, des situations nobles & des coups de théâtre heureux; d'ailleurs, les passions étant plus fortes & plus décidées dans les Héros que dans les Hommes ordinaires, l'imitation en devient plus facile & l'action du Pantomime plus chaude, plus vraie & plus intelligible." Alle Übersetzungen stammen von mir.
2   Vgl. z. B. Edward Nye, "Dancing Words: Eighteenth-Century Ballet-Pantomime Wordbooks as Paratexts", *Word & Image* 24:4 (2008), 403–412, Zitat 408: "staging the passions is almost universally accepted as a key objective of the *ballet-pantomime*, the feature which distinguishes it from other forms of dance which are allegedly less expressive and more mechanical."

schrieb der Schauspieler Joseph Uriot über eine Szene in Noverres Ballett *Médée et Jason* (Stuttgart 1763):

> der Anblick dieser Szene lässt alle vor Entsetzen erschauern; der folgende Augenblick, in dem Medea in dem Versuch, den Schrei der Natur zu ersticken, den Dolch über die Köpfe ihrer beiden Kinder erhebt, die ihr zu Füßen fallen und mit erhobenen Armen um ihr Leben bitten, bildet so eine entsetzliche Gruppierung, dass sie die Seele in Stücke reißt und den Zuschauer dazu bringt, die tränenerfüllten Augen abzuwenden, die fürchten, den Mord an diesen armen Unschuldigen mit ansehen zu müssen. [...] [D]ie Katastrophe bietet das tragischste Spektakel, das man in einem Theater darstellen kann.[3]

Noverre wollte das Publikum zutiefst berühren und Mitleid und Entsetzen hervorrufen; in seinen Augen war das Ballett hierfür nicht weniger geeignet als die Tragödie. Dem Ballettmeister, den sein Freund David Garrick angeblich den "Shakespeare des Tanzes" nannte, wird oft das erste Shakespeare-Ballett zugeschrieben, *Cleopatra* (Ludwigsburg 1765).[4]

Shakespeares *Romeo und Julia* entspricht nur bedingt Noverres Tragödienkonzept. Zwar enthält das Stück starke Leidenschaften, doch kann man die Protagonisten – ein sehr junges, relativ gewöhnliches Liebespaar – kaum mit den Helden der klassischen griechischen und der neoklassischen französischen Tragödie vergleichen, die Noverres Aussage inspirierten. Romeo hat wenig von einem klassischen tragischen Helden, der im Lauf des Werkes an seinen inneren Konflikten wächst; er und seine Liebe zu Julia scheitern an einer Verkettung ungünstiger äußerer Umstände. Die Stärke und Entschiedenheit der Leidenschaften, die Noverre zufolge den tragischen Helden auszeichnen, finden sich eher bei der weiblichen Hauptfigur; diese ist ihrem Partner mindestens ebenbürtig. Im ersten Teil des Stückes, in dessen Zentrum die Trennung ei-

---

3 Joseph Uriot, *Description des fêtes données à l'occasion du jour de naissance de Son Altesse, le duc régnant de Wurtemberg et Teck, le 11 février 1763, par Mr. Uriot* (Stuttgart: Cotta, 1763), 43–44: " le Spectacle de ce moment fait frémir d'horreur; l'instant qui le suit & où Médée s'efforçant d'étouffer jusqu'au cri de la Nature, lève le poignard sur ses deux Fils qui tombent à ses pieds les bras levés pour lui demander la vie, forme un Grouppe si épouvantable, qu'il déchire l'âme, & fait détourner les yeux qui baignés de pleurs, redoutent de voir donner la mort à ces pauvres Innocents. [...] [L]a Catastrophe offre le Spectacle le plus tragique qui puisse être présenté sur le Théâtre [...]."

4 Zu diesem Werk siehe mein Kapitel "Shakespeare Ballets in Germany: From Jean-Georges Noverre to John Neumeier", in Lynsey McCulloch und Brandon Shaw (Hg.), *The Oxford Handbook of Shakespeare and Dance* (New York: Oxford University Press, 2019), 359–386.

nes jungen Paares durch eine streitsüchtige ältere Generation steht, überwiegen Komödienelemente, die auch nach Mercutios Tod nicht vollkommen verschwinden. Die Thematik und Protagonisten des Stückes, die es manchen Kritikern seit A.C. Bradley als nicht ganz vollgültige Tragödie der Jugendjahre erscheinen ließen,[5] machen es zu einer exzellenten Vorlage für ein Ballett. Ähnlich wie die Oper eignet sich das Ballett besonders gut zur Darstellung starker gegensätzlicher Emotionen. Diese werden durch die Musik und die Unmittelbarkeit, welche durch das Verschwinden kommentierender und distanzierender Worte entsteht, noch akzentuiert. Die für eine Shakespeare-Tragödie ungewöhnliche Bedeutung der weiblichen Hauptfigur erleichtert die Umsetzung des Werkes in ein Genre, in dessen Zentrum oftmals die Ballerina steht und zu dessen wichtigsten Ausdrucksmitteln Pas de deux (Duos) zwischen einem Tänzer und einer Tänzerin gehören. Nicht zuletzt deswegen drehen sich fast alle Handlungsballette um eine Liebesthematik, was *Romeo und Julia*, die bekannteste Liebesgeschichte aller Zeiten, zu einem dankbaren Thema für den Tanz macht. So schrieb der Choreograph Maurice Béjart, der unter anderem auch ein *Romeo und Julia*-Ballett schuf:

> Besser als die Tragödie oder jede andere Ausdrucksform kann der Tanz die Liebe darstellen, denn es ist sehr schwierig [...], im Theater eine Liebesszene zu schreiben, ohne in Floskeln, Affektiertheit oder falsche Poesie zu verfallen. [...] [D]ie perfekte Liebesszene ist fast unmöglich zu schreiben. Allerdings ist es sehr leicht, sie zu tanzen. So gesehen ist der Tanz allen anderen Künsten überlegen.[6]

Neben der wachsenden Liebesleidenschaft der Hauptfiguren enthält das Stück ein breites Spektrum starker Emotionen, unter anderem Hass, Verzweiflung, Hoffnung und Trauer. Die Pole des Konflikts – Capulets und Montagues, die ältere und jüngere Generation – lassen sich optisch gut differenzieren, und die meisten Personen kann man leicht in helfende (Bruder Lorenzo, Amme) und

---

5 Siehe Gillian Woods, *Shakespeare: Romeo and Juliet* (Basingstoke: Palgrave Macmillan, 2013), 46–65.
6 Maurice Béjart, Vorwort zu Jean-Georges Noverre, *Lettres sur la danse et sur les ballets* (1760; Paris: Editions du Sandre, 2006), 21: "Mieux que la tragédie ou que toute autre forme d'expression, la danse peut traduire l'amour car il est très difficile [...] d'écrire une scène d'amour au théâtre sans tomber dans le verbiage, la préciosité ou la fausse poésie. [...] [L]a scène d'amour parfait est presqu'impossible à écrire. Il est, par contre, très facile de la danser. Vue sous cet angle, la danse est supérieure à tous les autres arts."

hindernde (die älteren Capulets, Tybalt) Figuren einteilen. Das tragische Ende eignet sich gut für den Abschluss eines Handlungsballetts, da dieses Genre wie die Oper oft mit einem emotionalen Höhepunkt endet. Andererseits enthält das Werk einige Elemente, die seine Umsetzung in ein wortloses Medium erschweren, beispielsweise Lorenzos Pläne für die Rettung des Paares und die Gründe für deren Scheitern, das zum tragischen Ende des Stückes führt. Zur Erklärung dieser Details verließen sich Choreographen aller Zeiten auf Handlungszusammenfassungen im Programm und die Bekanntheit des Stoffes.

Im Folgenden wird am Beispiel verschiedener Ballettfassungen von *Romeo und Julia* erläutert, wie sich das Tragische im wortlosen Medium Tanz ausdrücken lässt. Nach der Betrachtung einiger früher Adaptationen mit Happy End geht es darum, wie der Wandel des Stückes von einer potentiellen Komödie zur Tragödie mit den Ausdrucksmitteln des Balletts, vor allem Choreographie, Musik, Bühnenbild und Kostümen, dargestellt werden kann. Daraufhin werden verschiedene Mittel untersucht, durch die Choreographen Shakespeares Tragödie interpretieren und neue Perspektiven auf diese eröffnen können, beispielsweise die Hinzufügung kommentierender Figuren und von Visionsszenen, die Variation des choreographischen Tempos und der Bruch mit Konventionen ihres Genres.

Von der Komödie zur Tragödie

Die ersten Ballettadaptationen von *Romeo und Julia* entstanden in Italien in der zweiten Hälfte des 18. Jahrhunderts. Dem Vorwort der Libretti der ersten *Romeo und Julia*-Ballette zufolge ließen sich die Choreographen (damals Ballettmeister genannt) durch mehrere europäische Fassungen des Stoffes inspirieren. Sie veränderten die Quellen oft stark und ließen die Tragödie auf verschiedene Arten enden: In den meisten Balletten starben die Liebenden, wobei Julia häufig erwachte, kurz nachdem Romeo das Gift genommen hatte. Dies gab den Ballettmeistern Gelegenheit, einen hochdramatischen letzten Pas de deux für die Abschlussszene zu choreographieren. Manche Ballettmeister fügten eine letzte Konfrontation Julias mit ihrer Familie ein, bevor sie sich vor deren Augen das Leben nahm.[7] Einige ließen die Liebenden überleben. Dies entsprach mehreren literarischen Fassungen des Stoffes, beispielsweise Lope de Vegas Drama *Cas-*

---

7   Dies ist beispielsweise der Fall in Filippo Berettis *Giulietta e Romeo*, dem wohl ersten *Romeo und Julia*-Ballett, das 1784 in Padua uraufgeführt wurde.

telvines y Monteses (1647), Christian Felix Weißes Trauerspiel *Romeo und Julie* (1769) und Louis-Sébastien Merciers Drama *Les tombeaux de Vérone* (1782). So erwachte Julia etwa in Gaspare Ronzis 1799 in Neapel uraufgeführtem Ballett *Giulietta e Romeo* rechtzeitig, um Romeos Tod zu verhindern; der Ballettmeister erklärte, dass das Publikum Fassungen mit gutem Ausgang bevorzugte.[8] Dieser freie Umgang mit dem Stoff erstaunt keineswegs in einer Zeit, in der Shakespeares Stücke üblicherweise auch für das Theater umgeschrieben wurden. Im kontinentalen Europa erregte das Ende seiner Tragödien, in denen auch Unschuldige zugrunde gingen, häufig Anstoß. So reagierte beispielsweise das Pariser Publikum mit solcher Empörung auf Desdemonas Tod in Jean-François Ducis' *Othello*-Adaptation im Jahr 1792, dass sich der Autor gezwungen sah, das Ende neu zu schreiben.[9]

Im nicht textgebundenen Genre des Balletts waren der sehr freie Umgang mit Quellen und die Vermischung verschiedener Vorlagen seit jeher gang und gäbe, und man findet bis heute *Romeo und Julia*-Ballette mit glücklichem Ausgang. So fand beispielsweise Bronislawa Nijinskas *Romeo und Julia* (1926) in einem zeitgenössischen Ballettsaal während Proben zu einem *Romeo und Julia*-Ballett statt und endete mit der Entführung Julias durch Romeo in einem Flugzeug. Sergej Prokofjew, der 1935 die erste Fassung seiner höchst erfolgreichen Partitur für ein *Romeo und Julia*-Ballett komponierte, wollte das Werk ebenfalls zunächst glücklich enden lassen, da Tote nicht tanzen können.[10] Luke Jennings schrieb über das Libretto und die Partitur der ersten, nicht aufgeführten Fassung:

The original treatment [...] had been configured along strictly 'proletarian' lines. Shakespeare's tale had been given a happy ending, with the lovers escaping Verona's repressive, patriarchal society for a joyful Arcadia – an afterlife somewhere between

---

8   Siehe Gaspare Ronzi, *Giulietta e Romeo, Ballo Pantomimo Tragico-Urbano*, in Giacomo Tritto (Komponist) und Domenico Piccinni (Librettist), *Icaboro in Jucatan, dramma per musica di Domenico Piccinni da rappresentarsi nel Real Teatro di S. Carlo nel di'12. gennaro 1799* (Neapel: Flautina, 1799), 8–18, Vorwort 8.

9   Jean-François Ducis, "Avertissement" zu *Othello* (Paris: Théâtre de la République, 1792), in Renato Raffaelli (Hg.), *Otello* (Pesaro: Fondazione Rossini, 1996), 155–157, Zitat 157. Siehe auch Laurence Marie, "Gestuelles du crime shakespearien sur les scènes française et anglaise de la seconde moitié du XVIIIe siècle", *Littératures classiques* 67 (2008), 201–218.

10 Siehe Simon Morrison, "Romeo and Juliet's Happy Ending", Konferenzbeitrag zum *International Symposium of Russian Ballet*, Columbia University, 12. bis 13. Oktober 2007, 10, https://harriman.columbia.edu/files/harriman/International%20Symposium%20of%20Russian%20Ballet%20%20paper%20Morrison.pdf, letzter Zugriff 26. August 2020.

life and death. Prokofiev's music, meanwhile, was often leaner in construction than the 1940 version, with several scenes transposed.¹¹

Mark Morris schuf 2008 ein Ballett zu dieser Partitur. Von solchen Ausnahmen abgesehen, enden die meisten Ballettfassungen von *Romeo und Julia* wie Shakespeares Tragödie mit dem Tod der Liebenden.

Die meisten *Romeo und Julia*-Ballette, die vor dem 20. Jahrhundert entstanden sind, haben wenige oder gar keine Spuren hinterlassen. Die erste noch erhaltene Fassung ist Leonid Lawroswskis *Romeo und Julia* aus dem Jahr 1940 zu einer überarbeiteten Version von Prokofjews Partitur. Dabei handelt es sich auch um das älteste Shakespeare-Ballett, das heute noch mehr oder weniger in der Originalchoreographie aufgeführt wird. Lawrowski wollte ein dramatisches Ballett schaffen, das sich von den *divertissement*-artigen Märchenballetten mit Nummerndramaturgie des 19. Jahrhunderts unterschied. Prokofjews Musik trug stark zur Darstellung der Handlung bei, unter anderem durch Themen für verschiedene Figuren und Leitmotive.¹² Prokofjews 'narrative' Partitur, welche die große Mehrzahl von *Romeo und Julia*-Balletten seit den 1940er Jahren begleitet, hat zweifelsohne sehr viele Choreographen dazu inspiriert, dieses Thema zu wählen.

Der erste Teil des Balletts bis zum tödlichen Ausgang des Duells zwischen Mercutio und Tybalt im zweiten Akt enthält einige komische Passagen, unter anderem mehrere Szenen zwischen Romeo, Mercutio und Benvolio, Mercutios Solo beim Ball und ein paar bunte Marktszenen mit Prostituierten und einem Faschingstanz. Wie bei Shakespeare mischen sich auch hier die Familienväter in die erste Auseinandersetzung auf der Straße ein und bekriegen sich recht hilflos mit überdimensionierten Schwertern. Ihre sichtbare physische Unfähigkeit, die Fehde am Leben zu halten, deutet wie im Stück an, dass diese wie in einer Komödie von der jüngeren Generation überwunden werden könnte. Erst als der Streit von Tybalt weitergeführt wird und mit Mercutios Tod eskaliert, wird der potentiellen Komödie ein Ende gesetzt.

Dieser Wandel ist in Prokofjews Partitur hörbar, beispielsweise in der Variation von Leitmotiven, die Parallelen zwischen Szenen, aber auch die Entwicklung der Situation und der Protagonisten anzeigen. Diese erklingen unter anderem in den beiden großen Pas de deux des Hauptpaares, die unter Julias Balkon im

---

11   Luke Jennings, "Stalin's Star-Crossed Lovers: Romeo and Juliet, On Motifs of Shakespeare", *The Guardian*, 9. November 2008, www.theguardian.com/stage/2008/nov/09/markmorris-ballet, letzter Zugriff 24. August 2020.
12   Siehe z. B. Programm *Romeo und Julia*, Choreographie von Riccardo Duse, Opernhaus Halle, 18. März 1994, 11.

ersten Akt und in ihrem Schlafzimmer im dritten Akt stattfinden. Diese Duos veranschaulichen jeweils den Höhepunkt der Euphorie und der Verzweiflung im gemeinsamen Leben des Paares. Einige Choreographen haben diese Leitmotive in der Partitur aufgegriffen und sie in den Bewegungsabläufen der Protagonisten gespiegelt, beispielsweise John Cranko in seiner Fassung für das Stuttgarter Ballett aus dem Jahr 1962. In Crankos Balkon-Pas de deux legt Romeo zu einem wiederholten musikalischen Motiv zweimal seinen Kopf auf Julias Brust; diese umarmt ihn, blickt zum Himmel und streckt ihren Arm in die Höhe, wobei das erste Mal zarter, das zweite ekstatischer wirkt. Die Geste erscheint abermals zu einem leicht variierten musikalischen Motiv im Schlafzimmer-Pas de deux: Dieses Mal suggerieren Choreographie und Musik Trauer und Schmerz, und die Geste zum Himmel, die im ersten Duo Julias wachsende Leidenschaft ausdrückte, könnte nun als Bitte verstanden werden, ihren Geliebten zu schützen. Noch deutlicher wird die Entwicklung der Situation durch Julias jeweilige Geste signalisiert, als Romeo sie im Balkon- und Schlafzimmer-Pas de deux auf seine Schulter setzt: Im ersten Akt breitet sie glücklich die Arme aus, während sie im dritten Akt das Gesicht in den Händen verbirgt.

Manche musikalische Leitmotive in Prokofjews Partitur drücken selbst innerhalb einer kurzen Passage zahlreiche Stimmungswechsel aus. Ein Beispiel hierfür ist die Sterbeszene, in der dieselbe Melodie mehrmals unmittelbar hintereinander variiert wird und verschiedene gegensätzliche Emotionen aufscheinen lässt. In diesem Zusammenhang ist interessant, dass Prokofjew Teile seiner Musik für das nicht aufgeführte glückliche Ende in der Abschlussszene beibehielt; so begleitete die Musik für die glückliche Vereinigung des Paares später Julias Tod.[13]

Rudolf Nurejew schuf zu dem mehrfach variierten musikalischen Motiv in dieser Szene eine Choreographie, welche die wechselnden Nuancen der Musik und damit auch die Offenheit der Handlung, die tragisch oder glücklich enden kann, zum Ausdruck bringt. Das musikalische Thema, das der Zuschauer erstmals bei Julias Auftritt im ersten Akt hört,[14] erklingt in der Gruft am Ende des dritten Aktes schneidend und dissonant, nachdem Romeo das Gift genommen hat. Die geringe Lautstärke und das langsame Tempo der Musik suggerieren, dass Romeo stirbt und seine Lebenskräfte schwinden. Romeo wiegt Julia in seinen Armen und küsst sie mit letzter Kraft und letztem Lebensatem, bevor er leblos auf die Bahre sinkt. Die Sanftheit seiner schwachen letzten Liebesbekun-

---

13 Siehe Morrison (2007), 10–11.
14 Siehe Rudolf Nurejew, *Romeo und Julia* (Pariser Fassung von 1984), Ballett der Pariser Oper, 1995, mit Monique Loudières (Julia) und Manuel Legris (Romeo), auf www.youtube.com/watch?v=-hM0B70F1YM, ab 19:53, letzter Zugriff 15. August 2020.

dungen steht im Gegensatz zu der impulsiven Leidenschaft des Paares früher im Ballett. Bei Julias Erwachen (Julia beginnt sich langsam zu bewegen und richtet sich halb auf) klingt die Melodie wärmer und harmonischer, als gehe die Sonne auf. Da Julia noch benommen ist, bleibt die Musik hier ziemlich langsam. Die nächste Variation, die einen Ausbruch an Emotion suggeriert (die Musik wird schneller und lauter), begleitet den Moment, in dem Julia sich ihrer Umgebung bewusst wird, entsetzt in der Gruft umherläuft und abwehrende Gesten mit den Armen macht, zunächst, ohne ihren Geliebten zu bemerken. Schließlich erblickt sie Romeo auf der Bahre und glaubt, er sei noch am Leben: Die Melodie ertönt abermals harmonischer, als Julia mit weit ausgebreiteten Armen zu ihm läuft, ihn an sich drückt, umarmt und leidenschaftlich küsst; allerdings trübt die Orchesterbegleitung die Klarheit der Melodie unterschwellig (als deute sie an: er ist in Wirklichkeit tot). Ein letztes Mal erklingt das Motiv, als sie das Gift auf seinen Lippen schmeckt, ihn schüttelt und schließlich seinen Tod feststellt; diesmal unterstreicht es ihre Erschütterung und tiefe Verzweiflung (diese wird in der Choreographie durch einen stummen Schrei und Schluchzen ausgedrückt) und zeigt die endgültige Wandlung zur Tragödie an.[15]

Anders als in Shakespeares Stück, das auch nach Mercutios und Tybalts Tod einige Komödienelemente enthält,[16] gibt es in der zweiten Hälfte der meisten *Romeo und Julia*-Ballette keinerlei komische Auflockerung mehr. Dieser Wendepunkt zur Tragödie wurde von Lawrowski und Prokofjew stark akzentuiert und von manchen Choreographen sehr wirkungsvoll inszeniert, beispielsweise von Nurejew.

In Shakespeares Stück erfährt man nicht viel über den Ablauf des Kampfes zwischen Mercutio und Tybalt; man weiß lediglich aus dem Nebentext und Mercutios Vorwurf an Romeo ("Why the devil came you between us? I was hurt under your arm." [3.1.102–103]),[17] dass Mercutio den tödlichen Streich erhielt, nachdem Romeo die Kämpfer zu trennen versuchte. Regisseure und Choreographen haben relativ freie Hand mit der Interpretation dieser Szene: Handelt es sich um einen ebenbürtigen Kampf, oder hat einer der Duellanten die Oberhand? Tötet

---

15 Siehe Nurejew (1984), ab 2:17:05. Meine Analyse bezieht sich auf dieses Video; es muss berücksichtigt werden, dass in einer Vorstellung Tempo und Lautstärke variieren können.

16 Zu diesen gehören der Scheintod der Braut, um ihre Eltern zu täuschen und mit ihrem Geliebten zu fliehen – ein Element, das sich beispielsweise in Middletons späterer Komödie *A Chaste Maid in Cheapside* findet –, sowie die exzessive Trauer der Angehörigen und die Kommentare der Musiker in Akt 4, Szene 4.

17 Zitate aus *Romeo und Julia* beziehen sich auf William Shakespeare, *The Complete Works*, hg. von Stanley Wells und Gary Taylor (Oxford: Clarendon, 2005).

Tybalt Mercutio mit Absicht oder versehentlich? In jedem Fall wird den Umstehenden recht schnell klar, dass Mercutio tödlich verwundet ist. Er selbst drückt dies bereits unmittelbar nach dem Ende des Kampfes aus ("I am sped" [3.1.91]). Auf Romeos ermutigende Worte reagiert er mit zynischen Wortspielen und dem Fluch auf beide Familien, woraufhin Romeo keinen Zweifel mehr an Mercutios bevorstehendem Tod hegt.

In den meisten Ballettfassungen behält Mercutio während des Kampfes, der von seinem eigenen musikalischen Thema begleitet wird, klar die Überhand; nur eine Dissonanz, die Mercutios Musik durchbricht, deutet zwischendurch die Bedrohung für den übermütigen jungen Mann an. In Nurejews Fassung reizt er Tybalt, der einem wütenden Stier gleicht (Romeo fängt ihn später wie ein Torero mittels eines roten Tuches), mit frechen Scherzen, steht nach seiner vermeintlich tödlichen Verwundung gut gelaunt wieder auf und ringt Tybalt schließlich zu Boden. Der gedemütigte Tybalt wirft seinem bereits abgehenden Gegner einen Dolch nach, der diesen im Rücken verwundet. Da Romeo und seine Freunde den Dolch nicht sehen, halten sie Mercutios darauffolgende Sterbepantomime für ein Spiel. Diese Szene ist in Prokofjews Partitur sehr ausgedehnt; wie die Oper eignet sich das Ballett für unnatürlich langgezogene, emotionsreiche Sterbeszenen, die sich gut durch Musik und Körpersprache ausdrücken lassen. Mercutios musikalisches Thema wird variiert, erklingt stockender als zuvor und wird immer langsamer. In vielen Ballettfassungen wiederholt Mercutio in dieser Szene Teile seiner früheren Choreographie, was wie seine Wortspiele im Stück zeigt, dass sein unangepasster Charakter sich auch im Angesicht des Todes nicht ändert. Die besondere Tragik in Nurejews Umsetzung liegt darin, dass Mercutios Freunde die Hinweise in der Musik – Stocken, Langsamkeit und einige schwere, dumpfe Akzente, die das Straucheln des zuvor leichtfüßigen Mercutio begleiten – überhören und erst nach seinem Tod bemerken, dass das Spiel ernst war. Sie necken und quälen ihn mit Stößen, inszenieren sogar einen ironischen Leichenzug, wobei nur Mercutio selbst und das Publikum wissen, dass er wirklich verwundet ist. Dieser ausgedehnte Moment dramatischer Ironie ist nur in einem Genre möglich, das unabhängig von Shakespeares Text ist.[18]

Auch Bühnenbild und Kostüme tragen stark zur Interpretation des Geschehens bei. So wählte beispielsweise John Cranko ein sehr farbenfrohes, sonnendurchflutetes Bühnenbild und relativ leichte und schmucklose Kostüme von Jürgen Rose, wohingegen Kenneth MacMillan sich für eine schwerere, prunkvolle Ausstattung von Nicholas Georgiadis entschied. Ezio Frigerio und Mauro

---

18 Siehe Nurejew (1984), ab 1:24:30.

Paganos Ausstattung von Nurejews Fassung ist noch düsterer und bedrohlicher. Obgleich alle drei Ballette Prokofjews Musik verwenden, deutet der Rahmen unterschiedliche Interpretationen der jeweiligen Tragödie an: Crankos Ballett dreht sich um ein unschuldiges Paar, dessen absolute Liebe an unglücklichen Zufällen scheitert. Bei MacMillan zeigt das Bühnenbild, gegen welch ein übermächtiges, erdrückendes Milieu die Hauptfiguren, und vor allem Julia, ankämpfen müssen; das Paar ist weniger idealisiert als in Crankos Fassung. In Nurejews Ballett erscheinen die vor dem dunklen Bühnenbild meist sehr hell gekleideten Liebenden wie vereinzelte Lichtstrahlen in einer Umwelt, in der Gewalt und Tod allgegenwärtig sind; dies erinnert an die Metaphern im Stück, in dem Romeo und Julia einander oft mit Lichtern in dunkler Umgebung vergleichen. Ihre Liebe wird sowohl von einer erbarmungslosen Umgebung als auch von einem ungnädigen Schicksal zerstört, das mehrmals in Form ominöser Figuren im Ballett erscheint.

Schicksalsfiguren und Vorzeichen

In Shakespeares Tragödie schaffen kommentierende Figuren eine gewisse Distanz zum Bühnengeschehen, die in wortlosen Kunstformen vermindert wird. Der Prolog, der das tragische Ende von Anfang an ankündigt, und die abschließende Rede des Prinzen rahmen das Geschehen. Bruder Lorenzo unterbricht die Todesszene der Liebenden, die streitenden Familien versöhnen sich, und der Prinz beschließt das Stück mit folgenden Versen:

> Prince: A glooming peace this morning with it brings.
> The sun for sorrow will not show his head.
> Go hence, to have more talk of these sad things.
> Some shall be pardoned, and some punishèd;
> For never was a story of more woe
> Than this of Juliet and her Romeo.
> (5.3.304–309)

Diese Sätze lenken die Aufmerksamkeit auf die Bedeutung des doppelten Selbstmordes für die Gesellschaft: Er bringt der Stadt endlich Frieden, jedoch um den Preis eines düsteren Tages, an dem für niemanden die Sonne scheint. Das Vorgefallene soll in weitem Kreise besprochen und die Verantwortlichen zur Rechenschaft gezogen werden. Obgleich der Prinz mit den Namen der Liebenden endet, geht es nicht mehr um sie als Individuen: Ihr Schicksal soll den Überlebenden eine Lehre sein und sie sind bereits zur "story" geworden, welche die Menschen inner- und außerhalb der Welt des Stückes noch lange bewegen wird. In der Tat war die tragische Geschichte des Paares bereits zu Shakespeares Zeit eine wohlbekannte "story"; diese lebt bis heute aufgrund der Aufführungen und der Bearbeitung des Stoffes in vielen Medien weiter.

In den meisten Ballettfassungen von *Romeo und Julia* gehören die letzten Szenen den Titelfiguren. Die Versöhnung der Familien bleibt zwar in manchen Balletten bestehen, unter anderem bei Nurejew und in Lawrowskis sowjetischer Fassung, die auf die gesellschaftliche Bedeutung des individuellen Schicksals hinweist. Jedoch handelt es sich zumeist nur um einen kurzen Epilog, in dem sich die Vertreter der beiden Familien umarmen, was kaum von der Tragik des doppelten Selbstmordes ablenkt. Diese Akzentverschiebung erklärt sich unter anderem dadurch, dass im Ballett die Aufmerksamkeit oftmals weg vom sozialen Kontext auf Emotionen und von der älteren Generation auf junge, ballettgeeignete Protagonisten gelenkt wird. Auch die Rede der Autoritätsfigur, die der Wiederherstellung der Ordnung dient und die sich nicht leicht ohne Worte darstellen ließe, entfällt. Bleiben am Ende nur die Musik und das Bild der toten Liebenden, führt dies tendenziell zu einer stärkeren Identifikation des Publikums mit dem Paar.

Einige *Romeo und Julia*-Ballette enthalten allerdings chorähnliche Figuren, die ähnlich wie Shakespeares Prolog das tragische Ende ankündigen. So rahmt etwa in Nurejews *Romeo und Julia* eine Gruppe glatzköpfiger, in schwarze Mäntel gehüllter Würfelspieler das Geschehen. Diese schieben am Anfang Teile des schweren, prunkvollen Dekors beiseite und geben den Blick frei auf einen Leichenzug von Pestopfern; dazu erklingt die unheilschwangere Musik, die Prokofjew für den Beginn des dritten Aktes komponierte. Die Umstellung eines Teils der Partitur erlaubte Nurejew, von Anfang an die Allgegenwart des Todes zu unterstreichen und auf das tragische Ende hinzudeuten. Einer der Würfelspieler erscheint später als personifizierter Tod mit einer Totenkopfmaske. Er legt die totenstarre Julia auf eine Bahre und legt sich auf sie. Dies bezieht sich auf folgende Verse in Shakespeares Tragödie:

> *Juliet*:   I'll to my wedding bed,
> And death, not Romeo, take my maidenhead!
> (3.3.136–137)

Die Würfelspieler beschließen das Ballett, indem sie ungeachtet des Vorgefallenen geschäftig ihrem Spiel nachgehen. So wird der Selbstmord der Liebenden zu einer Episode in einem ständigen Karussell des Todes, der sich bereits seine nächsten Opfer aussucht. Das Schicksal eines einzelnen Paares hat in diesem

'Glücksspiel' kaum Bedeutung. Eine ähnliche Gruppe schwarz Gekleideter greift später in den Ausgang des Balletts ein: Einige Banditen ermorden Bruder Markus und zerreißen seinen Brief an Romeo in Mantua. Schließlich erfindet Nurejew als weiteres Zeichen des Schicksals einen Bettler, der stirbt, nachdem Romeo ihm ein Almosen gibt. Dies zeigt, dass Romeo unter einem unglücklichen Stern geboren ist und unwillentlich Tod um sich verbreitet.

Andere Choreographen setzten Shakespeares Prolog noch 'wörtlicher' um: In Tatjana Gsovskys 1948 an der Berliner Staatsoper aufgeführtem *Romeo und Julia*-Ballett trat ein Larvenverkäufer auf, der die Handlung in einem Commedia dell'arte-ähnlichen Prolog schilderte und Unheil prophezeite. Es ist zu vermuten, dass er dazu Worte verwendete, auch wenn dies aus dem Libretto nicht klar hervorgeht. Der Larvenverkäufer nahm auch am Geschehen teil, indem er die Gäste des Festmahls mit Masken versorgte. Romeo sprang auf seinen Rücken und erspähte von dort aus Julia. Am Ende des ersten Aktes erstarrte der Verkäufer mit seinem leeren Schellenbaum zu "einer Maske böser Ahnungen".[19]

In Bridget Breiners Gelsenkirchener Fassung aus dem Jahr 2018 betrachtete eine weibliche Figur die Vorgänge auf der Bühne und versuchte zuweilen in die Handlung einzugreifen – allerdings ohne Erfolg. So zeigte sie Romeo Bruder Lorenzos Brief, doch der junge Mann schien sie nicht zu bemerken.[20] Gleichzeitig rezitierten Stimmen Passagen aus dem Stück und andere Texte in verschiedenen Sprachen. Obgleich durch den Text ein weiteres Ausdrucksmittel hinzukam, das theoretisch einen Kommentar des Geschehens erlaubt hätte, wurde sein erklärendes Potential durch die unterschiedlichen Sprachen und die Vermischung von textinternen und -externen Elementen so untergraben, dass der Text zwischen verbalem Kommentar und einer musikähnlichen Begleitung des Geschehens changierte.

Auf ähnliche Weise beobachtete in Alicia Alonsos einaktiger *Romeo und Julia*-Adaptation für das Kubanische Nationalballett aus dem Jahr 2005 (Libretto: José Ramón Neyra) eine Figur, die Shakespeares Züge trug, die Protagonisten und schüttelte in der Schlussszene missbilligend den Kopf. Die Inszenierung suggerierte also, dass der Autor der Vorlage selbst nicht mehr in der Lage ist, den Gang der berühmten Geschichte zu verändern.[21]

---

19 Siehe Archiv Akademie der Künste Berlin, Sammlung Edith-Elke Harms-Horn 7, Tatjana Gsovsky, *Romeo und Julia*, Scenarium Deutsche Staatsoper Berlin, 1. Juli 1948.
20 Siehe www.omm.de/veranstaltungen/musiktheater20172018/GE-romeo-und-julia.html, letzter Zugriff 20. Februar 2018.
21 Siehe Tanzarchiv Leipzig, DVD 211: Ballet Nacional de Cuba, *Romeo and Julia in Havanna*, Choreographie: Alicia Alonso, Musik: Charles Gounod, Libretto: José Ramón Neyra, 2004.

Der tragische Konflikt in einem wortlosen Medium

Im Unterschied zu anderen Shakespeare-Tragödien durchlebt in *Romeo und Julia* vor allem die weibliche Hauptfigur einen tragischen Konflikt. Ihre zwei wichtigsten Entscheidungen, nämlich die Heirat mit Romeo und ihren Selbstmord, trifft Julia ohne zu zögern. Schwerer fällt ihr die Entscheidung gegen ihre Familie und für Romeo nach Tybalts Tod, die sie in ihrer Hochzeitsnacht besiegelt, sowie der Entschluss, Bruder Lorenzos Schlaftrunk zu nehmen, der ihren vollkommenen Bruch mit ihren Eltern und der Veroneser Gesellschaft bedeutet. Beiden Entscheidungen gehen lange Monologe voraus, die ihren Kampf mit sich selbst und ihre Entwicklung von der gehorsamen Tochter der Capulets zu Romeos leidenschaftlicher Gattin anzeigen.[22]

Diese Entwicklung wird in Prokofjews Partitur durch die Julia zugeordneten musikalischen Motive ausgedrückt.[23] Julias Überlegung, ob sie den Schlaftrunk einnehmen soll, wird bei Prokofjew und Lawrowski zu einer langen Szene, die choreographisch allerdings nicht leicht zu füllen ist, da sich die Gründe für Julias Zögern – ihre Angst, alleine in der Gruft neben Tybalts Leiche aufzuwachen und die Angst, es könne sich bei dem Trunk um Gift handeln – in einer wortlosen Kunstform schlecht ausdrücken lassen. John Neumeier schuf in seiner Fassung für das Frankfurter Ballett aus dem Jahr 1971 eine Visionsszene. So glaubt Julia nach Einnahme des Schlaftrunks, Tybalt und Romeo zu sehen. Allerdings drückt diese Szene keinen inneren Konflikt aus, sondern scheint eine Halluzination zu sein, die durch den Trunk ausgelöst wurde. Rudolf Nurejew hingegen machte aus dieser Szene einen regelrechten *agon*, in dem Mercutios und Tybalts Geist versuchen, Julia zur Einnahme des Trankes beziehungsweise zum Selbstmord zu bringen. Mercutio steht hier für Julias neue Loyalität zu ihrem Gatten und den Kampf um ihre Liebe, während Tybalt die ältere Loyalität zu ihrer Familie repräsentiert, deren Ehre durch Julias Tod bewahrt werden soll. Sie entscheidet sich schließlich für Mercutio und den Trunk.[24]

Nurejew schuf noch andere Visionen, die Julias Gedanken und Zwiespalt veranschaulichen. In all diesen Szenen erstarren die Umstehenden vorübergehend, was zeigt, dass die Szenen sich in Julias Kopf abspielen. Eine kurze Se-

---

22 Für eine ausführliche Untersuchung dieses Themas und der Art, wie verschiedene Choreographen die ungewöhnliche Geschlechterkonstellation in Shakespeares Tragödie umgesetzt haben, siehe meinen Artikel "Juliet's Mute Soliloquies: Visualizing Thought Processes in Rudolf Nureyev's *Romeo and Juliet*", *Women: A Cultural Review* 30:4 (2019), 440–464.
23 Siehe z. B. Humphrey Searle, *Ballet Music: An Introduction* (London: Cassel, 1958), 182–184.
24 Siehe Nurejew (1984), ab 1:53:10.

quenz in ihrem letzten Tanz mit Paris und ihren Eltern drückt aus, dass sie nur noch äußerlich der von ihrer Familie vorgeschriebenen Choreographie folgt: Julia verlässt vorübergehend ihren Platz in der Familienkonstellation, um ihrer Verzweiflung in einer Passage stummer Revolte Ausdruck zu verleihen.[25] In einem Moment, in dem sie eine Kreisformation mit Paris und ihren Eltern bildet, reißt sie sich von diesen los, rollt über den Boden, macht eine abwehrende Geste gegen Paris, als wolle sie ihn von sich wegstoßen, und streckt dann verzweifelt einen Arm in die Höhe, als rufe sie den Himmel an. Diese Szene zeigt, dass sie "no longer [...] a Capulet" (2.1.78) ist, wie sie Romeo in der Balkonszene versprach.

Zudem fügte Nurejew in der Szene nach Tybalts Tod eine kurze Vision ein, die Julias Entsetzen über Romeos Mord an ihrem Cousin veranschaulicht: Julia erscheint kurz nach dem Duell am Schauplatz des Geschehens, erblickt Tybalts Leiche und verleiht ihrer Verzweiflung durch weit ausladende Gesten Ausdruck. Daraufhin erblickt sie ihren Gatten, in dem sie den Mörder ihres Cousins erkennt; sie schlägt ihn und fällt ihm schließlich zu Füßen. Dies erinnert an ihren inneren Zwiespalt in Shakespeares Tragödie:

> *Juliet*: O serpent heart hid with a flow'ring face!
> Did ever dragon keep so fair a cave?
> Beautiful tyrant, fiend angelical!
> Dove-feathered raven, wolvish-ravening lamb!
> Despisèd substance of divinest show!
> Just opposite to what thou justly seem'st –
> A damnèd saint, an honourable villain.
>   (3.2.73–79)

Diese Rede erinnert an Raphael Lynes These: "[f]or Shakespeare, at key moments, rhetoric comes to look like a problem-solving process whose goal is to make sense of things that are not easily made into sense".[26] Julias Oxymora veranschaulichen ihren Versuch, Romeos strahlendes Äußeres und ihre Liebe zu ihm mit seiner Tat zu vereinbaren.

Anders als bei Shakespeare entscheidet sich Julia in Nurejews Ballett nicht unmittelbar im Anschluss an diese Szene für Romeo. Der Choreograph intensiviert ihren inneren Konflikt, indem er ihre Beziehung zu Tybalt am Anfang als eng

---

25 Siehe Nurejew (1984), ab 1:51:00.
26 Raphael Lyne, *Shakespeare, Rhetoric and Cognition* (Cambridge: Cambridge University Press, 2011), 11.

und vertrauensvoll darstellt und sie nach dem Duell direkt mit der Leiche ihres eben von Romeo ermordeten Cousins konfrontiert. Am Ende des Aktes bleibt Julia allein mit Tybalts Dolch in der Hand auf der Bühne. Dieser Dolch erscheint abermals in ihrer Vision im dritten Akt, in der Tybalts Geist sie zum Selbstmord bewegen will.

Zeit und Tempo

Das tragische Ende von Shakespeares *Romeo und Julia* wird unter anderem dadurch herbeigeführt, dass die ungeduldigen, impulsiven Liebenden mit einer anderen Geschwindigkeit leben als alle anderen. Julia gibt Romeos Werbung schneller nach, als es die gesellschaftlichen Gepflogenheiten erlauben: Bei ihrer ersten Begegnung erlaubt sie ihm, sie zu küssen, und bereits bei der zweiten Begegnung arrangiert sie die Hochzeit. Das Warten auf Romeos Antwort in Akt 2, Szene 4 scheint ihr unerträglich, und in Akt 3, Szene 2 drückt sie die brennende Ungeduld aus, mit der sie den Anbruch der Nacht und das Erscheinen ihres Geliebten erwartet:

> *Juliet*: Gallop apace, you fiery-footed steeds,
> Towards Phoebus' lodging. Such a waggoner
> As Phaëton would whip you to the west
> And bring in cloudy night immediately.
> Spread thy close curtain, love-performing night,
> [...]
>   So tedious is this day
> As is the night before some festival
> To an impatient child that hath new robes
> And may not wear them.
>   (3.2.1–30)

Immer wieder ruft sie die Nacht und Romeo an und versucht, ihr Erscheinen zu beschleunigen: Ihre Sehnsucht will nicht nur die Schritte ihrer fußlahmen Amme und ihres – durch den Streit mit Tybalt aufgehaltenen – Geliebten antreiben, sondern auch die Natur selbst. Stanley Wells zufolge drückt Julias gewagte Rede das Tempo ihrer Entwicklung aus: "she has matured with extraordinary rapidity from the girl who, in terms of the play's time scale, only a day or two earlier was speaking of marriage as 'an honour that [she] dreamt not of'. Now she looks forward to it, and to her sexual initiation, with passionate and impatient rapture."[27] Das Ende der Rede erinnert daran, dass sie nur wenige Szenen zuvor selbst ein Mädchen war, das auf den Capulet-Ball wartete; dies unterstreicht den schnellen Fortgang der Handlung. Anders als in Brookes *Tragicall Historye of Romeus and Juliet*, in dem sich das Geschehen innerhalb von mehreren Monaten abspielt, dauern bei Shakespeare Julias Entwicklung vom Mädchen zur reifen Frau und die Ereignisse, die zu ihrem Tod führen, nur wenige Tage.

Auch Romeo handelt wiederholt übereilt: So nimmt er Rache an Tybalt, obgleich dessen Leben durch den Mord an Mercutio bereits verwirkt ist. Später verlässt der junge Mann Mantua, begibt sich zu Julias Grab und bringt sich um, bevor Bruder Lorenzo ihn erreichen kann und bevor Julia erwacht. Sowohl Romeo ("O true apothecary, / Thy drugs are quick!" [5.3.119–120]) als auch Julia ("I'll be brief" [5.3.168]) sterben schnell, nachdem sie sich von ihrem leblosen Partner verabschiedet haben. Ihre Familien und der Prinz kommentieren die Unnatürlichkeit des frühzeitigen Todes der Kinder vor den Eltern:

> *Prince*: Come, Montague, for thou art early up
> To see thy son and heir more early down.
> [...]
> *Montague*: What manner is in this
> To press before thy father to a grave?
> (5.3.207–208, 213–214)

Einige Choreographen haben sowohl die schnelle Entwicklung der Protagonisten als auch ihren Umgang mit der Zeit hervorgehoben, durch den sie sich von anderen Figuren unterscheiden. So betonte etwa Nurejew die Geschwindigkeit von Julias Entwicklung, die er zu Beginn als besonders jung portraitiert, und die fiebrige Eile, mit der die Liebenden ihre Geschichte durchleben. Im ersten Akt spielt Julia, die ungestüm ist wie ein sehr junges Mädchen, noch kindliche Spiele mit ihrem Cousin Tybalt und später mit Romeo. Ihre Bewegungssprache ändert sich nach ihrem ersten Kuss beim Capulet-Ball. Die leidenschaftlichen Pas de deux der Liebenden sind sehr schnell, geradezu hektisch, und enthalten zuweilen mehr Schritte, als die Musik zu erlauben scheint; dieses Überschreiten des 'natürlichen' Tempos des Balletts erinnert daran, dass Julia im Stück die Natur zu beschleunigen sucht. Das Paar hält fast nie inne oder sieht einander auch nur an, was im Lauf des Balletts auf verschiedene Weise interpretiert werden kann: Im Balkon-Pas de deux werden sie von einem neuen Gefühl überwältigt und

---

27 Stanley Wells, *Shakespeare, Sex, and Love* (Oxford: Oxford University Press, 2010), 15.

scheinen sich kaum bewusst, wie ihnen geschieht. In der Schlafzimmerszene wirbeln sie umeinander herum, als wollten sie ein ganzes gemeinsames Leben in ihre Hochzeitsnacht kondensieren. Anders als in den meisten Ballettversionen, in denen die Szene wie in Shakespeares Stück ihren Abschied am Morgen zeigt, komprimiert Nurejew hier die ganze Begegnung von Romeos Erscheinen in Julias Zimmer bis zu ihrer Trennung in einer relativ kurzen Szene. Der Schlafzimmer-Pas de deux deutet auch bereits auf Julias spätere Verwandlung in eine scheinbare und später tatsächliche Leiche voraus: Als sie merkt, dass Romeo sie verlassen wird, sinkt sie wie zerbrochen zu Boden.

Die extreme Geschwindigkeit der Tänze der Liebenden unterscheidet sich vom langsameren Tempo und den kontrollierteren Tänzen anderer Figuren wie Rosalinde oder Paris. So wirken Romeos Tänze mit Rosalinde zu Beginn des Balletts kleinteilig und höfisch manieriert; beide Partner scheinen selbstverliebt und vor allem für sich und ihre Zuschauer zu tanzen. Nach Romeos Zusammenstoß mit Julia beim Ball werden seine Bewegungen schneller und energischer, so dass das Publikum seinen stärkeren Herzschlag zu sehen glaubt. Die kleinen Kreise, die er zunächst um Rosalinde zeichnet, werden zu großen Kreisen weiter Sprünge; die Liebe verleiht Romeo geradezu Flügel. Auch Julias Tänze mit Paris beim Capulet-Ball sind höfisch formaler und zielen mehr auf Präsentation vor einem Publikum als Kommunikation mit dem Tanzpartner. Rosalinde und Paris kontrastieren mit Julia und Romeo im Ballett: Auch sie sind schön und aus gutem Hause, aber ihr Tanz überschreitet nie die sozialen Konventionen.

Jenseits der klassischen Balletttragödie

Ähnlich wie Shakespeare, dessen Tragödie den Mustern des Genres nur bedingt entsprach, haben manche Choreographen von *Romeo und Julia*-Balletten mit den Konventionen ihrer Kunstform gebrochen. In verschiedenen Fassungen von *Romeo und Julia* wird die Tragik des Geschehens unter anderem dadurch ausgedrückt, dass die Protagonisten die für das Ballettgenre typische aufrechte Haltung und Kontrolliertheit der Bewegung aufgeben. So gleicht Julia in der Gruftszene einiger *Romeo und Julia*-Ballette einer zerbrochenen Puppe, die Romeo durch die Luft schleudert, als wolle er sie wieder zum Leben erwecken. Sie lässt Kopf und Füße baumeln, ihre Glieder verlieren die balletttypische Spannung und wirken schlaff. In MacMillans Fassung schleift Romeo seine Gattin sogar an einem Arm über den Boden. MacMillan, dessen *Romeo und Julia*-Ballett von Franco Zeffirellis radikaler Inszenierung der Tragödie im Old Vic Theatre (1960–1961) beeinflusst war, wollte mit dem stilisierten Ausdruck von Emotionen brechen und Leiden und Tod realistisch darstellen.[28] Nurejew und viele andere Choreographen von *Romeo und Julia*-Balletten teilten dieses Ansinnen.

Romeos Tanz mit Julias vermeintlicher Leiche in der Gruft veranschaulicht das Staunen des jungen Mannes über die lebendige Schönheit seiner Gattin:

> Romeo: Death, that has sucked the honey of thy breath,
> Hath had no power yet upon thy beauty.
> Thou art not conquered. Beauty's ensign yet
> Is crimson in thy lips and in thy cheeks,
> And death's pale flag is not advancèd there.
>
> (5.3.91–96)

Viele Choreographen gehen in dieser Szene allerdings weiter: So scheint Romeo etwa in Crankos, MacMillans und Nurejews Adaptationen Julias Tod nicht zu akzeptieren und versucht, die Choreographie ihrer glücklichen Zusammentreffen mit Julias vermeintlicher Leiche zu reproduzieren. Prokofjews Partitur in der Gruftszene nimmt Motive aus dem Balkon- und Schlafzimmer-Pas de deux wieder auf. Die besondere Tragik dieses Moments besteht darin, dass Julia in der Tat kurz vor dem Erwachen steht – mit einer totenstarren Frau wäre eine derartige Choreographie nicht denkbar. In Wirklichkeit muss die Ballerina größte Anstrengung aufwenden, um mit Romeo zu tanzen und dennoch leblos zu erscheinen; die Bildung gebrochener, ballettuntypischer Formen verlangt zuweilen sogar mehr Kraft von beiden Tänzern als ein gewöhnlicher Pas de deux.[29]

Dieses Duo ist nicht nur ein getanztes Äquivalent zu Romeos Anrede seiner lebendig erscheinenden Gattin in der Gruft. Es ermöglicht auch die Bildung einer Struktur, in der die Entwicklung der Geschichte auf einprägsame Weise in drei Pas de deux zusammengefasst wird: Diese zeigen das erste Erblühen der Liebe der Protagonisten, ihren Wendepunkt und ihr Ende. Dazu werden Musik und Choreographie der Szenen jeweils variiert und drücken die Veränderung der Stimmung und Situation aus. So illustriert am Ende der drei Teile des Balletts jeweils eine Begegnung der Protagonisten die Auswirkungen der vorhergehenden Handlung. Diese Struktur macht das Geschehen in einem visuellen Medium verständlich und trägt zur balletttypischen Akzentverschiebung hin zum jungen Hauptpaar bei.

---

28 Siehe Jann Parry, *Different Drummer: The Life of Kenneth MacMillan* (London: Faber & Faber, 2009), 278.
29 Privater Austausch mit Mathieu Ganio, Danseur Étoile der Pariser Oper, 28. August 2020.

Obgleich im Ballett tendenziell die Identifikation der Zuschauer mit den Hauptfiguren begünstigt wird, gibt es vor allem in jüngerer Zeit Fassungen, in denen die gesellschaftliche Bedeutung des individuellen Schicksals der Liebenden in den Vordergrund rückt. Wie in manchen Theateraufführungen und Filmadaptationen wird die Handlung oftmals in einen anderen zeitlichen und räumlichen Kontext versetzt, und zuweilen wird durch Spiegelungen des Hauptpaares angedeutet, dass dessen tragische Liebesgeschichte nur eine unter vielen ist. In Maurice Béjarts Fassung aus dem Jahr 1966 brachen neben Romeo und Julia in einer Anspielung auf den Vietnam-Krieg einige andere Paare unter Schüssen zusammen. Mauro Bigonzettis *Romeo und Julia* aus dem Jahr 2006, in dem ebenfalls mehrere Paare starben, spielte unter Motorradfahren im Italien des 21. Jahrhunderts, deren gefährlicher und leichtsinniger Lebensstil im Ballett portraitiert wurde. In beiden Fällen war das Schicksal der Liebenden nicht auf eine private Fehde zurückzuführen, sondern auf die Allgegenwart von Gewalt und Konflikt, die das Leben zahlloser anonymer Paare zerstörte. In einigen anderen Fassungen (Tom Schilling, Ostberlin, 1972; Angelin Preljocaj, Lyon, 1990) scheiterte die Liebe an einem Klassenkonflikt, und Birgit Scherzer machte in ihrer Trierer Fassung im Jahr 2014 aus Romeo einen Flüchtling. Diese gesellschaftskritischen Interpretationen adaptieren die Tragödie und übersetzen sie in Kontexte von zeitgenössischer Relevanz. Sie zeigen, dass das Ballett, dessen Handlung sich traditionell zumeist zwischen typisierten und idealisierten Protagonisten abspielt, aktuelle Themen kritisch zu kommentieren vermag. Scherzer fragte: "Was soll ich sonst erzählen als das, was uns heute bewegt?"[30]

Seit Noverres Zeit gehört die Darstellung der Leidenschaften und Berührung der Zuschauer zu den Hauptanliegen der Choreographen von Handlungsballetten. Das Publikum wird sowohl emotional bewegt, durch Identifikation mit den Figuren, als auch intellektuell durch die Auseinandersetzung mit den Verbindungen zu aktuellen Konflikten. Die besondere Unabhängigkeit des Ballettgenres vom Text erleichtert solche freien Adaptationen. Jedoch eröffnen auch die Ballette, die Shakespeares Tragödie genauer folgen, neue Perspektiven auf das Stück, da die Konventionen, Zwänge und Möglichkeiten ihres Mediums zu Akzentverschiebungen und Neuinterpretationen der Handlung führen können. Die Bandbreite der choreographischen Umsetzungen, die mit der Vielfalt der Theaterinszenierungen und Filmfassungen des Stückes konkurrieren kann, macht *Romeo und Julia* zu einem besonders geeigneten Fallbeispiel für die origi-

---

30 Birgit Scherzer auf www.youtube.com/watch?v=hqRSHYH9Tk0, letzter Zugriff 16. März 2020.

nellen Beiträge, die das wortlose Medium des Tanzes zur Interpretation literarischer Werke leisten kann.

Liste der im Text erwähnten Adaptationen
(Choreograph, Komponist, Titel, Ort der Uraufführung, Jahr)

Filippo Beretti, Luigi Marescalchi, *Giulietta e Romeo*, Padua, 1784.
Gaspare Ronzi, Luigi Marescalchi, *Giulietta e Romeo*, Neapel, 1799.
Bronislawa Nijinksa, Constant Lambert, *Roméo et Juliette*, Monte Carlo, 1926.
Leonid Lawrowski, Sergej Prokofjew, Ромео и Джульетта, Sankt Petersburg, 1940.
Tatjana Gsovsky, Sergej Prokofjew, *Romeo und Julia*, Berlin, 1948.
John Cranko, Sergej Prokofjew, *Romeo und Julia*, Stuttgart, 1962.
Kenneth MacMillan, Sergej Prokofjew, *Romeo and Juliet*, London, 1965.
Maurice Béjart, Hector Berlioz, *Roméo et Juliette*, Brüssel, 1966.
Tom Schilling, Sergej Prokofjew, *Romeo und Julia*, Berlin, 1972.
Rudolf Nurejew, Sergej Prokofjew, *Romeo and Juliet*, London, 1977.
Angelin Preljocaj, Sergej Prokofjew, *Roméo et Juliette*, Lyon, 1990.
Alicia Alonso, Charles Gounod, *Shakespeare y sus Máscaras*, Valencia, 2003.
Mauro Bigonzetti, Sergej Prokofjew, *Romeo and Juliet*, Reggio Emilia, 2006.
Birgit Scherzer, Sergej Prokofjew, *Romeo und Julia*, Trier, 2014.
Bridget Breiner, Sergej Prokofjew, *Romeo und Julia*, Gelsenkirchen, 2018.

Summary

This contribution exemplifies how tragedy can be expressed in the nonverbal medium of dance. It analyses different ballet adaptations of *Romeo and Juliet* – the most frequently choreographed literary work since the beginnings of story ballet in the second half of the eighteenth century. The article demonstrates how ballet and its means of expression – especially choreography, music, set design and costumes – not only lend themselves for contemporary adaptation and actualization, as do theatre and film, but can also develop new perspectives on the Shakespearean tragedy itself.

Dance of Death:
Hitler and the Morris Men

RICHARD WILSON

Magic Island

"To our German friends, England is still *Zauberinsel*, the land of Shakespeare's Histories and *The Tempest*, tenanted by historic ghosts and natural faeries."¹ The writer of that mystic encomium, who was introduced to the readers of the *Observer* in 1934 as "D. H. Lawrence in a Black Shirt [...] Mr. Rolf Gardiner, the English neo-Nazi", is remembered as a pioneering ecologist, early music reviver, naturist and folk-dancer, a Pied Piper whose interwar work camps inculcated "obedience to authority" by coercing youths in lederhosen into singing masses by William Byrd.² Hugo von Hofmannsthal idealized him in his 1924 play *Der Turm* as "a Children's king", whose legions sang in the fields "as men did of old"; and Patrick Wright excuses him as "a morris-dancing boy scout [...] overtaken by storm troopers".³ Yet, as Gardiner informed Joseph Goebbels, in a letter hailing "the Germanic revolution initiated by National Socialism", drafted on St George's Day, 23 April 1933, which the Propaganda Minister instantly published, this self-proclaimed "*Führer* of a young English generation" aimed "to bring about not

---

1   Rolf Gardiner, "Can Farming save European Civilisation?", extract from "European Husbandry Meeting", in *Wessex: Letters from Springhead*, Third Series 2 (Christmas 1950), repr. in *Water Springing from the Ground: An Anthology of the Writings of Rolf Gardiner*, ed. by Andrew Best (Fontmell Magna: Springhead, 1972), 196–203, quote 200.
2   "D. H. Lawrence in a Black Shirt", *Observer*, 4 February 1934. See E. Delaveney and W. J. Keith, "Mr Rolf Gardiner, 'The English Neo-Nazi': an Exchange", *D. H. Lawrence Review* 7 (1974), 292–293; "obedience to authority": Rolf Gardiner, "Reflections on Music and Statecraft", *North Sea and Baltic* (Summer 1934), repr. in Delaveney and Keith (1974), 95–105, quote 95.
3   Hugo von Hofmannsthal, "The Tower", in *Hugo von Hofmannsthal: Selected Plays and Libretti*, ed. and trans. by Michael Hamburger (London: Routledge & Kegan Paul, 1963), 348; see Matthew Jefferies and Mike Tyldesley, "Introduction", in Matthew Jefferies and Mike Tyldesley (eds), *Rolf Gardiner: Folk, Nature and Culture in Interwar Britain* (London: Routledge, 2016), 1–15, at 11, n. 54; Patrick Wright, *The Village that Died for England* (London: Faber & Faber, 2002), 228.

brotherhood but spiritual combat", indeed to smash the enemy by every "undemocratic and unpacifist" means.[4]

In another celebratory piece printed in Germany in 1933 Gardiner trumpeted the country's "National Revolution" as "the spring storm of a new Renaissance".[5] So, in her book *The Imagined Village*, folklorist Georgina Boyes infers he may have mixed with the *Freikorps* paramilitaries in the *Ostmark*, Germany's disputed Eastlands, about 1920.[6] The environmentalist's most enduring friendships would certainly be bonded with such "*völkisch Artamanen*", revanchist "Guardians of the soil", who "dreamed of re-settling 'the German East'".[7] Among them was the friend who called England Shakespeare's *Zauberinsel*: the future West German Refugee Minister Theodor Oberländer, whose "wide experience of Eastern Europe" included zealous ethnic cleansing.[8] For following in the steps of his "torch bearer and torch leader" Lawrence with a gap-year Alpine hike, Gardiner was fired up by the "terrifying earnestness" of a new breed of *Altwandervögel*, who were shedding the dreaminess of the pre-war *Bündische* youth groups, and "sought a return to the roots of all values", having grasped that "The *Bund* is an elite. It is a soil, for ever being self-raked, re-dug, re-manured, in which strong natures can grow."[9]

Gardiner saluted the leaders of Germany's post-war *Jugendbewegung* as "a new type of manhood", the "sons of gods, a race of heroes returning to conquer the

---

4   Rolf Gardiner to Joseph Goebbels, 25 April 1933, trans. and qtd. in Dan Stone, "Rolf Gardiner: An Honorary Nazi?", in Jefferies and Tyldesley (2016), 151–168, at 154. See also James Cain, "English Fuhrer and his Battle Plan for Teesside", *Middlesbrough Evening Gazette*, 24 February 2014.

5   Rolf Gardiner, "Die deutsche Revolution von England gesehen", in Rolf Gardiner, Arvid Brodersen and Karl Wyser (eds), *Nationalsozialismus vom Ausland gesehen: an die Gebildeten unter seinen Gegnern* (Berlin: Verlag die Runde, 1933), 10, qtd. and trans. in Richard Griffiths, "The Dangers of Definition: Post-Facto Opinions on Rolf Gardiner's Attitudes towards Nazi Germany", in Jefferies and Tyldesley (2016), 137–149, at 140.

6   Georgina Boyes, *The Imagined Village: Culture, Ideology and the English Folk Revival* (Manchester: Manchester University Press, 1993), 162, 191. See Rolf Gardiner, "Changing Carinthia", *Wessex: Letters from Springhead*, Fourth Series 5 (1966), 154.

7   Anna Bramwell, *Ecology in the 20th Century: A History* (New Haven: Yale University Press, 1989), 100.

8   Gardiner (1950), 200; Bramwell (1989), 206.

9   "torch bearer": Rolf Gardiner, *World Without End: British Politics and the Young Generation* (London: Cobden-Sanderson, 1932), 10; "terrifying earnestness": Rolf Gardiner, "German Youth Movements", *Youth* 9 (March 1923), 202; "The Bund is an elite": Gardiner (1932), 38.

kingdoms of the world", who "sing as they go".[10] Soon after he met Lawrence in 1926, the illustrator Maxwell Armfield portrayed the Dorset squire as just such a blond and blue-eyed "*Gauleiter* of Wessex" himself: "a cross between Baldur the Beautiful and a Boy Scout [...] Maypole in hand".[11] For in the journals *Youth* and *North Sea and Baltic*, which he financed and edited, Gardiner proclaimed the "kinship of German and English youth", and its rootedness in Nordic Europe, in contrast to the "restless" Wandering Jews, who were "without soil or tradition", yet carried the "smell of Asia in their beards".[12] As the historian of British fascism Richard Griffiths observes, Gardiner presents "almost a caricature of the 'blood-and-soil' fanatic".[13] His influence therefore arose not simply from his compulsion that "What is at stake is civilization and the preservation of the world from the roving sand-dunes of the East", but the inherited wealth he deployed to confront this supposed impending ecological disaster with such heaps of Shakespearean drama, dance and dung:

> The world is out of joint: O cursed spite
> That ever I was born to set it right!
> This is the horror of Hamlet. The age of darkness is upon us. This
> is the winter of our discontent and the approaching winter of
> Western Civilisation. And it will be cold.[14]

Every trope of racial regeneration was hyped in Gardiner's ecstatic pronouncements; but it was his belief that because "the wealth of a people" inheres "in their devotion to the same soil and its continuous culture", blood and soil could be reunited through drama, dance and song, that marked him as a follower of Hitler rather than Mussolini, he loudly announced.[15] Thus, "Whereas Jewish art

---

10 Rolf Gardiner, "The Outlook of Young Germany" (1929), Rolf Gardiner Papers, Cambridge University Library (henceforth RGP), A3/1/1; "sing as they go": Gardiner (1923), 202–203.
11 "*Gauleiter* of Wessex": Wright (2002), 235, citing "local gossip"; "Baldur the Beautiful": Arthur Bryant to H. J. Massingham, 29 November 1943, qtd. in Richard Moore-Colyer and Philip Conford, "A 'Secret Society'?: The Internal and External Relations of the Kinship in Husbandry, 1941–1952", *Rural History* 15 (2004), 189–206, quote 198.
12 Rolf Gardiner, "The Meaning of the German Revolution", *North Sea and Baltic* (1933), 2; "smell of Asia": Gardiner, "Die Deutsche Revolution" (1933), 15, trans. and qtd. in Stone (2016), 157.
13 Griffiths (2016), 144.
14 "What is at stake": Rolf Gardiner, *New Pioneer* (May 1939), 147–148, quote 143; "The world is out of joint": Rolf Gardiner, "Youth and Europe", *Youth* 2:11 (1923), 1–2: repr. in Gardiner (1972), 19–21, quote 19.
15 Rolf Gardiner, *England Herself: Ventures in Rural Restoration* (London: Faber & Faber, 1943), 7.

is analytic, individualistic, and self-expressive, that of the northern European is mythic, communal and religious", he wrote to *The Times* in the summer of 1933; so the coming "purge, despite the hardship it will cause many thousands of Jews, will release the Germans from an alien spell".[16] And long after he disavowed the concentration camps, his project for a Viking federation, stretching "between Whitby and Lübeck, Elsinore and Danzig", would persist in the Hamburg Shakespeare Prize he inspired.[17]

With an Egyptologist father, who inherited a textile fortune, and swanned between Berlin, London and family estates in Malawi, and an aristocratic half-Austro-Hungarian, half-Swedish-Finnish mother, who was herself of Jewish descent, Gardiner spent his life aspiring to be a horny-handed son of Anglo-Saxon soil. His debut publication in 1921, when he was nineteen, was therefore a Lawrentian paean to the anti-Jewish passion play at Oberammergau, which contrasted the Hamlet-like "indecision in the bodies" of the "pallid looking" tourists with the firmness of the Bavarian peasants on stage, for whom "past, present, and future are locked in one unity".[18] As Lawrence informed Gardiner, such "Germans take their shirts off and work in the hay" when not staging plays, since "they are still physical". By contrast, the novelist feared his protégé was "reaching for the earth", rather than rooting in it. So, he urged him to build a "hearth where you keep the central fire of your effort alive [...] if your song, dance and labour are to have a real source. – The German youth is almost ready to fuse into a new sort of fighting unity, it seems to me: us against the world". Gardiner had read in the *Hamlet* chapter of Lawrence's *Twilight in Italy* how Shakespeare mourned "the true phallic worship" which earthed such a "strong dominion of the blood" with masculine song and dance. This essay will follow his attempts to literally ground that Shakespearean vision in English and German soil.[19]

---

16   Rolf Gardiner, unpublished letter to *The Times*, undated (summer 1933), qtd. in Stone (2016), 157.
17   "between Whitby and Lübeck": Rolf Gardiner, "Meditations on the Future of Northern Europe", in Rolf Gardiner and Heinz Rocholl (eds), *Britain and Germany: A Frank Discussion Instigated by Members of the Younger Generation* (London: Williams & Norgate, 1928), 121–132, quote 126–127.
18   Rolf Gardiner, "Oberammergau", *The Saturday Review*, 13 May 1922, 485–487, quote 485–486; "potencies of the earth": Rolf Gardiner, "The Travelling Morrice and the Cambridge Morris Men", *Springhead Ring News Sheet* (1961), 10.
19   D.H. Lawrence, *Twilight in Italy*, in *The Cambridge Edition of the Works of D.H. Lawrence: Twilight to Italy and Other Essays*, ed. by Paul Eggert (Cambridge: Cambridge University Press,

Hail the Day

For the rest of his life Gardiner would quote Lawrence's warning that "the human race is like a great uprooted tree, with its roots in the air", which must be planted "again in the universe", as the inspiration for his neo-feudal organic farm at Springhead in Dorset, where his totem was the sacred ash tree of Norse myth, Yggdrasil, "with long lusty roots in the dark earth". There his Ring of initiates would obey the novelist's "ritual of dawn" with the "morning torture" of a naked "air bath", then weave a "serpentine dance" before raising the dragon flag of Wessex to a pagan hymn: "Hail the day, which in darkness lay".[20] But the scheme to "plant" the community in "the seasons, with the Drama and the Passion of the Soul embodied in processions and dances", would fuse into a "fighting unity" in a less pastoral setting: the "godly darkness" of the ironstone mining villages of North Yorkshire, where Gardiner imagined the steel weapons wielded in the region's sword dances "were really symbols of the rays of the Sun", which were "wreathed together into a pattern called the 'lock' or 'rose'", to form the figure of the solar wheel, or swastika:[21]

The North Riding is the home of one of the most vigorous regional cultures in England. Its Scandinavian population [...] is deeply attached to its earth, the moorland

---

2002), 138, 167–168; D. H Lawrence to Rolf Gardiner, 7 January 1928, *The Letters of D. H. Lawrence VI, 1927–28*, ed. by James Boulton and Margaret Boulton with Gerald Lacey (Cambridge: Cambridge University Press, 1991), 257–258.

20 D. H. Lawrence, *A Propos of "Lady Chatterley's Lover"*, qtd. in Gardiner, *England Herself* (1943), 13–14; "long lusty roots": Rolf Gardiner to D. H. Lawrence, 13 December 1926, qtd. in Edward Nehls (ed.), *D. H. Lawrence: A Composite Biography: III: 1925–30* (Madison: University of Wisconsin Press, 1959), 122; "morning torture [...] serpent dance": Rolf Gardiner, "A Report on the Hermannsburg Camp, Easter 1927", 7–8, qtd. in Matthew Jefferies, "Rolf Gardiner and German Naturism", in Jefferies and Tyldesley (2016), 47–64, quote 56; "air bath": Rolf Gardiner to Bettina Ostarhild, 16 January 1967, qtd. in Jefferies and Tyldesley (2016), 50; "Hail the day": Michael Pitt-Rivers, qtd. in Wright (2002), 190.

21 "the seasons": D. H. Lawrence, *Lady Chatterley's Lover and A Propos of "Lady Chatterley's Lover"*, ed. by Michael Squires (Cambridge: Cambridge University Press, 2002), 329; "godly darkness": Rolf Gardiner, *Wessex: Letters from Springhead*, Fourth Series 2 (1959), repr. in Gardiner (1972), 37–47, quote 37; "which were really symbols": Rolf Gardiner, "Prologue", in Gardiner (1972), 1–12, quote 4. For the symbolism of the interlocked weapons in the Yorkshire Sword-dances, see Rishona Zimring, *Social Dance and the Modernist Imagination* (London: Routledge, 2016), 141–142. See also Stephen Corrsin, "The Historiography of European Linked Sword Dancing", *Dance Research Journal* 25:1 (1993), 1–14.

soil, and it cherishes its native pastimes and recreations. Among these were such things as the long sword dance (the midwinter ritual of the North).[22]

No wonder Lawrence said he "would like to try a sword-dance with iron-stone miners".[23] The Cleveland dance was elevated by Gardiner into "one of the most ancient and persistent solar rituals", which endured, he believed, "wherever Germanic customs have taken root", its "solar symbolism" being derived from "Druidic times".[24] In her study of the toxic roots of Green ideology, Anna Bramwell relates how it was through the novelist that this "German brand of serious sun-worship" penetrated "the English nature tradition", after he witnessed the *Nacktkultur* of Hermann Hesse, Rudolf Laban and Rudolf Steiner, as they flocked to "dance in the sun" on Monte Verita – the Hill of Truth – at Ascona.[25] Bramwell remarks that if these nudist sunbathers wished to avert the apocalypse, "Lawrence did not"; and his disciple's role was to give the solar wheel a further violent twist, with his dogma that the sun-dance had always been the preserve of a *Blutsbrüderschaft*, an Aryan *Männerbund* sworn to enact the "killing of the old year" with the slaying of a totemic Fool in a dance of death and resurrection, as the swordsmen "speed in a frenzied spiral around the kneeling man", and lock swords in the wheel around his neck, and "the Fool falls sideways upon the ground".[26]

Gardiner's proselytizing against "the most unnatural" female membership of the English Folk Dance Society (EFDS) led to the formation in 1933 of an exclusively male Morris Ring of men's clubs, causing a schism which still persists.[27] One of his few woman collaborators would be the Dutch folklorist Elise van der

---

22 Gardiner, *England Herself* (1943), 33.
23 D. H. Lawrence to Rolf Gardiner, 22 July 1926, in *The Letters of D. H. Lawrence: V: 1924–27*, ed. by James Boulton and Lindeth Vaisey (Cambridge: Cambridge University Press, 1989), 501–502.
24 Ibid., 131; "solar symbolism [...] Druidic times": Gardiner (1961), repr. in Gardiner (1972), 53–56, quote 55.
25 Bramwell (1989), 107; "dance in the sun": Martin Green, "The Mountain of Truth", in Max Blechman (ed.), *Revolutionary Romanticism: An Anthology* (San Francisco: City Lights, 1999), 163–178, quote 173. See also Carl Krockel, *D. H. Lawrence and Germany: The Politics of Influence* (Amsterdam: Rodopi, 2007), 93. Bramwell's controversial thesis about the entanglement of environmental and racial politics has been vociferously contested by, among others, Piers Stephens in "Blood Not Soil: Anna Bramwell and the Myth of 'Hitler's Green Party'", *Organization and Environment* 14:2 (2001), 173–187.
26 Bramwell (1989), 113; Gardiner, *England Herself* (1943), 133–134.
27 Gardiner (1961), 10.

Ven-ten Bensel, whose Aryanization of the sword dance during the Nazi Occupation proved she fully shared his pan-Germanic prejudices.[28] For long before the wheel of fire became loaded with the apocalyptic menace of the *Hakenkreuze*, Gardiner scandalized the Society by describing the "voltaic commotion" of the clashing blades as a "purging flame of ecstasy, an exaltation, a cathartic frenzy" of immemorial "magical or priestly" significance.[29] So, when he led a "phalanx" of Yorkshire dancers to the World Congress for Leisure-Time and Recreation, convened as a curtain-raiser for the Berlin Olympics in Hamburg in July 1936, under the banner of "Strength Through Joy", and the presidency of Robert Ley, leader of the Reich Labour Front, his sinister words about the midwinter sacrifice were perfectly pitched:

> During the Congress you will have the opportunity of seeing a group of miners from the North of England who perform the old Nordic sword dance. This dance, which was also known throughout Germany and the neighbouring lands, forms part of a Midwinter play which is intended to represent the death and resurrection of the year. To this very day this dance is still performed [...] in some forty or fifty mining villages.[30]

In his speech to the Hamburg Congress, "The Muses and the People in England", Gardiner presented the sword dance as living proof "that the old German music and old English folk-dance" were "very closely related, for in the sixteenth and seventeenth centuries England and Germans alike lived together in one great common western civilization and with one common Germanic will".[31] Thus, at Cambridge he had been enchanted to learn about the Shakespearean travelling companies, who "during the heyday of our national arts, between 1550–1620, literally overran the Continent and were popular throughout the length and

---

28   Georgina Boyes, "'Potencies of the Earth': Rolf Gardiner and the English Folk Dance Revival", in Jefferies and Tyldesley (2016), 65–94, at 87–90. See Gardiner, "Prologue", in Gardiner (1972), 7.
29   "voltaic commotion": Rolf Gardiner, *The English Folk Dance Tradition: An Essay* (Hellerau: Neue Schule Hellerau, 1923), 12; "magical or priestly": Rolf Gardiner, "Summer Tour in Germany, 1928", *North Sea and Baltic*, New Series 4 (1938), 101.
30   Rolf Gardiner, "The Muses and the People in England", *Report of the World Congress for Leisure Time and Recreation, Hamburg July 23 to July 30 1936* (Hamburg: Hanseatische Verlagsanstalt, 1937), 150; "phalanx": Rolf Gardiner, "Homage to North Skelton", *Wessex: Letters from Springhead*, Fourth Series 2 (1959), repr. in Gardiner (1972), 37–47, quote 39.
31   Gardiner (1937), 151.

breadth of Northern Europe from Austria to Scandinavia". And it was the revelation of this "half-remembered tradition" of strolling players that spurred him to defy the objections of the Gandalf of the EFDS, Cecil Sharp, and organize the first ever English folk-dancing tour of Germany, where "Shakespeare's was a name to conjure with", for "Did not the Germans even claim him as 'unser Shakespeare'?"[32]

If Shakespeare provided Gardiner with a passport, it was to the provincial Germany Hitler voiced when he pledged to rescue the Bard from the "morbid monstrosities produced by insane and degenerate" directors.[33] The National Socialist Shakespeare would be an artisan and countryman, whose craft "was a communal work".[34] The nexus between such *völkisch* anti-urbanism and the origins of modern dance as "a purgative, regenerative mixture" remains contentious.[35] Gardiner would certainly attempt to meld Social Credit with "gymnosophy" in the nudist colony run by the Order of Woodcraft Chivalry at the well-named Hampshire village of Sandy Balls.[36] So, when this Rupert Brooke lookalike exhibited the "cathartic frenzy" of his dancing as the climax of the 1922 tour in the "organic community" at Hellerau, he was in step with the holistic ideas about *Handwerk* and *Lebensreform*, which drew the "music and movement" pioneers, Émile Dalcroze, A. S. Neil and Mary Wigman, to establish schools in this garden-suburb of Dresden. And it was the Dalcroze-*Schule* that printed Gardiner's orgasmic creed:

> The Morris is a great experience, like going through a cleansing fire, when the whole six of you, each striving for supreme individual technical excellence, swayed by the pulsing rhythm of the dance, the whole body and soul of you, singing to the ineffable loveliness of the melody [...] feel one surging electric fluid flowing through, fusing the whole six of you, feel one surging electric fluid in the great spasm of physical effort [...] [37]

---

32 Gardiner (1961), 55–56.
33 Adolf Hitler, *Mein Kampf*, trans. by James Murphy (London: Hurst and Blackett, 1935), 205–206. For Gardiner's career in Germany, see "Rolf Gardiner", in Hinrich Jantzen, *Namen und Werke: I* (Frankfurt am Main: DIPA, 1972), 77–81.
34 Hans Rothe, *Kampf um Shakespeare: Ein Bericht* (Leipzig: Paul List, 1936), 17, trans. and qtd. in Andreas Höfele, *No Hamlets: German Shakespeare from Nietzsche to Carl Schmitt* (Oxford: Oxford University Press, 2016), 210.
35 Bramwell (1989), 115.
36 Jefferies (2016), 54–56.
37 Gardiner, *English Folk Dance* (1923), 19.

"Clearly, dance implied a coming together of more than minds", smiles Boyes, of this "masturbatory display".[38] For in his Dresden manifesto Gardiner fantasized that the sword dancers merged into a single "man of superhuman power"; and in a later essay, "Music and Soil", he likened the electrified Yorkshire miners to the Jacobean courtiers in Enid Welsford's study of the masque, who knew when "to stop thinking and dance".[39] Spectators were therefore perhaps too thoughtful to join in, at places like Weimar or Wiesbaden, when the sword smashing was rounded with the "Cornish Furry Dance" or "Kemp's Jig". But the Morrismen were following in the footsteps of a host of whirling *Inflationsheiligen* – 'Inflation Saints' – such as the wild-eyed Friedrich Muck-Lamberty, whose "New Flock" of adolescents jubilantly "sang and danced the old German songs and dances" across Thuringia during the post-War economic breakdown. So, Gardiner was developing a network of contacts who shared his hope that although England had been "descended upon" by "Jewish-American finance", Shakespeare's countrymen could also be revitalized through an alliance with their "kin folk", the "kin tongued [...] Celtic-Germanic peoples", in a "union of the North Sea and Baltic, as in the heyday of the Hanseatic League".[40]

Music and Manure

It was likely at the "special festival in Hamburg" during this tour that Gardiner met the Baltic grain and shipping merchant whose agro-industrial fortune made the dream of sailing from England "to Stettin and up the Oder" a reality. Alfred Toepfer's matching conviction that the answer to "The Decline of the West" lay in the soil led him to share the belief that because "treatment of the earth as a food factory has the most dire consequences for civilisation", it was the "artist or poet,

---

38 Boyes (1993), 162–163.
39 Gardiner, *English Folk Dance* (1923), 12; Gardiner, *England Herself* (1943), 131, 141, quoting Enid Welsford, *The Court Masque: A Study in the Relationship Between Poetry and the Revels* (Cambridge: Cambridge University Press), 425.
40 "sang and danced": Martin Green, *Mountain of Truth: The Counterculture Begins: Ascona, 1900–1920* (Hanover, MD.: University Press of New England, 1986), 153; Walter Laqueur, *Young Germany: A History of the German Youth Movement* (London: Routledge and Kegan Paul, 1962), 115–117; Erin Sullivan Maynes, "Currency and Community: Labor, Identity and *Notgeld* in Inflation-Era Thuringia", *Bulletin of the German Historical Institute (Washington) Supplement* 14 (2019), 39–56. "England was being descended upon": Rolf Gardiner, "Stroemungen des englischen kulturellen und politischen Lebens", undated, RGP A3/1/1, trans. and qtd. in Stone (2016), 156; "Celtic-Germanic peoples": Gardiner (1928), 121–132.

as the unacknowledged legislator of mankind", who "should be the first to apprise the dangers of soil mobilization".[41] In 1922 he was just putting behind him his own service in the *Freikorps*, under the vicious anti-Semite Ludwig Maercker, beside Reinhard Heydrich, architect of the so-called 'Final Solution'.[42] But Toepfer's views about culture and agriculture had been shaped as a boy in the wanderers' movement, strumming beside campfires to "the rhythm of eternity", and the tunes of its chief songster, Hans Breuer: "Here is the focus: to find out about our life's project as early as possible [...] to plant this project in the nourishing soil of our home country where all roots still touch hands; then to develop it organically from a world which you have discovered by walking through it."[43]

Between motets sung by the Germans and galliards danced by the English, "there was an unmistakable affinity due to their 17th century roots", Gardiner recalled, and "In view of the friendships cemented" in Hamburg, and "activities that followed in both England and Germany, this was an historic turning-point".[44] His partnership with Toepfer would culminate in 1969 at the Schloss Fürsteneck in Hessen, where, as founders of the European Working Party for Landscape Husbandry, equally intent on creating a stink over chemical fertilizer, they ceremonially buried a copy of the Common Agricultural Policy under a gigantic heap of steaming manure.[45] But during their half-century collaboration Gardiner and Toepfer's "unshakeable belief in the regenerative power of a culture based on kinship and soil" would raise, with the Hamburg Shakespeare Prize, a monument to the confluence of music and manure that would cause, by the end, even more of a stench.[46]

Toepfer funnelled part of his profits to youth projects in "areas which bordered on the Reich".[47] One of these was the *Boberhaus* camp of "students, workmen and peasants" that "lay just beyond the *Ostmark*" in Silesia, which Gardiner also

---

41 "to Stettin": Rolf Gardiner to James Pennyman, 2 August 1929, RGP 73/17; "treatment of the earth [...] mobilization": Gardiner, *England Herself* (1943), 126.
42 Jürgen Schlaeger, "Introduction", in *Shakespeare Prize: 1937–2006* (Hamburg: Alfred Toepfer Stiftung F.V.S., 2013), 3–13, quote 7.
43 Hans Breuer, "Herbstschau 1913", *Der Wandervogel: Eine Monatsschrift für deutsches Jugendwandern* (October 1913), 282, trans. and repr. in Schlaeger (2013), 326. For the wanderers' songbook, *Der Zupfgeigenhansl*, see Robert-Jan Andriassen, *The Rhythm of Eternity: The German Youth Movement and the Experience of the Past: 1900–1933* (New York: Berghan, 2015), 40–42.
44 Rolf Gardiner, "Biographical Essays: Anna Helms-Blasche, 1877–1963", RGP A37.
45 Richard Moore-Colyer, "Rolf Gardiner, Farming and the English Landscape", in Jefferies and Tyldesley (2016), 95–119, at 116; RGP H3/1.
46 "unshakeable belief": Schlaeger (2013), 8.
47 Ibid., 7–8.

helped set up, to defend European soil, he avowed, from the encroaching "Asiatic desert".[48] There, and at the *Musikheim* art college in Frankfurt an der Oder, "music, speech and movement" proved to be the "essential links in the chain of discovery and growth" that led to the "recreation of the local community", the English folk-dancer headily reported. "As the basis of community health and wholeness", in "the home, the village, the region, the nation", indeed in "Christendom" itself, the "design and order" of "music, of ritual and figure dances, of choric masques and home-made drama, of rhythmic gymnastics", were keys to the repossession of the *Heimat*, Gardiner proclaimed.

For Gardiner and Toepfer song and dance were weapons in a *Kulturkampf* that expressly earthed "the rhythmic arts" in the revanchist "tasks of the German *Ostmark*", and the expansionist settlement of "a people without living space".[49] In his congratulation to Goebbels, the Englishman therefore boasted how he and his comrades in "the conservative-national section of German youth" had toiled "tirelessly" to bring about "the new order of a third Reich", and he implored the "Esteemed *Reichsminister*" to reward his colleague, the director of the *Musikheim*, Georg Götsch, as "a true executor of the ideas of the National Socialist state". Gardiner concluded his message hoping the "great development of the German *Volk*" would flow from the "Germanic world" to the British Isles, and that Goebbels would assist him in cultural exchanges that would amalgamate the resources of both "a tradition-rich England and a future-oriented Germany":

> We will pursue our work of renewing Germanic values in all countries around the North and Baltic Seas with renewed strength. For we believe that the new German state will be our protector. You, Herr *Reichsminister*, will understand us and assess our path correctly. In this sense we English, through you, greet the new German state.[50]

Gardiner later pretended he contacted Goebbels purely to help Götsch. But at the time he was euphoric, writing in *The Adelphi*, the journal edited by Lawrence's friend John Middleton Murry, that the reason "an astonishing number of Hitler's adjutants" had been *Wandervögel* was that "the aims of this post-War youth movement and those of Hitler and his storm troops were the same": the "resuscitation

---

48 Stone (2016), 154, quoting Rolf Gardiner, "The Musikheim, Frankfurt an der Oder", *North Sea and Baltic* (1930), 10.
49 Gardiner, *England Herself* (1943), 130; "people without living space": Schlaeger (2013), 8.
50 Gardiner to Goebbels, trans. and qtd. in Stone (2016), 159.

of yeoman, peasant values".[51] Here he spoke as a follower of the radical "National Bolshevik" wing of Germany's Conservative Revolution, whose magazine *Die Tat* was a hotline connecting what Martin Green terms the Lawrence-inspired "Asconan" anti-capitalist counter-culture with the Nazi regime.[52] Articles in *Die Tat* by the likes of Laban lived up to its decisionist name by prophesying the "fate change of our race" would be "the act" of the dance.[53] But when this so-called "Black Front" was suppressed, the journal was taken over, and in 1937 Toepfer was arrested, along with other *Tat* men of action.

The merchant of Hamburg was soon freed at the behest of the irredentist "Association of Germans Living Outside the Reich".[54] And a decade on, his imprisonment would prove a godsend during his de-Nazification. Likewise, his English friend's "National Bolshevik" disenchantment over Hitler's "league with machinery" provided a smokescreen after his Dorset neighbours accused him of planting a forest of Nordic Pine in the shape of a swastika.[55] Post-war patronage by the eco-minded Duke of Edinburgh then "restored the 'Prince of Denmark'" to his "production of *Hamlet*" he liked to say.[56] But as historian Dan Stone concludes, Gardiner's treasonous offer to Goebbels, "to be of assistance with propaganda work coming out of the German Academic Exchange Centre in London", in fact arose directly from his conviction that "Our generation has three tasks before it: to return to the England that was lost in the 17th century, to decentralize on our own soil, and to prepare for incorporation in a new system with Germany as the heart."[57]

---

51   Rolf Gardiner, "Correspondence", *The Adelphi* 8 (1934), 64, qtd. in Wright (2002), 227. Gardiner's letter was a reply to Leslie Paul, "The Decline of the Youth Movement", *The Adelphi*, 7 (1934), 317–327.
52   Green (1999), 218–222.
53   Rudolf Laban, "Symbole des Tanzes und Tanz als Symbol", *Die Tat* 33 (1919), 669–675, at 673–675, trans. and qtd. in Green (1999), 222–223: "The fate of our race is its awakening to dance".
54   Schlaeger (2013), 9.
55   Rolf Gardiner, "Money and Machine? Or Bread and Skill?", *The Springhead Ring News Sheet* 42 (1943), repr. in Gardiner (1972), 156–158, quote 157; "swastika": Wright (2002), 187.
56   Rolf Gardiner, "Speech to the Duke of Edinburgh's Conference 'The Countryside in 1970'", 12 November 1965, *Wessex: Letters from Springfield*, Fourth Series 4 (1965), repr. in Gardiner (1972), 264–265, quote 265.
57   Stone (2016), 161; Rolf Gardiner to "Alan" (Collingridge), 17 November 1930, RGP A2/6.

Gartenfest in Whitby

At Easter 1927 Gardiner teamed up with his Hamburg comates in a work camp at Hermannsburg, on Lüneburg Heath, where he saw dance and song weld "soul and soil" into a will to fight for the *Ostmark*, "like the Teutonic knights of old".[58] It was therefore while digging and playmaking in this *Arbeitslager* that his diffuse notions about dancing, hiking, eugenics, eurhythmics, farming, forestry, nudism, singing and race converged into an existential decision for an actual return to the Germanic earth. He had worked for two years as "Gleemaster" and international officer of the pacifist Kibbo Kift Kindred, and no one minded when he sported the Saxon hood and jerkin of the kinfolk in his roving role as "Rolf the Ranger".[59] But he now suspected the thrust of his "central idea", to "form a union between the kindred people of the North", based on "the homogeneity of the old Germanic culture", was "going too far" for the Travelling Morrice and the Cambridge Morris Men.[60]

Gardiner had always intended "to bring the Cambridge team to Jutland and Gothland", for "a men's expedition" that would dance like real "Norsemen" around the shores of the Baltic, as "the climax of our endeavours".[61] And during the tour of Germany he organized for them the following year, after a gig in the idyllic Schlosspark at Weimar, he was fortuitously offered a Nordic "hearth" for his "new system", and a base for operations beside the "tossing ferment" of the "German Ocean", among the Yorkshire sword-dancers of Teesside, where, as he recalled in his eco-fascist apologia, *England Herself*, "a local squire with roots in the soil" cared enough about "What became of the people and landscape when the pits closed", to join him in establishing an *Arbeitslager* twinned with the *Musikheim*.[62]

---

58 Rolf Gardiner, "The Triple Function of Work Camps and Work Service in Europe", *North Sea and Baltic* (Harvest 1937), New Series 2 (Springhead), repr. in Gardiner (1972), 109–125, quotes 113, 116.
59 David Fowler, *Youth Culture in Modern Britain* (Basingstoke: Palgrave Macmillan, 2008), 34–35.
60 Gardiner (1961), 10; "the homogeneity": Gardiner (1928), 127.
61 Gardiner (1961), 9.
62 Rolf Gardiner, "Travelling Morrice: Tour of Germany 1928", 1, in "Biographical Essays", RGP A3/7; "tossing ferment": Gardiner, "Homage to North Skelton" (1959), 37; "German Ocean": Oliver Soden, *Michael Tippett: The Biography* (London: Weidenfeld & Nicolson, 2019), 123; Gardiner, *England Herself* (1943), 34.

Faber and Faber would issue Gardiner's memoir of "muck and mystery" in the middle of the war only after advocacy by the like-minded T. S. Eliot.[63] That the name of Gardiner's stalwart Yorkshire squire, James Pennyman, was blanked out in the published text therefore indicates the embarrassment his continued ranting about "our Jew-controlled press, cinema, wireless and advertising" was by then causing the landowning territorial army officer, who had been eager enough on his return from the Berlin Olympics to update the *Middlesbrough Evening Gazette* on how "so much has been said about the bullying of the Jews that Hitler's constructive ideas had been overlooked", and in any case, "this was not the first time, that in a revolution, people had been deprived of their property".[64]

When Gardiner wrote to take up Pennyman's offer in 1929, his words were not rebuffed: "Our business is to create something new, something rooted in faith and obedience which may survive the storms which loom and break over England."[65] If that read like a coded incitement to prepare the North Sea bridgehead for a future German *Blitzkrieg*, Major Pennyman's response at the time was collaborative and unblinking: "As a national group, I want England and Germany one, with Scandinavia thrown in. Holland in automatically. As a cultural (save the word) group ditto." But the Conservative County Councillor also impressed on his impatient young Hotspur the need for discretion: "Don't go too fast […]. I think you may put people off if you so much as declare the whole of it publicly".[66]

"We have got to be dangerous and political, without telling anybody so", Gardiner agreed, informing the major that "the German Singers and English Players" would make their triumphal entry into the rebuilt *Musikheim* in Silesia on 17 August 1929, and promising to follow this move "by invading you" in Yorkshire: "Let us reconstruct and re-energise Cleveland […]. Let us change the people in dance and music, in play-acting […]. Let us have a *Gartenfest* in Whitby". Pennyman resided at stately Ormesby Hall, outside Middlesbrough; but he and his wife had listened to the Gleemaster preach on how to transform their Palladian mansion into "a nucleus of vital harmony" in "the sunny heart of Germany, in the old park at Weimar, sitting on a bench" outside the Belvedere. So, with his mystical sense

63 "muck and mystery": Richard Moore-Colyer, "Rolf Gardiner, English Patriot and the Council for the Church and Countryside", *Agricultural History Review* 49:2 (2001), 187–209, quote 187.
64 Rolf Gardiner, *Springhead Ring News Sheet* 23 (Winter Solstice 1938), qtd. in John Field, "An Anti-Urban Education? Work Camps and Ideals of the Land in Interwar Britain", *Rural History* 23:2 (2012), 213–228, quote 223; James Pennyman, qtd. in Cain (2014).
65 Rolf Gardiner to James and Ruth Pennyman, undated, c. 1929, Teesside Archives, qtd. in Cain (2014).
66 James Pennyman to Rolf Gardiner, 17 March 1931, RGP J3/17.

of sacred space, Gardiner was preaching a version of the "open-air theatre" cult to which both his listeners were already half-converted, but with ulterior purposes to which they also soon subscribed.[67]

The Pennymans' "stone Hall of simple elegance on the edge of the Moors" might become something of which D. H. Lawrence, and even Weimar's own Goethe would approve, Gardiner assured its compliant owners: a veritable "temple" for celebrating "changing social values [...] a centre for social ventures, meetings, conferences, communal recreations such as concert parties, play-productions", where "people of all classes, miners and farm-folk and guests and local gentry" could be "mixed together".[68] To bring Shakespeare to Teesside might be beyond the Pennyman's means. But now this seemingly romantic young visionary wrote from Frankfurt an der Oder with a concrete plan of action: "May I come to visit you in North Yorkshire? I should like to bring a Col. G. S. Hutchinson with me, who is a strong man. I believe he could help us. He wants to do something".[69]

"Here's your job!" Gardiner exhorted the Pennymans, "To initiate something new, and to kindle the life quality where it has been quenched", on "the foul sewer of the Tees beside poor, old maligned Middlesbrough".[70] So, to keep their "central fire" burning with "song, dance and labour", they would indeed need a "strong man", with hefty supporters. Admired by Lawrence, John Buchan, Ezra Pound and his correspondent Ernst Jünger, Graham Seton Hutchinson had inspired a march entitled "The Mad Major" with his wartime exploits, which included shooting forty of his own troops for retreating; thumped out Buchan-style thrillers, with titles like *Blood Money* and *Warrior*, which demonized "World Jewry" and foretold "the destruction of the Jewish financial system"; and was just then recruiting a "Cohort of Paladins", consisting of "men of Spartan habits, capable of sacrifice" in the crusade against the "woolly-minded degenerates" who were ruining Britain.[71]

---

67 Rolf Gardiner to James Pennyman, 2 August 1929, RGP J3/17. For Gardiner's esoteric ties to the open-air theatre cult, which originated in Theosophy, see Clare Button, "'A very perfect form of discipline': Rolf Gardiner, Folk Dance and Occult Landscapes", in Christine Ferguson and Andrew Radford (eds), *The Occult Imagination in Britain, 1875–1947* (Abingdon: Routledge, 2017), 58–74, at 67.
68 Rolf Gardiner, "Youth and the Land", in Gardiner, *England Herself* (1943), 34.
69 Rolf Gardiner to James Pennyman, 2 August 1929, RGP J3/17.
70 "This is your job!": Rolf Gardiner to James and Ruth Pennyman, undated, c. 1929, Teesside Archives, qtd. in Cain (2014); "foul sewer": Rolf Gardiner to James Pennyman, 2 August 1929, RGP J3/17.
71 Graham Seton Hutchinson, *Superman* (November 1930), 20–22; *Superman* (December 1930), 43–44, qtd. in Ina Zweiniger-Bargielowska, "Building a British Superman: Physical Culture

The colonel's plan perhaps involved a more immersive type of open-air theatre than the *Gartenfest* the Pennymans bargained for in Weimar, for Gardiner had persuaded Hutchinson that the dancing miners of Cleveland were the answer to the call that echoed through his books: "We want Men! A race of Supermen."[72] On the council of the New Health Society, and in the magazines *Superman* and *Health and Strength*, the mountaineering muscle-builder extolled the "Supermanity" of the male "body beautiful", and idolized Mussolini as a "He Man".[73] Gardiner, who was struck by the "bronzed bodies, naked to the hips, just as in Sparta", at the Prussian State Institute for Physical Exercise in Spandau, encountered Hutchinson in Upper Silesia, where the keep-fit fanatic was on the Border Commission, and agitated for German resettlement.[74] So, in the lead-up to Silesia's "invasion" of Yorkshire, Gardiner's dispatches to the Pennymans sounded ever more like this "Pocket Mussolini", as he excoriated usurious "money madness" and outlined their campaign.[75]

"What we have got to do, Jim and Ruth, is to break the superstitious, cringing belief in money, and teach men to respect and obey those in whom they can recognize a real life-superiority", Gardiner confided. Hutchinson had convinced the money-maddened Pound he could "talk economics to any workman or bunch of boys"; but in Middlesbrough his usefulness to the unluckily named Pennyman, in helping to lay on enough "recreation and entertainment to recapture the traditional spirit of 'Merrie England'", must have taken a more practical monetary form.[76] For as the name of his putative political grouping morphed, from the Paladin League to the National Worker's Movement, to the National Socialist Worker Party, Hutchinson's own funds remained mysteriously buoyant,

in Interwar Britain", *Journal of Contemporary History* 41:4 (2006), 595–610, quote 603–604; "World Jewry": Graham Seton Hutchinson, *Truth: The Evidence of the Case* (London: Hutchinson, 1936), 12, qtd. in Richard Griffiths, *Fellow Travellers of the Right: British Enthusiasts for Nazi Germany, 1933–39* (Oxford: Oxford University Press, 1983), 103.

72   Graham Seton Hutchinson, *Footslogger* (London: Hutchinson, 1931), 382, qtd. in Gavin Bowd, *Fascist Scotland: Caledonia and the Far Right* (Edinburgh: Birlinn, 2013), 52.
73   Zweiniger-Bargielowska (2006), 604.
74   Bowd (2013), 50; "bronzed bodies": Rolf Gardiner, unpublished ms., report on 1928 Travelling Morrice tour of Germany, 26 June 1928, 16–17, Nachlass Gardiner, N44/61, qtd. in Jefferies (2016), 56.
75   "pocket Mussolini": Richard Thurlow, *Fascism in Britain: A History, 1918–1985* (Oxford: Blackwell, 1987), 56; "money madness": Rolf Gardiner to James Pennyman, 2 August 1929, RGP J3/17.
76   "What we have got to do ... life-superiority": ibid.; "talk economics": Graham Seton Hutchinson to Ezra Pound, 25 July 1934, qtd. in Bowd (2013), 57; "recreation and entertainment": Graham Seton Hutchinson, *Meteor* (London: Hutchinson, 1933), 281, qtd. in Bowd (2013), 54.

and by 1933 British intelligence knew he was "in German pay", as "a great friend of Hitler". In fact, for several years Goebbels "had been seeing to it that all available means" were put into the strongman's capable hands.[77]

Heartbreak Hill

Sailing from Hamburg to Hull in the summer of 1931, the madrigalists of the *Musikheim*, led by Götsch, were joined at Ormesby by Gardiner's Dorset Morris dancers, who felt as much in "a foreign country" as the Germans.[78] From the Hall, the entire company, with females in rustic frocks and males in "blue baldrics", their bells and ribbons dangling from white flannels, paraded over to Darlington, and other run-down northern industrial cities, to exhibit, so a bemused *Leeds Mercury* reported, how "the happier spirit of former times can be attained through a revival of the songs and dances of the village greens of England".[79] Whenever harvest work was available for these ale-drinking wayfarers, the Germans "amused the farm hands by instantly taking off their clothes", and everywhere a commingling of "Counterpoint, Beer and Good Fellowship" was heartily encouraged.[80]

Back at the Hall after their "vagabondage", for evenings that ended with "the Horst Wessel Lied" and "God Save the King", the Silesian minstrels and Dorset mummers "mingled" with the local sword dancing miners, in what Gardiner liked to say was an "easy north-country fashion" that escaped "class distinctions", but which he had in fact carefully scripted with the Pennymans: "Try to get the young socialists and the communists to meet the 'Imps'" – members of the Imperial Fascist League – "Get them to report the result of their discussions to the united assembly afterwards, but be careful whom you put in charge".[81] As he relayed to another mentor, Prussian Culture Minister Carl Heinrich Becker, he was looking to identify an "uprising aristocracy, or caste of leaders", a "Cohort of

---

77 Griffiths (1983), 102, 104.
78 Jack Saunders to Rolf Gardiner, 18 September 1931, RGP D3/6.
79 "blue baldrics ... flannels": Fowler (2008), 44; "happier spirit": *Leeds Mercury*, 14 August 1931.
80 "amused the farmhands": Alan Collingridge, "Anglo-German Camp in Scotland", in Gardiner and Rocholl (1928), 270–272; "Counterpoint, Beer": Christopher Scaife, "Log of the Tour", RGP A5/14, 96–97.
81 'Horst Wessel ... the King'": *Skelton-in-Cleveland in History*, skeltonincleveland.com/wp-content/uploads/SkeltonE70.html, accessed 21 October 2020; "vagabondage": Rolf Gardiner to James Pennyman, 18 January 1931, RGP J3/17; "easy north-country [...] in charge": Rolf Gardiner to James Pennyman, undated, c. 1929, Teesside Archives, qtd. in Cain (2014).

Paladins" with the "fighting unity" to "take charge" in "preparing for the future".[82] So, behind the "creative irrelevance" of songs and dances, he was searching for "the hidden ore" in the youth of Teesside, and this meant sorting the "sheep and goats".[83]

Gardiner had observed how "The *Arbeitslager* is a most effective winnower of chaff from the grain of human personality [...] cowards, shirkers and weaklings quickly discover themselves in their true colours".[84] And so notable did Ormesby's model camp become that a procession of politicians, led by Neville Chamberlain, shuttled to Teesside, ostensibly to inspect the "poultry houses, pigsties" and furniture factory the unemployed miners were tasked to erect on aptly-named Heartbreak Hill, as the "singers, dancers and players" reclaimed the moorland, which was "double dug by hand".[85] Chamberlain's talks at the Hall are not on public record. But Gardiner was thinking of a "rural university" to "lay the foundations of a new social order", an elite academy to rediscover the "reverence for the earth" that Yorkshire's Cistercians once cultivated.[86] In fact, he had in mind the type of seminary for "knight monks" being set up throughout fascist Europe, to inspire "youth from different backgrounds to abandon liberal democracy".[87]

Another "strong man" Gardiner consulted early in 1932 was therefore W. H. Auden, then teaching near Edinburgh, where the poet had just written *The Orators*, "the diary of an Airman", inspired by *Coriolanus* and Lawrence of Arabia, which its author later confessed was conceived by a different person, who might, "in a year or two, become a Nazi".[88] A year later Auden would in fact burlesque Gardiner's power mania in his play *The Dance of Death*, with Death an extermi-

---

82   Rolf Gardiner to Carl Heinrich Becker, 2 December 1928, Archiv der Deutschen Jugendbewegung, N44–14, qtd. in Jefferies and Tyldesley, "Introduction", in Jefferies and Tyldesley (2016), 13.
83   Rolf Gardiner to James Pennyman, 2 August 1929, RGP J3/17.
84   Rolf Gardiner, "Reconstruction in Silesia", *In Northern Europe* (London: The Anglo-Germanic Academic Bureau, 1932), 41–42.
85   Gardiner, *England Herself* (1943), 35.
86   Moore-Colyer (2016), 102; "the foundations": Rolf Gardiner, "On the Functions of a Rural University", extract from *North Sea and Baltic*, September 1933, in Gardiner (1972), 88–94, quote 89.
87   John Hellman, *The Knight Monks of Vichy France: Uriage, 1940–45* (Liverpool: Liverpool University Press / Montreal: McGill-Queen's University Press, 1997), cover note.
88   Wystan Hugh Auden, "Introduction", *The Orators* (London: Faber & Faber, 1967), qtd. in Humphrey Carpenter, *W. H. Auden: A Biography* (London: George Allen & Unwin, 1981), 130.

nating dictator.⁸⁹ But at Helensborough they talked of "drama, the masque, the mummers' play", and Auden sent his guest to bed with the works of Martin Luserke, the pederastic headmaster of a floating boys' "School on the Sea" moored off Frisia, where the syllabus consisted of dancing, gymnastics, music, sunbathing and Shakespeare.⁹⁰ The poet's own skin reminded Gardiner of the "clayey mud" of ancient "country lanes". Praise came no higher than that; and after he obediently imbibed Luserke, Shakespeare became the core of the curriculum he proposed for Ormesby.⁹¹

Remains of the Day

May I offer you our hearty congratulations upon the success of last night's performance and presentation of *The Winter's Tale* – it was a sheer delight from start to finish. The glory of the night, the beauty of the scene and setting, the artistic colouring of the quaint costumes, the jolly country dances, the appeal of the old world music, the excellence of the acting (with my settlement friends bearing a good part) and a very talented Autolycus, the magical words of the old dramatist, falling like music on our ears in the still evening air, all combined to give us an abiding memory of real joy [...].⁹²

Few events better illustrate Roger Griffin's thesis that "Anchoring Britain's future in nostalgia for the Tudors played a major role in the 'naturalization' of continental fascism" than the Shakespeare shows produced at Ormesby.⁹³ And

---

89 W. H. Auden, *The Dance of Death*, in *The Complete Plays of W. H. Auden: Plays and Other Dramatic Writings, 1928–1938*, ed. by Edward Mendelson (Princeton: Princeton University Library, 1988), 81–108.
90 The *völkisch* educationalist Martin Luserke authored two influential books on Shakespeare in performance, *Shakespeare – Aufführungen als Bewegungsspiele* [Shakespeare Performance as a Moving Game] (Stuttgart: Walter Seiffert, 1921), and *Pan – Apollon – Prospero: Ein Mittsommernachtstraum, die Wintersage und der Sturm: Dramaturgie von Shakespeare-Spielen* (Hamburg: Christians, 1957).
91 David Bradshaw, "New Perspectives on Auden: Rolf Gardiner, Germany and *The Orators*", *W. H. Auden Newsletter* 20 (2000), https://audensociety.org/20newsletter.html#P54_40194; Rolf Gardiner, "Diary", Microfilm, RGP, MS95633.
92 Thomas Morris to Ruth Pennyman, 27 June 1933, Teesside Archives, UPEN (4) B6 E13.
93 Roger Griffin, "This Fortresss Built Against Infection", in Julie Gottlieb and Thomas Linehan (eds), *The Culture of Fascism: Visions of the Far Right in Britain* (London: I. B. Tauris, 2004), 45–65, quote 46.

the florid thanks offered to Ruth Pennyman by a trustee of the Cleveland land scheme, on her stage-management of *The Winter's Tale* in June 1933, testify to the way Shakespeare productions functioned as a "creative irrelevance", to screen meetings at the Hall, during the "dishonest decade" of Appeasement.[94] One such flying visit was paid to Ormesby that spring by Nazi-leaning Prince George, Duke of Kent. Shakespeare's romance of princes and peasants was accordingly turned back-to-front, opening in praise of "great creating nature" (4.4.88)[95] at its shepherds' feast, to foreground Gardiner's corporatist vision of a community where "farmers and squires, the miners and schoolmasters, the fisher-folk" and "university men from Leeds and Hull" were united in "singing and dancing", and "a man was recognised for his function and his character rather than for his title and his dress".[96]

The Winter's Tale had come to be valued as a version of the pastoralism piped by Conservative Prime Minister Stanley Baldwin, that "We country people have, by the mere fact of our birth and sojourn in the heart of England, learned something which stands us in good stead in the strange politics in which we are immersed".[97] But in a revolutionary essay of 1929 that was more relevant to Heartbreak Hill and Cleveland's Unemployed Miners Association in the year of the Crash than Baldwin's "Merrie England", the Shakespearean G. Wilson Knight launched his career arguing that the play had instead to be interpreted as a myth of sacrifice, in which we "progress from spiritual pain and despairing thought through stoic acceptance", and thence to the "serene and mystic joy" which "is a universal rhythm of the spirit of man [...]. Tragedy is never the last word".[98] And such was the exaltation that prevailed in "imperishable Ormesby".[99]

---

94 "dishonest decade": Wystan Hugh Auden, "September 1 1939", l. 5, *The English Auden: Poems, Essays and Dramatic Writings*, ed. by Edward Mendelson (London: Faber & Faber, 1977), 245.
95 All Shakespeare quotations are from *The Norton Shakespeare*, ed. by Stephen Greenblatt, Walter Cohen, Jean Howard and Katharine Eisaman Maus (New York: Norton, 2007).
96 "the farmers ... university men": Rolf Gardiner, "Work Culture amongst the Unemployed", in *North Sea and Baltic: An Autobiographical Record of the Younger Generation, 1926–1932* (unpublished), repr. in Gardiner (1972), 60–63, quote 62; "a man was recognised": Gardiner, *England Herself* (1943), 34.
97 Stanley Baldwin, speech to the Worcestershire Conservative Association, February 1929, qtd. in Peter Parker, *Housman Country: Into the Heart of England* (London: Little, Brown, 2016), 409.
98 G. Wilson Knight, "Myth and Miracle (1929)", in *The Crown of Life: Essays in Interpretation of Shakespeare's Final Plays* (London: Methuen, 1965), 29–30.
99 Rolf Gardiner to James Pennyman, 18 January 1931, RGP, J317.

With Knight's uplifting rhythm as a guide, *The Winter's Tale* became the first of a trio of Shakespeare productions at the Hall, each fiercely cropped to reassure the mining community that in Yorkshire tragedy would never have the last word. It would be followed by a *Romeo and Juliet* in 1934, lightened up with Tudor ballads, and starring Eliot's long-term theatrical collaborator, E. Martin Browne; and, to celebrate the Silver Jubilee of King George V in 1935, a pageant of the Agincourt scenes of *Henry V*, which was planned to show off the talents of Gardiner himself, as "Harry the King" (4.3.53). "We are going to have fun this year with *Henry V* Act IV as a Jubilee performance", Pennyman psyched his leading man, "with the audience entangled in the action – a torch light procession, a hymn, and the inhabitants of Ormesby – coming up the long stone walk way into the garden and onto the croquet lawn".

Like Lawrence and Hofmannsthal, the Pennymans were confident Gardiner had all the qualities of "He that plays the king" (*Ham*, 2.2.308), and "warlike Harry like himself" (*H5*, Prologue, 5), because "For this we want freshness, conviction and an appreciation of the beauty of the words, rather than dramatic experience or ability". Crucially, the squire of Springhead regularly "galloped" across his "ancient banks" and "Celtic Fields". For the major was determined that the victory cavalcade, when the "audience and English soldiers just returned from Agincourt mingle", would inspire the "groups of the unemployed", who would take part in larger numbers than ever before: "the sword dancers, the male voice choir" from the local British Legion, and the massed boys' clubs of Middlesbrough and Darlington.[100]

Crowned with the irresistible Anglo-German anthem of deliverance, "Now Thank We All Our God", the finale of the Ormesby *Henry V* owed everything to the techniques developed at the *Musikheim*. And Gardiner and Götsch would indeed revive "The Agincourt Song" at the close of the four-hour "Masque of the Seasons" they devised as the culmination of the Kassel Festival of Social Arts on 9 October 1938, when the choir of the Springhead Ring hymned the "dispensation of Providence" that was Chamberlain's timely Munich Agreement of the previous week, and Anglo-German kinship was solemnized with the gift to the *Musikheim* of a bowl of Dorset soil, donated with Kipling's Shakespearean "Charm":

---

100 James Pennyman to Rolf Gardiner, undated, 1935, RGP, J317; "galloped ... fields": Rolf Gardiner, "Harvest Rides in Wessex", *Wessex: Letters from Springhead* 2 (1942), repr. in Gardiner (1972), 159–166, quote 163.

> Take of English earth as much
> As either hand may rightly clutch.
> In the taking of it breathe
> Prayer for all who lie beneath.[101]

"English Earth with English humus goes abroad to a place of affinity, the ultimate cross-cultural fertilizer", is how David Matless describes this scene in *Landscape and Englishness*.[102] So, there was more than a touch of the lethal amateurism of Kazuo Ishiguro's fascist-following Lord Darlington in the novel *The Remains of the Day*, who was "the sort of gentleman who cared to occupy himself only with what was at the true centre of things", when the owner of Ormesby Hall careered the length of his grounds on his bold charger, playing the Duke of Exeter in *Henry V*, to read his audience the joyous "number of the slaughtered French" (4.8.68).[103] "We want no professionals", he had emphasized. Hence, if Gardiner could not take the role of Harry, "do you think it would be possible to get some young man from the English Mistery?"[104]

Jim Pennyman was restating his preference in light of his displeasure in previous years, when the composer Michael Tippett had been picked for the program by the Left-leaning Ruth, and involved the miners in communistic productions of *The Beggar's Opera* and his Brechtian *Singspiel Robin Hood*, before he ran off with the "Mercurial" Wilf Franks, Ormesby's "talented Autolycus" and Gardiner's personal trainer.[105] By contrast, if cast in the role of "noble Harry" (4.1.34), a sterling "young man from the English Mistery" could be counted on to toe the line of this "aristocratic-minded" circle of Nazi fellow travellers, which had been founded in 1930 by Gardiner's neighbour, the conservationist Gerald Wallop, Lord Lymington, "the most openly pro-German of the back-to-earthers".[106]

The English Mistery, and its medievalist successor the English Array, "mustered" beneath the flag of St. George and vowed "to restore the King to his rightful position"; but its "mystical obsession" was "the locally-baked loaf" and "un-

---

101 Rudyard Kipling, "A Charm", in *Rudyard Kipling: Selected Poems* (London: Penguin, 2000), 129; Rolf Gardiner, "The Kassel Festival", *The Springhead Ring News Sheet* 23 (5 November 1938), repr. in Gardiner (1972), 131–136, at 133–135.
102 David Matless, *Landscape and Englishness* (London: Reaktion, 1998), 173.
103 Kazuo Ishiguro, *The Remains of the Day* (London: Faber & Faber, 2005), 146.
104 James Pennyman to Rolf Gardiner, undated, 1935, RGP, J317. The part of Henry was taken by B. J. Rushby Smith, later a play-producing Headmaster of Southwell Minster Grammar School.
105 Soden (1943), 114, 139–144.
106 Griffiths (2016), 141.

pasteurized milk", its slogan "Save Our Soil".[107] For this Far Right league, "belief in healthy soil" went with dread of "erosion, desertification [...] decadence"; so Gardiner had been gripping its pledge-men with papers detailing how "urbanised society" was becoming "detached from the earth [...]. It is denying the Natural Order".[108] That this "Marshal of the Mistery" declined to lead the Shakespearean cavalry across Ormesby's greensward was therefore due to these pressing concerns, for he had just made his most influential connection, and was researching the policies of Walther Darré, as guest of the Reich Agriculture Minister and chief of the SS Race and Settlement Office at an even grander "giant spectacle", where he would watch the Führer presented with "a magnificent crown" of corn and flowers before a million peasant farmers, as "twenty thousand singers sang", at the 1936 Reich Harvest Thanksgiving high on the Bückeberg near Hamelin.[109]

At Hamelin, the Pied Piper came home. For Gardiner's friendship with Darré, which they maintained for the rest of their days, gave him a grandstand view onto the theatrics of Nazi agriculture. He subsequently claimed this experience led to his disillusion with the Third Reich's "pseudo-biological materialism mixed with a cloudy nature-worship".[110] But it actually brought the organicism of his Shakespeare cult close to the discourse of Darré himself, "the man who first invented the term 'Blood and Soil'".[111] As Herbert Marcuse pointed out, "glorifying earth and blood as the central forces of history" exempted fascism from rationality.[112] But soil and Shakespeare were mucked together by Gardiner in the National Socialist cause. And it was while attending the Reich Farmers' Congress at Goslar, that Toepfer, his soulmate "from his 'Wandervogel' years", raised with Gardiner the crowning glory of a Shakespeare Prize, to be awarded on behalf of the Hanseatic University of Hamburg.[113]

---

107 "mystical obsession [...] loaf": Moore-Colyer (2001), 205; "unpasteurized [...] Soil": Martin Pugh, *"Hurrah for the Blackshirts!" Fascists and Fascism in Britain Between the Wars* (London: Jonathan Cape, 2005), 72, 206.
108 Gardiner, *England Herself* (1943), 127; Stone (2016), 163–164.
109 "magnificent crown": Wright (2002), 234–235; "Twenty thousand singers": Gesine Gerhard, *Nazi Hunger Politics: A History of Food in the Third Reich* (Lanham, MD: Rowman and Littlefield, 2015), 43.
110 Rolf Gardiner, "Hitler's Reich and the Real Germany", *Wessex Letters From Springhead*, 4:5 (1948), qtd. in Wright (2002), 458, n. 68.
111 Jefferies (2016), 62.
112 Herbert Marcuse, *Negations: Essays in Critical Theory*, trans. by Jeremy Shapiro (Harmondsworth: Penguin, 1968), 30.
113 Jefferies (2016), 62; Schlaeger (2013), 16.

Soil Association

Gardiner would advise on the annual Shakespeare Prize until his death in 1971, and won Toepfer's Goethe Prize for "humanitarianism" the year before. Throughout that time his proposals scarcely wavered from the "volley of names" he submitted in 1936: ruralist writers Adrian Bell and Edmund Blunden, Browne, Eliot, and the Hitlerite novelist Henry Williamson, who was then urging the British Union of Fascists to pump "sewage sludge" back "on our land, our England", so salmon would leap again, "in both the Rhine and its ancient tributary Thames".[114] All Gardiner's nominees would join "the Society of Earth" he envisioned "germinating in the ashes" at the time of the Blitz, which became the post-war Soil Association. Though Toepfer lived to be nearly a hundred, preserving to the end the dream of a Nordic union, he died shortly before the smell from this natural history became unmistakable, resulting in the abandonment of the prize in 2006, by which time, as its chronicler Jürgen Schlaeger records, "everything reminiscent of the language of the Third Reich" had been cleansed from the statutes, and "Blood and kinship and common Germanic ancestry were out".[115]

The legacy of the merchant of Hamburg was enshrined in his conservation project on Lüneburg Heath; and Ormesby was detoxified in 1946, when it housed Joan Littlewood's Theatre Workshop.[116] Yet for the Hall's sword dancers there would be no finer hour than in August 1938, when Gardiner booked them to perform outside the Shakespeare Memorial Theatre, during the EFDS Stratford Summer School. Gardiner was still lamenting in *North Sea and Baltic* that current youth could not appreciate how "the values manifested by the Morris were part of the spiritual fabric of Shakespeare's England, and that that England was being destroyed by neo-Phoenician values".[117] But as the "sunburned sicklemen" (*Tem*, 4.1.134) from Yorkshire configured their wheel of fire, they were keenly applauded by members of the Society, one of them "a true specimen of Hitler Youth", who had audited every mumming, dance and song. Asked whether he intended to return to Shakespeare's birthplace in the future, this Siegfried "replied 'Sicherlich – es ist viel nötig'" ("Certainly: there is much to do"): "Subsequently, we learned that both he and Elise [van der Ven-ten Bensel] were being groomed

---

114 Ibid., 34, 46; Henry Williamson, *The Phoenix Generation* (London: Macdonald, 1965), 145.
115 Rolf Gardiner, "The Kaleidoscope of War", *Springhead Ring News Sheet*, 38 (1941), repr. in Gardiner (1972), 154–155; Schlaeger (2013), 33.
116 Howard Goorney, *The Theatre Workshop Story* (London: Eyre Methuen, 1981), 54–58.
117 Rolf Gardiner, "Postscript 1938", *North Sea and Baltic*, New Series 4 (1938), repr. in Gardiner (1972), 57–59, quote 58.

as 'Gauleiter' [...] he at Stratford (after the invasion) and she at Hilversum and Arnhem after the Nazis handed over and returned to base [...]. Neither she nor the Storm-trooper came to the 1939 Stratford."[118]

Zusammenfassung

Der englische Naturschützer Rolf Gardiner ist einmal als "Morris tanzender Pfadfinder, der von den NS-Sturmtruppen überholt wurde", beschrieben worden. Tatsächlich war seine Theorie des Tanzes eng mit Hitlers Politik verbunden. Er glaubte, dass Shakespeare einen globalen Winter vorhergesagt hätte, dass aber Hamlets Vorhaben, die Zeit wieder "einzurenken", antizipierte, wie Blut und Boden über Tanz und Gesang miteinander verbunden werden könnten. 1933 schrieb dieser "Gauleiter von Wessex" an Goebbels und machte ihm das Angebot, die "germanische Welt" der Shakespeare'schen Schauspieltruppen wiederzuvereinigen; er brachte englische Schwerttänzer zu den Olympischen Spielen nach Berlin, die den Sonnenkult als nordisches Sonnenwendritual präsentieren sollten. Gardiner teilte seine 'organischen' Vorstellungen mit dem Reichsminister für Ernährung und Landwirtschaft Walther Darré. Sein Gartenfest in Ormesby Hall in Yorkshire war als Brückenkopf für das Projekt einer Nordischen Föderation gedacht, das auch den Hamburger Shakespeare Preis seines Freundes Alfred Toepfer inspirierte.

---

118 Letter from Douglas Kennedy to Ewart Russell, 7 November 1984, repr. in *The Morris Dancer* 3 (1999), 190–191, at 191. Boyes has identified Stratford's "Hitler Youth" as SS-*Untersturmführer* Hans Ernst Schneider, who had been "ordered by his SS superior", the Austrian folklorist Richard Wolfram, "to attend various congresses abroad" (Boyes [2016], 87–88, 91). Schneider operated as an official of the Folklore and Homeland Department of the National Socialist Culture Community, and his responsibilities included the supply of devices used in lethal medical experiments in the occupied Netherlands. He was editor of the SS journal *Weltliteratur*. As Hans Schwertes, and the author of *Faust und das Faustische* (Stuttgart: Ernst Klett Verlag, 1962), he became Professor of German Literature and Rector of Aachen University. His Nazi identity was publicly exposed in 1995. For Schneider's reporting activities, see Joachim Lerchenmüller, "Hans Ernst Schneiders / Hans Schwertes Niederlande-Arbeit in den 1930er bis 1950er Jahren", in Burkhard Dietz, Helmut Gabel and Ulrich Tiedau (eds), *Griff nach dem Westen: Die "Westforschung" der völkisch-nationalen Wissenschaft zum nordwesteuropäischen Raum, 1919–1960*. Vol. 2 (Münster: Waxmann, 2003), 1111–1140.

Macbeth Dances in the Zār Ritual: The Significance of Dancing in an Iranian Adaptation of *Macbeth*

MOHAMMADREZA HASSANZADEH JAVANIAN

Introduction

William Shakespeare was among the first European writers whose works were translated into Persian. In the late nineteenth century, a group of Iranian translators who had travelled to Europe and studied there began to translate Shakespeare's works for Iranian readers. The interest in Shakespeare's plays witnessed a surge during the Persian Constitutional Revolution (1905–1911). It is not clear which of his plays was first performed in Iran, but various reports indicate that *The Taming of the Shrew* and *Othello* were staged in the cities of Tehran and Tabriz in the 1910s and 1920s.[1]

For a period spanning over a century, Shakespeare's plays have continued to feature prominently on the Iranian stage. In the last two decades, nevertheless, theatrical performances in Iran based on Shakespeare's drama have significantly departed from both the content and the context of their hypotexts. Iranian theatre directors have developed numerous structural and thematic innovations in staging Shakespeare's plays and their adaptations. In most cases, Shakespeare's classic plays have been adjusted to Iran's domestic cultural and social contexts. *Diabolic, Romeo and Juliet* (2018), for instance, places the familiar tragic love story in modern Iranian society. The play was directed by Atila Pesyani, who also adapted several other Shakespearean plays including *The Death Garden* (2010) based on *Macbeth*, *Richard III* (2011), and *Blood Lineage* (2017) based on *King Lear*. Hamidreza Naeimi, Mostafa Kooshki, Mohsen Sadeghi Esfahani and Ali Afzal are other notable Iranian directors who have adapted more than one of Shakespeare's plays in recent years.

Most of these productions dramatize Shakespeare's stories in either realistic or surrealistic contemporary urban settings. It is only in the adaptations of Ebrahim

---

1 Ali Amini Najafi, "Shakespeare in Iran: From the First to the Last Translations", *BBC*, 27 April 2014, https://www.bbc.com/persian/arts/2014/04/140427_l51_shakespeare_book_translation, last access 10 March 2020.

Poshtkoohi that Iranian rituals and traditions find a way into Shakespeare's plays. Poshtkoohi, who leads The Titowak Theater Group in his hometown of Bandar Abbas in southern Iran, has frequently brought old rituals of the southern Hormozgan and Boushehr provinces to national and international stages. In particular, he has adapted two tragedies of Shakespeare: *Macbeth-Zār; or, Hey Macbeth, Only the First Dog Knows Why It Is Barking* (2009)[2] (henceforth *Macbeth-Zār*) and *Hey Othello, Only Pet Crabs Nest in Bed Sheets* (2020). *Macbeth-Zār* was received positively by both theatre audiences and critics, with one critic describing the play as "one of the most successful Iranian adaptations of *Macbeth* ever".[3] Over the past ten years, the play has been staged over 100 times in Iran and other countries including Germany, Russia, Armenia, France and Azerbaijan. It won the awards for best theatre ensemble and best performance at the Moscow Nights Theater Festival in 2012. *Macbeth-Zār* also had highly acclaimed performances at the Theaterfestival Spielart (Germany, 2017), the High Fest International Performing Arts Festival (Armenia, 2011) and the Avignon Festival (France, 2011). The play also won the award of the New Experience Section at the 28th Tehran International Theater Festival in 2009.

In *Macbeth-Zār*, Poshtkoohi has incorporated the Zār rite into the story of *Macbeth*. This paper will explore the crucial role of dancing in *Macbeth-Zār* and its significance in the social, cultural and political atmosphere of Iran. The first section will investigate the healing function of the Zār dance. Next, the article will discuss the recontextualization of *Macbeth* in Poshtkoohi's adaptation. The focus will then turn to the elaborate choreography of *Macbeth-Zār* and highlight the redemptive dance of the protagonist. The final part of the discussion will illustrate how the play challenges Iran's power structures as well as gender stereotypes.

Zār, the Dance of Healing

Zār is an ancient ritual that has survived in Northeast Africa, the Arabian Peninsula and southern Iran. People in these regions, especially those who live in coast-

---

2   The play is for seven actors. The 2009 production was financially supported by The Titowak Theater Group. Although there is no official database for the box office sales of plays in Iran, reports by most theatre websites and newspapers demonstrate that *Macbeth-Zār* was one of the top box office earners in 2009.

3   "Drama News", *Tose'e Irani Newspaper*, 28 August 2019, https://www.toseeirani.ir, last access 14 September 2020.

al areas, believe that evil spirits can enter the human body in the form of winds and possess them. The winds are categorized into different groups in terms of their strength, specifications, temperament and geographical domain. Cultural critic and ethnographer Gholam-Hossein Saedi has carried out a comprehensive research on these winds in southern Iran. Saedi identifies the Zār as "one of the seven types of major winds (the other six types are *Noban*, *Mashayex*, *Jinn*, *Pary* [Peri], *Div* [Demon], and *Ghoul*)".[4] Saedi maintains that "the Zār is the most dangerous of all these winds. Like any other wind, it carries a jinn into the body of its target."[5] The treatment process of the affected individual includes two stages: the individual is initially quarantined for seven days. During this isolation phase, the chief organizer of the ritual, the Babazār or Mamazār, tends to the individual and gradually purges the jinn from their body. When the jinn is extracted, it is time for the Zār itself to be expelled in a ceremony; this is the second stage. A typical Zār ceremony includes much regional music and dance. There is a lot of food and fruit for the participants, called *ahle hava* (approximately meaning 'marked by the wind'), that is, those who have survived the Zār. Every Zār speaks the language of the region from which it starts to blow. A Zār can communicate with the Babazār or Mamazār only when the affected individual drinks the blood of the animal – usually a goat – sacrificed specifically for the ceremony. When the Zār is able to speak, the Babazār or Mamazār urges it to reveal the whereabouts of its origin. The Babazār or Mamazār opens the ceremony by playing the drum and singing a song which is echoed by all participants. The Babazār or Mamazār and *ahle hava* make a circle around the affected individual, who gradually begins to dance. While this person is dancing, the Babazār or Mamazār tries to speak to the Zār and convince the wind to leave the body of its target. This ceremony continues until the Zār agrees to depart from the body. There are reports that the healing process can last for as long as a week.

Several anthropologists like Erika Bourguignon[6] as well as a number of cultural critics and phenomenological theorists[7] have explored the healing power of the dance in their studies. Iris J. Stewart observes that "the dance of healing belongs to the oldest form of combined medicine and psychotherapy in which focused exaltation and the release of tensions transformed physical and mental

---

4   Gholam-Hossein Saedi, *Ahle Hava* [*Marked by the Wind*] (Tehran: Social Studies and Research Institute Press, 1966), 36–37. Translations are mine.
5   Ibid., 39.
6   Erika Bourguignon, *Trance Dance* (New York: Dance Perspectives, 1986), 45.
7   For a remarkable example, see Steven M. Friedson, *Dancing Prophets: Musical Experience in Tumbuka Healing* (Chicago: University of Chicago Press, 1996).

suffering into a new option on life. Rhythm and dance have a vitalizing effect, as does chanting and music".[8]

The ritual dance, in particular, has been investigated in terms of its healing function. Boston Soko, for instance, has studied the Vimbuza dance in Northern Malawi. Soko's observations about a Vimbuza ceremony closely resemble what has been reported about a Zār gathering. He writes that during a typical Vimbuza dance "through the songs and the gestures, the possessed gives the portrait of the genie or the genies that possess him or her",[9] after these evil spirits found a way to enter the body by means of wind or lightning. Chris Low has explored healing dances of the Khoisan people. Low opines that ritual dances among the Khoisan are not only performed for healing purposes, but that they are viewed as binding together the people "who need one another to survive".[10] Such studies are not limited to the African continent. Beth-Sarah White has underlined the "potential for healing through ritual dancing"[11] in her study of women's dance and performance in Jamaica. Also, Laura Shannon has stated how the function of dancing has developed from healing individuals and communities to preserving "the earth and all living beings".[12]

The Zār ritual is performed in Northeastern African and the Middle Eastern countries. While each region differs from the others regarding the details of the rite, the general framework – including the origin of the Zār and the isolation period for the affected person – is similar. The healing dance is also an indispensable constituent of every Zār ceremony. Simon D. Messing has recorded his observations of the Zār dance in Ethiopia. He contends that "the patient is therefore surrounded by sympathetic kinfolk, entertained with dance, and promises are made to fulfill any desires [of the evil spirit]".[13] Samir Sarhan has conducted an insightful research about the Zār in Egypt, where "a large variety of rituals still

---

8   Iris J. Stewart, "Transcendental Healing Dance", in Johanna Leseho and Sandra McMaster (eds), *Dancing on the Earth: Women's Stories of Healing through Dance* (Forres: Findhorn Press, 2011), 196–206, quote 196.
9   Boston Soko, *Vimbuza: The Healing Dance of Northern Malawi* (Zomba: Imabili Indigenous Knowledge Publications, 2014), 31.
10 Chris Low, "Khoisan Wind: Hunting and Healing", *The Journal of the Royal Anthropological Institute* 13 (2007), 71–90, quote 87.
11 Beth-Sarah White, "Latter-Day Emancipation! Woman, Dance and Healing in Jamaican Dancehall Culture", *Agenda: Empowering Women for Gender Equity* 58 (2003), 77–83, quote 80.
12 Laura Shannon, "Women's Ritual Dances: An Ancient Source of Healing in Our Times", in Leseho and McMaster (2011), 138–158, quote 157.
13 Simon D. Messing, "Group Therapy and Social Status in the Zār Cult of Ethiopia", *American Anthropologist*, New Series 60:6 (1958), 1120–1126, quote 1123.

form part of the daily existence of the population".[14] Sarhan maintains that "Zār is the name given by the popular classes in Egypt to a ritualistic performance that includes violent dancing and incantations".[15] He writes that this ancient tradition has inspired the Zār Beat: "one of the rare productions in contemporary Egyptian theatre that tries to tread completely new ground both in form and content".[16] The dancing performance of the Zār Beat, Sarhan notes, is presided over by a woman exorcist, or the Kodia, and the action is "centered around the conflict between the Kodia and a doctor, the representative of the rational scientific approach to reality".[17] In other words, the Zār dance downplays the ability of modern medicine to find a cure for patients. In a more recent study of the Zār in Egypt, Richard Johan Natvig has analyzed an old Zār song about a female character called Umm al-Ghulam ('mother of the boy'). Natvig argues that in the context of this song and its accompanying dance, it is Umm al-Ghulam's "powers as a saint and mediator that are sought".[18]

Hanadi Ismail's study of the Zār healing practices in Oman shows various similarities with the way they are carried out in the south of Iran.[19] The *Encyclopedia Iranica* refers to the Zār dance as a trance or healing dance: "In some parts of Persia, musical exorcisms are performed to relieve those thought to be afflicted with evil spirits. They include music and guidance of the afflicted into a trance, in which state he or she dances and eventually throws off the evil spirit. The form of the dance has little significance; each dancer moves as compelled by the music."[20] This description, though important, is partly flawed because in the Zār ritual, the form of the dance *does* have significance. What it fails to take into account is that every Zār dancer incorporates various elements of Persian, Arabic and African dances into their performance.[21] Thus, every individual dancer

---

14 Samir Sarhan, "The Zār Beat", *The Drama Review: TDR* 25:4 (1981), 19–24, quote 19.
15 Ibid., 20.
16 Ibid., 19.
17 Ibid., 20.
18 Richard Johan Natvig, "Umm al-Ghulam: Zār Spirit or Half-Forgotten Saint? Making Sense of an Egyptian Zār Song", *Folklore* 124:3 (2013), 289–306, quote 301.
19 Hanadi Ismail, "Communities of Healing Practice on al-Baṭinah Coast of Oman", *Proceedings of the Seminar for Arabian Studies* 43 (2013), 145–151.
20 A. Shapur Shahbazi and Robyn C. Friend, "Dance", *Encyclopedia Iranica*, 15 December 1993, http://www.iranicaonline.org/articles/dance-raqs, last access 20 March 2020.
21 Behnaz A. Mirzai (2002), for instance, has pointed to the establishment of Afro-Iranian communities in southern Iran during the nineteenth century and the ensuing influence of African dances on the Zār dance in Iran. See Behnaz A. Mirzai, "African Presence in Iran:

can mix these elements in their own specific way, hence different forms of the Zār dance exist even within a single community or region.

Macbeth-Zār: Macbeth Lives in Southern Iran

Researchers, ethnographers and even documentary filmmakers have recently investigated various aspects of the Zār ritual in Iran. The ritual has also found its way into a number of theatrical works in Iran.[22] However, the Zār has largely remained unexplored in terms of its potential for inspiring innovative adaptations from either contemporary or early modern non-Iranian dramatic literature. *Macbeth-Zār* thus was a pioneering work in Iran's theatre because it was the first attempt by any director in the country to build a bridge between an Iranian ritual and English Renaissance drama.

In Poshtkoohi's *Macbeth-Zār*, the setting of the story is transposed from the Scottish Highlands to a coastal area on Iran's Hormoz Island in the province of Hormozgan. The choice of the setting is noteworthy because Hormoz is a geopolitically significant region in Southern Iran but its residents have to cope with extreme poverty. Macbeth is a great warrior who lives on Hormoz Island. Other characters including Ross, Macduff, Banquo and Malcolm are sea captains. The witches, who introduce themselves as Zār winds, prophesy that Macbeth will be the next Babazār. As in Shakespeare's play, Macbeth murders Duncan with the assistance of his wife, Lady Macbeth. After the murder, Macbeth hears the dogs barking, which is inaudible to other characters. This originates from a common belief in southern Iran that when dogs detect evil spirits, they begin to bark. The use of "Only the First Dog" in the title is significant in the broader socio-political context of the play as it implies that the person who first detects an evil deed is usually forced to remain silent.

Identity and Its Reconstruction", in O. Pétré-Grenouilleau (ed.), *Traites et esclavages: vieux problèmes, nouvelles perspectives?* (Paris: Société Française d'Histoire d'Outre-mer, 2002), 229–246.

22 Mohammadali Khabari and Mohammadreza Pourjafar (2006) have studied what they call the "reflection" of the Zār ritual in four plays: *Flower and Jahleh* [*jahleh* designates a piece of Iranian pottery] (1993), *Mirror in the Ceiling* (1993), *Firouzeh, Who Sings* (1998) and *Moonlit Women, Sunny Man* (2000). All four plays were directed by Kourosh Zarei. Although they put the Zār ritual onstage in one way or another, the dancing part of the rite was eliminated. See Mohammadali Khabari and Mohammadreza Pourjafar, "Reflection of Zār Ritual in Four Plays", *Sahne* 51 (2006), 10–15.

In another prophecy, Macbeth is assured that his position will be safe until the roots of the trees in the Mangrove forests, or Hara forests, rise out of the water. Macbeth feels secure because he assumes such a phenomenon to be impossible. However, due to their peculiar nature, these trees, which grow in Hormozgan, are submerged at high tide, but their roots reappear at low tide. The substitution of the King of Scotland with the Babazār and the movement of Great Birnam Wood toward Dunsinane Hill with the roots of the trees in Hara forests, as well as other readjustments, have contributed to the recontextualization of Shakespeare's tragedy and increased the appeal of the adaptation for both domestic and international audiences.

In addition to such changes, the Zār ritual plays an important role in key scenes of Poshtkoohi's adaptation. The banquet scene in *Macbeth* where King Macbeth talks to Banquo's ghost has been transformed into a scene in which the *ahle hava* elderly – equal to the thanes of Scotland – pay Macbeth a visit. Like in Shakespeare's play, the Iranian Macbeth begins to act weirdly when Banquo's ghost enters and sits in his place. Unlike in the hypotext, however, where the banquet guests attribute Macbeth's unusual behaviour to a possible physical illness, the *ahle hava* in *Macbeth-Zār* assume that Macbeth has been stricken by the Zār wind.

In Act 2, scene 2 of Shakespeare's play, Macbeth's bloody hands represent his guilty conscience after the murder of Duncan:

> Macbeth: Whence is that knocking?
> How is't with me when every noise appals me?
> What hands are here? Ha! They pluck out mine eyes.
> Will all great Neptune's ocean wash this blood
> Clean from my hand? No, this my hand will rather
> The multitudinous seas incarnadine,
> Making the green one red.
>
> (2.2.57–63)[23]

Eugene R. Huber is among the critics who have pointed to the significance of the blood imagery in *Macbeth*. Huber notes that "throughout the play, Shakespeare uses the words 'blood,' 'bleed,' or 'bloody' a total of forty-eight different times,

---

23 William Shakespeare, *Macbeth*, ed. by A. R. Braunmuller. The New Cambridge Shakespeare (Los Angeles: Cambridge University Press, 1997). All quotes from the play are to this edition.

with the heaviest and most frequent occurrence in Act II".[24] In *Macbeth-Zār*, Poshtkoohi has retained much of Shakespeare's imagery because, as mentioned above, the blood of the sacrificed animal is an essential component of every Zār ceremony. He has even added to Shakespeare's blood imagery by using a large piece of red cloth for different purposes in most scenes of his play. In the words of one of the characters, the cloth was white before Macbeth, as the island's Babazār, used it for the Zār ceremonies. (In most ceremonies, the inflicted person is covered by a piece of white cloth. During the ritual dance, the Babazār splashes blood on the cloth.) The red cloth thus serves as what T. S. Eliot described as an "objective correlative"[25] for Macbeth's thirst for power, which sparks the bloody chain of events in the play.

The Intricate Choreography of *Macbeth-Zār*

As discussed above, dancing plays a central role in Poshtkoohi's adaptation of *Macbeth*. The dominating dance pattern of the play closely resembles the Zār dance practiced in Southern Iran. This special type of Zār dance consists of two interrelated dances: the rhythmic and slow group dance performed by the Babazār or Mamazār and the *ahle hava* present at the healing session, and the ecstatic and fast dance movements performed by the patient. As the healing process evolves, the latter dance form constantly changes but the former remains unchanged during the entire session.

In addition to the Zār dance, which is performed several times throughout the play, the Iranian director has made extensive use of three other types of Asian dances: Kathakali, Kabuki and Butoh. Kathakali is a seventeenth-century Hindu dance-drama performed mainly in the southwestern part of India. While this highly stylized art form is still under the influence of Hindu religious discourse, its extensive repertoire includes court performances designed for the Indian high-caste and more recent productions that seek to "to articulate a distinct regional and post-colonial identity".[26] Poshtkoohi's experimentation with

---

24 Eugene R. Huber, "A Note on Blood, Ambition, and Guilt in *Macbeth*", *Bulletin of the New York Shakespeare Society* 2:4 (1983), 20–21, quote 20.
25 T. S. Eliot. "Hamlet and His Problems", in *The Sacred Wood: Essays on Poetry and Criticism* (New York: Alfred A. Knopf, 1921), 87–95, quote 93.
26 Jenny Nilsson, "'The Sense of a Lady': An Exploration of Transvestite Roles in Kathakali and Their Relation to Keralan Gender Constructions", *The Cambridge Journal of Anthropology* 24:3 (2004), 1–40, quote 2.

this ritual dance in an adaptation of Shakespeare is not unprecedented. In July 1999, *Kathakali King Lear* was performed in Shakespeare's Globe Theatre in London. Kathakali scholar, Diane Daugherty, has described the play as a successful adaptation, "both in terms of theatrical impact and proper intercultural practice".[27]

Butoh and Kabuki have both engaged with the plays of Shakespeare. Butoh, which developed in Japan in the late 1950s, is an avantgarde dance form which includes full-body makeup, a bizarre environment and improvised but controlled movements. The number of adaptations from Shakespeare's plays which were inspired by Butoh has surged in recent years. *Lady Macbeth* (2017), performed at the United Solo Theatre Festival in New York, *Old Lear* (2019), *A Tale of Star-Crossed Lovers* (2018; based on *Romeo and Juliet*) and *Laments of the Dead* (2016; based on *Richard III*) were all staged at the KL Butoh Fest in Malaysia and are notable examples blending Shakespearean stories with elaborate choreography.

Several Kabuki scholars including Leonard C. Pronko[28] have detailed points of similarity between Elizabethan drama and Kabuki, arguing that Shakespeare's plays and the classic Japanese dance theatre seem to be natural partners due to their baroque spirit and universal subject matters. Brandon notes that Kabuki producers "looked to Shakespeare for new play material"[29] in the early years of the twentieth century because their arch-rival, the Shinpa theatre, had successfully added over forty Shakespeare plots to its repertoires between 1901 and 1915.

Despite the apparent differences between Kathakali, Butoh and Kabuki, the unique combination of these Asian dances within the context of the Zār ritual has created highly innovative cross-cultural moments in the performance of *Macbeth-Zār*. For instance, in one of the Kathakali dance scenes of the play, Macbeth and a character with an unknown identity don the traditional *burqe*[30] instead of the face masks worn by Kathakali dancers. The choreography of the scene includes the fast and ecstatic dance of Macbeth and the Kathakali dance of

---

27 Diane Daugherty, "The Pendulum of Intercultural Performance: 'Kathakali King Lear' at Shakespeare's Globe", *Asian Theatre Journal* 22:1 (2005), 52–72, quote 53.
28 Leonard C. Pronko, "Kabuki and the Elizabethan Theatre", *Educational Theatre Journal* 19:1 (1967), 9–16.
29 James R. Brandon, "Kabuki and Shakespeare: Balancing Yin and Yang", *TDR* 43:2 (1999), 15–53, quote 29.
30 *Burqe* is part of the traditional costume in the southern provinces of Iran. It was traditionally worn by women to protect their faces from the blazing sunshine. However, the use of *burqe* has evolved over time. It is now mostly known as part of the hijab of women in southern Iran.

the other character marked by martial art leaps. The combination of such seemingly unrelated dances, rituals and costumes has yielded a cross-cultural adaptation of *Macbeth*. In an interview in 2017, Poshtkoohi pointed to the hybridity of his adaptation, stating that "I think the success of this play is the result of the incorporation of Eastern culture as well as dances such as Zār, Kathakali, and Kabuki in a Western play."[31]

The regional music is tightly interwoven with the choreography of the play. Poshtkoohi had a music band from Southern Iran play *bandari* [from *bandar*, the Persian word for port] music live for every production of the play. Throughout the play's narrative line, the music inspires dancing, changes its pace and even puts an abrupt and unexpected end to it. The music band of *Macbeth-Zār* also plays Indian and African music which is reminiscent of Zār rituals in those regions. The combination of *bandari*, African and Indian music is yet another hybrid aspect of Poshtkoohi's adaptation.

Macbeth and the Dance of Redemption

Like most rituals, the Zār rite involves a dance performance that is aimed at healing the individual who has been inflicted by the dangerous Zār wind. This ancient dance is believed to be an effective treatment for both physical illnesses[32] and mental disorders.[33] In *Macbeth-Zār*, Poshtkoohi has turned the healing aspect of the Zār dance into an integral part of the story.

As Babazār, Macbeth is expected to perform healing dances for two patients affected by evil spirits: Hormoz Island (sickened by the corrupt Babazār Macbeth) and himself (sickened by the witches, who are actually the Zār winds). As a result, Macbeth is the main dancer of the play. He dances to heal and at the same time to be healed. Like Scotland in Shakespeare's *Macbeth*, Hormoz Island is plunged into chaos and disease after the murder of Duncan. This point of affinity is even reflected in the language of the play. The language in *Macbeth-Zār* is mainly based on a modern-day Persian translation of *Macbeth* mixed with the dialect of southern Iran. However, Poshtkoohi draws attention to the illness of Hormoz

---

31 "Interview with Ebrahim Poshtkoohi: Bandar Abbas Will Host *Macbeth-Zār*", *IranTheatre*, 8 July 2017, https://theater.ir/fa/95999, last access 2 September 2020.
32 Howaida El Guindy and Claire Schmais, "The Zār: An Ancient Dance of Healing", *American Journal of Dance Therapy* 16 (1994), 107–120.
33 Edith H. Grotberg, "Mental Health Aspects of Zār for Women in Sudan", *Women & Therapy* 10:3 (1990), 15–24.

Island and the plight of its people by translating the exact words that Ross uses in the source text to describe the misery of Scotland in the post-Duncan era:

> Ross: Alas, poor country!
> Almost afraid to know itself. It cannot
> Be called our mother, but our grave, where nothing,
> But who knows nothing, is once seen to smile;
> Where sighs and groans and shrieks that rend the air
> Are made, not marked; where violent sorrow seems
> A modern ecstasy. The dead man's knell
> Is there scarce asked for who, and good men's lives
> Expire before the flowers in their caps,
> Dying or ere they sicken.
>
> (4.3.166–175)

Despite the restoration of peace after the death of Macbeth in both plays, the ending of the adaptation significantly differs from the way Shakespeare ended his tragedy. The final battle of the source play, where Macduff beheads Macbeth, is eliminated from the Iranian version. Instead, Macbeth performs a dancing scene while he is covered by the red cloth. But when at the end, the cloth is removed, the protagonist slowly collapses and dies. The omission of all direct confrontations in Shakespeare's text and the simultaneous retention of its blood imagery suggest that the major conflict of the adaptation involves Macbeth's internal struggle to overcome those wicked spirits that wreaked havoc on him as well as on the other inhabitants of Hormoz Island.

With this in mind, it is of note that in Poshtkoohi's adaptation, Macbeth fails to prolong his rule as Babazār because he is eventually defeated by the corrupt spirits. This is highlighted in the Zār context of the play where the final healing dance of Macbeth as Babazār inevitably leads to his own death. It remains unclear who will succeed Macbeth as the next Babazār, but we are invited to believe that Macbeth's life was a necessary price for his redemption and for the redemption of Hormoz Island, the other patient sickened by evil spirits.

The Zār Dance and Power Structures

The interpretation of dances in theatrical works necessitates the study of the culture in which they are produced. In this regard, Alexandra Carter has suggested that dance needs to be interpreted not "as an isolated artistic phenomenon but as a mode of cultural production".[34] Ted Polhemus also stresses that "dance styles, instead of being arbitrary, constitute a 'natural' expression of the cultural system within which they are found."[35] Every dance performance, therefore, is a discursive act that engages with various social, historical, political, economic and cultural discourses. These discursive interactions influence the way a particular dancing scene in a play is produced and then received by its audiences. Given the highly political importance of the year of the play's staging (2009) in the recent history of Iran, *Macbeth-Zār* invited its spectators to view the play in a broader socio-political context of a country that had just experienced a contentious presidential election.

An inclusive analysis of dancing in *Macbeth-Zār* is also contingent upon our understanding of the Iranian socio-cultural context. Staging dance performances in the Iranian theatre in recent decades has remained a contentious issue. The subject is even more sensitive when female actors are given roles that require them to dance onstage. Ida Meftahi observed that due to contemporary debates on the moral propriety of dancing for the public, "the preview and permission process for the movement-based works, especially the full-length rhythmic movements productions, have been more challenging compared to regular plays".[36] Meftahi's use of the word 'regular' for plays without a dance performance indicates that those *with* at least one dance scene are designated as irregular. She also notes that female actors in Iran's theatre are not permitted to perform movements that "involve rotations of the wrist, hip, and/or chest, as these are thought to signify *raqs* [dance] for the public".[37] While some of the restrictions for performing dances in the theatre have been eased in the past few years and this growing tolerance has made the inclusion of dance scenes in *Macbeth-Zār* possible, dancing is mostly restricted to male actors in religious plays.

In *Macbeth-Zār* Poshtkoohi thus inevitably faced a social taboo as the dance segment of the Zār ritual could not be omitted. As a result, the director made a number of modifications to the traditional Zār ritual to secure a place for his play in the predominant socio-cultural context of Iran. Firstly, mixed-sex

---

34 Alexandra Carter, "Feminist Strategies for the Study of Dance", in Lizbeth Goodman and Jane de Gay (eds), *The Routledge Reader in Gender and Performance* (London: Routledge, 1998), 247–251, quote 249.
35 Ted Polhemus, "Dance, Gender and Culture", in Helen Thomas (ed.), *Dance, Gender and Culture* (Basingstoke: Macmillan, 1993), 3–16, quote 8.
36 Ida Meftahi, *Gender and Dance in Modern Iran: Biopolitics on Stage* (New York: Routledge, 2016), 162.
37 Ibid., 163.

dancing is almost absent from the play although, as Ismail underlined, the Zār ritual "is an outlet for the community whereby, unlike weddings for example, mixed-sex ecstatic dance and music are socially sanctioned and celebrated".[38] In *Macbeth-Zār*, the mixed-sex dance is omitted from the play, since none of the *ahle hava* are female. Secondly, the majority of dance scenes in the play are performed by Macbeth or other male characters while not a single dance performance has been designed for major female characters such as Lady Macbeth and Lady Macduff.

Nevertheless, female characters have their limited dance parts in this adaptation. Their most significant dance is perhaps the one performed by the witches – or the Zār winds – when they inform Macbeth that he is destined to be the next Babazār. In this scene, the two female characters (there are two witches in the play as opposed to three witches in Shakespeare's *Macbeth*) perform an elaborate traditional dance of southern Iran mixed with the Japanese Butoh dance. At a certain point of their dance, Macbeth joins them, which shows that he has fallen prey to their prophecy. The witches and Macbeth thus create a mixed-sex dance, which is a rare phenomenon not only in the Iranian theatrical adaptation of Shakespeare but in Iran's theatre in general.

Conclusion

The history of Shakespearean adaptations in Iran now counts over one hundred years. Some of these adaptations have closely stuck to the original plays while others have recontextualized the works for their specific purposes. *Macbeth-Zār*, directed by Ebrahim Poshtkoohi, certainly belongs to the latter category. Poshtkoohi has recreated Shakespeare's tragedy within the framework of the ancient Zār ritual in Iran; a rite in which a healing dance plays a central role. Accordingly, the role of dancing in this *Macbeth* adaptation is essential. Dance performances have replaced all battle scenes of the play, including the initial battle where Macbeth appears triumphant and the final one which marks his death. The director's focus on dancing is also apparent in the intricate choreography of the play in which the Zār dance patterns are mixed with Kathakali, Kabuki and Butoh.

While Poshtkoohi's adaptation contains a number of Zār ceremonies, the whole play seems to be a rite held for the healing of Hormoz Island plunged into

---

38   Ismail (2013), 150.

corruption under the rule of Macbeth as its Babazār. Therefore, the only healing dance that can lead the community back to prosperity is the one that leads to the corrupt Babazār's demise.

Macbeth-Zār can also be studied in terms of the social and cultural significance of dancing. This version of *Macbeth* suggests that not only the design and arrangement of movements but even the *inclusion* of dance performances within Iranian adaptations of Shakespeare is subject to the country's social hierarchies, macrocosmic power relations and socio-cultural formations. However, *Macbeth-Zār* shows that Iranian adaptations of Shakespeare can challenge these power structures and yield productions that resist being simply labelled as 'regular'.

Zusammenfassung

Mit *Macbeth-Zār; or, Hey Macbeth, Only the First Dog Knows Why It Is Barking* (2009) hat der iranische Regisseur Ebrahim Poshtkoohi eine Adaption von Shakespeares *Macbeth* geschaffen, in deren Zentrum ein Ritual aus dem Nahen Osten und Teilen Afrikas steht: das heilende Zār-Ritual, in dem der Tanz eine Schlüsselrolle spielt. Poshtkoohis Adaption enthält eine Reihe von kunstvollen Tanzszenen, bei denen der Zār-Tanz mit dem indischen Kathakali-Tanz und den japanischen Tanzkünsten Kabuki und Butoh kombiniert wird. In *Macbeth-Zār* tötet Macbeth Duncan, nachdem ihm die Hexen mitgeteilt haben, dass er dazu bestimmt sei, das Ritual als Babazār, als Leiter der Zeremonie, anzuführen. Der einzige heilende Tanz, der zur Wiederherstellung der Ordnung und des Friedens führen kann, ist allerdings jener, der zu Macbeths Tod führt. Somit wird in dieser Bearbeitung die große Schlacht am Ende der Shakespeare'schen Tragödie durch einen Tanz ersetzt. Der Beitrag erörtert, wie die Tänze in *Macbeth-Zār* iranische Machtgefüge und soziale Hierarchien infrage stellen.

Performing *Macbeth* in India's Endangered Sanskrit Theatre Art of *Kutiyattam*

THEA BUCKLEY

Why adapt Shakespeare in another time, land and culture, let alone for the world's oldest orally transmitted performance art form, India's Sanskrit *kutiyattam*?[1] One answer lies in local practitioners' perspectives, in an intercultural conversation inflected by shifting notions of hybridity, postcolonialism and decreasingly binary East-West and local-global relationships. In Asia, the colonizers' legacy "is self-explanatory: Shakespeare made into the official curricula".[2] Despite this, intercultural theatre "thrives, consciously accentuating differences between Shakespearean theatre and Asia's cultural and performance traditions".[3] Of India, Dennis Kennedy and Yong Li Lan point out that it "cannot be said to contain a unified approach to Shakespeare any more than it does to theatre".[4] Crucially, individual artistic perspectives are increasingly valued in intercultural Shakespeare Studies, within which Alexa Huang cogently notes a post-millennial "paradigm shift from seeking authenticity to foregrounding artistic subjectivity".[5] Correspondingly, this essay foregrounds Indian theatre artist Margi Madhu's first-hand perspective as adapter, director and performer of William Shakespeare's *Macbeth*.

Hereditary *kutiyattam* artist Madhu premiered his *Macbeth* in 2006 at Vijnanakalavedi, a classical arts school in his state of Kerala. The occasion was "the first time that a Koodiyattom [sic] version of a foreign play was being per-

---

1　In preparing this essay I am grateful for the support of a Leverhulme Trust Early Career Fellowship.
2　Bi-qi Beatrice Lei, "Shakespeare's Asian Journeys: An Introduction", in Bi-qi Beatrice Lei, Judy Celine Ick and Poonam Trivedi (eds), *Shakespeare's Asian Journeys: Critical Encounters, Cultural Geographies, and the Politics of Travel* (New York and London: Routledge, 2016), 1–15, quote 1.
3　Ibid.; *kutiyattam* is a performance form that mixes elements of dance and drama.
4　Dennis Kennedy and Yong Li Lan, "Introduction: Why Shakespeare?", in Dennis Kennedy and Yong Li Lan (eds), *Shakespeare in Asia: Contemporary Performance* (Cambridge: Cambridge University Press, 2010), 1–24, quote 6.
5　Alexa Huang, "The Visualization of Metaphor in Two Chinese Versions of *Macbeth*", in Alexa Huang and Charles S. Ross (eds), *Shakespeare in Hollywood, Asia, and Cyberspace* (West Lafayette: Purdue University Press, 2009), 98–108, quote 104.

formed".⁶ For his orally transmitted heritage art form, first-person perspectives are increasingly rare. Unique to Kerala, *kutiyattam* claims an antiquity of two millennia of oral transmission (written records date to c. 10 CE), which would make it the world's oldest surviving theatrical form. *Kutiyattam* performers are living resources for an art form so fragile that it has gained UNESCO protection as a "Masterpiece of the Oral and Intangible Heritage of Humanity".⁷ To better understand Madhu's self-expressed "cultural translation" of *Macbeth* into endangered, elite Sanskrit theatre, I interviewed the artist, and I include his observations on his work in this essay.

First, I give an overview of Madhu's hereditary *kutiyattam* temple art form of Kerala, situating his cultural translation of *Macbeth* in both intercultural performance theory and that of Bharata's *Natyasastra*, India's fundamental performance art treatise.⁸ Concurrently, I highlight Madhu's use of Shakespeare as a medium through which to attract new audiences and democratize his declining temple-theatre form. Next, I locate his portrayal of Macbeth in the tradition of *kutiyattam* anti-heroes from the Hindu *Ramayana* and *Mahabharata* epics. Here I outline Madhu's strategic negotiation of tensions between the strictures of *kutiyattam*, the *Natyasastra* and Shakespearean tragedy. In the third section, I examine Madhu's 2011 performance of *Macbeth* at the Indian-language "Hamara Shakespeare Festival", Chennai, India. To conclude, I analyse Madhu's cultural translation into the world's oldest theatre, looking at its implications for intercultural cross-fertilization and the evolving postmillennial identities of Keralan and global Shakespeares.

Kutiyattam: An Overview

In producing *Macbeth* for *kutiyattam*, Madhu exploits his art form's potential for depicting scenarios of imagination and the otherworldly. David Shulman depicts the theatre form as "staged in a dimension distinct from the ordinary plane of perception", where a performer can hold an audience's attention for

---

6   Radhakrishnan Kuttoor, "All the World's a Stage", *The Hindu*, 11 March 2006.
7   Leah K. Lowthorp, "Voices on the Ground: Kutiyattam, UNESCO, and the Heritage of Humanity", *Journal of Folklore Research* 52:2–3 (2015), 157–180, quote 157.
8   Arya Madhavan, *Kudiyattam Theatre and the Actor's Consciousness* (Amsterdam: Rodopi, 2010), 19; G. Venu, *Into the World of Kutiyattam with the Legendary Ammannur Madhavachakyar* (Irinjalakuda: Natanakairali, 2002), 179. For more, see Bharata, *Bharata: The Nātyaśāstra*, ed. and trans. by Kapila Vatsyayan (New Delhi: Sahitya Akademi, 1996).

hours on a bare stage.⁹ In Madhu's *Macbeth* and *kutiyattam*, the set is bare as that of original-practice Shakespeare, with only a hand-held curtain and a wooden stool. Costumes are opulent, augmented by richly coloured face paint coded to stock heroic or demonic character types. The performer stands downstage centre, facing the audience. Upstage, musicians play instruments including the oboe, cymbals, conch and drums, which alternately announce and accentuate the performer's movements. The metre-high copper *mizhavu* hand-drums, said to possess souls of their own, provide the heartbeat of the largely mimetic performance, which typically unfolds over the course of one or more nights.¹⁰ The stage is lit by the flames of a large foreground oil lamp that burns throughout, illuminating the action and representing the divine spectator.

Madhu defines his *Macbeth* as a "cultural translation".¹¹ He avers that this means his *Macbeth* is indistinguishable from a traditional *kutiyattam* performance: "the same costume, the same tradition, the same [dance] steps and stage". Instead, Madhu's version radically alters the Shakespearean original in its language, setting, staging, narrative trajectory and thematic focus. Yet his definition is apt. Madhu's production recalls Poonam Trivedi's proposed postcolonial "cannibalisation" of Shakespeare, where intercultural performance is a translation that subsumes Shakespeare's work utterly to then reconstitute it in a perverse homage.¹² Conversely, Madhu's production reconstitutes *Macbeth* in homage to *kutiyattam*. His *Macbeth* therefore rather resembles Sangeeta Mohanty's concept of "transculturation", which is "a transformation of the whole cultural setting and background but [with the] plot remaining the same as the original".¹³ It is an intercultural *Macbeth* but not in the sense of Patrice Pavis's definition of interculturalism: "a hybridization such that the original forms can no longer be distinguished".¹⁴ Instead, Yong's revision of Pavis's definition fits better: she pro-

---

9   David Shulman, *More than Real: A History of the Imagination in South India* (Cambridge, Mass.: Harvard University Press, 2012), 16.
10 K. Kunjunni Raja, *Kutiyattam: An Introduction* (Delhi: Sangeet Natak Akademi, 1964), 9.
11 Unless otherwise specified, I quote Madhu from our personal interview on 22 November 2013.
12 Poonam Trivedi, "'Filmic' Shakespeare", *Literature/Film Quarterly* 35:2 (2007), 148–158, quote 158. Trivedi paraphrases Oswald de Andrade and Leslie Bary, "Cannibalist Manifesto", *Latin American Literary Review* 19:38 (1991), 38–47.
13 Sangeeta Mohanty, "The Indian response to *Hamlet*: Shakespeare's reception in India and a study of *Hamlet* in Sanskrit poetics" (doctoral thesis, University of Basel, 2010), 65, *Edoc Universitätsbibliothek Basel*, https://edoc.unibas.ch/1168/1/finalversionJan2010.pdf, last access 30 May 2020.
14 Patrice Pavis, "Introduction: Towards a Theory of Interculturalism in Theatre?", in Patrice Pavis (ed.), *The Intercultural Performance Reader* (London: Routledge, 1996), 1–21, quote 8.

poses that in postmillennial productions of intercultural Shakespeare, rather than an erasure of two forms, what is "desired is the signature of Shakespeare in another authentic performance style".[15]

Madhu presents *Macbeth* in authentic *kutiyattam*, with episodic enactment of a story rather than a text and minimal verbal recitation and elaboration in mime and dance. As Suresh Awasthi and Richard Schechner observe, a "*kutiyattam* actor speaks 40 to 50 words and then his/her body "speaks" for 40 to 50 minutes, transforming the speech through gestures and movements into "a performance text of plastic, visual images".[16] In these, Madhu's hereditary art form, like India's other classical performance forms *kathakali*, *bharatanatyam* and *kuchipudi*, adheres largely to the strictures of India's comprehensive *Natyasastra* scripture.[17] This Sanskrit treatise prescribes classical performance practice and theory, including the appropriate *mudra* or sign-language 'gesture' to enact, the fitting *rasa* or 'emotional flavour' and *bhava* or 'mood' to display, the *tala* or 'tempo' to dance, and the suitable, colour-coded *vesha* or character-typed 'costume and makeup' to apply. It even outlines the dimensions of the *kuttampalam* or 'temple-adjacent performance hall'. Yet the *Natyasastra* remains only a text; it is in the interpretation of its rules, of the movements for its gestural language and of the expressions for the eyes to show each mood that *kutiyattam* performers must receive years of oral instruction.

Kutiyattam's oral corpus of Sanskrit plays, composed between the second and tenth centuries, is based on India's Hindu epics *Ramayana* and *Mahabharata*.[18] Abbreviated plays and rules of enactment have also been passed down in the palm leaf manuscript manuals *Attaprakaram* and *Kramadeepika*.[19] A play can be presented and elaborated over days, with only a segment spoken as the day's invocatory Sanskrit *shloka* or 'quatrain', such as Madhu's opening verse in *Macbeth*. Following this recitation, the actor enacts the first half of the plot as a flashback, through *nirvahanam* or 'plot elaboration', before enacting the rest of the narrative forward in real time.[20]

---

15   Yong Li Lan, "Ong Keng Sen's *Desdemona*, Ugliness, and the Intercultural Performative", *Theatre Journal* 56:2 (2004), 251–273, quote 261.
16   Suresh Awasthi and Richard Schechner, "'Theatre of Roots': Encounter with Tradition", *TDR* 33:4 (1989), 48–69, quotes 54, 52.
17   Mundoli Narayanan, "Over-Ritualization of Performance: Western Discourses on Kutiyattam", *TDR* 50:2 (2006), 136–153, at 146.
18   Lowthorp (2015), 160.
19   Ibid.
20   G. Venu, *Production of a Play in Kūṭiyāṭṭaṁ* (Irinjalakuda: Natanakairali, 1989), 100.

Figure 1. Margi Madhu performs *Macbeth* at Kalakshetra, 2011.

Madhu's *Macbeth* co-opts Shakespeare to invigorate and sustain his endangered tradition. Until recently, *kutiyattam* had been practiced exclusively by six high-caste families.[21] Performances had taken place purely inside temples before an elite audience of high-caste Brahmin *sahrydaya*s, or 'aficionados'. With India's Independence in 1947, Kerala witnessed the dissolution of kingdoms and feudal Hindu caste hierarchies and the election of a Communist government.[22] Suddenly, "the system which had sustained Kutiyattam as an elite, temple-based occupation for nearly one thousand years crumbled beneath the artists'

---

21 Rustom Bharucha, "Foreign Asia/Foreign Shakespeare: Dissenting Notes on New Asian Interculturality, Postcoloniality, and Recolonization", *Theatre Journal* 56:1 (2004), 1–28, at 11.
22 Now illegal yet still widespread, India's caste system fixed people by birth into a social hierarchy, in descending order: *brahmins* or 'priests and scholars', *kshatriyas* or 'warriors and rulers', *vaishyas* or 'farmers and traders', and *shudras* or 'labourers and servants'. Lowest were the casteless – tribespeople and *dalits* or 'broken' castes, treated as untouchable.

feet".²³ It was only when Kerala's new economic climate "threatened the very survival" of their art that the *chakyars* or 'masters' "relaxed their orthodoxy and consented to give performances outside temples".²⁴ Significantly, Madhu's *Macbeth* secularizes a Hindu traditional art; Madhu has never performed his cultural translation inside the usual temple theatre.

Madhu's performance of *Macbeth* at South India's premier classical arts academy, Kalakshetra, took place in the art school's open-air rehearsal space instead of its reconstructed traditional *kuttampalam*, hinting at a deliberate break with tradition. Architecturally the *kuttampalam* is auxiliary to the temple and represents a spiritual locus for performer and audience, underlaid with Hindu symbolism. One among a handful still in use, the *kuttampalam* at Thrissur's Vadakkunnatha Temple is a "22 m by 15 m rectangle", with a capacity of five hundred and "excellent" acoustics.²⁵ Replica *kuttampalam* theatres have been constructed at performing arts schools including Madhu's own Nepathya. By creating a cultural rupture with new work that is performed outside the temples, secularizing *kutiyattam* presents it with "both danger and opportunity".²⁶

Not only has Madhu's *Macbeth* been performed outside the temple, but his work has further "entailed innovation", with new "performance manuals".²⁷ Madhu has composed several *kutiyattam* manuals: *Macbeth, Doothaghatothkacham, Kanchukeeyam* and *Karnabharam*, the latter three based on *Mahabharata* characters.²⁸ Madhu explains how *kutiyattam* has incorporated innovations while retaining its core tradition, using the metaphor of an heirloom dagger, repaired and renewed over generations:

> One man, he [...] got a knife from his father. [...] But after some years, this blade is cut off [...]. So, he [...] change[s] it. [At] last, [after] six or seven generations, *every-*

---

23 Lowthorp (2015), 160.
24 Venu (1989), 6.
25 David Mason, "Architecture and Stage of Traditional Indian Theatre: India", in Siyuan Liu (ed.), *Routledge Handbook of Asian Theatre* (Abingdon: Routledge, 2016), 222–225, quote 223; K. G. Paulose, *Introduction to Kūṭiyāṭṭam: The Living Tradition of Ancient Theatre* (Kalady: Sree Sankaracharya University of Sanskrit, 1998), 36.
26 Bruce Sullivan, "Kerala's *Mahābhārata* on Stage: Texts and Performative Practices in Kūṭiyāṭṭam Drama", *The Journal of Hindu Studies* 3:1 (2010), 124–142, quote 136.
27 Ibid., 137.
28 Margi Madhu (trans.), "Text and Performance [of *Kanchukeeyam*]", in K. G. Paulose (ed.), *Improvisations in Ancient Theatre* (Thrippunithura: International Centre for Kutiyattam, 2003), 1–151, at 36; Nita Sathyendran, "'The kalari and the arangu are not the same'", *The Hindu*, 25 September 2009.

thing [on the knife] is changed. But they [the descendants] said, this is my father's-father's-father's-father's, it is more than 2,000 years [old]. [Such] is the tradition. We can't keep it, the same thing, from 2,000 years [ago]. It is changing. But it is the continuity.

In the twenty-first century, the "most important audience" for *kutiyattam* remains "the ordinary people irrespective of caste or creed".[29] Madhu avers that "*kutiyattam* was [a] ritual, at the same time, [it] is a culture also". If Yong proposes that intercultural performance is a mode in which culture is "basically sustained *by and as performance*", Madhu's cultural translation represents the evolution of *kutiyattam* from religious ritual to humanist theatre, sustained by and as the performance of Shakespeare.[30]

Performing *Macbeth* in Cultural Translation

Madhu's solo performance of 12 February 2011 was set in the front yard of South India's premier classical performing arts academy, Kalakshetra. The event took place underneath the boughs of a banyan tree and the night sky, a setting reminiscent of *Macbeth*'s: "Stars, hide your fires / Let not light see my black and deep desires" (1.4.50–51).[31] Although set in an elite locus of artistic tradition, the free public performance ensured that *kutiyattam* was no longer restricted to a high-caste audience. As Bi-qi Beatrice Lei, Judy Celine Ick and Poonam Trivedi argue suggestively, "Shakespeare can also liberate a society from fixed cultural identity".[32] Here, colonial Shakespeare was both reclaimed and requisitioned to act as the midwife for *kutiyattam*'s newest production.

Madhu's cultural translation rewrites Shakespeare's *Macbeth* along linguistic, geographic, cultural and artistic dimensions. Madhu declares that he translates *Macbeth* selectively, aiming "to not do the full text. I just [aim] to use the [narrative] thread". Madhu's authentic *kutiyattam* performance distils *Macbeth*'s trans-

---

29 G. Venu, *Kathakali, Kūṭiyāṭṭaṁ and Other Performing Arts: Fifty Years of Theatrical Exploration* (Irinjalakuda: Natanakairali, 2005), 118.
30 Yong Li Lan, "Shakespeare and the Fiction of the Intercultural", in Barbara Hodgdon and William B. Worthen (eds), *A Companion to Shakespeare and Performance* (Oxford: Blackwell, 2005), 527–549, quote 532.
31 William Shakespeare, *The Complete Works*, ed. by Stanley Wells et al. The Oxford Shakespeare, 2nd ed. (Oxford: Oxford University Press, 2005).
32 Lei, Ick and Trivedi (2016), 11.

lated text to an opening Sanskrit *shloka* and cuts the narrative heavily. His version retains only a few central characters, including Macbeth, Duncan, Macduff and Lady Macbeth; he compresses the witches into one, presumably the easier to enact during his solo performance, and he omits her dialogue aside from a single prophecy conflating 1.3 and 4.1. His production ends with Macbeth fainting upon realizing defeat as Birnam Wood approaches. Outwardly, Madhu's *Macbeth* is indistinguishable from *kutiyattam*, maintaining its performance elements intact: "If I [do] not say [so], nobody can tell this is a Shakespeare play." While preserving *Macbeth*'s Scottish names, Madhu nativizes geographical and cultural markers to suit the South Indian resetting.

In adapting Shakespearean tragedy for *kutiyattam*, Madhu further underscores a fundamental difference between his art form and Sanskrit drama. The *Natyasastra* states that "a drama's hero is not to be killed on the stage" – unless "he is brought back to life before the drama ends".[33] Any onstage tragic "incidents might be compared to the supposed death of Hermione in *The Winter's Tale*, of Imogen in *Cymbeline*, or of Hero in *Much Ado About Nothing*".[34] For in the *Natyasastra* "the tragic does not exist, and Sanskrit plays always have a happy ending".[35] However, *kutiyattam* convention permits onstage death scenes, especially of anti-heroes, the better to display the performer's artistry. In *kutiyattam*, anti-heroic villains such as the demon king Ravana wear codified facial makeup signifying that their nature is only semi-evil (see Figure 1). Significantly, Madhu chose Ravana's anti-heroic make-up for Macbeth, revising Shakespeare's tyrant into a more sympathetic character. The performer declares, "I think Macbeth is a human. [...] I am not sure Shakespeare is thinking like that, but in my mind, Macbeth is a very nice man". His view evokes Duncan's opening tribute "noble Macbeth" (1.2.67) rather than Macduff's closing depiction, "hell-hound" (5.10.3). Departing further from Shakespeare, Madhu's adaptation features Duncan's murder onstage, while cutting Macbeth's death. Madhu avers that he enacts the scene expressly to illustrate Macbeth's psychological conflict, arguing that Duncan's "death is not the important thing. [...] But, before the killing, [...] [Macbeth's inner] conflict, that is the important thing". Madhu thus both employs and subverts Shakespeare's narrative as a means to incorporate new material, invigorating his art form.

---

33 Sullivan (2010), 7–8.
34 Virginia Saunders, "Some Literary Aspects of the Absence of Tragedy in the Classical Sanskrit Drama", *Journal of the American Oriental Society* 41 (1921), 152–156, quote 155.
35 Eugenio Barba and Nicola Savarese, *A Dictionary of Theatre Anthropology: The Secret Art of the Performer*, 2nd ed. (London: Routledge, 2006), 106.

Ultimately, Madhu's *Macbeth* functions successfully as a medium of improvisation in performance, rather than its end. *Kutiyattam* playtexts are prized primarily for "their ability to stimulate the actor's imagination to create interesting improvisation on the text".[36] John Russell Brown suggests that Shakespearean drama appears static in contrast to the infinite realm of imagination of both actor and character create for the *kutiyattam* audience.[37] Shakespeare's *Macbeth* is an excellent text to facilitate this creation, with scenes of magic, dreaming, sleepwalking and hallucination, its "horrible imaginings" (1.3.137). Acting as the narrator, a *kutiyattam* actor may mime different characters while remaining in his/her own costume and in his/her own character. Likewise, Madhu narrates Macbeth's story through this method of *pakarnnattam* or 'multiple parts'. The action takes place entirely onstage; Madhu notes that characters are presented through Macbeth's viewpoint as narrator, rather than as independent entities, and that he externalizes Macbeth's internal monologue. This technique presents the audience with an unusual unifocal insight into the protagonist's perspective and motivations during Madhu's two-hour performance.

Kutiyattam Macbeth: The Performance

On the night of 12 February 2011, Madhu performed his *Macbeth* outdoors, under the overarching banyan tree with twisted roots that glowed red in the lamp flame, and on flat flagstones that resounded with the flat-struck beats of the artist's bare feet, evocative of Macbeth's line "Thy very stones prate of my whereabout" (2.1.58).[38] Despite its non-traditional setting and secular story, Madhu's two-hour solo *Macbeth* began much like any other typical *kutiyattam* performance. Breaking the reverent silence, one musician blew the conch ceremonially; simultaneously, another percussionist lit the wicks of a tall brass oil

---

36   Kevin J. Wetmore, Siyuan Liu and Erin B. Mee, *Modern Asian Theatre and Performance 1900–2000* (London: Bloomsbury, 2014), 197.
37   John Russell Brown, *New Sites for Shakespeare: Theatre, the Audience, and Asia* (London: Routledge, 1999), 84.
38   *Macbeth*, directed and performed by Margi Madhu, introduced by Indu G. (Prakriti Foundation, 2011) [VCD]. This and other descriptions of Madhu's performance relate to the Prakriti Foundation's archival recording of his 12 February 2011 dance as part of its annual Hamara Shakespeare Festival (a segment can be seen here: https://youtu.be/nygaToljxrw, last access 30 May 2020).

PERFORMING "MACBETH" IN KUTIYATTAM · 133

lamp that stood centre front. Although the performance took place outside the temple *kuttampalam*, these male accompanists were bare-chested according to the traditional respectful dress code for male worshippers. Seated upstage rear, the first drummer started the slow invocatory beat, the drum steady in its wooden holder, as two accompanists raised a bedspread-sized curtain and held it horizontally between them at eye level. Invisible behind the curtain continued the steady resonant beat of the holy *mizhavu* hand-drum. Its introductory rhythm typically raises the audience's anticipation in first announcing the start of the performance and then, rising in speed, strength and complexity, signalling the behind-the-scenes entrance of the main character, concealed by the curtain.

The curtain here was a typical *kutiyattam* prop, white with a red centre and gold trim. Above its top edge appeared the rim of a rounded red, white and gold headdress, bobbing in time as the rhythmic thrumming was joined by the even chime from a pair of finger cymbals played by Madhu's wife Indu G., herself an accomplished performer, seated stage right and maintaining the regular *thalam* or 'tempo'.[39] The second *mizhavu* drummer joined in, as did that of the small cylindrical *edakka* or 'side-drum' to his left, the tandem beat creating a trance-like effect. Here, it was also a beat that simultaneously, if perhaps unconsciously, evoked the play's original text: "A drum, a drum – / Macbeth doth come" (1.3.28–29). This build-up heightened the anticipation for the expectant audience of approximately fifty local and foreign visitors. Seated cross-legged on the ground, they had been briefed beforehand by Indu with an English plot summary and lecture-demonstration on *kutiyattam*. This audience further reflected a secular, democratic interculturalism that transcended the socio-religious stratifications formerly imposed by the *kuttampalam*.

As the drumming intensified, the curtain slowly lowered to reveal Madhu, a slim, energetic performer in his forties, already in character as Macbeth. Macbeth was seated centre stage on its sole furniture, a wooden stool that became his throne. Buoyed by the turbulent rhythm of a tri-drum-ensemble that heralded his appearance and presence with increasing intensity, the king surveyed the scene in a typical regal opening pose. His arms were firmly crossed, holding long neck-scarves with mirrors embedded in their ruffled ends, so that these reflected the light from the lamp flames at the audience; his eyes, with their pre-reddened whites, radiated pride and intrigue, narrowing and widening expressively. The

---

39 Female performers enact female *kutiyattam* roles; the *nangiar koothu* branch of *kutiyattam* is performed only by *nangiars* or 'hereditary female performers' channelling the goddess.

ruler created a terrific effect, fierce and bold, seated centre stage resplendent in the traditional *vesham* or 'make-up style' for the demon king Ravana. His bloodshot eyes contrasted with his face, painted in a thick, mask-like base make-up of bright parrot-green, with red lips, black eye designs, white paper cheek rills and white papier-mâché ball on the tip of his nose and forehead. This codified *vesham* marked him instantly for those in the know as a valorous yet evil character.[40]

The full moon of Macbeth's halo-like gilded wooden crown gleamed, as did the wooden jewellery of multiple necklaces, bracelets and belt that shone against his long-sleeved shirt of red, striped with black. His white cotton skirt was streaked with gold among its red and black stripes. It covered his bare calves and feet in front, while at the rear it was gathered up into a multi-layered ruff over white shorts that allowed greater movement. A dark blue headdress-apron covered the back of his head, glimpsed in the rare moments when he turned away from the audience; he held his rose-tinted palms occasionally towards the audience, showing a vulnerable, human side of the murderous protagonist amidst his demonic, royal outward lustre.

This combined effect of valour and evil was instantly evocative of Shakespeare's *Macbeth* and its supernatural prophecy, both eerie and fascinating. The protagonist's every gesture and expression were accompanied by appropriately soft or loud sharp taps or broad thrums on the drums. The *mizhavu* artists followed the artist's movements in minutiae, providing individual accompaniment in addition to the sustained backdrop beat.

The play began directly in the middle of the rising action of Shakespeare's narrative, at the start of 3.1. Madhu's Macbeth emerged as a king at the height of his glory and uncertainty, fearful of losing his tenuous grasp on the throne. From the outset, his semi-demonic make-up indicated that his baser nature would undermine his good fortune. In his sole speech during the performance, Macbeth recited the invocatory Sanskrit *shloka* in a sonorous, sing-song voice:

> *Nrupa padha adhirodhim dhuskaram naasthi kinchit*
> *Adhigatha bharanambho kashtamevam nrupanam*
> *Sahaja mahitha bhavam pasya Banquogatham than*
> *Prahaniranudhinam mam bheethi bhajamvidhathe.*

The verse corresponds to the following lines in the Shakespearean text:

---

40 Raja (1964), 24.

Macbeth: To be thus is nothing
But to be safely thus. Our fears in Banquo
Stick deep, and in his royalty of nature
Reigns that which would be feared.
(3.1.49–53)

An English translation of the Sanskrit lines was included in *Macbeth*'s programme leaflet:

Macbeth: There was not at all any difficulty for me to become the king.
To protect the throne and the kingdom thus gained is the most difficult task.
Why is that?
See the wise and mature posture that is natural to Banquo
The impact of that keeps me sacred [sic (scared)] all the time.[41]

Madhu clarifies that these lines could be interpreted to hold a contemporary political moral: "'I got the country very easily, but [it] is very difficult to maintain.' [...] In the contemporary society [it] is also happening. The politicians, they get the power [...] but [it] is not easy to maintain." With the opening Sanskrit verse, Madhu presented the translated Shakespearean text in a few sung lines that served as an introduction for the two-hour rendering of the plot in elaborate performance. His spoken portion completed, Madhu arose, pushed aside the stool and began to enact the story.

Macbeth's performance consisted of typical *kutiyattam* patterns: rhythmic swaying movements, hand and arm gestures, slow twirls and organized step combinations that remained within a small square area. For much of the performance, Madhu remained facing the audience with opened, bent knees in a typical narrative pose. More importantly for his cultural translation of Shakespeare, in deferring to established *kutiyattam* performance convention, Madhu recapitulated *Macbeth*'s narrative for the audience. He narrated the first half as flashback in mime, dance and expression, and enacted the second half forward in real time.

In beginning his *Macbeth*'s dramatic action at the midpoint of the Shakespearean narrative, Madhu foregrounds the protagonist's psychological conflict. Macbeth enters alone, an act that locates the audience in his first-person perspec-

---

41 *Macbeth* programme brochure (Chennai: Prakriti Foundation, 2011), 1; Madhu noted in our interview that this verse was composed for him by E. N. Narayanan.

tive, heightening its immediacy, unlike Shakespeare's third-person exposition. By telescoping the narrative to a single viewpoint, Madhu draws the audience deeper into the realm of Macbeth's psychology. Introducing Macbeth amid the throes of his post-murder guilt, Madhu heightens the accessibility of his portrayal as a symbol of universal human corruptibility: "How a man [can] *change* through these kind[s] of ambitions – power and money [...] maybe is a message also, to the world."

Here, after briefly proclaiming his guilty fears in verse, Macbeth mimed the events that had brought him to murder Duncan. While travelling home from *Macbeth*'s opening battle, Macbeth had met only one witch, who had prophesied he would become King of Scotland. Madhu clarified in interview that the "witches are female; but in my play, only one [...]; [she says] only one word: 'You['ll] become a king'". After the recapitulation, Macbeth enacted a compressed narrative, omitting scenes such as Lady Macbeth's sleepwalking and taking the action forward to an early close at the approach of Birnam Wood.

Madhu's cultural translation of *Macbeth* uses Shakespeare as a medium to showcase not only *kutiyattam* but also his own Keralan culture, including set performance pieces that highlight local customs. Indu explained that Macbeth recounted his victorious return from war with a typical *kutiyattam* interlude, enacting various celebratory musicians with their "Kerala percussion, like *chenda, maddalam, timila, edakka* ['drums'] and *shankh* ['conch']".[42] Here, Madhu's mimicry of each instrument was accompanied by the appropriate real-life percussion, showing off multiple performers' skills.

Madhu's *Macbeth* also incorporates an extended meal-serving scene, allowing him to showcase a typical *kutiyattam* performance sequence.[43] Here, his (imaginary) guest Duncan was seated on the floor while the host laid out the typical Keralan *sadya* or banquet. Madhu explains that Duncan's meal was served "Kerala style" and that "chewing the *paan*" ('tobacco') formed part of the dramatic action. This stimulant and digestive aid is offered to esteemed Indian guests after a meal, putting them in a mood evocative of Duncan's "unusual pleasure" (2.1.12). Thus, Madhu extends Shakespeare's dramatic action in places where it serves his own creative agenda.

---

42 In quoting Indu G., I refer to her 12 February 2011 pre-performance lecture.
43 Madhu explains that in *kutiyattam* a depiction of food often accompanies a philosophical point made by the traditional *koothu* or 'jester'. This role derives from the *vidusaka* or 'fool' in Sanskrit drama, similar to the Shakespearean fool who speaks in the vernacular, provides social commentary and mocks people; see Raja (1964), 27.

Madhu's cultural translation of the play's symbolism further echoes *Macbeth*'s guilt metaphors, here paralleled in Keralan omens, both Hindu and Christian.[44] His Macbeth signified Duncan's impending doom by miming the howling of a jackal, an inauspicious omen. As Indu recounted: "he thinks that this is a sign [...] telling him that this is the time to kill King Duncan". Here, the fatal howl also evoked a tolling bell, occurring at the interlude that precedes Shakespeare's lines: "Hear it not, Duncan; for it is a knell / That summons thee to heaven, or to hell" (2.1.63–64). After murdering Duncan, Indu explained, Macbeth feels that "from the drops of the blood, snakes are coming to him". Madhu elaborates: "a snake, attack[ing] him. So that is also Keralite [...] the sign of the *paapa* ['sin']". This metaphor echoes Macbeth's eventual prick of his guilty conscience: "O, full of scorpions is my mind, dear wife!" (3.2.37).

Moreover, to depict *Macbeth*'s dagger scene (2.1), as aforementioned, Madhu inverts Shakespeare's text by bringing onstage the offstage bedchamber murder. Madhu mixes other Keralan dance choreography with "*kutiyattam*-type stylised movements" to show the "hallucination that a sword is hanging in front of him, and he tries to catch hold of that sword and it disappears", as Indu put it. She described the action: "on seeing the face of the king, he is reluctant to kill the king. There happens a big struggle in his mind [...], and after two-three times, he takes courage and he kills the king". This dagger scene, too, is constructed to depict Macbeth's internal struggle, rather than highlight his murderous nature. In dramatizing Macbeth's vacillation and Duncan's murder with the dagger (here, a wooden prop sword), Madhu innovates and borrows a choreographed sequence from *kutiyattam*'s derivate performance form *kathakali*, used in the story *Rukmangada Charitham* (*The Tale of King Rukmangada*). Here, a king agonizes over God's secret test via his wife's order to kill his innocent relative. Madhu explains: "in *kathakali*, [that scene is] very famous [...]. [I use that] choreography [...], take that sword with the rhythm, steps".[45] The artist should "come [towards Duncan] and back, come, and back. He is just starting [to kill him]; then he sees his face, he is remembering, he love[s] him [...]. Then he is thinking, he can't". The

---

44 The 2011 census puts Kerala's population as 55% Hindu, 26% Muslim and 19% Christian. See "Population by religious community – 2011," *Census of India*, 2011, https://censusindia.gov.in/meta-data/metadata.htm#/tab3/subtab1, last access 26 May 2016.

45 In the legend, the virtuous king Rukmangada is urged by his wicked new second wife Mohini to kill his young son, on penalty of breaking his oath; see K. Bharatha Iyer, *Kathakali, the Sacred Dance-Drama of Malabar* (New Delhi: Dev Publishers and Distributors, 2011), 39, 94. While Mohini's incitement evokes that of Lady Macbeth, Mohini is actually a heavenly damsel sent by God to test the king's integrity.

resulting mimed murder was particularly chilling. After narrating this incident, Macbeth's recapitulation ended and the storyline returned to the present, resuming at the midpoint described in the opening *shloka*. This scene of Macbeth's guilt thus forms the keystone of the narrative arc of the protagonist's psychological journey, mirroring that of the Shakespearean character.

Madhu notes that while he does not alter Shakespeare's plot in cultural translation, "I avoid so many things" including the Macduffs' killing or Lady Macbeth's hand-washing scene. Madhu explains that in his view, Lady Macbeth's death represents a psychological turning point in the narrative, where Macbeth begins to taste fear again (5.5.9). He elaborates: "Lady Macbeth is the power of Macbeth. Then after Lady Macbeth [dies], he is very poor and very helpless", averring: "Man and woman; if they [are] together, they can do anything." Madhu's interpretation echoes the Indian classical categorization of *tandava/lasya*, or 'masculine and feminine dance styles' that balance these life forces that together complete a person or art form.[46] Here, on losing his other half, Macbeth loses his desire for life.

Madhu's innovation rewrites *Macbeth*'s ending to coincide with the terminus of the protagonist's inner journey. The artist states, "I am not killing Macbeth [...] that is not important in the play. [...] Because when he saw the Birnam Vanam [Wood], [...] he is already finished". As Indu elaborated, "And then he faints. There, the story ends." Consequently, in Macbeth's first-person narrative, his story ends with his loss of consciousness, culminating in his psychological rather than physical destruction.

Conclusions: Shakespeare as an Intercultural Bridge

In performing *Macbeth*, Madhu appropriates Shakespeare as a marker of international theatrical excellence to demonstrate and market his own creativity. Madhu's *Macbeth* reimagines Shakespeare's supernatural narrative as a *kutiyattam* morality play for contemporary audiences. His interpretation suggests that our inner demons possess the dangerous potential to destroy our natural humanity with the lure of wealth and power. Equally, Madhu performs Shakespeare to both highlight his own artistry and modernize his endangered heritage

---

46 The concept of *tandava/lasya* resembles *yin/yang* in its symbiosis of mirror-opposites; it recalls the Hindu construct of Shiva-Shakti, in which the male and female deities and life forces merge into one complete and ultimate being.

art form, updating its repertoire to facilitate its continued survival with wider audiences in a capitalist, secular, globalized twenty-first century. Madhu's Nepathya school "includes traditional performances but also innovative adaptations such as 'Macbeth' [...] and sends out all over the globe their monthly email announcements of scheduled performances".[47] The artist explains that "market forces are changing *kutiyattam*". Whereas Madhu is the first *kutiyattam* artist to adapt Shakespeare (previously, performers had only introduced new Sanskrit plays), Keralan *kathakali* artists have for decades adapted Shakespeare's tragedies. Yet *kutiyattam* is a particularly strictured art form, its former hierarchical rigidity contributing to both its longevity and fragility. To encourage flexibility, Madhu's own institution actively dismantles the formerly sacred hierarchy of the guru-disciple relationship. He states in a press article: "I started Nepathya [...] with the aim of creating a democratic work space where the traditions of training are intact but with a whole new outlook, which I feel is necessary for the survival of Koodiyattam [sic]".[48] Clearly, Madhu's wish to eliminate cultural gatekeeping and democratize *kutiyattam* drives his eagerness to produce new secular works such as *Macbeth*, reverse-engineering high-status Shakespeare as a leveller. The uninitiated audience is growing, and must grow, for *kutiyattam*'s survival. For this purpose, Madhu's *Macbeth* is perfectly placed to capture the imagination of an audience already familiar with Shakespeare, whether encountered through the stage or through the vestiges of the British Empire in our English classroom education. Time will tell whether Madhu's cultural translation brings *kutiyattam* its due wider recognition.

I have argued here that Shakespeare in cultural translation can serve as a cultural bridge enabling Madhu's fragile regional art form to attain a wider outreach, both nationally and internationally. Perceptively, Kennedy and Yong remark that "some worry that when his text is aggressively transformed into a new language and a radically unfamiliar performative mode, something essential in Shakespeare disappears".[49] Yet Brown maintains that in watching Madhu perform *kutiyattam*, he experienced an enhanced understanding of Shakespearean theatre through their very differences.[50] It is not only for *kutiyattam* that Madhu's *Macbeth* may be iconoclastic, but also for Shakespeare, whom "when we call on [...]

---

47 Bruce Sullivan, "How Does One Study a 'Masterpiece of the Oral and Intangible Heritage of Humanity'? Ethnographic Reflections on Kerala's Kutiyattam", *Method and Theory in the Study of Religion* 21:1 (2009), 78–86, quote 80.
48 Sathyendran (2009).
49 Kennedy and Yong (2010), 3.
50 Brown (1999), 83.

[we] almost necessarily allude to an icon, even an idol".[51] Even as Madhu's radical cultural translation of *Macbeth* challenges rigid notions regarding Kerala's *kutiyattam* or Shakespeare, it can effect a greater global understanding of both.

Zusammenfassung

Warum sollte man Shakespeare zu einer anderen Zeit, in einem anderen Land oder einer anderen Kultur inszenieren, und dann noch in der ältesten Theaterform der Welt, dem Sanskrit Tanzdrama *Kutiyattam* in Kerala, Indien? Um die 'kulturelle Übersetzung' von *Macbeth* in diese gefährdete Kunstform besser zu verstehen, hat die Autorin den *Kutiyattam*-Tänzer Margi Madhu interviewt. Sein zweistündiges Solostück *Macbeth* wird von einem König erzählt, der wie der Dämonenkönig Ravana gekleidet ist und nur eine kurze Shakespeare-Passage spricht, in Sanskrit. In dieser Adaption gibt es nur Duncan, Macduff, Lady Macbeth und eine Hexe, die Morde von Banquo und Macduff sowie Lady Macbeths Schlafwandeln sind gestrichen. Das Stück endet mit dem Herannahen von Birnam Wood. Madhus radikal säkuläre Übersetzung von *Macbeth* in die differenzierte Zeichensprache, die Mimik und den Tanz des *Kutiyattam* hinterfragt sowohl *Kutiyattam*- wie auch Shakespeare-Traditionen, bringt beide aber gleichzeitig in einen Dialog und kann somit zu einem besseren Verständnis von beiden führen.

---

51   Kennedy and Yong (2010), 3.

Movement, Music and Silence in Cheek by Jowl's *Measure for Measure*, *The Winter's Tale* and *Périclès, Prince de Tyr*

LINDA MCJANNET

> [A] character often speaks to you with words, but you also have to listen to the gentle tap-tapping behind them [...] like two prisoners trying to communicate through a cell wall.
> (Declan Donnellan)[1]

> [In addition to attending to] the directorial eye, we should not forget the directorial ear.
> (A. J. Ledger)[2]

Dance in or based on Shakespeare's plays has received a welcome surge of attention in the last few years, as this special issue of the *Jahrbuch* attests, but some have called for greater attention to the music that accompanies the dance. As Amy Rodgers and Lynsey McCulloch have noted, "despite the co-dependent nature of music and dance, Shakespeareans have been slow to examine this intermedial relationship".[3] Their point applies particularly to dance adaptations based on pre-existing classical scores, such as Prokofiev's *Romeo and Juliet* or Mendelssohn's *A Midsummer Night's Dream*,[4] but the accompaniment for social dancing called for in the plays (at the Capulet's feast or the Bohemian sheep-shearing festival) also merits closer attention. Thirteen of Shakespeare's plays

---

1   Declan Donnellan in Nicole Fayard, "Making Things Look Disconcertingly Different: In Conversation with Declan Donnellan", *Multicultural Shakespeare* 19:34 (2019), 139–159, quote 147.
2   Adam J. Ledger, *The Director and Directing: Craft, Process, and Aesthetic in Contemporary Theatre* (London: Palgrave Macmillan, 2019), 18.
3   Amy Rodgers and Lynsey McCulloch, "Shakespeare, Music, and Dance", Seminar at the 48th Annual Meeting of the Shakespeare Association of America, http://www.shakespeareassociation.org/annual-meetings/seminars-workshops/, last access 14 April 2020.
4   See Nona Monahin, "Prokofiev's *Romeo and Juliet*: Some Consequences of the Happy Ending", *Borrowers and Lenders* 10:2 (April 2017), n.p., www.borrowers.uga.edu/783442/show, last access 14 April 2020.

explicitly call for dance, and many contemporary directors *add* choreographed sequences to their productions, both period and non-period. This is particularly true of body-centred or physical theatre companies who tackle Shakespeare.[5] In these productions, dance and movement are integrated throughout the performance, sometimes accompanied by music and sometimes by non-instrumental sound or extended passages of silence. The practices of these companies thus extend the field of inquiry from traditional forms of music and dance to a broader range of movement and sound.

Prominent – perhaps pre-eminent – among such companies is Cheek by Jowl. Founded by director Declan Donnellan and designer Nick Ormerod in 1981, the company has produced fourteen plays by Shakespeare and five by other early modern playwrights. Their productions tour internationally, win awards and are often revived, so they constitute a major force in performed Shakespeare. While it does not call itself a physical theatre company, Cheek by Jowl emphasizes the centrality of the actor and the human body. Donnellan takes exquisite "care for the text" of any play he directs;[6] Peter Kirwan attests that a "well-thumbed Arden 2 edition of *The Winter's Tale* sat on the production table throughout rehearsal, and the actors understood every word".[7] Nonetheless, Donnellan has expressed dismay at "a world [...] dominated by the word".[8] He was an Irish dancer as a child and cites Peter Brook's 1970 *Midsummer Night's Dream*, arguably the first physical theatre production of Shakespeare, as a seminal influence.[9] Typically,

---

5   My review of the repertoires of thirteen physical theatre companies show that six have produced one or more Shakespeare plays. For the list, see K. C. Wright, "13 Innovative Physical Theater Companies", *Back Stage*, 4 November 2014, https:www.backstage.com/news/13-innovative-physical-theater-companies, last access 27 March 2020. For the origins of physical theatre, see Linda McJannet, "Incorporating the Text: John Farmanesh-Bocca's *Pericles Redux* and Crystal Pite's *The Tempest Replica*", in Lynsey McCulloch and Brandon Shaw (eds), *The Oxford Handbook of Shakespeare and Dance* (Oxford: Oxford University Press, 2019), 545–567, esp. 545–546. Some critics use "physical theatre" to describe what I would call dance adaptations – versions that include no spoken text; see Sheila T. Cavanaugh, "'A Delightful Measure or a Dance': Synetic Theater and Physical Shakespeare", in McCulloch and Shaw (2019), 569–583.
6   Aleks Sierz, "Declan Donnellan and Cheek by Jowl", in Maria M. Delgado and Dan Rebellato (eds), *Contemporary European Theatre Directors* (London: Routledge, 2010), 145–164, quote 146.
7   Peter Kirwan, *Shakespeare in the Theatre: Cheek by Jowl* (London: Bloomsbury Publishing, 2019), 20.
8   Qtd. in Charlotte Runcie, "Shakespeare in Russian? Why Language Is no Bar to the Bard", review of *Measure for Measure*, dir. Declan Donnellan, *The Telegraph* (London), 20 April 2015.
9   Sierz (2010), 145 and 152.

Donnellan begins rehearsals with the actors "moving around the space" already off-book, not with a read-through sitting at a table.¹⁰ Like singing, he argues, verse-speaking involves the whole body, not just the head.¹¹ He often envisions relationships in terms of dance. A rehearsal tango (for Rosalind and Orlando) became a permanent part of the performance;¹² a flamenco sequence appeared in *The Changeling* and an Irish step-dance in *Cymbeline*.¹³ In addition, Donnellan and Ormerod make important use of ensemble movement, putting the entire cast in motion, so the line between dance and other kinds of movement in their work is fluid, even erased.

I propose to analyse the interplay of movement and sound in three recent Cheek by Jowl productions: *Measure for Measure* (choreography by Irina Kashuba, music by Pavel Akimkin, in Russian with the Pushkin Theatre of Moscow, 2013–2018), *The Winter's Tale* (movement by Jane Gibson, music by Paddy Cunneen, in English, 2016–2017) and *Périclès, Prince de Tyr* (no choreographer given, sound designed by Kenan Trevien, in French with Les Gémeaux/Sceaux/Scène Nationale and Théâtre du Nord, 2019). I base my comments on the performance of *Measure for Measure* I attended in Boston in the fall of 2018 and on the edited "live capture" recordings of all three productions kindly provided in the Education Packs on the company's website.¹⁴ My analysis is partly modelled on studies of the "soundscape" of a particular play.¹⁵ In an essay on *The Tempest*, for example, Michael Neill explored mutually reinforcing patterns created by music, other sound effects and the prominence of aural imagery in the dialogue itself. He demonstrated the "extent to which the meaning of the play – what we might call its 'burden' – is expressed through the orchestration of inarticulate sound as

---

10   Declan Donnellan, qtd. in Sierz (2010), 154.
11   Declan Donnellan, ARTE Documentary on Cheek by Jowl's *Cymbeline*, Part 2, 16 January 2008, https://youtube.com/watch?v=YFfACZhp800, last access 9 January 2019.
12   Declan Donnellan, "All You Need Is Love: Adrian Lester and the Miraculous All-Male *As You Like It*", *The Guardian*, 12 November 2014.
13   Kirwan (2019), 19–20.
14   On the effects of different recording protocols, see Peter Kirwan, "Cheek by Jowl: Reframing Complicity in Web-Streams of *Measure for Measure*", in Pascale Aebischer, Suzanne Greenhalgh and Laurie E. Osbourne (eds), *Shakespeare and the 'Live' Theatre Broadcast Experience* (London: Bloomsbury Publishing, 2018), 161–173.
15   The concept of the "soundscape" was developed by communication theorists to identify "a space within which groups of people […] experience the world through sound" (Bruce Smith, "[Review of] *The Sound of Shakespeare* by Wes Folkerth", *Shakespeare Quarterly* 54:4 [2003], 463–466, quote 463).

much as through the eloquence of speech".[16] Rather than analysing sound called for or alluded to in the text, however, I will address the integrated sound- and kineto-scapes created for these productions, which I take to be one way to access the "tap-tapping behind [the words]" referenced by Donnellan in my first epigraph. My discussion will focus on three categories of onstage action: movement-based prologues; social dancing, whether called for in the texts or added by the director; and closing tableaux. Following the company's lead, I will attend to choreographed movement and artful stasis as well as familiar forms of dance. Just as the line between dance and other kinds of movement is fluid, the distinction between music and other kinds of sound needs to be decided on a case-by-case basis – consider the clacking keys in LeRoy Anderson's *Typewriter* or the cannons in Tchaikovsky's *1812 Overture*. Applying this wider lens to these productions, one finds that movement and sound make meaning in remarkably varied ways and that the sound of a body in motion can be the most eloquent accompaniment of all.

Moving Prologues

A prologue in sound and movement – an adaptation of the early modern dumb-show – is a hallmark of Cheek by Jowl productions. *Measure for Measure* began with a darkened stage and loud clanging noises, like the closing of jail house doors.[17] When the din subsided, on-stage metallic, hanging lamps were cued part-way, and the cast members entered in a tight group and regarded the audience intently. For the next few minutes, they circulated among five large red cubes that dominated the set. They moved, paused, crouched, arose, gazed in different directions and circulated again. Eventually, one figure (the Duke) separated from the group, and the rest interacted with him, blocking his exits, gesturing toward a "chair of state" (a simple side chair), imploring him to sit. Then a second character (Escalus) emerged from the group, and the first scene began. When it ended, Escalus and the Duke were reabsorbed into the ensemble, which remained onstage throughout.

---

16 Michael Neill, "'Noises, / Sounds, and sweet airs': The Burden of Shakespeare's *Tempest*", *Shakespeare Quarterly* 59:1 (2008), 36–59, quote 37–38.

17 Emma Davis (ed.), "Measure for Measure Livestream Screenplay" (2015), https://www.cheekbyjowl.com/resources/measure-for-measure-livestream-screenplay/, quote 1, last access 14 April 2020.

As Paul Prescott and Aleks Sierz have observed, Donnellan's use of wordless prologues "locates the labour and the pleasure of the evening to come in the actors' bodies, presence and their attentiveness to us, their audience"[18] and "emphasizes [the actors'] role as story-tellers, 'the makers of the tale'".[19] They possess the stage as a cry of players, before they enter as characters. During this particular sequence, the ensemble moved "as if in subconscious communion",[20] wheeling unpredictably like a "school of fish",[21] a "swarm of bees",[22] or a "flock of birds".[23] The reviewers' zoological similes captured the uncanny cohesion of the group – it moved as one organism.[24] After the ominous clangs, the audience heard only footsteps, the jingle of the jail-keeper's keys and the swish of Isabella's and Friar Peter's religious habits. The essentials of theatrical performance were thus highlighted: the actors' bodies, their intense focus and presence, the minimalist set and the costumes that hinted at their fictional identities. In the sometimes uncomfortable silences that alternated with the sound of their movements, they gently confronted the spectators, "mirroring and intensifying [their] expectation[s]".[25] (See Figure 1.)

Reviewers saw the members of the ensemble variously. One compared them to the chorus of classical drama;[26] another saw them as "ghoulish" at

18 Paul Prescott, "Declan Donnellan", in John Russell Brown (ed.), *The Routledge Companion to Directors' Shakespeare* (London: Routledge, 2009), 69–85, quote 76–77.
19 Sierz (2010), 147.
20 Dominic Cavendish, "*Measure for Measure*, Cheek by Jowl, Barbican: Like a Punch to the Guts", *The Telegraph* (London), 17 April 2015.
21 Noah Birksted-Breen, "Review of Shakespeare's *Measure for Measure* (directed by Declan Donnellan for Cheek by Jowl and the Pushkin Theatre), at the Silk Street Theatre, Barbican Centre, London, 16 April 2015", *Shakespeare* 12:1 (2016), 88–91, quote 88.
22 Peter Marks, "If Shakespeare in Russian is on your bucket list, here's your chance to cross it off", review of *Measure for Measure*, dir. Declan Donnellan, Kennedy Center for the Performing Arts, *Washington Post*, 11 October 2018.
23 Honour Bayes, Review of *Measure for Measure*, dir. Declan Donnellan, Barbican Theatre, London, *The Stage*, 17 April 2015.
24 Ormerod said that the group was "led primarily by Barnardine", but Barnardine gave no visible cues (Nick Ormerod, "*Measure for Measure*: Design", Cheek by Jowl, Archive Interviews, 17 June 2015, www.youtube.com/watch?v=3Lh9MHOyjnA, last access 6 January 2019).
25 Prescott (2009), 76.
26 Lyn Gardner, "*Measure for Measure* Review – Punchy Reminder that Power Corrupts", *The Guardian*, 19 April 2015, https://www.theguardian.com/stage/2015/apr/19/measure-for-measure-russian-language-declan-donnellan-barbican-london-review, last access 23 January 2018.

Figure 1. The intense solidarity of the ensemble. Photograph by Johan Persson. Used by permission.

times.²⁷ Still others saw them as emblematic of the victims – or the supporters – of the government or even as a stand-in for the surveillance state itself.²⁸ To me, they were mute witnesses hovering at the edges of the action, participant-observers whose bodies registered horror at injustice and sometimes intervened to protect a fellow character. When Angelo pressured Isabella during their second interview, the group inched up to his desk, and when he sat her horrified body on his desk, removed her stockings and unzipped his trousers, the ensemble "burst into life [...] and forced him to withdraw".²⁹ Equally important, accompa-

---

27 Drew Lichtenberg, "*Measure for Measure*, presented by Cheek by Jowl and the Pushkin Theatre, Brooklyn Academy of Music, 16–20 October 2018", *Shakespeare Bulletin* 37:2 (2019), 261–265, quote 263.
28 See Jacek Fabiszak, "*Measure for Measure*, dir. Declan Donnellan for Cheek by Jowl and Moscow Puskin Theatre, Gdańsk Shakespeare Theatre, 21st International Shakespeare Festival in Gdańsk, 4 August 2017", *Cahiers Élisabéthains* 95:1 (April 2018), 98–101, quote 99; and Kirwan (2018), 170.
29 Kirwan (2019), 171.

nied only by the sounds of their own movements, the somewhat motley group seemed pitted against the cavernous set, in which oppressive clamour and metallic fixtures seemed poised to dominate mere flesh and fabric. Thus, to my eye and ear, the prologue previewed the theme of the people vs. a soulless state that proved central to this production.

The opening sequence of *The Winter's Tale* also relied on the eloquence of bodies at rest and in motion and on the sounds of bodily movement. The play began with two tableaux involving a single figure. In the first, a woman in a red (winter) parka sat on the long modular bench that dominated the set, her back to the audience, while the lights slowly rose and then blacked out.[30] She was replaced by a male character (Leontes), who sat facing the audience on the same bench, staring intently into the middle distance. The first figure was seen in silence, but Leontes's troubled gaze was emphasized by tinkling piano, nervous strings, a bleaching spotlight and a blackout with thunderclap, which, like the clang in *Measure for Measure*, set an ominous tone. These moments of intense immobility were followed by a contrasting three-minute sequence in which two men (Leontes and Polixenes) lolled in close physical contact on the bench and then chased each other about the stage. As Justin Hopkins described it, they "tackled, and wrestled, [...] apparently reliving the days of their youth, but with a noticeably aggressive edge".[31] Polixenes repeatedly escaped the embrace of his friend and ran away, sometimes suitcase in hand, pursued by Leontes. The movement was athletic, and the only sounds were those their bodies produced: hard-shoe footfalls as they ran or jumped over the bench, a squeak of fabric as they slid along it, gasps and grunts as they wrestled on the floor.

In addition to calling attention to fundamental elements of theatre – bodies at rest or in motion, an almost bare stage, sound and lighting – this sequence illuminated character, especially Leontes's competitiveness[32] and his "emotional neediness".[33] The vigour of the movement and the emphasis on bodily sounds also underscored the age-inappropriateness of their rough-housing. One could imagine even the tolerant Hermione asking them to "take it outside" when she entered with Mamillius, who was bug-eyed at the spectacle. Equally important, the aggressive movements of the prologue pointed to similarities between Leon-

---

30 This figure returned later as Time and shed her winter coat.
31 Justin B. Hopkins, "*The Winter's Tale*, presented by Cheek by Jowl at the Brooklyn Academy of Music, 6–10 December 2016", *Shakespeare Bulletin* 35:2 (2017), 339–342, quote 340.
32 Ibid.
33 P. B. Roberts, "*The Winter's Tale*, dir. Declan Donnellan, at Theatr Clywd, Mold, 25 March 2017", *Shakespeare* 13:4 (2017), 356–358, quote 356.

tes and his children. P. B. Roberts noted that the adolescent Mamillius "shared his father's constant desire for affection and contact" and his emotional instability; when Hermione asked her ladies to tend to him, Mamillius threw a tantrum, "pummelling the stage with his hands and feet".[34] Perdita was also seen as "her birth father's daughter";[35] at the beginning of the sheep-shearing scene, she and her adoptive brother punched and bit each other and wrestled (much as the two men did at the beginning).

The mock violence of the prologue was also a hint of worse to come. In the grip of his delusions, Leontes loudly slapped both his son and Camillo, knocking the latter to the floor; during the trial, he assaulted Hermione, initiating her premature labour. More shockingly, Autolycus (dressed as a customs officer) savagely beat the dim-witted Clown as he and the Old Shepherd navigated their way to Leontes's court. After a parody of modern airport procedures, Autolycus dragged the Clown upstage and executed a semi-visible but highly audible barrage of foot-stomps and baton blows. The beating, as rhythmic as a tap dance, was its own accompaniment. In addition to underscoring the meta-theatrical bond between audience and players, as in *Measure for Measure*, this prologue puzzled, established specific character traits (especially Leontes's) and prepared the spectators for the physical violence just under the surface of court *and* country life.[36]

In *Périclès*, Cheek by Jowl began with ambient sound, routinized movement and catatonia. Unlike the abstract designs for *Measure for Measure* and *The Winter's Tale*, the set was "an intriguingly illusionistic hospital ward".[37] Seven actors took all the roles (with minor costume adjustments), entering and exiting through a pair of swinging doors, or moving to and from a waiting area furnished with a table, two chairs, a box of tissues and magazines. As the play began, the room was empty, except for Périclès in his bed, and silent except for voices from a bedside radio. Two orderlies entered quietly, used sanitizer on their hands, adjusted Périclès's position, plumped the pillows and exited by pushing the doors with their elbows (practising good hygiene). A doctor entered briskly, with an authoritative *tap-tap* of her boots, sanitized *her* hands, checked the chart at the foot of the bed and took the patient's vital signs. We heard the wheeze

---

34   Ibid., 356. Hopkins (2017), 341, also noted Mamillius's "inherited intemperance".
35   Hopkins (2017), 341.
36   This interpretation was viewed as gratuitous by Roberts, who lamented that the ugliness of Leontes's behaviour "carried over" to Bohemia, and that Donnellan made the rustics "as charmless as possible" (Roberts [2017], 357).
37   A[nne-] V[alérie] Dulac, "*Périclès, Prince de Tyr*, presented by Cheek by Jowl, Les Gémeaux/Sceaux/Scène Nationale, 7–25 March 2018", *Shakespeare Bulletin* 36:3 (2018), 534–537, quote 534.

of a blood pressure bulb and the scratch of her pen before she *tap-tapped* out again. One by one, two women and a man eased through the doors. The women bent over the patient and whispered anxiously. Their words may have been only semi-audible in the theatre, but the video recording captured their queries and reassurances: "Monsieur?" (or perhaps "Mon cher?") and "Papa?" and, more clearly, "Je resterai avec toi" ('I will stay with you'). When the doctor re-entered, she spoke with the visitors *sotto voce* and ushered them to the waiting area at stage left. Then, a full five and a half minutes into the performance, the lighting warmed, Périclès stirred and looked about, and, as Peter Kirwan put it, "the play took over the bodies and objects that inhabit[ed] the ward".[38] Gower's prologue having been replaced by an introduction in movement, the first scene began.

The unexpected setting was controversial. Laura Cappelle called it a "hackneyed device", "a gimmick", but to Ian Shuttleworth it was a welcome change from the company's stylized "spatial" approach and Donnellan's "freshest work in ages".[39] Some reviewers were untroubled by the hero's adventures being cast as a dream, or a "morphine-induced fantasy",[40] or a mad hallucination,[41] or (as I read them) a traumatic memory, perhaps part of an endless cycle of amnesia and remembering. Others found the set "so separate and odd" as to prevent audience engagement.[42]

While the design provoked strong reactions, few observers commented on sound or movement (one noted that the radio was on).[43] To my mind, diegetic sound (footsteps, the radio, medical equipment) and what might be described as "standard hospital choreography" emphasized the challenges the company had set itself (pun intended). *Pericles* is noted for the scope of its action – sea voyages, shipwreck, birth and burial at sea, chivalric tournaments, the attempted rape and murder of innocents, and an improbable rescue by pirates, not to mention a visit from the goddess Diana herself. For anyone acquainted with the play, the

---

38   Kirwan (2019), 186.
39   Laura Cappelle, "Two Theater Worlds Collide in Paris", *The New York Times on the Web*, 16 March 2018, https://www.nytimes.com/2018/03/15/arts/two-theater-worlds-collide-in-paris.html, last access 28 October 2020; and Ian Shuttleworth, "Theatre: *Périclès, Prince de Tyr*", *The Financial Times* (London), 11 April 2018.
40   Michael Billington, "Shakespeare's Epic Checks into the Emergency Ward: Barbican, London", *The Guardian*, 10 April 2018.
41   Kirwan (2019), 186, identifies the setting as a "psychiatric hospital", and his judgment is borne out when the straitjacket is produced.
42   Ann Treneman, "*Périclès, Prince de Tyr* at Barbican, Silk Street Theatre, London", *The Times* (London), 10 April 2018.
43   Ibid.

prologue instilled curiosity as to how it could be enacted in so constricted a space. The "medical solutions" were "ingenious",⁴⁴ sometimes quirky, often ironic. An overturned bedpan stood in for ship-destroying waves, and a straitjacket replaced Périclès's "rusty armour". (See Figure 2.)

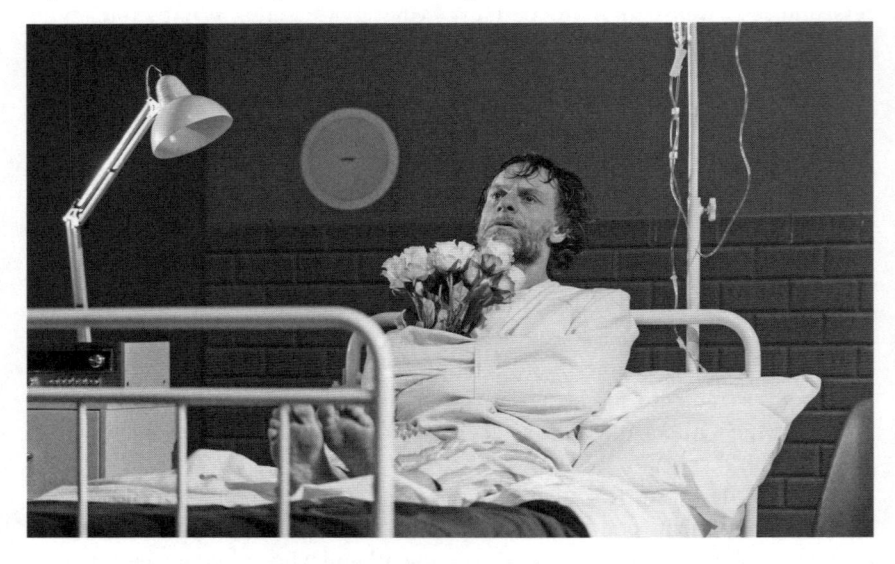

Figure 2. The bedside radio and Pericles in his "armour" holding the tourney bouquet. Photograph by Patrick Baldwin. Used by permission.

Ann Treneman complained that it was not "enough to signify high-seas drama with wave sounds and people pointing out from the hospital ward",⁴⁵ but Kirwan argued that the "complex slippage between the world of the play and the world of the hospital ward" resulted in a "commentary on a more quotidian but deeply felt emotional situation – the present absence of the comatose patient from his family's lives".⁴⁶ Certainly, the (apparent) destruction of the family, a major theme in the text, was emphasized in this production. At the same time, one element of the soundscape pointed to a threat to families that was more than quotidian. Dulac reported that the radio interview concerned "the death and rescuing of

44 Billington (2018).
45 Treneman (2018).
46 Kirwan (2019), 186.

immigrants in the Mediterranean", repeating the phrase "sauvetage en mer" ('rescue at sea') three times.[47] At least for a francophone audience, the production linked the travails of Périclès with the refugee crisis in the news at the time. The hospital setting, the choreography and soundscape of this prologue suggested that displaced persons suffer mentally and emotionally, as well as physically, and that their suffering does not necessarily cease at journey's end.

In each of these "physical epigraphs", to borrow Prescott's felicitous phrase,[48] choreography and the sounds of bodies in motion played a major role. In *Measure for Measure*, the ensemble created a communal identity as they moved and gazed, while the sounds of their footfalls and their costumes emphasized their weight, literally and figuratively, and their vulnerability. In *The Winter's Tale*, aggressive movement combined with gestures of affection hinted at Leontes's character, framed his relationship with Polixenes and laid down a marker for familial resemblances to come. In *Périclès*, the routinized movements and sounds of modern hospital care insisted on the unexpected setting and suggested a link to contemporary issues. In all cases, bodies moving without musical accompaniment invited, even required, an audience to attend to ordinary movement and sound with more than usual care.

Scenes of Social Dancing

As one would expect, the social dances in these productions were performed to music. Sometimes these sequences reinforced romantic or festive emotion; at other times they were instruments of diversion and control. In *The Winter's Tale*, before Leontes's soliloquy about Hermione's imagined infidelity, the couple danced a few measures of a gentle waltz to offstage music, remembering her acceptance of his marriage proposal. In the sheep shearing-scene, Perdita and Florizel and their friends enjoyed a country waltz accompanied by accordion and acoustic guitar. When the villagers froze, focusing our attention on the lovers, Florizel and Perdita turned two-hands and waltzed while Florizel declared his love: "When you do dance, I wish you / A wave o' th' sea" (4.3.140–141).[49] While, as noted, Bohemia was far from an idealized pastoral world in this production, the music and dancing in this part of the scene conveyed communal festivity,

---

47   Dulac (2018), 536.
48   Prescott (2009), 76.
49   All quotations are from G. Blakemore Evans et al. (eds), *The Riverside Shakespeare*, 2nd ed. (Boston, MA: Houghton Mifflin, 1996).

and the lovers' duet provided a conventional example of dance and music amplifying romantic feeling.

Less conventional, the soldiers' dance in *Périclès* unfolded to synthesizer club music, which King Simonides (formerly the doctor) cued up on the radio. Each "knight" posed provocatively and then performed a sexually explicit solo, grinding his hips or pole-dancing on the bedframe to impress an increasingly nonplussed Thaisa. The effect was a grindhouse parody of a TV dating show. When Périclès took his turn, he was comically hampered by his straitjacket-armour, so Thaisa, who was attracted to him straitjacket and all, took the initiative, embracing him and swaying her hips seductively. They danced not to the club music, but to a ballad by Jean Sablon from 1939: "J'attendrai le jour et la nuit [...] ton retour" ('I shall wait day and night [...] for your return').[50] For audience members who recognized the source of the melody as the "Coro a bocca chiusa" from *Madame Butterfly*, the music further distanced the lovers' dance from that of the suitors.[51] Once Périclès (triumphantly) freed his arms, the couple performed a pornographic, modern-dance pas de deux, to the surprising delight of Simonides, Thaisa's father, and the obvious envy of the other suitors.[52] While ever more daring sexual poses were depicted, decorum was preserved. The music was elegant, crooning not throbbing, and a modern-dance vocabulary replaced the bump-and-grind of the strip joint. There was usually space between the lovers' bodies, and their expressions remained demure. The effect, to my mind, was at once comic, sweet and sardonic.

Social dancing in *Measure for Measure* was more pervasive and complex than in the later productions. After Isabella's failure to convince Claudio that she had to reject Angelo's extortion of her virginity, Claudio, in his despair, nearly enacted the "incest" of which she accused him ("Is't not a kind of incest to take life / From thine own sister's shame?", 3.1.139–140). More aggressive than when Angelo assaulted her, the ensemble lifted his splayed body and carried it upstage. A few moments later, a bass violin was produced. Claudio sat astride the instrument and plucked out the baseline of a waltz "as if his life depended on it".[53] As he was joined by off-stage concertina and violin, the cast members took hands and danced serpentine patterns around the stage, a prominent element of many folkdance traditions. (See Figure 3.)

---

50 Dulac (2018), 537.
51 Ibid, 535. Dulac notes that the musical connection was further exploited when Marina hummed (literally *a bocca chiusa*) the same melody to Périclès in the recognition scene.
52 In *The Winter's Tale*, during Leontes's jealous soliloquy, he arranged the bodies of his wife and friend into sexual poses that were the more shocking for being imposed on their 'frozen' figures.
53 Kirwan (2019), 173.

Figure 3. The ensemble dances around Claudio in *Measure for Measure*. Photograph by Johan Persson. Used by permission.

The footwork began with "giant steps" on the downbeat and accelerated to a more energetic pattern of *slow-step, slow-step, one-two-three*.[54] While it was preceded by Claudio's sexual assault, this sequence seemed to me to focus on ethos rather than Eros: it suggested the ensemble (the "folk") rallying to support Isabella and Claudio with increasing urgency. Donnellan and Omerod intended to evoke the medieval Dance of Death, famously captured in Ingmar Bergman's *The Seventh Seal*[55] and some observers noted the parallel.[56] For Drew Lichtenberg, however, at this moment "the evening [...] blossom[ed] into something richer and more mysterious".[57] But these readings are not entirely incompatible. Death indeed seemed immanent for Claudio, but, unlike the tortured postures of Bergman's sinners forcibly escorted to judgment, the erect postures of the dancers and their smooth, unison movement around Claudio suggested communal

54 Surprisingly, this "bravura sequence" "only emerged in the final days of rehearsal" (ibid.).
55 Ormerod (2015).
56 See, for example, Kirwan (2019), 173.
57 Lichtenberg (2019), 264.

sympathy more than the writhing of the damned. While compassionate onlookers in this production were often unable to act, compassion is a quality that the play ultimately (however ambiguously) endorses.

On other occasions, social dancing and music in these productions were instruments of deflection and control. While morally distasteful, such stratagems are effective. People turn to music for solace, and rhythm is powerful: it's difficult to tango if the band is playing a waltz. The motive for and outcome of such manipulations varied widely. When the Duke proposed the bed-trick, Isabella, Mariana and Angelo performed a dumbshow in three-quarter time. Angelo and Mariana mimed their broken engagement, rehearsing the past. Isabella blindfolded Angelo, and Mariana took her place and triumphantly swooped him into ballroom hold. They waltzed around the stage, froze in a posture that suggested sexual climax, and danced off. From then on, the bed-trick was a *fait accompli*, and later scenes related to it were cut. The waltz thus enacted the Duke's plan – and Donnellan's desire to streamline the narrative. It also highlighted the artificiality of the bed-trick: instead of a *narratio* or simple pantomime, the characters danced out the story like mechanical dolls. As Lichtenberg noted, the dumbshow-in-dance also marked a shift not only from "tragedy to comedy" but "from the Duke's passivity to his active orchestration of the plot".[58]

A second waltz sequence (surprisingly) involved the Duke and Barnardine. Donnellan and Ormerod saw Barnardine as the Duke's alter-ego.[59] When the Duke visited the jail (in 4.3), Barnardine manhandled him into a waltz, swinging him about like a child and ultimately throwing him to the floor. As they danced, the red cubes rotated to reveal grim tableaux: Lucio sodomizing a prostitute, Claudio in an electric chair and Isabella, arms raised in supplication. For Kirwan, the waltz was "a macabre reprisal of the dance of death" and highlighted Barnardine's "infernal confidence that resisted control" even from the Duke.[60] In this instance, the very same music and dance form used by the Duke to control the plot ironically marked the limits of his power and underscored Barnardine as a force no social system (or jail) could control.

While the motive and results of the Duke's choreographic interventions were arguably benign (a subject to which I will return), Autolycus, in a freely adapted version of the sheep-shearing scene in *The Winter's Tale*, used music and dance to manipulate potential customers. In a jarring musical change, he interrupted the country waltz, entering from the audience to blasts of electric guitar and

---

58 Ibid.
59 Ormerod (2015).
60 Kirwan (2019), 174.

Figure 4. Autolycus (second from right) leads the line dance, while the villagers show off their purchases. Photograph by Johan Persson. Used by permission.

percussion, with a microphone, a cowboy hat and a camera crew. Led by Autolycus ("Over here, over here!", "Follow me!"), the couples responded to the beat and boogied around the stage. The loud music and Autolycus's patter-song whipped up desire for his trinkets ("Lawn as white as driven snow", 4.4.218). As villagers lined up to buy, he snapped up their cash in time to the music, as if to underscore his complete control of the group. The festive energies of the sheep-shearing were thus artificially amplified (in all senses of the word) and diverted to his benefit. When Mopsa and Dorcas's argument over the Clown became a hair-pulling-fight, Autolycus took charge, interviewing them à la Jerry Springer or Jeremy Kyle, treating the spectators as if they were a studio audience.[61] When the Clown's revelation of Perdita's status as "a changeling" (relocated from line 688 in the scene)[62] provoked an altercation between the Clown and the Old Shepherd, Autolycus distracted the group with a line dance of the type popular in the American southwest. (See Figure 4.)

61 The two television hosts were referenced by several reviewers. See Hopkins (2017), 341, and Roberts (2017), 357.
62 In most performances, the term was "immigrant" or "stranger", uttered in scorn.

Although it did not feature "four threes of herdsmen", one of whom was reputed to "[jump] twelve foot and a half" (4.4.336, 339), the line dance stood in for the satyrs' dance called for in the text. It made everyone forget their differences; even Mopsa and Dorcas hugged as they exited the stage.[63] It also excited sexual desire: left alone, Perdita and Florizel embraced passionately and began to remove their clothes, only to be discovered *in flagrante* by Polixenes ("How now, fair shepherd?", 4.4.345). The music and dancing that filled Autolycus's pockets both purged and excited emotions in his on-stage audience, a suitable outcome for a bacchanal.

Apart from the final tableaux (to be discussed shortly), Donnellan's use of social dancing was surprising. Sometimes social dancing expressed joy, as it usually did in early modern Europe and still does today,[64] but in these productions it was often associated with manipulation, oppression and even doom. Autolycus manipulated the villagers with a line dance, and Barnardine dominated the Duke in an aggressive waltz. Social dancing was also a target of parody. The vulgar sexuality of the soldiers' solos in *Périclès* was contrasted with the lovers' balletic pas de deux, so as to parody both forms. Dance music also modulated in unexpected and sometimes jarring ways: the sheep-shearing waltz was blasted by Autolycus's electric guitar; the honky-tonk accompaniment of the soldiers' dance in *Périclès* gave way to a ballad based on a melody by Puccini. Paradoxically, social dancing in these productions, involving familiar forms such as line dances and waltzes, contravened audience expectations and challenged easy interpretations.

Final Tableaux

Movement, music and silence figured powerfully in the final tableau of each production. After the revelations that conclude *Measure for Measure*, the waltz music returned. As the couples paired up, the choreography defined each rela-

---

63 Roberts (2017), 357, read this detail as evidence of their being "only capable of transient emotions" and as further gratuitous coarsening of the Bohemian characters.
64 As Emily Winerock's archival work has demonstrated, outside the socio-political milieu of the court, social dancing was a form of "merriment" enjoyed at "social gatherings, civic celebrations, and [even] church fundraisings". Prior to Puritan times, it was suspect only if it led to excessive drinking or gaming or if unmarried partners were suspected of "inappropriate intimacy off the dance floor" (Emily Winerock, "'The Heaven's True Figure' or 'An Introit to All Kind of Lewdness'? Competing Conceptions of Dancing in Shakespeare's England", in McCulloch and Shaw [2019], 21–48, quotes 22 and 34).

Figure 5. As this 'screen grab' shows, Mariana (far right) takes the man's position in the final waltz in *Measure for Measure*.

tionship and (somewhat) resolved the question of whether Isabella would accept the Duke's offer of marriage. Claudio and Juliet danced with their baby nestled between them. When they paused, Mariana, as in the dumbshow of 3.1, abruptly gathered Angelo into ballroom hold. In this case, however, she was leading: she adopted the man's position, with her left arm extended, while Angelo's left arm, which should have been leading her, trailed limply. (See Figure 5.)

Finally, the Duke again extended his hand to Isabella. As in the text, she had ignored his previous overtures ("But fitter time for that" and "I have a motion much imports your good", 5.1.489, 530). However, while staring at her brother's newly formed family, which seemed to soften her resolve for a religious life, Isabella had removed her novice's veil. As the other couples waltzed, she eventually accepted the Duke's hand, but when he attempted to take her veil, she snatched it back, not yet ready for a complete change of heart. As they danced, she began to make eye-contact, suggesting she might accept him in the end. The production ended with all three couples waltzing as the lights faded to black.

Some (including myself) were tempted to view the final frame as a restoration of communal harmony, or at least a "compassionate" outcome building to "a sad, unsettling poignancy".[65] Jacek Fabiszak found the "nostalgic waltzes" consti-

---

65 Laura Collins-Hughes, "Sex, Lies and Vindication", *New York Times* (East Coast), 18 October 2018, C7.

tutive of the "decadent, resigned, lethargic, and passive atmosphere" of the piece. He argued that as a result, for better or for worse, "one accepted and yielded to even the most outrageous metatheatrics" of the ending.[66] Others read the final moments as even more deeply problematic. Lichtenberg, alluding to Vladimir Putin's cynical alliance with the Russian Orthodox Church, saw "death, sex, and religion locked together in an eternal waltz, united by the power of the state".[67] While this view is powerful, each couple waltzed differently. In the case of Claudio and Juliet, Skiles Howard's distinction between popular and elite dancing is helpful.[68] Initially they slow-danced, a form that requires no teaching and amounts to a gently swaying hug. When they began to waltz, however, they did so with grace achieved only by rigorous instruction; as a result they seemed to establish a private emotional space before joining the public display engineered by the Duke. Mariana enthusiastically waltzed with Angelo, but she did so on her own terms, taking the man's position. As for Isabella and the Duke, we had witnessed her reluctance to dance and his public humiliation when she ignored him. (In a wonderful gesture, rising from his knee, he carefully brushed a smudge from his trouser leg.) Further, Isabella retained her veil as she danced and kept her eyes partly downcast. Thus, while the waltz could be seen as an imposed celebration, the choreography for each couple created important nuances.

In *The Winter's Tale*, the ending seemed reverential rather than cynical or ambiguous. The music Paulina calls for was provided by low "communal humming" and "an insistent chord" played on a toy piano featured earlier in the play.[69] As the sequence progressed, the music diminished and bodily sounds became more salient. When Hermione's statue 'awoke', Leontes approached her on his knees, like a penitent in a church, and the shuffling sound was achingly audible. His courtiers also inched forward, one by one, knelt with an occasional creak of a shoe or knee, and joined the "odd but strangely moving huddle" around Hermione.[70] While some found the effect of this sequence "exquisite"[71] or even "sacral",[72] Pascale

---

66 Fabiszak (2018), 101.
67 Lichtenberg (2019), 265.
68 "Courtly dancing reinscribed hierarchy through codified movement, and popular dancing celebrated affinity with traditional motion" (Skiles Howard, "Hands, Feet, and Bottoms: De-centering the Cosmic Dance in *A Midsummer Night's Dream*", *Shakespeare Quarterly* 44:3 [1993], 325–342, quote 326).
69 Roberts (2017), 358. In the opening scene, the piano calmed Mamillius's tantrum when his mother asked her women to take the boy, another example of music as diversion.
70 Hopkins (2017), 242.
71 Ibid.
72 Roberts (2017), 358.

Aebischer argued that Leontes' "shuffl[ing] on his knees to hug [Hermione and Perdita] from behind" amounted to a "pathetic attempt at rebuilding a family".[73] At the same time, having almost destroyed it, what course was open to him besides abject penance? Another striking instance of movement-plus-sound was Perdita's running to embrace her mother for the first time. In the sheep-shearing scene she had displayed a "rough-hewn forthrightness",[74] shaking hands like a boy and clapping Polixenes and Camillo on the back. Here, even though she was barefoot, her rapid footsteps broke the silence, a marker of her straightforward character and urgent filial love. They also recalled the footfalls of the ensemble in *Measure for Measure* as it reacted to injustice: Perdita, like the ensemble, voted with her feet.

Little remarked upon by reviewers, the dance in the final scene of *Périclès* also seemed to celebrate the restoration of the family and the promise of a daughter's marriage. The ballad "J'attendrai" was reprised, and Périclès slow-danced with his daughter and his wife, recalling the image of Claudio and his family in *Measure for Measure*. Périclès released Marina to dance with Lysimachus, but moments later, he collapsed. The orderlies carried him back to bed, the song faded, and the radio interview about refugees was heard again. Thaisa and Marina embraced Périclès on the bed, while Lysimachus hovered protectively, and the lights dimmed. While the slow dances clearly signalled love restored, the possibility that the play might begin again and that Périclès would relive his ordeal qualified the 'happy ending'. Moreover, the sombre tones of the radio interview re-emphasized a link to the present: while Périclès and his family survived, others fleeing violence in the Middle East have not.

Thus, in two of these final sequences, music and dancing signalled a restoration of love and harmony, but other movement or sound inserted an asterisk, a contrary element. The elegance of the final waltzes in *Measure for Measure* was humanized by details specific to each couple, but it still recalled the mechanical way the characters danced out the Duke's plan to defeat Angelo's cruelty. In *Périclès*, the slow-dance was qualified by Périclès's inability to sustain it and the re-emergence of the radio interview as the dominant element of sound. By contrast, in *The Winter's Tale*, I infer, the loss of Antigonus, Mamillius and years of family life were beyond the power of conventional music and dance to heal; rather, the surviving members of family and court embraced in relative silence,

---

73 Pascale Aebischer, "*The Winter's Tale*, Presented by Cheek by Jowl at the Silk Theatre, Barbican, London, 5–22 April 2017, dir. by Declan Donnellan", *Shakespeare Bulletin* 35:4 (2017), 721–725, quote 725.
74 Ibid., 724.

broken only by the sound of Leontes's penitent knees and Perdita's footsteps. In all three cases, Donnellan's orchestration of movement and music created specific effects that illuminated his vision of each play and juxtaposed closure with unresolved questions.

Conclusion

In *The Sound of Shakespeare*, Wes Folkerth explored the sounds of early modern London and their echoes in the plays to suggest that play-texts are less "a species of writing in which conventional semantic meaning or narrative is advanced" than something akin to musical notation, "which describes, or eventuates in, a[n] [...] experience [...that] occurs in time".[75] His claim gains strength when dance and movement are considered as well as sound. When faced with stage directions – "*A dance*" or "*Hoboys*" – directors, composers and choreographers join forces to realize the "notation" and create a multi-sensory, multi-layered experience. Cheek by Jowl consistently rises to the challenge, creating dance and movement sequences that, whether accompanied by music, non-instrumental sound or near silence, shape our experience of the production and bear much of its "burden", to use Michael Neill's term. Speaking of *Measure for Measure*, Lichtenberg wrote that, by "granting the language of gesture and physical presence the same prominence as Shakespeare's words, Donnellan granted the body the multivalent resonance of his poetry".[76] I would argue that the body *has* a multivalent resonance of which Donnellan is exquisitely aware and which he fully exploits. As a result, quotidian movements (walking, crawling, crouching, running, wrestling) accompanied by natural sounds often achieve an impact as great or greater than dancing to instrumental music. The ensemble footing it about the stage or standing in silent vigilance; Leontes jumping over a bench or inching toward Hermione on his knees; a gratuitous beating choreographed to "hard shoe and baton"; Perdita's footsteps as she ran to meet her mother – these moments stay in the mind's eye and ear long after the performance ends. In addition to familiar dances performed to music, movement that foregrounds the actor's body, its physicality and weight, are essential to Cheek by Jowl's kinetic approach to Shakespeare and even their most controversial productions' "near-hypnotic hold" on audiences.[77] The artful interplay of movement, music, sound

---

75 Wes Folkerth, *The Sound of Shakespeare* (London: Routledge, 2002), 21.
76 Lichtenberg (2019), 262.
77 Marks (2018).

and silence supplements, penetrates and illumines text and subtext by engaging, more than is usual in Shakespearean performance, our aural and kinaesthetic receptors, as well as our cognitive responses to language and plot.

Zusammenfassung

Die Forschung zum Tanz in oder in Anlehnung an Shakespeares Dramen hat in den letzten Jahren an Fahrt aufgenommen; in diesem Zusammenhang wurde angeregt, sich eingehender mit der Musik zu beschäftigen, die den Tanz begleitet. Körperorientierte Theaterensembles wie Cheek by Jowl integrieren Tanz und Bewegung in ihre Produktionen, manchmal mit Musikbegleitung, manchmal ohne. Solche Inszenierungen erfordern eine Betrachtung, die sich nicht nur auf die in Shakespeares Stücken geforderten Formen von Musik und Tanz konzentriert, sondern auch solche berücksichtigt, die eigens für die Aufführung konzipiert werden. Aus dieser Perspektive analysiert Linda McJannets Beitrag das Zusammenspiel von Bewegung und Ton in drei Inszenierungen von Cheek by Jowl. Anhand von Prologen, die hauptsächlich aus Bewegung bestehen, von Gesellschaftstänzen (sowohl auf dem Text beruhende wie auch hinzugefügte) sowie von Schlusstableaus wird gezeigt, dass ein bewusstes Spiel mit Bewegung, Ton und Stille sowohl die kognitive als auch die emotionale Wirkung einer Inszenierung verstärkt – und dass das Geräusch eines sich bewegenden Körpers manchmal die eloquenteste aller akustischen Begleitungen ist.

"Like an old tale": *The Winter's Tale* on the Balletic Stage

JONAS KELLERMANN

> That she is living,
> Were it but told you, should be hooted at
> Like an old tale.
> (5.3.116–118)[1]

Paulina's comment, addressed to her wonderstruck audience upon revealing Hermione's statue in the final scene of *The Winter's Tale*, applies to the other works commonly grouped under Shakespeare's romances just as well. Filled with far-flung exotic locations, shipwrecks, miraculous reunions of presumed-lost relatives, and supernatural *deus ex machina* interventions, these plays – more so than any other generic subcategory of Shakespeare's oeuvre – urge spectators on- and offstage to "awake your faith" (5.3.95), as Paulina says, and to willingly suspend their disbelief. The dramatic idiosyncrasy of these plays, while arguably part of their ongoing appeal, has both fascinated and confused critics. The term *romance*, in itself an anachronistic labelling of Shakespearean drama, is but one of several generic descriptors, also including *tragicomedy* and *late play*, with which scholars have attempted to unify those late works of Shakespeare that on first glance appear in line with the "ahistorical realm of fantasy"[2] more than anything else. *The Winter's Tale* certainly encapsulates this categorical evasiveness in its profound "intent on probing the weird magic of the theatrical medium" and "its theorizing of theatrical art".[3] Given the current interest in the intermedial relationship between Shakespeare's verbal works and the non-verbal art form of

---

1   Unless noted otherwise, all Shakespeare citations refer to *The Norton Shakespeare: Romances and Poems*, ed. by Stephen Greenblatt, 2nd ed. (New York: W. W. Norton, 2008).
2   Cyrus Mulready, *Romance on the Early Modern Stage: English Expansion Before and After Shakespeare* (Basingstoke: Palgrave Macmillan, 2013), 20.
3   Simon Palfrey, "Formaction", in Henry S. Turner (ed.), *Early Modern Theatricality* (Oxford: Oxford University Press, 2013), 346–367, quote 358.

dance,⁴ the idiosyncrasy of Shakespearean romance begs another question: if the events in these plays, many of which only take place offstage and are reported afterwards, so ostentatiously challenge and push the boundaries of dramatic form and theatrical representation, how may this challenge be adapted into an art form that eschews any verbal communication – such as dance, or more specifically ballet? If we consider the choreographic adaptation of Shakespeare as "a series of re-materializations, as a work both theatrical and literary phases in and out of shades of materiality and embodiment",⁵ then what shapes and materiality do the distinctive dramaturgies of the romances assume in dance? Rather than establishing a false hierarchy between 'original' and 'predecessor', the concept of re-materialization offers a productive framework for adaptational comparisons between literature and dance in order to explore how the verbal materiality of one art form re-appears in the physical materiality of the other. Unsurprisingly perhaps, the romances have received comparatively less attention on the balletic stage than some of Shakespeare's other genres, such as comedy (*A Midsummer Night's Dream*, *The Taming of the Shrew*) or tragedy (*Romeo and Juliet*).⁶ One notable exception to this tendency has been Christopher Wheeldon's commercially and critically lauded adaptation of *The Winter's Tale* for the Royal Ballet in 2014.⁷ This article therefore conducts a generic comparison of Shakespeare's play and Wheeldon's reworking, showcasing how the simultaneous oldness and newness of the romance form re-materializes in Wheeldon's ballet, both in its self-reflec-

---

4   On the current interest in Shakespeare and dance, see Adeline Chevrier-Bosseau, "Dancing Shakespeare in Europe: Silent Eloquence, the Body and the Space(s) of Play within and beyond Language", *Cahiers Élisabéthains* 102:1 (2020), 3–17.
5   Joseph Campana, "New Directions: Dancing Will: The Case of *Romeo and Juliet*", in Julia Reinhard Lupton (ed.), Romeo and Juliet: *A Critical Reader* (London: Bloomsbury, 2016), 153–176, quote 155.
6   Out of the four romances, *The Tempest* has received the most attention both by classical choreographers like Rudolf Nureyev (1982) and contemporary ones like Crystal Pite (2008). On the choreographic reception of Shakespeare's romances, see Elizabeth Klett, *Choreographing Shakespeare: Dance Adaptations of the Plays and Poems* (London: Routledge, 2019), 131–152.
7   *The Winter's Tale* premiered on 10 April 2014 and won the prestigious Prix Benois de la Danse the following year for Best Choreography (Wheeldon), Best Male Dancer (Edward Watson as Leontes) and Best Composer (Joby Talbot). Since then, it has entered the repertoires of the National Ballet of Canada and the Bolshoi Ballet and was revived by the Royal Ballet in their 2015/2016 and 2017/2018 seasons; its scheduled premiere by the Hamburg Ballet in June 2020 was cancelled due to the Covid-19 pandemic. The description of Wheeldon's *The Winter's Tale* in this essay is based on the DVD recording by Opus Arte from 2015 and a live performance that I attended at the Royal Opera House, Covent Garden, on 24 February 2018.

tive outlook on the classical story ballet and its adaptational lens on Shakespeare's play.[8] In the first step, I outline some of the most distinguishing features of Shakespeare's complex dramaturgy, making the case for the term *romance* as a contested yet productive label. In the second step, I discuss selected scenes from Wheeldon's three-act ballet – the emergence of Leontes's jealousy in Act 1, the sheep-shearing feast in Act 2, and the duet scene between Leontes and Paulina in Act 3 – to examine how Shakespeare's romantic dramaturgy re-materializes in Wheeldon's adaptation. This comparison reveals a striking parallelism between the two: just as Shakespeare's *The Winter's Tale* relies upon pre-existing generic templates from predominantly non-dramatic literature to dramatize these in a highly unique way, so too does Wheeldon choreographically narrate the Shakespearean story by both adhering to and innovating the traditional form of the classical story ballet, or *ballet d'action*, from a twenty-first-century perspective.

The Mixed Mode

The term *romance*, as indicated above, was not yet used as a generic label for dramatic writing during Shakespeare's lifetime. Plays that qualify as dramatic romances first emerged on the early modern English stage in the 1570s and, following a decline in popularity in the early 1600s, experienced a resurgence in and after 1607.[9] While the denominator "dramatick romance" in itself was first recorded in the 1670s, it was not until 1875 that Edward Dowden would establish the tradition of classifying *The Winter's Tale* alongside *Cymbeline*, *Pericles* and *The Tempest* as romances.[10] Antecedent to this tradition, the First Folio had listed *The Tempest* and *The Winter's Tale* as comedies and *Cymbeline* as a tragedy, with *Pericles* – as well as *The Two Noble Kinsmen*, another play nowadays often classified as a romance, for example in the Norton Shakespeare – not being included at all. Thus even before the attribution of the term *romance* to Shakespeare's late

---

8   The idea that art works should be viewed through the perspective of their creative afterlives goes back to T. S. Eliot and has recently gained new currency in literary and cultural theory. See Elisabeth Bronfen, *Crossmappings: On Visual Culture* (London: I. B. Tauris, 2018), 7.
9   See chapter 3, "The Development of Dramatic Romance: 1570–1610", in Christopher J. Cobb, *The Staging of Romance in Late Shakespeare: Text and Theatrical Technique* (Newark: University of Delaware Press, 2007), 60–116, for an overview.
10 Mary Ellen Lamb and Valerie Wayne, "Introduction: Into the Forest", in Mary Ellen Lamb and Valerie Wayne (eds), *Staging Early Modern Romance: Pose Friction, Dramatic Romance, and Shakespeare* (London: Routledge, 2009), 1–20, quote 5–7.

works and the critical debates that this would eventually spark, generic placement had proven an editorial issue concerning those Shakespeare plays that, irrespective of labelling, overtly appropriate what Helen Cooper has termed "the memes of romance".[11] This generic tension is particularly apparent in *The Winter's Tale*, adding to the standing of the play as "the most powerful and challenging of the romances",[12] two qualities that are interconnected. On first glance, the play with its two halves and the speech of Time in 4.1 as a conjunction reads as starkly dichotomous, more suggestive of the hybridized term *tragicomedy* than of *romance*. As critics have long pointed out, the story of Leontes's inexplicable suspicion of adultery between his wife Hermione and his childhood friend Polixenes as staged in Acts 1 to 3 resembles Shakespeare's earlier tragedy *Othello*,[13] sans an Iago figure to instigate Leontes's paranoia, though; rather, it is Leontes's very own "hallucinatory gaze"[14] that drives forward his jealousy and the plot. The play has also been discussed for its historical echoes of the downfall of the second Queen consort to Henry VIII and mother of Elizabeth I, Anne Boleyn,[15] who was unjustly executed on charges of treason, adultery and incest in 1536. The generic expectations that these various allusions may have evoked in contemporary audiences are certainly fulfilled by the end of 3.2 in the revelation of Leontes's fallacy and the deaths of Hermione and Mamillius. Leontes may not be punished for his deeds by his own physical death, yet at least on a metaphorical level he is nonetheless "killed off to us, consigned to a tomb of self-immolation and stagnancy".[16]

By contrast, the tragedy of the first three acts of *The Winter's Tale* appears even further heightened through the sudden time jump of sixteen years and the

---

11   Helen Cooper, *The English Romance in Time: Transforming Motifs from Geoffrey of Monmouth to the Death of Shakespeare* (Oxford: Oxford University Press, 2004), 4.
12   Michael O'Connell, "The Experiment of Romance", in Alexander Leggatt (ed.), *The Cambridge Companion to Shakespearean Comedy* (Cambridge: Cambridge University Press, 2001), 215–229, quote 224.
13   Paul Innes, "Seeing the Spider: The Jealous Rage of Exchange in *The Winter's Tale* and *Othello*", *Anglica* 25:3 (2016), 69–80, quote 69–72.
14   Maria Del Sapio Garbero, "A Spider in the Eye/I: The Hallucinatory Staging of the Self in Shakespeare's *The Winter's Tale*", in Ute Berns (ed.), *Solo Performances: Staging the Early Modern Self in England* (Amsterdam: Rodopi, 2010), 133–155, quote 138.
15   M. Lindsay Kaplan and Katherine Eggert, "'Good queen, my lord, good queen': Sexual Slander and the Trials of Female Authority in *The Winter's Tale*", *Renaissance Drama* 25 (1994), 89–118, quote 91–92.
16   R. S. White, *Let Wonder Seem Familiar: Endings in Shakespeare's Romance Vision* (New Jersey: Humanities Press, 1985), 149.

change of scenery from Sicilia to the inherently pastoral Bohemia by the sea in Act 4, anticipating the climactic transcending and reversal of tragedy in Act 5. This generic contrast is often emphasized in stage productions of the play by employing different design aesthetics for the opposing settings, for example in the 2015 Garrick Theatre production by the Kenneth Branagh Theatre Company or Wheeldon's ballet adaptation as discussed below. At the same time, several scholars have challenged dichotomous readings of *The Winter's Tale*, arguing that the play features a common dramaturgical thread that infuses both halves in equal measures. Lawrence Danson, for example, has claimed that "more remarkable than the division are the ways in which the play mixes rather than separates genres, infusing the expectations aroused by each half with the destabilizing generic potential of the other".[17] Subsuming therefrom his definition of romance as "an intrinsically mixed mode that holds in suspension tragedy, comedy, and even history", he argues that Shakespeare's romances do not stand apart from his other works, but instead exemplify the idea that "the mixed mode is the Shakespearean default mode".[18] Christopher Cobb has similarly suggested that "it is better for critics to think of the late plays as not working within a single genre, even a highly mixed one like 'romantic tragicomedy' or 'tragicomic romance': their genre is not simply mixed but changeable and changing".[19] This paradoxical simultaneity of generic uniformity and hybridity, of solidity and fluidity of the romance form also applies to their dramatic content, specifically in the case of *The Winter's Tale*. As Gillian Woods has shown, the play "probes at the possibilities of dramatic fiction in romantic space, in part through articulating the ideological awkwardness that attends some of its generic features".[20] This probing quality, she continues, pertains in particular to the central question of Hermione's 'death' and subsequent resurrection:

> The structure of *The Winter's Tale* provides Leontes and his audience with a paradox at a conceptual level: the play maintains a sense of the absolutely fictional on the one hand and the logically explainable on the other. [...] It is through the conceptual paradox that underpins the plot that *The Winter's Tale* celebrates fictional transcen-

---

17   Lawrence Danson, "The Shakespeare Remix: Romance, Tragicomedy, and Shakespeare's 'distinct kind'", in Anthony R. Guneratne (ed.), *Shakespeare and Genre: From Early Modern Inheritances to Postmodern Legacies* (Basingstoke: Palgrave Macmillan, 2011), 101–118, quote 115.
18   Ibid., 116, 102.
19   Cobb (2007), 19.
20   Gillian Woods, *Shakespeare's Unreformed Fictions* (Oxford: Oxford University Press, 2013), 170.

dence, celebrates the way that fiction can remove us from ourselves and show us something entirely other.[21]

That "something entirely other" which the ending of *The Winter's Tale* shows us is the idea, the mere fictional possibility, of a stone statue coming to life and bringing back Hermione from the dead. The play does not force its audiences to 'pick sides' as to whether Hermione did (not) in fact die in Act 3. Instead, it creates an epistemologically liminal space in which the fiction that it brings forth is in the literal sense "wonderful",[22] manifesting the most overtly romantic moment in the drama as an incomplete reversal of tragedy.[23] Taking the paradoxical quality of *The Winter's Tale* with regard to both its form and content into account, the play may thus be called a romance in that it bears its identity as an "old tale" on its dramaturgical (and even titular) sleeves, while daring its audience to embrace said tale all the same. Like other dramatic romances at the time, *The Winter's Tale* does not shy away from showcasing its own literary inheritances of Greek and medieval as well as contemporary romance narratives and motifs, while at the same "transform[ing] narrative romance into a powerful theatrical mode".[24] My own preference of the term *romance* is not intended as an implicit discrediting of its competing terminological alternatives, an exhaustive discussion of which would certainly exceed the scope of this paper. Yet, as I will show in the following, it is the peculiarly romantic quality of an 'old tale newly told' that re-materializes in Wheeldon's balletic adaptation of *The Winter's Tale*.

The Literature Ballet

The Royal Ballet has a long-standing history of Shakespeare-based creations, due in particular to Frederick Ashton's one-act *The Dream* in 1964, based upon *A Midsummer Night's Dream*, and Kenneth MacMillan's ground-breaking *Romeo and Juliet* the following year. Christopher Wheeldon's adaptation of *The Winter's Tale* follows this tradition, retelling the Shakespearean play as a cohesive and easy-to-follow story ballet that aims for dramatic "legibility and

---

21   Ibid., 208.
22   Ibid.
23   The reversal remains incomplete since both Mamillius and Antigonus, unlike Hermione, do not return from the dead.
24   Mulready (2013), 19.

intelligibility",[25] as opposed to the more formally abstract and experimental Shakespeare adaptations that Susan Jones has recently surveyed in the field of modern dance.[26] The story ballet, or *ballet d'action*, emerged in eighteenth-century France in the wake of the so-called *ballet reform* as a performance art that conveys a dramatic plot solely through choreographic movement and instrumental music without the use of spoken or sung word.[27] Ballet thus emancipated itself as a dramatic art form from both spoken-word theatre and opera, in which it had merely functioned as an ornamental *divertissement*. While few of the story ballets created in the eighteenth century are still regularly performed today, the theoretical and practical revisions surrounding them laid the foundation for the rise of the romantic ballet in the nineteenth century with its now canonical masterpieces like *Giselle* or *Swan Lake*. Wheeldon's ballet also follows a traditional premise on a musical level. Rather than appropriating non-balletic music for his choreography as has become a standard in the twentieth and twenty-first centuries, the Royal Ballet commissioned Joby Talbot to compose a full-length original score specifically intended for the three-act ballet, reminiscent of Tchaikovsky's highly thematic ballet scores of the nineteenth century. Talbot had previously been commissioned to compose the score to Wheeldon's 2011 adaptation of *Alice's Adventures in Wonderland*, also for the Royal Ballet. On first glance, then, Wheeldon's ballet appears to be approaching its Shakespearean source in a decidedly traditional manner – and thus to be reiterating the romance's parading of its own generically old-fashioned qualities.

Upon closer consideration, however, one can identify in Wheeldon's production a highly nuanced dramaturgical engagement with both Shakespeare's play and its own balletic form, thus continuing the tendency that Iris Julia Bührle has identified in a number of twentieth-century creations as "literature ballet".[28] By the end of the nineteenth century, the romantic ballet had produced a significant divide between virtuoso, but essentially 'meaningless' dancing on the one hand and pantomimic 'meaningful' acting on the other. As Susan Leigh Foster

---

25 Klett (2019), 131.
26 Susan Jones, "Shakespeare, Modernism, and Dance", in Lynsey McCulloch and Brandon Shaw (eds), *The Oxford Handbook of Shakespeare and Dance* (Oxford: Oxford University Press, 2019), 287–302.
27 Christina Thurner, *Beredte Körper – Bewegte Seelen: Zum Diskurs der doppelten Bewegung in Tanztexten* (Bielefeld: Transcript, 2009), 50–53.
28 Iris Julia Bührle, *Literatur und Tanz: die choreographische Adaptation literarischer Werke in Deutschland und Frankreich* (Würzburg: Königshausen & Neumann, 2014), 202–207.

has shown, "[a]ny sense of physicality as a discourse, and of dance as an endeavor that investigated and then celebrated that physicality, had vanished".[29] This sterilization of the romantic ballet and its depletion of dramatic meaning led to the rejection of ballet aesthetics and practices in newly emergent, non-balletic dance forms in the first half of the twentieth century such as *Ausdruckstanz* or modern dance, but also subsequently to significant innovations within the field of ballet itself. These included the revolutionary productions of the Paris-based *Ballets Russes* as well as the emergence of a variety of creations based upon literary works, which differed in their more profound interest in character psychology and narrative realism from the more fairy-tale-like qualities of the romantic ballets. Significantly these ballets, some of the most noteworthy examples of which were created by choreographers like John Cranko and John Neumeier, sought to overcome the dramaturgical divide between pantomimic acting and abstract dancing inherited from the romantic period, by effectively conveying their dramatic plots and characters *through* the choreography, not *beside* it.[30] The discursive complexity that Foster had found to be lacking in late nineteenth-century ballet was thus gradually reclaimed throughout the following century in the intertextual engagement with literary works, including Shakespeare.

As I will argue in the remainder of this essay, Wheeldon's adaptation of *The Winter's Tale* can certainly be placed within the tradition of the literature ballet. While the piece as a whole displays the overall premise of a conventional *ballet d'action*, Wheeldon nevertheless uses the structural toolkit of the ballet vocabulary to provide a modern and poignant perspective on Shakespeare's idiosyncratic play. Furthermore, the meta-reflections on the classical ballet form that one can subsume from this perspective establish another intermedial bond to Shakespeare's play and its meta-dramatic reflection of both romance and theatricality. To illustrate these connections, I have chosen a few scenes from Wheeldon's ballet, which I will discuss in detail. This selection includes moments from all three acts, thereby not only demonstrating the dramaturgical complexity of the piece, but also the variety of balletic structures that Wheeldon uses to navigate that complexity: solo, ensemble and duet dances.

---

29   Susan Leigh Foster, *Choreography & Narrative: Ballet's Staging of Story and Desire* (Bloomington: Indiana University Press, 1996), 254.
30   Bührle (2014), 194.

Solo

The solo has undergone a considerable artistic development in its transition from classical to non-classical theatre dance, as Laurence Louppe has observed in her *Poetics of Contemporary Dance*:

> The solo was one of the great innovations of contemporary dance in a civilisation where it had practically been lost since the solo entrances (*entrées seules*) of the *danse noble* (either in the theatre or the ballroom) in the 17th and 18th centuries. Soloists certainly existed but they always appeared at a specific moment during the ballet. The solo in academic dance of the 19th century could not be a whole or a proposition by itself. By contrast, contemporary dance made the solo one of its pinnacles, as a form best corresponding to its original project: to affirm the presence of a subject in the immediacy and wholeness both of her/his being and movement.[31]

The Winter's Tale appropriates this idea of the subject's presence in movement for the purpose of balletic storytelling. Act 1 of Wheeldon's ballet gives Leontes several solo passages to signify the emergence of jealousy and his increasing mental and physical anguish. It should be noted that these solo passages only constitute a temporal fraction of the piece as a whole, lasting only little over a minute each. They are thus even briefer than some of the already short modern dance solos of the twentieth century,[32] like Martha Graham's four-minute *Lamentation*. Unlike the stereotypical soliloquy in Shakespearean drama, all of these soli occur in the presence of other characters, who continue their scenic actions either in the background of the stage or freeze in their positions, as for example during Leontes's very first solo. Nevertheless, these solo passages convey to the spectator Leontes's growing isolation from the Sicilian court and his worsening descent into deluded paranoia, as David Fuller has aptly described for Leontes's initial outbreak of jealousy:

> Leontes' vividly choreographed agonies, with a new style of movement, more angular and contorted, opposite to the free, exuberant style of Polixenes; a distinct orchestral colouration for the agonized distortions of his jealousy (bass drum, gongs, low brass, muffled trumpets and shrieking soprano clarinets) [...]: all this induces greater sympathetic engagement with Leontes than the play's vivid but more distinctly diseased

---

31   Laurence Louppe, *Poetics of Contemporary Dance*, trans. by Sally Gardner (Alton: Dance Books, 2010), 205.
32   Ibid.

fantasies, experienced through report. The audience is taken, visually and aurally, into Leontes' mind. The scene also initiates a series of tortured solos for Leontes, so that in total the ballet gives a more extended Othello-like presentation of his experience.[33]

Similarly, Elizabeth Klett has described Leontes's first solo as a "sickness that creeps into his mind and infects his body, through the medium of the convulsive spider-like image".[34] This convulsive quality that Klett and Fuller discuss within the context of Wheeldon's ballet gains further significance if we consider it in regard to the equivalent language of its source material.

Russ McDonald has worked in depth on what he considers to be Shakespeare's late style, which he has described as "ellilptical, syntactically involuted, and flagrantly extrametrical".[35] The stylistic features typical in this late period range from ellipsis, convulsion of syntax, and parenthesis to repetitions, rapid succession of metaphors and a striking irregularity of blank verse.[36] In *The Winter's Tale*, this style can be found in several of Leontes's speeches throughout the first three acts, for example in his elaboration on the nature of "affection" in 1.2:

> Thou dost make possible things not so held,
> Communicat'st with dreams – how can this be? –
> With what's unreal thou coactive art,
> And fellow'st nothing.
>
> (1.2.141–144)

The disruption of syntactical structures is particularly apparent in this monologue as Leontes uses multiple parentheses to interrupt himself, adjust his own argument and express his incredulity at the implications of his own words, such as "may't be" (1.2.139) or "how can this be" (1.2.142). Furthermore, the concluding lines of the speech read like three short individual thought-fragments without

---

33 David Fuller, "Communities in the Theatre and in the World: Three Ballets and a Masque", in Paul Edmondson and Ewan Fernie (eds), *New Places: Shakespeare and Civic Creativity* (London: Bloomsbury, 2018), 65–82, quote 72–73.
34 Klett (2019), 144.
35 Russ McDonald, "Late Shakespeare: Style and the Sexes", in Catherine M. S. Alexander (ed.), *Shakespeare and Language* (Cambridge: Cambridge University Press, 2004), 267–287, quote 267.
36 Russ McDonald, *Shakespeare's Late Style* (Cambridge: Cambridge University Press, 2006), 33.

verbs, linked together rather crudely by the repeated "and" at the beginning of each line, as opposed to a continuous flow of argumentation.

> Thou mayst co-join with something, and thou dost –
> And that beyond commission; and I find it –
> And that to the infection of my brains
> And hard'ning of my brows.
>
> (1.2.145–148)

Further onwards in the same scene, phrases such as "inch-thick, knee-deep" (1.2.187) disrupt the iambic pentameter through the sequential use of multiple stressed syllables, highlighting the disturbing quality of Leontes's sexual fantasy on a mere acoustic level. This poetic convulsion notably differs from the more lyrical style in some of Shakespeare's earlier works, such as *Romeo and Juliet* and *Richard III*, but also from the sophisticated blank verse of the later tragedies.

If we conceive of dance as the metaphorical 'language' of ballet[37] and bear in mind the semiotic difficulties of a one-to-one analogy between dance and verbal language, we can identify in Leontes's convulsive solo passages a corresponding deconstruction of the more classically graceful ballet style that is on display for example in the pas de trois between Leontes, Hermione and Polixenes during the Prologue. This deconstruction can be exemplarily seen in Leontes's second solo as he imagines Hermione and Polixenes committing adultery behind his back. At one point, Leontes himself turns his back towards the audience, inverting the conventional frontal focus in ballet and denying spectators his facial expression as an emotional signifier. Very slowly, Leontes slides across the stage, alternately bending his knees into *grand pliés* and raising his legs angularly into *passés*, while his arms are contorting behind his slightly hunched back as if tying himself up. The passage creates a dichotomy between a classically rooted lower body in Leontes's leg movements and his non-classical upper posture, culminating in the exaggerated fifth position at the end of the sequence: Leontes's feet are turned outwards; yet, because of the extreme crossing of his legs, they actually point inwards and towards one another, before his right leg rises into a rigid *développé*. Leontes's movements thus oscillate between abandoning the classical lines altogether and heightening them to the point of hyper-distortion, establishing an aesthetic of deformity that mirrors the poetic deformity of Shakespeare's Leontes. His capability to adhere to the ideally balanced gracefulness of ballet

---

37 Bührle speaks of "Sprache des Balletts" (2014), 202.

is drastically corrupted as his adulterous suspicions take over his mind. Even when he reverts back to a more noticeably classical movement vocabulary in his later confrontation of Hermione, including "a series of *grand jetés* and powerful *développé* kicks", his movements express vengeful anger towards his wife, rather than the attempt to re-establish marital harmony.[38] The linguistic complexity of Shakespeare's Leontes and his paranoia thus re-materializes choreographically in the equally complex stylistic negotiation of (non-)classical form in Wheeldon's Leontes.

Ensemble

Wheeldon's negotiation of classical ballet form can also be seen in his varied use of ensemble and duet dances throughout the piece. The elaborate sheep-shearing feast, the longest scene in all of Shakespeare, takes up the entirety of the second act in the ballet, marking "an exuberant celebration of community",[39] in which a large part of the choreographic action is devoted to the corps de ballet after the more protagonist-focussed first act. The pastoral scenery, with a large tree as its main set piece, further emphasizes the overall contrast to the cold and stony sombreness of the Sicilian court. This stark aesthetic and dramaturgic contrast between the two acts, while potentially jarring in a Shakespeare play as discussed above, was however far from atypical in the romantic ballet of the nineteenth century, which introduced the so-called *ballet blanc* – scenes in which the female ensemble dancers as well as the prima ballerina would perform in purely white tutus. These scenes, famous examples of which are the second act of *Giselle* as well as the second and fourth acts of *Swan Lake*, would typically feature little narrative progression but focus instead on the technical virtuosity of the female dancers and thus exemplify the aforementioned divide between choreographic abstraction and dramatic enactment. Even though Perdita's prominent role somewhat resembles the position of the prima ballerina in a ballet blanc, the second act of *The Winter's Tale* displays neither the monochromatic colour scheme nor the female-only focus. Instead, it presents lively exchanges of colourfully costumed male and female dancers, alternating between individual duets by Perdita and Florizel, all-male and all-female group sections, and synchronized parts that divide the ensemble into multiple male-female pairs. All

---

38   Klett (2019), 138.
39   Fuller (2018), 73.

sections equally display fast-paced choreography that underline the natural vitality and liveliness of the pastoral setting as symbolized by the tree, including various turns (*fouettées, piqués, chaînes*) and jumps (*grand jetés, sauts de chat, changements*). These step also establish the thoroughly classical foundation of the Bohemian choreography, exemplified most purely in the duets between Perdita and Florizel whose traditional arabesque lifts and fish dives contrast noticeably with Leontes's earlier (non-)classical distortions. In doing so, the choreography of Act 2 retrieves the aesthetic innocence that was corrupted and eventually lost in Act 1. Furthermore, the scene follows the principle of the ballet blanc in that it is "almost pure dance"[40] in which the narrative, aside from the later intrusion by Polixenes, comes to a complete standstill – much like in Shakespeare's play. The most explicit case of "literalised dance"[41] in Shakespeare's *The Winter's Tale* thus becomes the perhaps most overtly conventional scene in Wheeldon's adaptation.

The structural analogy of the two scenes is also significant concerning the dramaturgic implications of dance in the play. As Steven Swarbrick has recently argued, Florizel's commentary on the dancing Perdita,

> [...] When you do dance, I wish
> A wave o'th'sea, that you might ever do
> Nothing but that, move still, still so,
> And own no other function. [...]
> (4.4.140–143),

encapsulates the play's paradoxical stance towards temporality:

> [T]ime captures the very essence of dance, [...] just as dance brings into focus the peculiarities of time. Although *The Winter's Tale* uses a number of figures to represent time's oddities – including subjects on 'crutches' and a statue of living stone – it is the image of Perdita dancing that provides the grammar of those images and, in the end, makes sense of the coexistence of 'fixture' and 'motion' – a kind of sense-making that, as Leontes rightly observes, "No settled sense of the world can match".[42]

---

40 Ibid.
41 Maria Marcsek-Fuchs, "Literature and Dance: Intermedial Encounters", in Gabriele Rippl (ed.), *Handbook of Intermediality: Literature – Image – Sound – Music* (Berlin: De Gruyter, 2015), 562–583, quote 563.
42 Steven Swarbrick, "Dancing with Perdita: The Choreography of Lost Time in *The Winter's Tale*", in McCulloch and Shaw (2019), 197–216, quote 213.

If we connect Swarbrick's reading to the earlier debate on the generic nature of *The Winter's Tale*, we can see in his co-aligning of fixture and motion yet another paradoxical simultaneity that distinguishes the romantic quality of the play. As Perdita's body assumes movement, her environment comes to a narrative halt, both in Shakespeare and in Wheeldon's ballet, a fixture of movement in an unmoving world. The fact that Wheeldon transposes this scene into one of the most traditional moments in the piece demonstrates that the intertextual relation between source and adaptation goes beyond mere thematic correspondences such as light and dark[43] and encompasses meta-reflective commentary on the forms of romance and ballet as well. Just as the dancing in Shakespeare's play serves to highlight its literary heritage in the legacy of pastoral romance, so too does the scene firmly anchor Wheeldon's piece in the framework of the romantic *ballet d'action*. Notably, one of the most prominent characters in Shakespeare's version of this scene, Autolycus, is missing from the ballet. The absence of the ballad-selling rogue cannot simply be explained with the non-verbal nature of dance, however, given that the equally word-playing Mercutio, for example, is just as present in most ballet adaptations of *Romeo and Juliet* as he is in the play itself. Rather, the omission of Autolycus underlines the "unalloyed picture of a harmonious community"[44] in Act 2 and its playful depiction of uncorrupted love both in the many unnamed ensemble couples and in the duets by Perdita and Florizel that alternate with the corps de ballet throughout.

Duet

While Wheeldon's use of the pas de deux in Act 2 echoes back to the conventional purpose of the form as a choreographic representation of romantic love as it emerged in the nineteenth century, he likewise modulates the form in striking manners to illustrate the more emotionally complex dynamics in Acts 1 and 3. The first act includes a couple of "combative"[45] duets between Leontes and Hermione, taking place prior to the latter's arrest and during her trial. These duets differ significantly from the harmonious scenes of Act 2, both in their choreographic material and dramatic effect. Here, the choreography is marked by frantic movements, tense body postures and almost aggressive-seeming lifts and pulls, showcasing two individuals who are not dancing in amicable unison *with*,

---

43   Klett (2019), 131.
44   Fuller (2018), 73.
45   Klett (2019), 138.

but full of agony *against* one another. During some of Hermione's lifts, Leontes even holds by her the shoulders, as opposed to her waist, apparently seeking to control his pregnant wife instead of supporting her. While on a performative level the two dancers must be in accord with one another to successfully execute the intricate movements, that very intricacy conveys an inherent sense of discord between them on a narrative level. This sense of discord eventually gives way to a more harmonious, albeit highly poignant portrayal of support in the couple's reconciliatory duet that concludes the ballet.

In addition to the pas de deux between Leontes and Hermione, Wheeldon adds yet another dimension to the form of duet dancing in the encounters between Leontes and Paulina, particularly their visitation of Hermione's and Mamillius's statue at the beginning of Act 3. The scene opens with Paulina holding Leontes's bowed head in her hands and guiding him towards the statue. She then performs a brief solo passage, featuring a series of arabesque steps, as Leontes kneels down in front of the statue. Once she joins him on the floor, the two perform a series of synchronized motions, at first bowing down to the statue in deference and grief and then reaching out towards it. As Leontes moves to stand by the statue, Paulina initiates another gracefully elegant solo passage including a couple of *tours jetés*, in which Leontes subsequently joins her. At the end of the scene, Leontes again kneels in front of the statue and Paulina stands upright behind him, both of their left arms extending towards the statue and their right arms pointing backwards. Aside from its melancholic tone, which had already informed their encounter at the end of Act 1 following Hermione's death, the scene is noteworthy for the lack of physical contact between Leontes and Paulina in their synchronized passages. The two characters move in synchronization with one another, establishing their grave relation as a shared devotion to the deceased Hermione and Mamillius, yet they do so without touching each other – the very element that had triggered Leontes's outbreak of jealousy and then dominated the illicit movements of the imaginary Hermione and Polixenes in Act 1. The few moments of touch consist of Paulina holding Leontes's head and placing a comforting hand on his shoulders. The elaborate lifts of the female dancer by the male dancer that typify the traditional pas de deux are absent. Even though the scene may not qualify as a fully formed pas de deux in the way that the duets between Leontes and Hermione as well as Florizel and Perdita do, the scene nevertheless opens up a new perspective on male-female duet dancing in classical ballet. It establishes through choreographic means, yet with little physical contact, a strong emotional relation between a male and a female character, yet a relation that cannot be categorized as amorous as is usually the case in classical pas de deux. This novel perspective also singles out the unique dramatic role of Paulina in the story. Not only is she the sole character 'in-the-know' of the climactic reveal at the end, but she also speaks the second-most lines in the play (behind only Leontes),[46] despite her complete absence from Acts 1 and 4. The comparison of the various duets in Wheeldon's ballet thus reveals an outlook onto the pas de deux form that is conservative and investigative at the same time.

Old Tales

In conclusion, both Shakespeare's *The Winter's Tale* and Wheeldon's adaptation for the Royal Ballet qualify as 'old tales', in more than one way. Both works contain narrative material, the origins of which partially date back as far as to the myth of Pygmalion as told in Book 10 of Ovid's *Metamorphoses*. Furthermore, both engage with this narrative material in a highly self-reflective manner, blatantly signalling their generic embeddedness into long-existing art forms while at the same time offering a decidedly contemporary perspective onto them. In Walter Cohen's words, "much of the sophistication of the romances consists in Shakespeare's deliberate recourse to a threadbare stagecraft",[47] a statement perhaps nowhere more evident than in *The Winter's Tale* with its exiting bears and living statues. Nevertheless, this threadbare quality, both in form and content, is appropriated and strategized into astounding dramaturgic effect by a playwright at the height of his generic virtuosity. This dualism of antiquated romance tropes on the one hand and contemporary early modern theatricality on the other re-materializes in Christopher Wheeldon's adaptation in a balanced negotiation between the traditional *ballet d'action* and the more self-exploratory literature ballet. While Wheeldon's *The Winter's Tale* features many hallmarks of a romantic story ballet, it likewise stages these hallmarks in a contemporary, twenty-first-century light that is reflected both in its larger form and its more minute choreographic material. The intertextual and intermedial network that this re-materialization produces should however not be mistaken as a one-sided primacy of the Shakespearean text over its non-literary adaptation. Instead, the comparison of the two brings forth a bidirectional understanding of *The Winter's*

---

46 David Crystal and Ben Crystal, "Characters by Part Sizes", *Shakespeare's Words*, https://www.shakespeareswords.com/Public/LanguageCompanion/CharactersParts.aspx, last access 5 May 2020.

47 Walter Cohen, "Shakespearean Romance", in William Shakespeare, *The Norton Shakespeare: Romances and Poems*, ed. by Stephen Greenblatt, 3rd ed. (New York: W. W. Norton, 2016), 127–138, quote 128.

Tale in which the adaptation, especially a non-verbal one, offers just as much a perspective onto the play, itself an adaptation, as vice versa. For one, the three-act structure of Wheeldon's ballet sharpens the generic hybridity of Shakespeare's play in that the tragedy of Act 1 and the pastoral comedy of Act 2 come together in Act 3, narratively and aesthetically. Furthermore, the moving pas de deux between Hermione and Leontes at the climax of Act 3 only accentuates the contrast to her lack of agency at the end of Shakespeare's play, in which she speaks no more than eight lines. The duet also reprises Hermione's trial solo from Act 1 both musically and choreographically, signalling that in this version of the story she certainly has not forgotten the injustices that Leontes committed against her. Similarly, the very last image in Wheeldon's ballet is not of the happily reunited family, but of Paulina lying down in front of Mamillius's statue, whose death in Act 1 takes place *on stage* to immense tragic effect, given the impossibility of verbal reporting in ballet. In choreographically telling a story that hinges upon the condition "if that which is lost be not found" (3.2.133–134), Wheeldon diverts attention away from what has been romantically found again towards what has been and remains irretrievably lost, even more so than Shakespeare.[48] What is gained in that loss, however, is a reinforced awareness of the vast narrative potential in generic transformations, whether from a non-dramatic to a dramatic text or, even more radically, from a literary text to movement and music. Both Shakespeare's and Wheeldon's versions of *The Winter's Tale* may be old tales that have been told since long ago, but perhaps it is that very 'oldness', in all its facets, that constitutes the unbroken fascination of telling it anew.

Zusammenfassung

Der vorliegende Aufsatz vergleicht Shakespeares Romanze *The Winter's Tale* in generischer und dramaturgischer Hinsicht mit der choreographischen Adaptation des Dramas durch Christopher Wheeldon für das Royal Ballet aus dem Jahr 2014. Der Vergleich offenbart dabei zahlreiche formtheoretische Verbindungspunkte, die über die rein inhaltliche Ebene hinausgehen. Während Shakespeares Stück von mehreren Paradoxien gezeichnet ist, welche seinen dezidiert antiquierten Status als Romanze herausstellen, überträgt Wheeldons Adaptation diese Charakteristika in das tänzerische Spannungsfeld zwischen dem romantischen *ballet d'action* des neunzehnten Jahrhunderts und dem Literaturballett des zwanzigsten und einundzwanzigsten Jahrhunderts. Beide Werke lassen sich somit als

---

48   Klett (2019), 140; Fuller (2018), 73.

old tales lesen, die formal wie inhaltlich das Erbe tradierter Kunstformen wie der antiken und mittelalterlichen Romanze oder des klassischen Handlungsballetts fortführen, diese aber zugleich auch aus zeitgenössischer Perspektive hinterfragen und erneuern. Zudem eröffnet Wheeldons Ballett einen aus adaptationstheoretischer Sicht interessanten rückwärts gerichteten Blick auf Shakespeares frühneuzeitliches Drama.

Von Shakespeare zum Ballett und zurück – Der intermediale Blick auf eine polydirektionale Shakespeare-Adaption: Christopher Wheeldons *The Winter's Tale*[1]

MARIA MARCSEK-FUCHS

> When you do dance, I wish you
> A wave o'th' sea, that you might ever do
> Nothing but that, move still, still so,
> And own no other function.
> (4.4.140–143)[2]

Christopher Wheeldon konsultierte 2014 Nicholas Hytner mit der Frage, welches Shakespeare-Stück der renommierte Theater- und Filmregisseur für eine Ballettadaption empfehlen würde, das noch nicht mehrfach choreographiert worden war. Es sollte zum Shakespeare-Jubiläum nämlich keine Neufassung von *Romeo und Julia*, *Der Widerspenstigen Zähmung* oder des *Sommernachtstraumes* geben, die im Schatten von Größen wie Kenneth MacMillan, John Cranko, Frederick Ashton oder George Balanchine stünde. Hytners Antwort war ebenso treffend wie überraschend: "Well, *The Winter's Tale* has proved really challenging for directors. I've got a feeling it might work for dance. I think some of the problems may sort themselves out if there's no one actually talking!"[3] Doch was genau soll es in Shakespeares Spätwerk sein, das im Tanz leichter umzusetzen ist: die

---

1 Dieser Aufsatz ist Prof. Dr. Dieter A. Berger (Universität Regensburg) zu seinem Geburtstag in Dankbarkeit gewidmet. Seine Shakespeare-Vorlesungen, Seminare, gerade auch zu den Komödien, und seine Publikationen zum Humor waren und sind eine große wissenschaftliche Inspiration.

2 William Shakespeare, *The Winter's Tale*, hg. von John Pitcher. The Arden Shakespeare, Third Series (London: Bloomsbury, 2010). Alle weiteren Zitate folgen dieser Ausgabe.

3 Lyndsey Winship, "Interview: Jeté, Pursued by a Bear: Dancing *The Winter's Tale*", *The Guardian*, 7. März 2016, https://www.theguardian.com/stage/2016/mar/07/the-winters-tale-christopher-wheeldon-shakespeare, letzter Zugriff 29. September 2020.

König Leontes zerfleischende Eifersucht, der aus Jonsons Masque *Oberon* übernommene Tanz oder die am Ende zum Leben erwachende Statue Hermiones? Und wie genau soll man ein so komplexes, mehrere Genres verbindendes und durch narrative Elemente geprägtes Theaterstück in Tanz übertragen, wenn das Wichtigste fehlt, nämlich die vieldeutige und bilderreiche Sprache Shakespeares? Französische Symbolisten am Ende des neunzehnten Jahrhunderts, unter ihnen Bewunderer von Diaghilevs *Ballets Russes*, hätten bei letzterer Frage auf das bedeutungsgenerierende, der Dichtung ebenbürtige Potential des Balletts hingewiesen: Paul Valéry beschrieb die Kunstform des Tanzes beispielsweise als "quite simply *a poetry that encompasses the action of living creatures in its entirety*".[4] Stéphane Mallarmé ging sogar so weit, den Künsten eine symbiotische, sich gegenseitig ergänzende Beziehung zuzuschreiben:

> [T]he ballerina *is not a girl dancing*; [...] but a metaphor which symbolizes some elemental aspect of earthly form: sword, cup, flower, etc. [...], *she does not dance* but rather, with miraculous lunges and abbreviations, writing with her body, she *suggests* things which the written work could *express* only in several paragraphs of dialogue or descriptive prose. Her poem is written without the writer's tools.[5]

Nun wird die Frage, wie sich Christopher Wheeldon als Choreograph zusammen mit dem Komponisten Joby Talbot und dem Bühnenbildner Bob Crowley Shakespeares *The Winter's Tale* nähern sollten, noch komplizierter, wenn man bedenkt, dass bei einer Tanzadaption in der Regel nicht nur ein linearer Adaptionsprozess, sondern mehrere palimpsestartig[6] überlagerte Kreationsprozesse in verschiedenen Medien bzw. Kunstformen gleichzeitig stattfinden. Das ist zwar bei einer Inszenierung und einer Verfilmung ähnlich, doch wie so häufig im Ballett bedingen sich auch in Wheeldons Fall Tanz und Musik gegenseitig und lassen sich für die Tänzer*innen sowie für die Betrachter*innen nicht voneinander trennen. Alle Ausdrucksformen ergänzen und überlagern sich, ähnlich wie

---

4 Paul Valéry, "Philosophy of Dance", in Marshall Cohen und Roger Copeland (Hg.), *What Is Dance? Readings in Theory and Criticism* (Oxford: Oxford University Press, 1983), 55–65, Zitat 64–65; Hervorhebung im Original.
5 Stéphane Mallarmé, "Ballets", in Cohen und Copeland (1983), 111–115, Zitat 112; Hervorhebungen im Original.
6 Linda Hutcheon benutzt die Metapher des Palimpsests wie folgt: "we experience adaptations (as adaptations) as palimpsests through our memory of other works that resonate through repetition with variation." (Linda Hutcheon, mit Siobhan O'Flynn, *A Theory of Adaption*, 2. Aufl. [New York: Routledge, 2013], 8.)

es William Butler Yeats so treffend in seinem Gedicht "Among School Children" ausdrückt: "O body swayed to music, O brightening glance, / How can we know the dancer from the dance?"[7] Kompositionsprozesse laufen dialogisch, Rezeptionsprozesse sogar gleichzeitig ab. Das heißt für Wheeldons *The Winter's Tale*: Der Choreograph, der Komponist und Bühnenbildner sowie alle Tänzer*innen sind gleichzeitig zunächst Interpreten des Shakespeare-Textes; in Absprache und Zusammenarbeit adaptieren sie diesen in ihr jeweiliges Medium. Die Ergebnisse werden dann durch alle Beteiligten (Tänzer*innen, Musiker*innen und den gesamten Theaterapparat) zu einer künstlerisch symbiotischen und gleichzeitig plurimedialen Interpretation des Shakespeare-Textes zusammengeführt und auf der Bühne präsentiert.

In diesem Aufsatz wird anhand der Fusionierung zweier Ansätze, nämlich der eher medial orientierten Intermedialitätsforschung mit der eher kontextuell angedachten neueren Adaptionsforschung, die Vielschichtigkeit der Signifikationspotentiale aufgezeigt, die speziell bei einer Ballettadaption eines Shakespeare-Werkes entstehen.[8] Dazu wird Christopher Wheeldons *The Winter's Tale* zunächst in zwei Schritten als Adaption gelesen: nämlich in Anlehnung an Linda Hutcheons Differenzierung zuerst als Prozess und dann als Produkt,

---

7   William Butler Yeats, "Among School Children", in William Butler Yeats, *The Major Works: Including Poems, Plays, and Critical Prose*, hg. von Edward Larrissy (Oxford: Oxford University Press, 2001), 113–115, Zitat 113.

8   Für eine Gegenüberstellung der Adaptionsansätze siehe Thomas Leitch (Hg.), *The Oxford Handbook of Adaptation Studies* (Oxford: Oxford University Press, 2017); Dennis Cutchins, Katja Krebs und Eckart Voigts (Hg.), *The Routledge Companion to Adaptation* (London: Routledge, 2018); und v. a. Jørgen Bruhn, Anne Gjelsvik und Eirik Frisvold Hanssen (Hg.), *Adaptation Studies: New Challenges, New Directions* (London: Bloomsbury, 2013). Meinem Aufsatz liegt ein weiter Medienbegriff zugrunde, wie ihn z. B. Werner Wolf in seinen Publikationen verwendet. Zu Intermedialität vgl. im Allgemeinen auch Irina Rajewsky (z. B. *Intermedialität* [Tübingen: Francke, 2002]) und im Speziellen zu Intermedialität und Tanz Maria Marcsek-Fuchs, *Dance and British Literature: An Intermedial Encounter (Theory – Typology – Case Studies)* (Leiden: Brill, 2015). Auch wenn es natürlich kontextuell angedachte Intermedialitätskonzepte und medial semiotisch konzipierte Adaptionsansätze gibt, ist für diesen Aufsatz die Gegenüberstellung dieser beiden Pole für die Analyseperspektive wichtig. Hier wird davon ausgegangen, dass die eher im europäischen Raum angesiedelte Intermedialitätsforschung tendenziell den medialen Charakter eines Medienwechsels (Rajewsky) bzw. einer intermedialen Transposition (Wolf) im Blick behält, während sich in der neueren Adaptionsforschung der kontextuelle Ansatz immer weiter durchsetzt. Eine Fusionierung der Konzepte findet sich z. B. bei Regina Schober, "Adaptation as Connection – Transmediality Reconsidered", in Bruhn et al. (2013), 89–112.

wobei sich beide Perspektiven gelegentlich überlagern.[9] Während es im ersten Teil um die von Hutcheon kontextuell angedachten Fragen geht, um das 'Wer', 'Wann' und 'Wie' des Entstehungsprozesses, steht der zweite Teil ganz im Sinne der inhaltlichen und intermedial ausgerichteten Besprechung des Balletts. In einem dritten Schritt folgt dann der Blick auf das kinetische Werk über einen Interpretationsaspekt der Shakespeare-Forschung. Damit soll gezeigt werden, dass die verschiedenen Perspektiven auf die Ballettadaption nicht nur eine Vielzahl an Interpretationsmöglichkeiten zu Wheeldons Werk eröffnen, sondern auch weiterführende, intermedial orientierte Denkimpulse für die Re-Lektüre von Shakespeares *The Winter's Tale* bereithalten.

Bevor wir nun in diesen drei Schritten tief in die Welt von Wheeldons Ballettwerk eintauchen, seien hier noch drei abschließende Gedanken zu dem der Diskussion zugrunde liegenden Verständnis von Adaption angeführt: erstens zum Begriff und den damit zusammenhängenden Implikationen für das Ballettwerk, zweitens zum dialogischen bzw. polylogen Verhältnis von Prä- und Posttext und drittens zur Rolle von Shakespeare-Adaptionen im Kontext der Rezeptionsgeschichte. In der Auseinandersetzung mit Adaptionsprozessen geht es hier nicht um die Suche nach Abweichungen zum Shakespeare-Text, um diese dann im Sinne des hochproblematischen Fidelity Criticism als sekundär oder im Sinne eines medienspezifischen Ansatzes als gegensätzlich auszuarbeiten. Adaption wird vielmehr mit Jørgen Bruhn als dialogischer Prozess verstanden. Bruhn schreibt dazu: "Any rewriting or adaptation of a text is always influencing the original work and even the most 'loyal' or repetitive adaptation imaginable is bound to be unsuccessful in terms of copying the original."[10] Er schlägt vor, sowohl Original wie auch Adaption als Quelle für den jeweils anderen Text zu betrachten: "[W]e should study *both* the source and result of the adaptation as two texts, infinitely changing positions, taking turns being sources for each other in the ongoing work of the reception in the adaptational process."[11] Diese gegenseitige Beeinflussung weitet sich gerade auch bei Tanzadaptionen auf weitere mediale Bereiche aus, die zudem noch den Rezeptionsprozess sowohl der Tanzschaffenden als auch des Publikums mit in den Blick nehmen. Regina Schober führt unter Einbeziehung von Konzepten wie Netzwerk und Rhizom[12] mediale und kontextuelle Perspektiven zusammen:

---

9   Hutcheon (2013), 7–8.
10 Jørgen Bruhn, "Dialogizing Adaptation Studies: From One-Way Transport to a Dialogic Two-Way Process", in Bruhn et al. (2013), 69–88, Zitat 70.
11 Ibid., 73. Hervorhebung im Original.
12 Schober (2013), 100–101.

> I suggest that adaptations are embedded in complex intermedial, cultural and perceptional configurations shaped by dynamic and reciprocal interactions. [...] I propose a view of intermediality that emphasizes the dynamic, reciprocal and relational nature of media adaptations as opposed to traditional approaches built on the presupposition of clear-cut medial borders and unidirectional cause and effect relationships.[13]

Eckart Voigts beschreibt den gesamten Prozess der Adaption als "reception in action",[14] eine Beobachtung, die auf Wheeldon ebenso zutrifft wie auf den Komponisten, den Bühnenbildner, eine*n jede*n Tänzer*in und das Publikum, sei es im Theater, bei Screenings in Kinos weltweit oder aber auch auf der privaten Couch beim Genuss der DVD.

Das plurimediale Netzwerk: auf dem Weg zu einer Shakespeare-Choreographie

Im ersten der drei Schritte steht der Entstehungsprozess von Wheeldons *The Winter's Tale* als Quelle für Interpretationsansätze im Mittelpunkt. Dabei geht es um den Adaptionsansatz, die Bedeutung von literarischen Genres und plurimedialen Quellen sowie die multimodale Komposition. Jede Adaption im Allgemeinen, und jede tänzerische im Besonderen, erfordert als erstes Grundsatzentscheidungen. Soll das Werk, um mit Julie Sanders' Unterscheidung zu sprechen, eher eine textnahe Adaption oder eine sich offen zur Distanz bekennende Appropriation werden?[15] Im Fall Wheeldon zeigt der Blick in den Kontext des Entstehungsprozesses und auf den Titel, dass hier – sicherlich auch aus Prestigegründen – ein wiedererkennbarer Bezug zu Shakespeares *The Winter's Tale* beabsichtigt war, gerade vor dem Hintergrund des Jubiläumsjahres 2014. Bei einer der viel gezeigten öffentlichen Proben zu Wheeldons *The Winter's Tale* betont der Choreograph die Bedeutung der ikonischen Shakespeare-Adaptionen des Royal Ballet, die ihn in seiner Arbeit geprägt haben, allen voran Frederic Ashtons *The Dream* (1964) und Kenneth MacMillans *Romeo and Juliet* (1964) – letzteres Werk

---

13 Ibid., 91.
14 Eckart Voigts, "The Performative Self: Reception and Appropriation under the Condition of 'Spreadable Media' in 'Bastard Culture'", *Anglistik: International Journal of English Studies* 24:2 (2013), 151–168, Zitat 161.
15 Julie Sanders, *Adaptation and Appropriation*, 2. Aufl. (London: Routledge, 2016).

wiederum inspiriert durch ein Vorgängerstück, und zwar John Crankos Version der "star-crossed lovers".[16] Wheeldons, Ashtons und MacMillans Shakespeare-Ballette haben vieles gemeinsam, allem voran den Entstehungskontext. All diese Werke wurden für das Royal Ballet für ein Shakespeare-Jubiläum choreographiert und dienten der Zelebrierung sowohl des Barden als auch der Kompanie. Gleichzeitig sollten so die Autorität und das Renommee der Kompanie sowie deren Stellung in der britischen Kultur untermauert und sichtbar gemacht werden. Elinor Parsons betont in ihrem Artikel zu drei anderen Shakespeare-Balletten die Doppelrolle dieser Werke, die sowohl Shakespeare als auch das Royal Ballet als Kulturträger und Grundlage britischer Identitätsbildung feiern.[17] Seit 1995 ist Wheeldons *The Winter's Tale* nach seiner *Alice*-Adaption (2011) allerdings erst das zweite abendfüllende Handlungsballett des Royal Ballet. Wheeldons Entscheidung ist insofern bezeichnend, da lange Zeit abstraktere Werke bevorzugt wurden und die Neukreation eines Handlungsballetts den Choreographen eher in Rechtfertigungsnot brachte. Zwar wurden und werden die ikonischen Shakespeare-Adaptionen von Ashton, Cranko, MacMillan und Balanchine an renommierten Fünf-Sparten Häusern regelmäßig aufgeführt und gehören zum Aushängeschild eines jeden Stars, doch war bislang bei neueren Werken Originalität durch Abstraktion gefragt. Umso mehr lastete auf Wheeldons Entscheidung für Shakespeares Spätwerk ein mehrfacher Erfolgsdruck, zum einen durch die Wahl des Stücks und zum anderen durch die Wahl des Ballettgenres – beides wurde aber letztendlich mit großem Erfolg belohnt. Ähnlich wie schon bei Shakespeare mehrere Prätexte als Inspiration dienten, allen voran Robert Greenes *Pandosto* (1588), so spielten auch 2014 sowohl intermediale als auch intramediale Quellen im Schaffensprozess eine prägende Rolle: Neben Shakespeares Text, inklusive seiner eigenen Hauptquelle, erkennt man zusätzlich zu den schon genannten Vorbildern auch choreographische Bezüge zu Crankos *Romeo und Julia* und *Eu-*

---

16 Sowohl auf der DVD als auch auf YouTube finden sich etliche Interviews mit Christopher Wheeldon, die Aufschluss über den Entstehungsprozess seiner Shakespeare-Adaption geben. Im Folgenden beziehe ich mich bei Referenzen zum Ballett auf folgende DVD: *The Winter's Tale*. Chor. Christopher Wheeldon, Comp. Joby Talbot, Bühnenbild Bob Crowley, Perf. Laura Cuthbertson, Edward Watson, et al. Royal Opera House in Cooperation with the National Ballet of Canada, 2015. Zu Interviews zum Entstehungsprozess vgl. "The Royal Ballet Rehearse *The Winter's Tale*", *Royal Opera House YouTube Channel*, 30. Januar 2018, https://www.youtube.com/watch?v=OFNcQHlJfro, letzter Zugriff 28. September 2020.

17 Elinor Parsons, "Therefore Ha' Done With Words: Shakespeare and Innovative British Ballets", in Lynsey McCulloch und Brandon Shaw (Hg.), *The Oxford Handbook of Shakespeare and Dance* (Oxford: Oxford University Press, 2019), 387–404, Zitat 388.

gen Onegin sowie zu Wheeldons eigener *Alice*-Adaption.[18] Insofern teilt Wheeldon mit Shakespeare die mutige Überblendung von Tradition und Innovation: Shakespeare hat neben der Wiederaufnahme von schon in früheren Werken behandelten Themen wie z. B. Eifersucht (*Othello, Cymbeline*) auch eine nicht ganz risikolose Mischung von Genres gewagt, indem der Tragödie der ersten drei Akte und der ungewöhnlich langen, mit Musik und Tanz durchsetzten pastoralen Komödie des vierten Aktes die damals umstrittene Gattung der Tragikomödie folgt.[19] Auch für den Choreographen und Komponisten sowie für alle beteiligten Kreativen des Balletts stellt der Aspekt der Gattungsmischung eine Herausforderung dar, welche durch choreographische, musikalische, licht- und kostümtechnische Motivbildungen gelungen umgesetzt wurde. Während am königlichen Hof von Leontes in Sizilien elegante Schwere, dunklere Farben und schwermütigere Bewegungen den Eindruck prägen, wirkt Böhmen in Bild, Musik und Tanz leicht und bunt. In der Mitte der Bühne steht ein Lebensbaum ("tree of life"[20]) vor blauem Hintergrund, auf der Bühne sind Live-Musiker im Stil fahrender Künstler in die Handlung eingebunden und das *sheep shearing* steht als folkloristisches, handlungsarmes Fest des ländlichen Tanzes im starken Kontrast zur emotionsgeladenen Tragödie des ersten Teils. Erstaunlicherweise hat sich Wheeldon dagegen entschieden, Shakespeares eigenen intermedialen Tanzbezug einzubinden, nämlich den Tanz der Satyren (4.4.347 SD).

Die Entstehung von Wheeldons *The Winter's Tale* stellt ein Netzwerk an intermedial verwobenen und multidirektional wirkenden künstlerischen Prozessen dar: Drei Adaptionsprozesse laufen in der Regel gleichzeitig bzw. kurz versetzt nacheinander ab und bedingen sich gegenseitig: Shakespeares *The Winter's Tale* wird vom Choreographen Christopher Wheeldon in Bewegung, vom Komponisten Joby Talbot in eine musikalische Ballettkomposition und vom Bühnenbildner Bob Crowley in ein Bühnenbild übertragen – ein kreatives und symbiotisches Dreiergespann, das schon bei Wheeldons *Alice*-Adaption ein plurimediales

---

18 Zu weiteren Beispielen und Anwendungen dieser Analyseperspektiven siehe Maria Marcsek-Fuchs, "*Romeo and Juliet* Re-danced: Choreographic Remakings of Shakespeare's Tragedy", in Rüdiger Heinze und Lucia Krämer (Hg.), *Remakes and Remaking: Concepts – Media – Practices* (Bielefeld: Transcript, 2015), 131–152. Zu theoretischen Überlegungen zur Intermedialität von Text und Tanz siehe Marcsek-Fuchs (2015).

19 Vgl. den Eintrag zu "Tragicomedy" in Michael Dobson und Stanley Wells (Hg.), *The Oxford Companion to Shakespeare*, 2. Aufl. (Oxford: Oxford University Press, 2015).

20 Luke Jennings, "*The Winter's Tale* Review – 'a Ballet to Keep'", *The Guardian*, 13. April 2014, https://www.theguardian.com/stage/2014/apr/13/winters-tale-christopher-wheeldon-british-ballet, letzter Zugriff 10. November 2020.

Meisterwerk geschaffen hatte. Dabei ist ein Erlebnis der Kollaboration und Stile entstanden, das auch diese Produktion prägt. Wie Wheeldon und Talbot im Interview im Rahmen einer Live-Probe[21] darlegten, ging der Impuls der Übertragung vom Dialog des Choreographen mit dem Komponisten aus. Nach eingängiger Textarbeit durch dramatisierende Lektüre im heimischen Wohnzimmer und nach der theaterwissenschaftlichen Beratung durch Nick Hyntner[22] legten Wheeldon und Talbot zunächst den übergreifenden Handlungsstrang und dann die Mikrostruktur des Stücks fest. Die Auswahl der zu übertragenden Handlungsmomente fußte laut Talbot auf der Frage, welche dieser Momente sich in Bewegung und welche sich besonders gut mittels musikalischer Komposition darstellen lassen.[23] Wheeldon begründete die Wahl von Shakespeares Spätwerk mit der Tiefe der im Stück dargestellten Gefühle sowie mit den Handlungsmomenten "of operatic size".[24] In diesem Prozess kommt es zwangsläufig zu Kürzungen und Veränderungen, denn während Shakespeare auch faktische Informationen vermitteln kann, basiert die Ausdrucksweise im Ballett auf Suggestion und kinetischem Ausdruck von Gefühlen.[25]

Vom Narrativen zum Kinetischen

Edward Watson, der tänzerische Star, auf dessen Persönlichkeit als Künstler Wheeldon die Rolle des Leontes zugeschnitten hat, bemerkt im *Making of* treffend, dass Szenen, die bei Shakespeare im Stil eines Botenberichtes dialogisch erzählt sind, nicht tänzerisch dargestellt werden können.[26] Das betrifft die Kindheitserzählung über das Prinzenpaar durch Camillo und Archidamus gleich zu Beginn in Akt 1 (1.1.22–31) ebenso wie die Nachricht von Mamillius' Tod in Akt 3 (3.2.141–144). Erzähltes muss auf der Bühne gezeigt und tänzerisch dargestellt werden, was wiederum Prozesse des Umschreibens sowie auch neue Interpretationsansätze zum Stück mit sich bringt. Ganz im ursprünglichen Sinn

---

21 "The Royal Ballet Rehearse *The Winter's Tale*" (2018).
22 Judith Mackrell, "Royal Ballet: *The Winter's Tale* Review – 'A Game-Changer for Wheeldon'", *The Guardian*, 11. April 2014, https://www.theguardian.com/stage/2014/apr/11/royal-ballet-winters-tale-review-christopher-wheeldon, letzter Zugriff 29. September 2020.
23 "The Royal Ballet Rehearse *The Winter's Tale*" (2018).
24 "From Page to Stage: Dancing *The Winter's Tale*", Extra-Feature auf der DVD zu Wheeldons Ballett (2015).
25 Vgl. Parsons (2019), 387.
26 "From Page to Stage" (2015).

des Wortes 'Choreographie'[27] schreibt Wheeldon in Analogie zur Exposition des Shakespeare-Stücks einen tänzerischen Prolog, welcher durch Talbot musikalisch als Ouvertüre konzipiert wird. Er etabliert dadurch die Kindheitsgeschichte wie auch die Dreiecks- und Freundschaftsbeziehung zwischen Leontes, Polixenes und Hermione. Sowohl im Programmheft als auch im visuellen Paratext der DVD ist dieser Teil nicht wie gewöhnlich als Ouvertüre, sondern als Prolog tituliert, was die Nähe des Balletts zum Theaterstück signalisiert. Wie Wheeldon und Talbot beide betonen, spielt der Aspekt der Zeit – ein bedeutendes Motiv des Shakespeare-Stücks – und die Dynamik bei der wechselseitigen Dramaturgisierung und Komposition des Stückes eine wesentliche Rolle. Nebenhandlungen und wichtige Figuren wie die des Autolycus werden weggelassen, dafür aber ein Schmuckstück zum Wiedererkennungsmerkmal von Perdita als Leontes' Tochter eingeführt. Beide Künstler stellten sich die Frage, wie lange welcher Moment musikalisch und tänzerisch dauern und wo die Schwerpunkte liegen sollten. Dabei verlief dieser mal musikalische, mal choreographische Adaptionsverlauf nicht nur wechselseitig, sondern es wurden zunehmend mehr Akteure mit ihren eigenen Interpretationen in den Prozess einbezogen. So trugen neben dem Bühnenbildner Bob Crowley auch die Tänzer*innen durch ausführende und szenische Beiträge zu den Adaptionsvorgängen bei. Der Choreograph und mit ihm die Tänzer*innen erhalten durch die Kraft des Tanzes, auf nonverbale Art und Weise Bedeutung zu stiften, die Rolle von (Ko)Autor*innen. Der Choreograph und die Interpreten 'schreiben' an den Text 'zurück'. In ihrer Bedeutung als Inspiratoren ähneln die ersten Tänzer*innen einer neuen Ballettadaption den ersten Schauspielern Shakespeares, so wie Richard Burbage Inspiration für Shakespeares Schaffen war. In diesem Zusammenhang ist es interessant, sich das Casting von Hermione und Paulina im Ballett anzusehen. Laura Cuthbertson in der Rolle der Königin war schon Inspiration für Wheeldons Alice, und Zenaida Yanowsky, jetzt Paulina, war 2011 als beängstigende Queen of Hearts zu erleben. Wheeldon beschreibt die drei weiblichen Hauptfiguren in *The Winter's Tale* als starke Frauengestalten. Für ein Publikum, das die zwei erwähnten Stars schon in *Alice* gesehen hat, wird die Stärke der Figuren über die intramediale Referenz und zusätzlich über die Ähnlichkeit des musikalischen, choreographischen und tänzerischen Stils unterstrichen, was interessierte Shakespearerezipient*innen zu der Frage führen kann, wie sich die Stärke der Frauen im Prätext äußert.

---

27 Die Etymologie des Wortes Choreographie stammt aus dem Griechischen und verweist auf den Akt des Tanz-Schreibens; vgl. hierzu Debra Craine und Judith Mackrell (Hg.), *Oxford Dictionary of Dance* (Oxford: Oxford University Press, 2004).

Alternativer Prolog – Interpretativer Epilog

Der Blick auf Wheeldons *The Winter's Tale* als Produkt des oben skizzierten polydirektionalen Adaptionsprozesses bietet die Möglichkeit, nun weitere Ansätze für Auslegung und Weiterschreiben aufzuzeigen. Im folgenden Schritt werden daher einige für die Interpretation sowohl des choreographischen als auch des dramatischen Textes relevante Aspekte im Ballettwerk, dem Adaptionsprodukt, beleuchtet. Das schließt die Diskussion der Übertragung von narrativen Elementen, Theaterkonventionen und Bühnenanweisungen mit ein. Im Anschluss daran werden zwei Beispiele für die inhaltliche und intermediale Weiterschreibung des Shakespeare-Stücks skizziert.

Wheeldon fasst die Exposition und damit den narrativen Einstieg des Stückes, wie er aus dem Dialog zwischen Archidamus und Camillo hervorgeht, choreographisch auf eine ganz besondere Art und Weise zusammen, bindet dabei sogar den genealogischen Ablauf von Großvater über den Vater (Leontes) zum Sohn (Mamillius) ein und leitet dann in die Darstellung der Beziehung von Leontes, Polixenes und Hermione über. Der Anfang lässt an einen Renaissance-Reigen denken, aus dem zunächst die jungen Prinzen als befreundete Kinder heraustreten, bevor der Tanz dann sanft in dem Duett der erwachsenen Könige mündet. Die königliche Dignität wird durch die Performanz der professionell tanzenden kleinen Ballettschüler unterstrichen. Da Wheeldon (ganz im Sinne von Jean-Georges Noverre) narrative Elemente immer anhand inhaltlich, emotional oder musikalisch motivierter Bewegungen des Ballett- und Modern-Dance-Kanons darstellt und – mit Ausnahme des gewollt tänzerisch abstrakter gehaltenen pastoralen Aktes – Pantomimisches mit virtuosen Passagen verbindet, werden auch Übergänge hinzugeschrieben, die zur Motivation der Figuren beitragen, so z. B. eine Szene, in der Hermione dem Jugendfreund und Gast Polixenes vorgestellt wird. In einem Pas de quatre (einem Tanz zu viert) etabliert Wheeldon die Beziehung sowohl der zwei Herren zu Hermione als auch die des Polixenes zu Mamillius, eine Leerstelle im Shakespeare'schen Prätext. Ganz besonders interessant wird hier die Überblendung von Ballettkonventionen und Figurenkonstellation. Während es im Gegensatz zu Greenes *Pandosto* bei Shakespeare keinen klaren Eifersuchtsgrund gibt und Leontes' Rage (fast) ausschließlich in seiner sich immer weiter steigernden Imagination von Betrugsszenarien begründet ist, wirkt Wheeldons Pas de trois mit den wiederholten Hebefiguren, bei denen einmal Leontes, einmal Polixenes die in der Szene zunehmend schwangere Hermione kunstvoll durch die Luft hebt, widersprüchlich. Die Musik, die Szene und auch der Tanz sollen zwar freundschaftliche Harmonie ausstrahlen, nur verschwimmen die Grenzen zwischen Freundschaft und Liebe durch das Ballettvokabular des Partnertanzes zunehmend. Damit wird Hermiones Bemerkung noch mehrdeutiger, zumal das Wort *friend* laut Annotation sowohl Freund als auch Liebhaber bedeuten kann:[28]

> Hermione: [...] Why, lo you now, I have spoke to th' purpose twice.
> The one for ever earned a royal husband;
> Th' other for some while a friend.
> [*Gives her hand to Polixenes*]
> (1.2.106–107)

Besonders interessant war Talbots Frage, wie denn Eifersucht, seiner Meinung nach das am wenigsten kinetische der Gefühle, in zwei Medien übertragen werden kann, denen Bewegung inhärent ist.[29] Der Höhepunkt einer festlichen Tanzszene des gesamten Hofes markiert den entscheidenden Moment, der die Leerstelle in Shakespeares Text zum Grund für den Ausbruch von Leontes' Eifersucht füllt: Das Pas de trois kommt zum plötzlichen Stillstand, alle werden in Schatten getaucht, und nur Leontes steht im Spot. In diesem Moment legt Hermione beider Hände auf ihren schwangeren Bauch, um die Bewegung des ungeborenen Babys mit ihnen zu teilen. Die verbale Ambiguität im Shakespeare-Text und die Bühnenanweisung werden durch eine Klarheit schaffende Geste ersetzt. Wheeldon gelingt es darüber hinaus, Talbots sehr eindringlicher Musik durch die Mischung von Ballett und Modern-Dance-Elementen Dramatik zu verleihen. Besonders auffallend dabei ist seine Übertragung der Spinnenmetapher (2.1.40–45), die Leontes im Text dazu nutzt, um seinem Ekel Ausdruck zu verleihen. Im Ballett wird die Spinne durch die Hand so dargestellt und geführt, als ob sie vom Magen quer durch den Körper zum Rückenmark laufen würde.

Im Gegensatz zu der Ambiguität der Liebesverhältnisse in der Choreographie des Prologs sind die erotischen Beweise nun ganz klar nur in Leontes' Gedanken verortet und wird Leontes' Unsicherheit, "May't be / Affection?" (1.2.137–138), plurimedial amplifiziert: Das Zusammenspiel von Licht und Dunkelheit, die Einbindung von anzüglichen Statuen in die Choreographie und der Wechsel von mal lyrisch freundschaftlichem, mal erotischem Pas de deux lassen dies sichtbar werden. Denn während die Statuen von hinten an künstlerische Darstellungen der griechischen Mythologie erinnern, kommen, sobald Leontes sie bei seinen Eifersuchtsattacken nach und nach umdreht, laszive Szenen zum Vorschein. Dieses Oszillieren zwischen Realität und Imagination wird durch Licht- und

---

28 Shakespeare (2010), 158, FN 108.
29 "The Royal Ballet Rehearse *The Winter's Tale*" (2018).

Choreographiewechsel eindeutig gekennzeichnet. Immer dann, wenn es hell ist, flanieren Hermione und Polixenes gemeinsam tänzerisch wie durch ein Museum, doch sobald nur noch Leontes im Spot steht, zeigt das Schattenspiel des flanierenden Paares Szenen eines Liebesaktes. Dem Publikum wird so im wahrsten Sinne vor Augen geführt, dass dies nur in Leontes' Imagination passiert.

Komplizierter ist die Umsetzung von starken Frauenfiguren. Zwar gibt es, wie oben bereits angedeutet, die Möglichkeit, Hermione und Paulina über die Besetzung und das choreographische Schrittmaterial stärker zu zeichnen. Da jedoch Frauen in den starren Konventionen der Ballettgeschichte häufig die strahlende, aber untergeordnete Rolle eines nur durch Heirat erlösbaren Opfers hatten (so beispielsweise in *Schwanensee*, *Giselle* oder *Dornröschen*), was sich auch in der Rollenverteilung des Paartanzes widerspiegelt, ist es nicht leicht, weibliche Rollen als die Stärkeren tänzerisch darzustellen, zumal das Publikum eben diese Paartanzchoreographien auch im einundzwanzigsten Jahrhundert von einem Ballett erwartet. Dennoch schafft es Wheeldon durch die Solos von Hermione und Paulina, welche wie im Fall von Leontes die Tanzstile mischen, Stärke auszudrücken. Der Moderne Tanz in der Tradition von Mary Wigman, Gret Palucca und Martha Graham hatte sich Anfang des zwanzigsten Jahrhunderts von den Zwängen eines starren Ballettvokabulars befreit, und zwar durch Soli, barfüßigen Tanz und die Konzentration auf ausdrucksstarke, auf Improvisation beruhende Bewegungen. Wheeldon nutzt an markanten Stellen den aus dem modernen Tanzvokabular bekannten freieren Ausdruck, um emotionale Tiefen und Stärken, vor allem auch der weiblichen Figuren, zu unterstreichen. Paulinas Soli zur Überzeugung bzw. Verurteilung von Leontes sind dafür eindeutige Beispiele. Auch Hermione bekommt einen sehr aussagekräftigen Moment, in dem klar wird, dass Wheeldon sie zwar analog zum Shakespeare-Text in der unschuldig verurteilten Opferrolle verortet, ihr aber auch Würde verleiht. Im Moment der Verhaftung reicht eine einzige kleine Handbewegung Hermiones aus, um die Soldaten davon abzuhalten, sie zu berühren.

Die zwei größten Herausforderungen an jeden Regisseur und noch viel mehr an jeden Choreographen sind gleichzeitig die berühmtesten: nämlich die Bühnenanweisung *"Exit, pursued by a bear"* (3.3.57 SD) und die zum Leben erwachende Statue Hermiones in Akt 5, Szene 3 des Shakespeare-Textes. Beide sind Leerstellen, deren Füllung große Auswirkungen für die Interpretation sowohl der Adaption als auch des Prätextes hat. Im Anschluss an die Erscheinung des Bären und den Tod von Antigonus wandelt sich das Shakespeare-Stück von einer Tragödie zu einer pastoralen Komödie. Wheeldon selbst warnte für seine Adaption vor einer komischen Interpretation und wählte daher durch die Einbindung des Puppenspielkünstlers Basil Twist ein eher romanzenhaft magisches Bild. Der

Bär wird durch ein sehr leichtes wehendes Seidentuch repräsentiert, das ähnlich einer Meereswelle Antigonus verschlingt. Der Tanz der Figur und der 'Tanz' des Tuches verschmelzen Schönheit und Grauen.

Wheeldons und Crowleys Lösung für die Statuenszene wurde schon viel besprochen[30] und ist bemerkenswert, ähnlich wie das Ende des Stückes: Anstatt einer einzelnen Statue sieht Leontes, nachdem Paulina den Vorhang beiseite gezogen hat, Mutter und Sohn, doch nur Hermione kommt auf Paulinas Anweisung "'Tis time; descend; be stone no more" (5.3.99) herab. Eine Uminterpretation erfolgt auch, wenn Hermione zwar am Anfang abweisend erscheint, es dann aber sie ist, die den vor Reue zusammengekauerten Leontes an ihre Hochzeit zurückdenken lässt und aufrichtet. Die Entwicklung bis dahin erinnert stark an das Flehen Eugen Onegins in John Crankos gleichnamiger Choreographie, die am Ende in der Zurückweisung Onegins durch Tatiana mündet. Auch wenn bei Wheeldon ein ähnlicher Ausgang möglich scheint, endet das Ballett im Gegensatz zum Shakespeare-Text in einem friedlichen Familientableau, nachdem Hermione Perdita anhand ihres Schmuckstücks erkannt hat. Obwohl gemäß der Ballettkonventionen zuvor eine Hochzeitsszene für das junge Paar hinzugeschrieben wird und das Familientableau einen glücklichen Ausgang des Stücks suggeriert, schafft es Wheeldon, die Klammer zur Tragödie des ersten Teils zu schließen. Leontes versucht nun, auch den Sohn herabsteigen zu lassen. Der traurige Nachklang, dass eben doch nicht alles verziehen werden kann, wird durch Paulinas leichtes Kopfschütteln und ihre einsame Schlusspose vor der Statue des Jungen auf den Punkt gebracht. Zwar wurde das Schweigen von Hermione, die im Theaterstück nur Perdita, nicht aber Leontes adressiert, ins scheinbar Positive umgeschrieben, doch mit dem umgestalteten Schluss wurde ein noch tragischerer Schlusspunkt gesetzt als im Text durch die Verheiratung Paulinas mit Camillo (5.3.135–146). Die Betrachtung der jeweiligen Dénouements in Drama und Ballett bieten so gegensätzliche Interpretationsansätze an.

Der Blick von der Forschung auf die Bühne – und zurück

Die bisherige Betrachtung von Christopher Wheeldons *The Winter's Tale* einerseits als Adaptionsprozess, andererseits als Adaptionsprodukt soll abschließend um einen weiteren Aspekt ergänzt werden: nämlich die gleichzeitige Re-Lektüre

---

30 Vgl. Judith Buchanan, "*The Winter's Tale*'s Spectral Endings: Death, Dance and Doubling", in Sarah Hatchuel und Nathalie Vienne-Guerrin (Hg.), *Shakespeare on Screen:* The Tempest *and* Late Romances (Cambridge: Cambridge University Press, 2017), 110–132.

sowohl des Shakespeare-Textes als auch der Ballettadaption mittels einer anglistischen Interpretationsthese. Während erstere Strategie natürlich den Alltag der Shakespeare-Forschung ausmacht, eröffnet letztere einen noch genaueren Blick auf das Ballett. Man kann die kinetische Ballettadaption mit dem dramatischen Prätext Shakespeares, bei gelegentlicher Heranziehung der einen oder anderen Inszenierung oder einem anderen Werk der Ballettliteratur, in Verbindung bringen.[31] Alternativ kann man die Adaption mit den Analysekriterien der eigenen Disziplin betrachten: im Fall von Wheeldons *The Winter's Tale* also entweder aus tanzkritischer oder aus tanzwissenschaftlicher Sicht. Was aber zu einer noch vertiefteren Lektüre des Balletttextes beitragen kann, ist das Herantragen spezifischer, aus der anglistischen Shakespeare-Forschung stammender Interpretationsansätze an den plurimedialen Balletttext. Die Shakespeare-Forschung gewährt eine neue Perspektive auf die Auslegung des Stücks im Ballett, welche wiederum den Blick auf den Shakespeare-Text schärft. Hier ein Beispiel: W. H. Auden hielt im April 1947 eine Vorlesung zu Shakespeares *The Winter's Tale*.[32] Darin nahm er die Frage der Unschuld und damit die Figuren der Hermione und des Mamillius in den Blick, welche schuldlos Gewalt erfahren.[33] Auden schreibt: "People suffer in the play, and one must consider the degree to which their suffering is innocent and the degree to which it is voluntary. Mamillius's suffering is wholly innocent, quite involuntary, and his death brings Leontes to his senses."[34] Nimmt man nun die Perspektive von Mamillius ein und bedenkt, was das Kind erleben muss, wird die Tragödie, die sich an Leontes' Hof abspielt, umso grausamer. Dies beginnt schon mit den zunächst harmlos scheinenden Fragen des Vaters:

> *Leontes:* [...] – Mamillius, – Art thou my boy?
> *Mamillius:* Ay, my good lord.
>
> (1.2.117–119)

---

31 Zu Christopher Wheeldons *The Winter's Tale* siehe Elizabeth Klett, "The Concord of this Discord: Adapting the Late Romances for the Ballet Stage", *Borrowers and Lenders: The Journal of Shakespeare and Appropriation* (2019); Linsey McCulloch, "Shakespeare and Dance", *Literature Compass* 13:2 (2016), 69–78.
32 W. H. Auden, *Lectures on Shakespeare*, hg. von Arthur Kirsch (Princeton: Princeton University Press, 2000), 284–294, Zitat 288.
33 Ibid.
34 Ibid.

Auch einem so jungen Kind müssen die Reaktionen des Vaters zunehmend verwunderlich anmuten, wenn dieser dann weiterfragt: "Art thou my calf?" oder "Will you take eggs for money?", und anschließend sinniert, ob der Junge ihm ähnlich genug sei, um sein Sohn zu sein, bevor er sich an seine eigene Kindheit erinnert (1.2.127–161). Auch während er sich mit seinem sechsjährigen Sohn unterhält, bestärken Leontes' Gedanken ihn zunehmend in der Überzeugung, von Hermione betrogen worden zu sein, und so schwingt ein ständiges und sich zunehmend steigerndes sexuelles Innuendo in sogar harmlosesten Fragen und Andeutungen mit. Umso furchtbarer ist es für den Jungen, nicht nur die wachsende und für ihn unverständliche emotionale Zerrissenheit seines Vaters mitzuerleben, sondern anschließend auch mitten im glücklichen Spiel und Geschichtenerzählen aus den Armen der Mutter gerissen zu werden – für immer, wie sich später herausstellt:

> *Leontes*: Bear the boy hence: he shall not come about her.
> Away with him, and let her sport herself
> With that she's big with, [*to Hermione*] for 'tis Polixenes
> Has made thee swell thus. [*Mamillius is taken away.*]
> (2.1.59–62)

Die Tragödie um den Jungen kulminiert während der Gerichtsverhandlung, als Leontes seine eigene Frau und Mutter seines Sohnes trotz ihrer Unschuldsbekundung und des positiven Orakelurteils verurteilt. Genau in diesem Moment wird Leontes und dem Hof durch einen Bediensteten mitgeteilt, dass Mamillius aus Sorge um seine Mutter an gebrochenem Herzen gestorben sei:

> *Servant*: O sir, I shall be hated to report it.
> The prince your son, with mere conceit and fear
> Of the queen's speed, is gone.
> *Leontes*: How, 'gone'?
> *Servant*: Is dead.
> (3.2.140–144)

Nun lässt sich fragen, wie Wheeldon die Unschuld des Jungen und die durch Leontes' zügellose Eifersucht verursachten und schmerzhaft tragischen Tod des Kindes in seinem Ballett darstellt. Dabei fallen gleich drei medienspezifische Aspekte in den Blick, die gleichzeitig eine Kommentarfunktion erfüllen und weitere Interpretationsansätze für den Shakespeare-Text anbieten: Dies betrifft erstens das Casting des Jungen, zweitens die tänzerische Weiterschreibung von

Figurenkonstellationen und drittens den choreographischen Umgang mit einem Botenbericht.

1. Auch in Bühneninszenierungen von *The Winter's Tale* spielt die Entscheidung, wie Mamillius besetzt wird, eine bedeutungsgenerierende Rolle. Wenn das Kind von einem filigranen Mädchen gespielt wird, wie der neunjährigen Ellen Terry in Charles Keans Inszenierung aus dem Jahr 1856,[35] einer jungen Frau im Rollstuhl, wie Emily Bruno in Gregory Dorans Inszenierung von 1999, oder von einem Jungen wie jüngst in der RSC-Inszenierung,[36] dann werden mit dieser Entscheidung weiterführende Impulse und Interpretationen sowohl der Figur als auch der mit ihr zusammenhängenden Handlungsstränge angeregt. Wheeldons Mamillius wird von einem Jungstudenten der Royal Ballet School gespielt, dessen Anmut, schauspielerisches Talent und tänzerische Technik zur tragischen Darstellung der Rolle beitragen. Gerade die für das Ballett so charakteristische Haltung schenkt der Figur aristokratische und gleichzeitig ästhetische Züge und unterstreicht dadurch Camillos Feststellung im Text: "It is a gallant child." (1.1.38)
2. Der spielerische Tanz von Mamillius mit Polixenes zu Beginn des Balletts, welcher während eines Pas de deux des Königspaars stattfindet, etabliert eine Beziehung, die im Text nur implizit angedeutet wird, wenn nämlich Polixenes von seiner Liebe zu seinem eigenen Sohn schwärmt (1.2.164–169).
3. Wheeldon überhöht die Tragik von 3.2 dadurch, dass Mamillius in der Ballettfassung das Urteil, dargestellt durch ein auffällig durch Brutalität gekennzeichnetes Pas de deux der Eltern, mit einem Teddy in der Hand miterleben muss, bevor er in Paulinas Armen stirbt. All diese choreographischen Umschreibungen unterstreichen tänzerisch und dramaturgisch die Rolle des Mamillius, der im Text nur wenige Zeilen sprechen darf. Zwar hat er

---

35 Vgl. Richard Foulkes, "Lewis Carroll, Ellen Terry and the Stage Career of Menella 'Minna' Quin: 'A Very Kind and Christian Deed'", in Katherine Cockin (Hg.), *Ellen Terry, Spheres of Influence* (London: Pickering & Chatto, 2011), 93–106, 93. Siehe auch Katherine E. Kelly, "The After Voice of Ellen Terry", in Cockin (2011), 65–76, 68.

36 Für diese Rolle wurden vier Jungen des Silhouette Youth Theatre aus Northhampton ausgewählt, einem Jugendtheater, das sowohl als Kooperationspartner als auch Talentschmiede für die Royal Shakespeare Company dient. Vgl. "Casting Announced for the RSC's 2020 Production of *The Winter's Tale*", in *What's On: Warwickshire's Essential Entertainment Guide*, https://www.whatsonlive.co.uk/warwickshire/news/casting-announced-for-the-rscs-2020-production-of-the-winters-tale/46937, letzter Zugriff 29. September 2020; "Production History: *The Winter's Tale* Production History in Pictures", *Royal Shakespeare Company*, https://www.rsc.org.uk/the-winters-tale/past-productions/production-history, letzter Zugriff 29. September 2020.

im Ballett auch keine Soli, doch die choreographische Inszenierung führt zu einer Aufwertung des Jungen, dessen zentrale Rolle für Leontes' Umkehr im Shakespeare-Text kaum zu unterschätzen ist und die im Schlussbild des Balletts noch einmal hervorgehoben wird.

Kinetische Paratexte als Symbiose von Text, Interpretation und Tanz

Nachdem eine Vielzahl an Interpretationsansätzen beleuchtet wurde, bleibt als kleine Perle noch der Ausblick in einen Intermedialität und Adaption verbindenden Paratext: Im Rahmen der Shakespeare-Feierlichkeiten 2016 präsentierte das Royal Ballet einen ungewöhnlichen, als Probe markierten Filmclip,[37] welcher im Ballettsaal Leontes' Monolog und Solo als plurimediale Symbiose zeigte. Der Schauspieler Geoffrey Streatfield rezitierte Shakespeares Zeilen, während der Tänzer Edward Watson Wheeldons Adaption der Szene präsentierte. Dieser Film war Teil eines gemischten Beitrags der Royal Opera, welcher Wheeldons *The Winter's Tale* mit Ausschnitten aus MacMillans *Romeo and Juliet* und den Verdi-Opern *Falstaff* und *Otello* kombinierte – für sich genommen eine interessante Vereinigung von intra- und intermedialen Bezügen zu Shakespeare-Adaptionen. Die Simultanität von Wheeldons Choreographie und Shakespeares gesprochenem Text visualisiert und kondensiert den palimpsest- und netzwerkartigen Adaptionsprozess von Wheeldons *The Winter's Tale* in einem kurzen plurimedialen Erlebnis. Geoffrey Streatfield und Edward Watson zeigen mit ihrem kurzen Beitrag im Kleinen, was sich bei dem intermedialen Vergleich von Shakespeares und Wheeldons *The Winter's Tale* im Großen beobachten lässt, nämlich wie sich beide Ausdrucksformen symbiotisch ergänzen, wie sich Aussagen über die jeweiligen Subtexte und medialen Eigenheiten multiplizieren und wie durch das vertiefte Studium der Einzelheiten im Ballett die von Symbolisten geschätzte Mehrdeutigkeit des Tanzes auch die Re-Lektüre des Shakespeare-Texts mit neuen Blickwinkeln bereichert. Nun wäre es an einer/m Musikwissenschaftler*in und weiteren Kenner*innen des Theaterapparates, die Feinheiten der anderen Medien an diese Studie heranzutragen, die die Perspektiven der Anglistik und Tanzwissenschaft entwickelt hat.

---

37 "Ballet vs Theatre – Two different interpretations of Shakespeare's *Winter's Tale* (The Royal Ballet)", *Royal Opera House YouTube Channel*, 10. Mai 2016, https://www.youtube.com/watch?v=IMu_tIli6Qg, letzter Zugriff 29. September 2020.

Summary

William Shakespeare's *The Winter's Tale* is a romance that combines tragedy with comedy, dramatic with narrative elements, and verbal complexities with music and dance. It is a play full of ambiguities and gaps, difficult to stage, and even more so to adapt, especially in cases where the most central means of communication is missing: Shakespeare's words. This paper studies Christopher Wheeldon's ballet version as an adaptation that fuses several processes of medial interpretation into a multidirectional web of signification. By combining intermedial and contextual approaches, and by studying Wheeldon's *The Winter's Tale* (2014) both as a process and as a product of adaptation (Hutcheon), the readings reveal how the interpretations that were gained from this multidirectional view not only provide insight into the complexities of this Shakespeare ballet, but also show how the findings reflect back onto Shakespeare's play.

Theaterschau

Shakespeare auf deutschsprachigen Bühnen

2019/2020

Spektakel und Drastik: Shakespeare im Norden

Die Neuinszenierungen der Spielzeit auf den norddeutschen Theatern sind leider im Lockdown verschwunden, bevor wir Gelegenheit fanden, sie zu besuchen. Zwei neue Produktionen in den großen Hamburger Häusern – *Hamlet* im Thalia Theater und *Falstaff* in der Staatsoper – widmeten sich Extremen des Shakespeare'schen Figurenensembles: dem gern zum vergeistigten Grübler stilisierten dänischen Prinzen einerseits und dem Lebemann und Frauen verführenden englischen Ritter andererseits. Beide Inszenierungen werden wir im Rückgriff auf das (über)regionale Presseecho kurz skizzieren.

Jette Steckels Inszenierung der *Hamlet*-Tragödie (Übersetzung: Frank-Patrick Steckel) beginnt bereits im Foyer, in dem Rosenkrantz (Julian Greis) und Guildenstern (Björn Meyer) das digitale Streaming des bevorstehenden Amtsantritts Claudius' (Bernd Grawert), des neuen Königs von Dänemark und Hamlets Onkel, vorbereiten. Auf der Bühne tritt Prinz Hamlet (Mirco Kreibich) mit dem Kopf in einer Kugel auf, die er zwar später ablegt, doch rollt im Verlauf des Stücks eine riesige schwarze Kugel – vielleicht eine "Sonne der Depression" (Peter Laudenbach, *Süddeutsche Zeitung*, 2.3.2020) oder ein "toter Planet" (Stephan Grund, *Die Welt*, 27.1.2020) – auf die Bühne (Florian Lösche), wo sie den Raum verengt und die Figuren bedrängt. Das Stück schließt mit einem waffenlos vollzogenen, händisch-gestischen Fechtkampf zwischen Hamlet und Laertes (Rafael Stachowiak). Dabei entkommt der skrupellose Machtmensch Claudius – abweichend von der Vorlage – der Todesspirale am Hof. Erweitert wird die Inszenierung durch Passagen aus Heiner Müllers *Hamletmaschine* und vielfältige musikalische Akzente (Samuel Savenberg und Sängerin Dominique Dillon de Byington).

Die Rezensentinnen und Rezensenten feiern einhellig die herausragende Leistung Mirco Kreibichs als Hamlet, und auch die anderen Rollen ernten größtes Lob. Darüber hinaus differenziert sich die wohlwollende Gesamtbewertung sehr wohl aus: Irene Bazinger ist entzückt vom anspielungsreichen "Kinderspielspektakel", das sich selbstironisch dem Medium des Theaters überlässt und so eine "amüsant-elegante Inszenierung" schafft (*Frankfurter Allgemeine Zeitung*, 26.1.2020), währen Katja Weise, ebenfalls beeindruckt von dem, "was Schauspiel kann", einen "aufwühlenden, aber auch anstrengenden Abend" erlebt hat (*NDR.de – Kultur*, 24.1.2020). In dieser Runde erscheint Stefan Grund zwar nicht als Spielverderber, moniert aber, die Regisseurin habe sich "verzettelt" (*Die Welt*, 27.1.2020). Peter Laudenbach schließlich sieht hier die "Effektvirtuosin" Steckel am Werk, die unterhaltsam eine "Enzyklopädie der Theaterstile" der letzten Jahrzehnte durchspiele, ohne dabei allerdings größeres Interesse für das komplexe und widersprüchliche Seelenleben Hamlets zu zeigen, das traditionell als Kern und Rätsel der Figur beschrieben wird (*Süddeutsche Zeitung*, 2.3.2020).

An der Staatsoper inszenierte Calixto Bieito *Falstaff*, Guiseppe Verdis letzte Oper, für deren Libretto Arrigo Boito Szenen aus Shakespeares Falstaff-Darstellung in den *Merry Wives of Windsor* und den Historienstücken *Henry IV*, Teil 1 und 2 geschickt verwoben hat. Auf der Hamburger Drehbühne (Susanne Gschwender) bestimmen eine Kneipe und eine Wohnung einschließlich deren Obergeschoss (Parallelhandlung im Bett) das Gesamtbild. Jedoch steht der Pub nicht im historischen Windsor, sondern im heutigen Dublin, und der Ritter (Ambrogio Maestri, Bariton) trägt beim Austernschlürfen Turnschuhe, Jeans und ein gelbes T-Shirt (Kostüme: Anja Rabes). Die beiden von Falstaff hintergangenen Frauen, Alice Ford (Maija Kovalevska, Sopran) und Meg Page (Ida Aldrian, Mezzosopran), unterstreichen ihren Protest mit einem großen Transparent; aber auch andere Einfälle, wie etwa die gläserne Toilette, auf der Falstaff sein Geschäft und Nanette, Fords Tochter, einen Schwangerschaftstest macht, erscheinen nicht gerade subtil. In einem mitternächtlichen Verkleidungsspektakel ist die drastische Demütigung des halbnackten Falstaff bald verwunden und die Ehe zwischen Nanette und ihrem Liebhaber Fenton wird gestiftet.

In der Kritik herrscht Einigkeit über die das Ensemble weit überragende Leistung Ambrogio Maestris, einem der derzeit führenden Interpreten der Rolle des Falstaff, der zudem die dafür gern gesehene Körperfülle mitbringt. "Trotz einiger Stressmomente [...] ein imponierendes Portrait", befindet Jürgen Kesting (*Frankfurter Allgemeine Zeitung*, 21.1.2020), und Elisabeth Richter urteilt: "Maestri [bewies] mit kernig-rundem Bariton, exzellenter Textverständlichkeit und nur minimalen Premierenunsicherheiten auch in Hamburg seine Klasse" (*Deutschlandfunk*, 20.1.2020).

Highlights in der Darstellung der Frauenrollen und des Ehemanns Ford werden differenziert gewürdigt, ebenso wie das Orchester, das allerdings unter der Leitung des Düsseldorfer Generalmusikdirektors Axel Kober die Geschwindigkeit zu sehr anzieht. Dagegen fällt die Bilanz für die Schauspielregie deutlich verhaltener aus. Sören Ingwersen erklärt das buhende Publikum damit, dass Bieito es wage, "in die Abgründe einer Gesellschaft zu blicken, die ein Opfer braucht, um sich selbst feiern zu können" (*Concerti.de*, 19.1.2020). Dagegen beklagen Richter und Kesting, man habe dem Falstaff den Geist ausgetrieben. Richter nennt die Inszenierung "deftig und temporeich", doch dabei "klischeehaft und szenisch banal", wiewohl sie im Mitternachtsspuk ein Moment von Poesie erkennt (*Deutschlandfunk*, 20.1.2020). "Banalität", punktuell "hochnotpeinlich", sieht auch Kesting, der wiederum gerade im "missratenen Massentreiben" der

Schlussszene Verluste ausmacht. "Von der rhythmischen Symmetrie der Szenen und von dem mehrschichtigen szenischen Geschehen ist nichts zu erkennen" (*Frankfurter Allgemeine Zeitung*, 21.1.2020).

UTE BERNS

Kann das Theater nach Hause kommen? *Romeo und Julia* im Chat, *Hamlet* kurz vor dem Lockdown, Berliner Shakespeare *on demand* und Stimmen aus leeren Theatern

Am Mittwoch, dem 11. März, wurde vom Kultursenator veranlasst, dass im Rahmen des Lockdowns zur Eindämmung der Corona-Pandemie alle öffentlichen Theater Berlins bis zum 19. April geschlossen bleiben sollten – und bekanntlich blieben sie noch wesentlich länger geschlossen. Vereinzelt wurde zunächst noch ein Angebot auf den kleineren Bühnen aufrechterhalten, aber auch dies musste bald eingestellt werden. Betroffen war davon auch das Festival Internationale Neue Dramatik (FIND), das an der Berliner Schaubühne stattfinden sollte und in diesem Jahr erstmals bereits vor seinem Start ausverkauft war (*Tagesspiegel*, 13.3.2020). Nach dem ersten Schock entwickelten die Häuser unterschiedliche Strategien, um die Kommunikation mit dem Publikum aufrechtzuerhalten. Abgesehen von Informationen über soziale Netzwerke gab es bald etliche Streamingangebote.

Auch Shakespeare war so gelegentlich *on demand* verfügbar. In der Regel waren diese Angebote allerdings eher ein Blick zurück als ein Versuch, das aktuelle Repertoire online anzubieten. Unter den Shakespeare-Konserven waren z.B. die zwei bekannten Shakespeare-Inszenierungen von Thomas Ostermeier an der Schaubühne: *Hamlet* (2008) und *Richard III* (2015). Eine Ausnahme stellt eine Produktion des Jungen DT dar, die laut Website motiviert war durch den Wunsch, weiter zu proben. In nur zwei Wochen entstand so *Zoom in: Romeo + Julia*, eine kleine Webserie in 13 Folgen mit einer Gesamtlänge von 49 Minuten (https://www.deutschestheater.de/junges-dt/programm/junges-dt-live-und-digital/zoom-in-romeo-julia/). In kurzen Ausschnitten werden zentrale Passagen als Videochats à drei bis vier Minuten inszeniert. Das Projekt verzichtet praktisch komplett auf Kostüme, Requisiten und Bühnenbild, aber auch weitgehend auf digitale Effekte. Durch den Rahmen des Chatfensters blicken wir in Privatwohnungen oder folgen den Figuren, wie sie sich mit wackliger Handykamera einsam durch Zimmer oder Straßen bewegen. Sprache und Mimik treten auf diese Weise stärker hervor als in einer konventionellen Inszenierung. Die letzte Folge der Miniserie kann als knappe Illustration des Grundproblems von Theater in Corona-Zeiten gelesen werden: Auf dem geteilten Bildschirm folgen wir Romeo (rechts) und Julia (links), die sich, von einem Voiceover begleitet, mit suchendem Blick durch ein fast leeres Berlin bewegen. Schließlich bemerkt man, dass sich die Umgebung der beiden Bildschirme zunehmend ähnelt, bis die zwei Liebenden sich endlich in einem Park gegenüberstehen. Die Perspektive wechselt; wir sehen nun beide vereint in einem Rahmen. Sie gehen aufeinander zu, doch bevor der Sicherheitsabstand unterschritten werden kann, verschwimmt das Bild – die Liebenden sind vereint, aber nur im Pixelmatsch des verlöschenden Bilds. Keine Umarmung, kein Applaus, das Stück ist aus.

Andere Berliner Theater haben die Pandemie ebenfalls mehr oder minder explizit zum Thema künstlerischer Darstellungen gemacht – wenn auch ohne Shakespeare-Bezug. Besonders eindrucksvoll ist eine kleine Monolog-Reihe des Berliner Ensembles (*Stimmen aus einem leeren Theater*; https://www.berliner-ensemble.de/stimmen-aus-einem-leeren-theater). In jeweils ca. zehnminütigen Clips machen einzelne Schauspielerinnen und Schauspieler das gesamte Haus zur Bühne. Die Kamera folgt ihnen durch leere Gänge, über die Bühne und durch Türen, die einem sonst verschlossen bleiben. Die Körper und Stimmen der Schauspielerinnen und Schauspieler vermitteln dabei fast schon beklemmend intensiv die Leere und Stille des verwaisten Hauses. Insbesondere Kathrin Wehlisch gelingt es so tatsächlich, einen – aller Distanz zum Trotz – in das Theater hineinzuziehen und über das Theater nachdenken zu lassen. Vordergründiger ist der Kommentar auf die aktuelle Lage in einer knapp sechzigminütigen Quarantäne-Variante von *Die Pest* nach dem Roman von Albert Camus (Deutsches Theater Berlin, Premiere der ursprünglichen Fassung: 15.11.2019). Am 15.6.2020 wurde diese Version online zugänglich gemacht. Ähnlich wie bei der Monolog-Reihe des BE folgen wir Božidar Kocevski, der auch regulär für das Stück besetzt ist, durch die leeren Flure und Säle des DT. Allerdings beginnt dieses Stück bereits vor dem Eintritt in das Theater. Am Eingang durchläuft man so die mittlerweile nur allzu vertrauten Rituale: Kocevski unterbricht kurz seinen Vortrag, setzt mit routinierten Handgriffen seine Maske auf, desinfiziert seine Hände, grüßt den Pförtner und tritt ein. Nachdem er durch diese Schleuse getreten ist, setzt Kocevski seine Maske wieder ab und setzt sein Spiel fort. Er spricht alle Rollen selbst, jeweils mit leichten Wechseln in Tonart, Akzent und Gestik, mal selbstvergessen lustwandelnd, mal direkt der Kamera zugewandt. Es ist erstaunlich, welche Intensität Camus' unerbittlich sachliche Schilderung der Ausbreitung der Pest dabei entfaltet. "Corona ist nicht die Pest", wie die Überschrift einer Rezension zur Aufführung des Stücks auf der improvisierten Open-Air-Bühne des DT feststellt (*Die Zeit*, 15. 6. 2020), doch mit dieser beeindruckenden Lesung drängen sich diverse Parallelen auf (Isolation, Stillstand, Kontrollverlust und der Widerstreit zwischen Egoismus und Solidarität), die die Vorstellung zu einem beeindruckenden 'Theatererlebnis' machen. Nicht zuletzt der Schluss stimmt nachdenklich, indem er gewissermaßen einen Blick in die Zukunft wirft. Am Ende scheint die Pest besiegt, die Menschen vergessen und machen weiter wie zuvor. Wird die Corona-Krise das deutsche Theater und die deutsche Gesellschaft nachhaltig beeinflussen?

Parallel zu den verschiedenen Online-Angeboten bemühten sich viele Theater, ein Angebot unter freiem Himmel zu schaffen. DT und BE nutzten dazu ihre Innen- bzw. Vorhöfe und boten so zumindest für ein kleineres Publikum Live-Theater. Die Deutsche Oper verlegte die Premiere von Wagners *Rheingold* (geplant für den 12. Juni) und spielte eine angepasste Variante des Stücks auf dem hauseigenen Parkdeck. Die auf mehrere Termine verteilten 1000 Tickets waren innerhalb weniger Minuten ausverkauft (*Frankfurter Allgemeine Zeitung* 11. 6. 2020). Und auch die Angebote des Sprechtheaters waren offenbar stark nachgefragt. Shakespeare unter freiem Himmel boten allerdings nur solche Theater, die ihr Programm ohnehin für die Freiluftbühne konzipiert hatten. Die Shakespeare Company Berlin zeigte (voraussichtlich zum letzten Mal im Natur-Park Schöneberger Südgelände) unter anderem *Was ihr wollt* und *Maß für Maß – Coronaversion*. Beide Stücke sind allerdings schon länger im Programm. Eine *Othello!*-Inszenierung ist noch im Entstehen begriffen, war aber zumindest schon als Leseversion zu sehen/hören.

Mit den zwischenzeitlichen Lockerungen der Beschränkungen nahmen die Theater auch in Berlin wieder einen minimalen Spielbetrieb in ihren (baulich angepassten) Räumlichkeiten auf. Bereits im Mai, lange vor Wiedereröffnung, hatte das BE Fotos des Zuschauerraums mit ausgedünnten Sitzreihen veröffentlicht – die Bilder gingen um die Welt und wurden zum Symbol für Theater in Corona-Zeiten. Aus 700 wurden 200 Sitzplätze. Einige Rezensentinnen und Rezensenten können den neuen Gegebenheiten durchaus etwas abgewinnen. Claus Löser schreibt etwa über die Saisoneröffnung im Gorki Theater: "Unter Sicht- und Fläzaspekten ist das zugegebenermaßen gar nicht so unangenehm, zumal man im Sog dieser berührenden erzählerischen Inszenierung [von *Berlin Oranienplatz*], in der es um Einsamkeit geht, ohnehin auf sich [zurück] geworfen wird" (*Berliner Zeitung*, 29. 8. 2020). Auch die Angst vor einem dünnen Applaus bleibt laut Löser an diesem Abend unbegründet. Das Schrumpfen des Publikums wird durch eine "gesteigerte Verbindlichkeit" und "herzliche Wucht" kompensiert: "Ein schönes Ritual ist diese Klatscherei, wie einem bei dieser Gelegenheit mal wieder auffällt" (*Berliner Zeitung*, 29. 8. 2020).

Schwieriger ist es, der Ausdünnung des Programms etwas Positives abzugewinnen. So feierte beispielsweise vor dem Lockdown eine sehr interessante Shakespeare-Inszenierung Premiere: Christian Weises *Hamlet* am Gorki Theater. Nach der Premiere am 1. Februar 2020 gab es gerade einmal drei weitere Aufführungen des Stücks, bevor der Betrieb eingestellt und das Programm komplett umstrukturiert wurde. Dabei hatte das Stück viel Anklang bei der Presse gefunden, nicht zuletzt aufgrund eines raffinierten Bühnenbilds von Julia Oschatz, von dem praktisch alle Rezensionen schwärmen. Katrin Pauly beschreibt es als "eine windschiefe Pappkulissen-Welt [...], die so einfallsreich, so detailbewusst, so liebevoll gestaltet ist, dass man sich gar nicht sattgucken kann" (*Berliner Morgenpost*, 2. 2. 2020). Ulrich Seidler hebt die erstaunliche Vielfalt des Spiels hervor: "Die Spielweise in dieser [...] Bilderbuchwelt wechselt zwischen Stummfilm, Stand-up, Puppentheater, Musical, Drama und gefühlsechter Großaufnahme à la Hollywood" (*Berliner Zeitung*, 2. 2. 2020). Irene Bazinger meint, Weise sei eine "eindrucksvoll intelligente und amüsante Interpretation geglückt, so hauptstädtisch und modern wie historisch informiert und bedacht" (*MOZ*, 8. 2. 2020). Insgesamt sei es "[e]in schöner, vollgestopfter, verspielter dreistündiger Abend, an dem man das Theater entdecken und lieben lernen kann", schreibt Seidler (*Berliner Zeitung*, 2. 2. 2020). Vom Spiel und Ideenreichtum ist auch Fabian Wallmeier überzeugt, "[d]och wo [Weise] eigentlich hin will, bleibt [für ihn] unklar" (*rbb24*, 2. 2. 2020).

Das Gorki spricht, in Anspielung auf seine neue Spielstätte auf dem Vorplatz, selbstbewusst und selbstironisch von einer "Containervariante" des großen Klassikers. Auch die Ankündigung im Spielzeitheft ist geprägt von Ironie: "[M]it dieser Leuchtturmproduktion sollte das Gorki endlich in der deutschen Hochkultur ankommen [...]. Eigentlich. Aber leider war die große Bühne nicht mehr zu haben, und da die Stars der Reihe nach abgesprungen sind [...], musste auf das Gorki-Ensemble zurückgegriffen werden." So erläutert das Heft dann auch erst am Ende und eher beiläufig, worum es in dem Stück geht bzw. gehen soll: "In Shakespeares Komödie *Hamlet* über die Unmöglichkeit, ein richtiges Leben im falschen zu führen, geht es um den amerikanischen Filmregisseur Horatio, der mit Berliner Schauspieler*innen versucht einen düsteren Film über die ideologischen Abgründe des schief vereinigten Deutschland zu drehen." Nicht alle Rezensentinnen und Rezensenten goutieren die Ironie, nicht alle verzeihen der Inszenierung ihre 'losen Fäden', wie Seidler es in Anspielung auf die zahlreichen gestrickten Requisiten formuliert. Barbara Behrendt klagt, "Shakespeares Stücke sind zwar viel zu brillant, als dass eine Theatermode sie kaputt machen könnte. Dass Weise im *Hamlet* nun aber die deutsche Wiedervereinigung finden möchte, ist doch ziemlich abenteuerlich. [...] Als hätten sich ein paar Theaternerds zum Brainstorming getroffen und sich dann von ihren Lieblingsgags nicht mehr trennen können" (*rbbKultur*, 3.2.2020). Svenja Liesau als berlinernder Hamlet findet jedoch auch bei Behrendt Anklang. Man schaue ihr gerne zu, so Behrendt: "Ihren Hamlet gibt sie als anstrengenden Charakter, der zu viel redet, zu viele böse Witze macht, zu viel im Kopf hat und mit seinen Extravaganzen allen auf die Nerven geht" (*rbbKultur*, 3.2.2020). Offenbar wurden hier Prioritäten gesetzt. Wer auf einen vordergründig politischen und grüblerisch-philosophischen *Hamlet* hoffte, wurde wohl enttäuscht. Im Zentrum standen nach einhelliger Meinung der Rezensentinnen und Rezensenten metadramatische Elemente, die Lust am Spiel sowie Shakespeares Witz und dessen popkulturelles Potential. Peter Laudenbach zeigt allerdings zugleich, dass eine politische Lesart des Stücks durchaus möglich ist – auch wenn er dies eher als eine typisch berlinerische Form von Nostalgie abtut: In Berlin am Gorki-Theater, "wo man sich gerne am Old-School-Linksradikalismus wärmt [...], ist Hamlet hier nicht unbedingt ein Prinz, sondern die Tochter von Karl Marx. Sein Mörder Claudius (Aram Tafreshian) erweist sich als Karrierist und Funktionär, der mit Vollbart und nach hinten gespachtelten Haaren eine gewisse Ähnlichkeit mit August Bebel aufweist: Wer hat uns verraten? Sozialdemokraten wie dieser Realpolitiker Claudius. Marx hat die Ehre, von Ruth Reinecke gespielt zu werden, womit die Sympathien klar verteilt sind" (*Süddeutsche Zeitung*, 3.2.2020). Wo Laudenbach eine Ähnlichkeit mit Bebel sieht, sehen andere eine Ähnlichkeit mit einem großen Hamlet-Darsteller: Kenneth Branagh. Beide Assoziationen lassen die metatheatrale Dimension der Aufführung erkennen. "Dass Hamlet hier von einer Frau gespielt wird, spielt übrigens [...] gar keine Rolle", meint Behrendt (*rbb24*, 2.2.2020).

Traut man Peter Laudenbach, kann man Weises *Hamlet* trotz aller Zweifel vielleicht dennoch als eine "Leuchtturmproduktion" sehen: "Auch mit diesem Hamlet-Comic erweist sich das Haus als das derzeit vitalste, anarchischste, spielfreudigste Theater Berlins, mindestens" (*Süddeutsche Zeitung*, 3.2.2020). Denkwürdig ist die Inszenierung in jedem Fall, denn für Ruth Reinecke (als Geist von Hamlets Vater) war es nach über vierzig Jahren am Gorki die letzte Premiere. Liest man Kritiken zur Aufführung (erschienen im Februar), kann man streckenweise meinen, es handele sich schon um eine 'Coronaversion': "Ein Trommelwirbel und los geht's – aber erst einmal für lange Zeit nur per Video: Die gesamte Bühnenfront ist an diesem *Hamlet*-Abend im Container des Maxim-Gorki-Theaters eine riesige Projektionsfläche" (*rbb24*, 2.2.2020). Trotz Trennwand und Videoprojektion dürfte es aber schwer sein, die Inszenierung Corona-tauglich zu machen. So wurde dieser interessante *Hamlet* in gewisser

Weise ein prominentes Opfer der Pandemie, auch wenn seine Premiere noch vor dem Lockdown stattfinden konnte. Allerdings lässt das Zauberwort 'Repertoire' hoffen, dass am Ende doch noch mehr Menschen in den Genuss dieser Inszenierung kommen werden.

LUKAS LAMMERS

"Das ist keine Komödie mehr!" Theater in NRW erteilen Absage an die unerträgliche Leichtigkeit des Scheins

Auch in Nordrhein-Westfalen läuteten die Theaterschließungen ein vorzeitiges Ende der Spielzeit 2019/2020 ein, sodass insgesamt leider nur drei Shakespeare-Inszenierungen (und eine Adaption) zur Aufführung gelangten. Nichtsdestoweniger fällt diesmal der eher reflektierte als reflexhafte Umgang mit den politischen Anliegen ins Auge. Im vierten Jahr ihres Bestehens war es erneut vor allem die #MeToo-Bewegung, die die Regisseurinnen und Regisseure bei ihrer künstlerischen Arbeit bewegte – und dies aus unverändert aktuellem Anlass, wird doch die Auseinandersetzung mit sexualisierter Gewalt einen langen Atem erfordern. Freilich sind, bei aller Bardolatrie, Shakespeares Dramen keine plakativen Plädoyers für Frauenrechte und Gleichberechtigung.

Wie lässt sich Shakespeare mit progressivem Anspruch inszenieren? Die eine Möglichkeit: Man setzt zur Entlarvung struktureller, also im System angelegter Gewalt bei der Täterperspektive an. Hier findet man in Shakespeare den idealen Gewährsmann, denn wie zuletzt Stephen Greenblatt in *Tyrant: Shakespeare on Politics* (2018) dargelegt hat: Zu Machtmissbrauch, Narzissmus, Größenwahn und vermeintlichem Gottesgnadentum haben die Dramen einiges zu sagen. *König Lear* ist hierfür ein gutes Beispiel – und in der Tat wäre diese Tragödie gleich zweimal zu sehen gewesen (in Bonn und in Bochum), hätte sie in der Ruhrgebietsstadt nicht verschoben werden müssen. Auch Angelo, der mit eisernem Besen durch Wien kehren möchte, solange der Herzog auf Abwegen ist, ein geeigneter Kandidat für den Club der wahnsinnig Mächtigen und mächtig Wahnsinnigen. Dass Greenblatt ihm in seiner Studie die Aufnahme verweigert, verwunderte bereits bei ihrem ersten Erscheinen den Rezensenten des *Guardian* (6.7.2018); nun holte zumindest das Theater Münster Angelo in einer Inszenierung von *Maß für Maß* auf die große Bühne.

Ein anderer Zugang zu Shakespeare im Kontext von #MeToo läge indes in der Einsicht, dass auch jene Komödien, denen die Forschung nicht das explizite Label *Problemstück* verpasst hat, mehr sind als Plattformen für jene burlesken Späße, die wir in den vergangenen Jahren mehrmals kritisierten – zumindest dann, wenn das Niveau ins Tiefparterre verlegt wurde (vgl. *ShJB* 156 [2020], 247). Dass in Komödien kritisches Potenzial schlummert, auch für eine Auseinandersetzung mit dem an sich ernsten Gender-Thema, bewies diesmal die Bürgerbühne des Düsseldorfer Schauspielhauses: Ihr gelang mit einer metatheatralen Inszenierung von *Was ihr wollt*, die die 'gerechte' und 'natürliche' Rollenverteilung bei den Proben zu ebenjenem Stück hinterfragt, eine gleichermaßen kluge und unterhaltsame Aktualisierung. Es gibt daher Hoffnung, dass auf der Bühne auch in Zukunft beides möglich ist: Haltung und künstlerische Imagination.

Das jugendliche Ensemble der Bürgerbühne des Düsseldorfer Schauspielhauses (13 Schauspielerinnen und Schauspieler im Alter von 14 bis 22 Jahren) machte in seiner Inszenierung von *Was ihr wollt* (Premiere: 28. 9. 2019) den Titel zum Programm und nahm das Stück zum Anlass, die Frage nach der (sexuellen) Wunschidentität zu stellen. Die in der Presse vielgelobte Inszenierung ("Darsteller, die […] glaubwürdig wie Profis agieren", *www.rp-online.de*, 29. 9. 2019) beginnt mit einem visuellen Paukenschlag: Ein weißer Vorhang teilt Bühne und Auditorium in zwei Hälften. Für das Publikum ist jeweils nur eine Bühnenhälfte direkt sichtbar; das Geschehen auf der anderen Seite wird als Video projiziert. Regisseurin Joanna Praml hat zusammen mit der Dramaturgin Dorle Trachternach eine Textfassung erstellt, welche uns die Komödie als Metatheater erfahren lässt. Gespielt wird, was wir sehen: Eine jugendliche Theatergruppe will Shakespeares *Was ihr wollt* aufführen und überlegt, wie das am besten zu bewerkstelligen sei. Dabei wird nicht nur über die Aktualität und Relevanz des Stücks, sondern auch über die beste Inszenierungspraxis gestritten. Der Vorhang markiert die Gendergrenze, die männlichen Darsteller sollen links, die weiblichen rechts spielen: "Die Trennung der Geschlechter war die einzig richtige Entscheidung", konstatiert ein Ensemblemitglied noch am Anfang. Doch diese Trennung erweist sich recht schnell als künstlich und nicht aufrechtzuerhalten, denn einige wollen auch "einmal auf der anderen Seite spielen". Man entscheidet sich, die Teilung aufzugeben, und dieses ist der erste magische Moment in dieser erfrischenden Inszenierung. Der Vorhang wird zurück- und hochgezogen, verändert sich in ein segelähnliches Gebilde, das nunmehr die gesamte Bühne überspannt und die Handlung mit dem Schiffbruch im Sturm vor der illyrischen Küste beginnen lässt. Die Handlungsebene bricht in die Darstellungsebene ein und im Wirbel des Sturms werden "mit anarchischer Lust Geschlechterstereotype durcheinandergewirbelt" (Homepage des Düsseldorfer Schauspielhauses, *www.dhaus.de/programm/a-z/was-ihr-wollt*). Dass die Überlagerung der beiden Ebenen so gut gelingt, ist auf mehrere Faktoren zurückzuführen. Zum einen ist da natürlich die Nähe der jugendlichen Darstellerinnen und Darsteller zu dem Leitthema der Inszenierung: Wer im Alter von 14 bis 22 Jahren setzt sich nicht mit der eigenen (Geschlechts-)Identität auseinander? Es wäre aber zu kurz gegriffen, allein hierin das Gelingen des Inszenierungskonzepts zu sehen. Auch Pramls Wahl von *Was ihr wollt* ist ein sehr kluger Griff, da das Spiel mit Geschlechtsidentitäten der Komödie wie keiner anderen eingeschrieben ist (mit Ausnahme vielleicht von *Wie es euch gefällt*). Wenn Frau Viola als Mann Cesario sowohl von Orsino als auch von Olivia umworben wird, dann fällt es den Beteiligten zusehends schwer zu erkennen, was sie denn eigentlich wollen, genauso wie auch die Figuren in Pramls und Trachternachs Textfassung erkennen müssen, dass es gar nicht so einfach ist zu wissen, was man wirklich will. Die von einem Ensemblemitglied geäußerte Einsicht, "[i]ch will nur das, was die anderen wollen", legt dann auch die fragile Grenze zwischen Selbstbestimmung und Fremdbestimmung offen und verweist auf das Illusionäre eines gänzlich autonomen und autarken Ichs. In der Inszenierung spiegelt sich diese Verwirbelung von Identitätsgrenzen und Geschlechtsidentitäten nicht nur in der Tatsache wider, dass Darsteller auch

Was ihr wollt, Düsseldorfer Schauspielhaus (Bürgerbühne), Regie: Joanna Praml
Foto: Thomas Rabsch

weibliche Figuren und Darstellerinnen auch männliche Figuren spielen, sondern auch darin, dass die Rolle der Olivia auf mehrere Schauspielerinnen verteilt wird (markiert durch T-Shirts mit Namensaufdruck; Bühne und Kostüm: Jana Denhoven, Inga Timm).

Nachdem das Ensemble erkennen muss, dass das Experiment der Geschlechtertrennung missglückt ist ("Wir hatten Schiffbruch"), beginnt mit der Ankunft in Illyrien nicht nur Shakespeares Handlung; es wird auch deutlich, dass dieser Ort ein 'U-Topos', ein Nicht-Ort ist, ein "Ort ohne Regeln, ohne Moral", wie es ein Ensemblemitglied formuliert, an dem die traditionelle Geschlechtertrennung nicht mehr greift bzw. nicht mehr gelten muss. Existieren Viola und Sebastian vor dem Sturm noch als zwei getrennte Identitäten, zeigen die emotionalen Irrungen und Wirrungen von Orsino, Viola und Olivia, aber auch das *cross-casting* und die Verteilung einer Rolle auf mehrere Darstellerinnen, dass es in Illyrien keinen Platz für Geschlechtsbinarität und Heteronormativität gibt. In der metadramatischen Düsseldorfer Bearbeitung wird somit das Theaterspiel selbst zu einer Utopie, einem Experimentierfeld, das alternative Identitätskonzepte ver- und aushandeln kann. Die Gefahr einer realitätsfremden utopischen Schwärmerei benennt allerdings eine Schauspielerin nach der Ankunft in Illyrien, wenn sie fragt: "Heißt das, dass wir uns keine Fragen mehr stellen?" Das illyrische Projekt operiert zwar mit utopischen und alternativen Konzepten, gibt aber gleichzeitig zu erkennen, dass zu diesen eine kritische Distanz eingenommen wird.

Dass die kritische Reflexion über utopische Entwürfe nach der Ankunft in Illyrien nicht aufhört, wird zudem an Malvolio deutlich. Getreu seiner bei Shakespeare angelegten Rolle und Funktion als *spoil sport*, will er wiederholt dem frivolen Rollen- und Gendertausch ein Ende machen. "Ich gehe jetzt zum Intendanten und werde das alles beenden", ruft er. Zum Schluss wird er jedoch in ein überdimensionales Vulva-Kostüm gesteckt und per Seilwinde an die Bühnendecke verbannt, sodass selbst Maria Mitleid mit Malvolio hat: "Das ist keine Komödie mehr."

Das Fazit der Inszenierung bleibt dennoch dem utopischen Blick verpflichtet und schaut zuversichtlich in die Zukunft. Am Ende umarmen sich die jungen Akteurinnen und Akteure gegenseitig und versichern sich und uns, dass es "nie wirklich einen Vorhang" gegeben habe. Während eine Darstellerin erkennt, dass alle "Rollen durch mich hindurchfließen", kommt eine andere Figur zu der Einsicht, dass "ich ich bin". Wenn auch diese etwas naiv anmutenden Botschaften am Ende etwas enttäuschen und der ansonsten sehr erfrischenden Ambivalenz der Inszenierung entgegenwirken (zudem hätte das Ensemble von mehr Stimm- und Sprechtraining profitiert; es wird sehr viel geschrien), gelingt der jungen Bürgerbühne eine mutige und intelligente Auseinandersetzung mit Shakespeares Komödie.

Mit *Maß für Maß* wurde am Theater Münster ein weiteres Stück unter Betonung der Gender-Thematik und der sozialen Machtmechanismen inszeniert (Premiere: 16.11.2019). Im Gegensatz zu den Jugendlichen in Düsseldorf, die der Sichtweise den Vorzug gaben, Gender als kreatives Potenzial zu begreifen und sich äußeren Zuschreibungen zu widersetzen, legte Regisseur Ronny Jakubaschk den Fokus seiner ersten Arbeit für die Westfalenmetropole eindeutig auf die Toxizität patriarchaler Herrschaftsformen und maskulinen Machtmissbrauchs. Für diesen zeitgemäßen Ansatz war die Inszenierung mit einigen Vorschusslorbeeren bedacht worden: Sie "zielt auf Aktuelles ab", lobten die *Westfälischen Nachrichten*, denn "Shakespeare kannte 'MeToo'" (14.11.2019). Kritisch anzumerken ist freilich, dass man Shakespeare nicht zu einem Feministen *avant la lettre* verklären sollte: Was er kannte, waren nicht die Anliegen der heutigen Bewegung, sondern die grundsätzliche Bedeutung von sozialen Machtgefällen und gesellschaftlichen Zwängen – Aspekte, die er überdies durchaus ambivalent behandelte, so etwa in der Komödie *Der Kaufmann von Venedig*, die im Vorjahr in Münster gezeigt wurde. Das erfreulich facettenreiche Programmheft stellt zunächst mit Frank Günther das Stück als Justizdrama vor, um sodann mit Margarete Stokowski, Laurie Penny und Silvia Federici Einblicke in die gegenwärtige feministische Publizistik und Kulturforschung zu gewähren. Fraglos weist das Drama um den sittenstrengen Angelo (Jonas Riemer), der während der vermeintlichen Abwesenheit des Herzogs Vincentio (Wilhelm Schlotterer) für Zucht und Ordnung sorgen möchte, zahlreiche Anknüpfungspunkte für eine Diskussion über das Wesen der Macht und der Mächtigen auf. Zum Problem wird die Indienstnahme der Literatur durch das Tagesgeschehen erfahrungsgemäß oft dann, wenn der allegorische Deutungsansatz dem Stoff gleichsam übergestülpt wird. Laut dem Drama stürzt Angelo über den Gegensatz von Selbstbild und Begierde: Während er Claudio wegen Unzucht zum Tode verurteilt, gelüstet es ihn selbst nach Claudios keuscher Schwester Isabella (Sandra Schreiber). Die Münsteraner Vorberichterstattung begeisterte sich für die "in Zeiten von '#MeToo' […] erschreckende Parallele", dass "ein Verfechter von Sittenstrenge über seine eigenen Prinzipien stolpert" (*Westfälische Nachrichten*, 14.11.2019). Heuchelei und Doppelmoral sind jedoch gar nicht das zentrale Anliegen von #MeToo, auch wenn sie mittelbar eine Rolle spielen; der Filmproduzent Weinstein war jedenfalls nie als Feminist ins öffentliche Bewusstsein getreten. Der entscheidendere Aspekt ist *entitlement*: der von Narzissmus und Anspruchsdenken getriebene Machtmissbrauch durch einzelne Männer (und, wie zum Beispiel Stokowski betont,

Frauen) in entsprechenden Positionen sowie die gesellschaftlich verankerten Strukturen, die derlei Verhalten ermöglichen.

Vielleicht sind es solche kleinen Ungereimtheiten im Ansatz, die dazu beitragen, dass die Inszenierung letzten Endes nicht zu überzeugen wusste. So gelten dem Premierenkritiker der *Westfälischen Nachrichten* die drei Hauptfiguren zwar als "aus dem Ensemble ideal besetzt", zugleich seien sie jedoch "seltsam unscharf" (16.11.2019). Die Zuspitzung von Shakespeares ambigen Dramen auf eine bestimmte theoretische Lesart oder das Zeitgeschehen ist stets eine Gratwanderung: Belässt es die Regie bei subtilen Andeutungen, riskiert sie, dass andere Themen in den Vordergrund rücken; wird sie explizit, läuft sie Gefahr, zu didaktisieren und ihren eigenen Witz zu erklären. Im aktuellen Fall reagierte die Presse enttäuscht auf ein augenscheinlich nicht eingelöstes Versprechen: "Die Themen 'Männliche Macht' und '#Me too-Debatte' kamen [...] nur am Rande vor" (ibid.). Allzu naiv – und dies ist eine plausible Kritik – gerät vor allem bei dem ostentativ komödiantischen Ausklang des Dramas die Darstellung des strategisch denkenden Politikers Vincentio als "der gute Onkel, der alles richtet" (ibid.). Auch die Ausdeutung der (wenigstens optisch bis auf die Unterwäsche ausgezogenen) Figuren bleibt an der Oberfläche. So muss offenbleiben, ob Angelo "ein kühler Bürokrat, ein früher Robespierre oder doch nur ein dumpfer Egoist" (ibid.) ist.

Das Bühnenbild (Bühne und Kostüm: David Gonter) greift die sogenannten Wiedertäuferkäfige aus den 1530er Jahren auf, in denen die Führungsfiguren des örtlichen radikalreformatorischen Regimes nach ihrer Hinrichtung zur Schau gestellt wurden; als Wahrzeichen und Touristenattraktion sind die Käfige noch heute an der Lambertikirche angebracht. Es ist eine faszinierende Idee, diese auf der Bühne in einen neuen, verfremdenden Kontext zu stellen; die Inszenierung positioniert sich damit auf nuancierte Weise gegen den Gesinnungsterror, der historisch sowohl von den reformatorischen Eiferern (vom Schlage Angelos) als auch den wieder an die Macht gekommenen Eliten (vom Schlage Vincentios) ausging. Eine solche kluge Akzentuierung und Konturierung wäre jedoch auch der Figurenregie zu wünschen gewesen.

Ein waschechter Tyrann gemäß Greenblatts Typologie – und damit ein weiterer Mann, der seine Mitmenschen leiden lässt, weil ihm die Herrschaft zu Kopf gestiegen ist – stand am Theater Bonn im Mittelpunkt: König Lear (Bernd Braun). Für die Inszenierung der gleichnamigen Tragödie (Premiere: 28.2.2020) zeichnete Luise Voigt verantwortlich, die neben der Regie auch die Bühnengestaltung übernahm. Bei einem Stück über die Unfähigkeit, Macht abzugeben, drängen sich Witze über diese Kompetenzballung auf – sie wären jedoch fehl am Platz:

Nach mehrheitlicher Kritikermeinung gelingt der Theatermacherin tatsächlich eine Interpretation wie aus einem Guss.

Voigt entscheidet sich für einen bewusst verfremdenden Ansatz: Die karge Bühne und die opulenten Kostüme (Maria Strauch) sind in Weiß- und Silbertönen gehalten – eine "weiße Hölle", "kalt" und "klinisch" (*theater:pur*, 4.3.2020), die die Empathielosigkeit vieler Figuren versinnbildlicht, die sich aus den Herrschaftsstrukturen an Lears absolutistischem Hof speist. Die Figuren tragen Schminke und Rokoko-Perücken; auch "der großartige Schauspieler Bernd Braun" (*theatergemeinde-bonn.de*, 7.5.2020) ist in der Rolle des Lear "auf alter weißer Mann geschminkt" (*General-Anzeiger*, 2.3.2020). Auf eine derart pauschale Maskulinitätskritik ist Voigt freilich nicht aus; das rheinische Kulturportal *choices.de* spekuliert im Gegenteil sogar hoffnungsfroh, dass Voigt sich dem vermeintlichen Zwang zur Political Correctness entziehen wolle, denn Ästhetizismus habe "mit Formwillen, aber auch dem Schutz vor einer (moralischen) Indienstnahme der Kunst zu tun – was in Zeiten der Hypermoral nicht schlecht sein muss" (16.4.2020).

Für das Verständnis von Voigts *Lear* dürften diese Überlegungen allerdings zweitrangig sein. Das formstrenge Konzept der Regisseurin ist nämlich kein Selbstzweck, sondern erfüllt eine einleuchtende interpretative Funktion: Voigt sieht alle Figuren in bestimmten öffentlichen Rollen gefangen. Freiheit existiert kaum (wenngleich sie nicht unmöglich ist, wie Cordelia eingangs durch ihre Gewissensnöte beweist); alle Höflinge agieren wie Uhrwerke. Die Regisseurin wendet diesen Ansatz konsequent an und etabliert in Zusammenarbeit mit dem Schauspieler Tony de Maeyer, einem Experten für die theatrale Biomechanik nach Meyerhold, sogar einen spezifischen Bewegungsablauf für jede Figur.

Die Darstellung des Menschen als Automaten hat allerdings eine Kehrseite: "Die Figuren bleiben blutleer, sie berühren nicht" (ibid.). Diese Wahrnehmung deckt sich mit Henri Bergsons Theorie, dass das Komische die mechanische Steifheit des Menschen sichtbar mache, die durch das Lachen bestraft werde – und dass das Lachen seinerseits einer *Anästhesie des Herzens* bedürfe. Gelingt es Voigt auch eindrücklich, die roboterhafte Gefühllosigkeit der Figuren aufzuzeigen, so reproduziert sie eine solche *nolens volens* im Publikum: "Die Künstlichkeit [...] entzieht dem Drama seine emotionale Kraft. Das Schicksal dieser Menschen wird niemand im Parkett beweinen" (*General-Anzeiger*, 2.3.2020).

Voigt will freilich ohnehin kein psychologisches Drama entfalten, erteilt also der romantischen Vorstellung des zwischen den Naturgewalten zu Güte und Menschlichkeit bekehrten Lear eine Absage. Ihre Lesart ist vielmehr konsequent historistisch (und gerade damit für die Entdeckung unpersönlicher, verselbständigter Machtstrukturen von Interesse): Voigt möchte bloßlegen, wie wenig

König Lear, Theater Bonn, Regie: Luise Voigt, Lear (Bernd Braun)
Foto: Thilo Beu

Lear als Individuum existiert – und wie sehr als höchster Amtsträger, als Fleisch gewordene Funktionsstelle einer patriarchalischen Gesellschaft. Diesem Zweck dient insbesondere das zentrale Element des Bühnenbildes: eine überlebensgroße aufblasbare Puppe, die die Gesichtszüge von Lear-Darsteller Braun trägt. Laut Programmheft bezieht sich Voigt damit auf Ernst Kantorowicz' Theorie der *zwei Körper* des mittelalterlichen Königs: dem *natürlichen*, sterblichen, und dem alterslosen, *politischen*, der sich beim Tod eines Herrschers augenblicklich mit dem nächsten verbindet, sodass – zumindest in der kulturellen Fiktion – niemals ein Machtvakuum herrscht. Voigts spannende Idee besteht darin, auch Lears politischen – also symbolischen, unsichtbaren – Körper mittels der Puppe auf der Bühne in Erscheinung treten zu lassen. Wenn etwa Lear zu Beginn des Stückes angekleidet wird, d.h. die Insignien seiner Macht anlegt, erhebt sich hinter ihm die Lear-Puppe; wenn er seine Macht abgibt, also den politischen Körper ablegt, fällt die Puppe in sich zusammen. Dies ist sinnfällig: Lears wesentlicher Fehler im Drama besteht ja – abgesehen von der Fehleinschätzung seiner Töchter und seiner Unkenntnis über die Lebensverhältnisse im Volk – in dem Irrglauben, er könne ohne die Königsrolle an seiner Autorität (etwa seinem großen Gefolge) festhalten.

Die Ästhetik der Inszenierung weiß allgemein zu überzeugen: Der *General-Anzeiger* lobt, dass die Aufführung "dank eigenwilliger Bewegungschoreografie und der originellen Puppe" für einige bleibende Erinnerungen sorgt (2.3.2020). Auch die *nachtkritik* sieht "ein mit feinen Bizarrerien stilsicher angerichtetes Großpuppenspiel" (28.2.2020). Das Konzept, durch die besondere Ästhetik das Primat von Machtstrukturen auf Kosten individueller Autonomie erkennbar zu machen, entgeht ihr allerdings: "hübsch und flach", so das etwas verwirrende Gesamturteil (ibid.).

Aufschlussreich wäre es im Übrigen gewiss gewesen, den ästhetizistischen Bonner Ansatz mit der am Schauspielhaus Bochum geplanten Fassung von *König Lear* (in einer Auftragsübersetzung durch die Dramatikerin Miroslava Svolikova) zu vergleichen. Da diese in die folgende Spielzeit verschoben werden musste, wird diese Gegenüberstellung leider noch ein Jahr auf sich warten lassen. Ähnlich verhält es sich mit der provokanten Düsseldorfer Lesart von *Was ihr wollt*: Eine Inszenierung derselben Komödie war am Theater Paderborn angesetzt, musste jedoch bis auf Weiteres abgesagt werden. Verlegt wurden ferner eine Inszenierung von *Romeo und Julia* in Wuppertal sowie eine Bühnenproduktion von *Shakespeare in Love* am Rheinisch-Westfälischen Landestheater in Neuss. In Neuss entfiel ebenso das jährliche Shakespeare Festival.

Auf die Besprechung einer weiteren (zu) kurz gezeigten Inszenierung im Rheinland, die in der kommenden Spielzeit wiederaufgenommen wird, möchten wir indessen einen kleinen Vorgeschmack bieten: David Böschs Regiearbeit *Henry VI & Margaretha di Napoli* (Premiere: 14.12.2019) stützt sich auf Tom Lanoyes gleichnamige Bearbeitung der Shakespeare-Trilogie um Heinrich VI., die bereits 1999 als Teil von *Schlachten!* bei den Salzburger Festspielen Premiere feierte. Im Zentrum der Bearbeitung steht Margarete, die Frau Heinrichs VI., die im Gegensatz zu ihrem Mann perfekt auf der Klaviatur der Macht zu spielen weiß und durch Verführung ebenso wie Mord an ihre Ziele gelangt. Dabei zeichnet sich ab, dass das Prinzip der Umkehrung der patriarchalen Hierarchie schwierige, aber umso wichtigere und spannendere Fragen aufwirft: "Will die Inszenierung Heinrich wirklich deshalb verulken, weil dieser Kindkönig von seiner Natur her nicht die Macht ausüben kann, die nötig wäre, in die heldischen Fußstapfen seines früh gestorbenen Vaters Heinrich V. zu treten und England Halt zu geben? Brauchen wir heute nicht gerade die Friedfertigkeit in der Welt, zu welcher der vermeintlich naive, kasperlhaft gezeichnete Heinrich trotz aller Intrigen um ihn herum immer wieder aufruft?" (*www.rp-online.de*, 15.12.2019).

Zu guter Letzt möchten wir einen kurzen Überblick über die verschiedenen Maßnahmen und Projekte geben, mit denen die Theater in Nordrhein-Westfalen den Lockdown zu überbrücken versuchten. Auffallend ist dabei, dass zunächst dieselbe Unsicherheit in der Einschätzung von Ausmaß und Tragweite der Pandemie wie in anderen Bereichen der Gesellschaft herrschte. Auch hinsichtlich der Frage, ob es überhaupt eine Pandemie und nicht nur eine Epidemie sei, war man sich in den ersten Wochen nicht einig. Nur sehr langsam wich der Gedanke einer lediglich kurzen 'Überbrückung' der Erkenntnis, dass es sich um eine langfristige und auch existenzielle Krise handelt, für deren Bewältigung es tragfähiger digitaler Konzepte bedarf. So finden sich bereits ab April durchdachte Projekte in einigen Notspielplänen, allerdings auch allerlei Albernes und Belangloses. Tatsächlich setzten sich manche Theater sogar schon vor der Krise mit digitalen Strategien auseinander – so musste z. B. das Dortmunder "Labor zu Kunst und Theater im Digitalen Zeitalter", das für Mitte März als Präsenzveranstaltung geplant war, auf das Internet ausweichen und sich somit gleich in der Praxis bewähren. Dennoch: Obwohl es in der Theaterwelt schon länger ein Bewusstsein davon gegeben hat, dass sich die fortschreitende Digitalisierung auch zunehmend auf das eigene Metier auswirkt, hat die Krise die Theater, wie auch den Rest der Gesellschaft, weitestgehend unvorbereitet getroffen.

Am 11. März, als bereits erste Fußballspiele vor leeren Rängen ausgetragen wurden, fragte die ZEIT noch, ob dem Theater nun dasselbe bevorstünde: "Beginnt nun das Geistertheater?" (*zeit.de*, 11.3.2020). Aufführungen vor leerem Publikum waren jedoch zunächst keine Option, da Theater als Menschenansammlungen "mit risikogeneigter Zusammensetzung" (so die Landesregierung in Nordrhein-Westfalen) schließen mussten. Viele der Projekte, die die Theater unmittelbar nach dem 'Lockdown' Mitte März online anboten, zeigten, dass man sich des Ausmaßes der Pandemie am Anfang noch nicht einmal ansatzweise bewusst war. In den sozialen Netzwerken der Theater, sei es Facebook oder YouTube, findet sich in dieser Zeit vieles, was man 'Durchhaltevideos' nennen könnte. Die Botschaft ist: "Keine Angst, wir sind noch da und kommen bald zurück."

Viele dieser Angebote zeichneten sich durch einen spielerisch-ironischen Tonfall aus, den man, nunmehr aus der besser informierten Perspektive der Rückschau, als naiv und trivial bezeichnen kann. Emblematisch hierfür ist ein knapp zweiminütiger Clip aus einem anderen Bundesland, der vom Hans-Otto-Theater Potsdam am 22.3. über Facebook geteilt wurde. In ihm führen zwei Schauspieler auf klamaukige Weise vor, wie Theater unter Abstandsregeln aussehen könnte. Da sieht man Kampfszenen, die mit zwei Metern Distanz ausgefochten werden, eine Umarmung und einen Kuss auf die Ferne sowie eine alternative Form der

Begrüßung, bei der man sich nicht die Hand reicht, sondern stattdessen mit Ellenbogen und Füßen berührt – alles bewusst ins Lächerliche gezogen.

Als sich jedoch abzuzeichnen begann, dass es mit der Corona-Pandemie länger dauern würde und die Theater auch nach dem 19. April voraussichtlich nicht würden öffnen können, schon gar nicht unter den üblichen Bedingungen, entwickelten die Häuser vermehrt den Anspruch, ein ernsthaftes kulturelles Ersatzangebot zu erstellen. "Nicht nur ein Trost für die abgesagten Veranstaltungen, sondern auch eine tolle neue Art, sich mit dem Kulturhaus zu verbinden", urteilte z. B. das Kulturmagazin Coolibri über die Pläne des Duisburger Theaters (*coolibri.de*, 30. 3. 2020).

Eine der populärsten, da wohl auch praktikabelsten und am schnellsten realisierbaren Formen stellten in Nordrhein-Westfalen Lesungen dar, die viele Theater online zu veröffentlichen begannen. Zwischen März und Mai initiierte zum Beispiel das Schauspielhaus Bochum eine auf elf Teile angelegte Reihe aus drei- bis fünfminütigen Kurzfilmen unter dem Titel *Ich ist ein Robinson*. Hier wird aus dem Off aus Defoes Roman vorgelesen, während bunt kostümierte Schauspielerinnen und Schauspieler an verschiedenen Orten der Stadt und des Theaters die Szenen nachstellen. Bisweilen entsteht so eine recht gelungene Spannung zwischen Bild und gesprochenem Wort. Die Analogie zwischen Robinsons einsamem Inseldasein und der Isolation in der Großstadt ist zwar nicht neu, jedoch wird das Medium des Films in der Auseinandersetzung durchaus kreativ genutzt. Die Online-Reihe verrät einen ernsthaften künstlerischen Anspruch und geht weit darüber hinaus, lediglich ein Lebenszeichen in den digitalen Raum zu entsenden. Auch in den *Bochumer Shortcuts*, kurzen Lesungen von Ensemblemitgliedern und anderen Personen des öffentlichen Lebens (wie z. B. Norbert Lammert), ist dieser Anspruch deutlich zu erkennen. Naturgemäß wurde bei allen Theatern immer wieder auf Werke zurückgegriffen, die einen Bezug zur Seuchen- und Isolationsthematik haben. Das Theater an der Ruhr in Mülheim bemühte das *Dekameron* (wie übrigens auch das Deutsche Theater Berlin), Ausschnitte aus Albert Camus' *Pest* fanden sich (Theater Oberhausen) ebenso wie Paul Celans Gedicht "Corona" (Schauspielhaus Bochum). Am Theater Aachen rief man einen "Theaterversand" ins Leben: Interessierte wurden ermutigt, dem Theater ihre Wünsche mitzuteilen und so im Gegenzug ein persönliches Kulturprogramm zu erhalten. So konnte man sich seine Lieblingsarie vorsingen oder Einschlafgeschichten für die Kinder vorlesen lassen oder sich über verlorengegangene Socken, den Sinn des Lebens oder peinliche Lieblingssongs unterhalten. Auch am Theater Duisburg versuchte man mit einer experimentellen Livestream-Theaterreihe, das Publikum einzubinden. Das Düsseldorfer Schauspielhaus zeigte sich mit einem breit gestreuten Programm aus

u. a. Online-Magazin (*D'mag*), Blogs (u. a. mit Quarantäne-Tipps) und Streams von vergangenen Produktionen als eines der aktivsten und vielseitigsten Theater, das zudem ein umfangreiches Online-Angebot für Kinder und Jugendliche bereitstellte.

Auf den Lockdown, so könnte man es zusammenfassen, reagierten die meisten Theater also in zwei Phasen: zunächst mit dem Versuch, möglichst schnell auf die Krise zu reagieren und (irgend)etwas in das Netz zu stellen, z. T. auch auf Kosten der Qualität und des eigenen Anspruchs, danach mit der Einsicht in die Ernsthaftigkeit der Lage und der Entwicklung durchdachter und künstlerisch anspruchsvollerer Angebote. So war also neben viel Sehenswertem auch einiges Banales zu sehen. Impressionen von einer leergefegten Stadt hatte schließlich jeder selbst zu Genüge beim täglichen Einkauf, auch Führungen durch die Privatwohnungen von Schauspielern dürften nicht alle gleichermaßen interessiert haben. Vor allem die vielerorts angebotenen digitalen Theaterrundgänge waren wohl eher dem Zwang geschuldet, schnell Präsenz zu zeigen und den Menschen 'da draußen' zu kommunizieren, dass das Leben im Theater weitergeht.

Es bleibt abzuwarten, welche Herausforderungen auf die Theater in der nächsten Spielzeit zukommen und inwieweit einige der digitalen Formate Einzug in die Spielpläne auch nach Corona finden werden.

SARAH BRIEST, JAN MOSCH, SARA TUCKWELL,
ROLAND WEIDLE UND JAN WILLING

Menschliche und familiäre Abgründe an der Corona-Kante: *Lady Macbeth von Mzensk* und *Otello* an der Oper Frankfurt

Auch die Theater im Südwesten hat die Pandemie schwer getroffen. Die meisten stellten, wie die Frankfurter Städtischen Bühnen und der Mousonturm, den Spielbetrieb im März ein, einige, beispielsweise das Theater Heilbronn, beendeten nach Rücksprache mit den städtischen Behörden die Spielzeit 2019/20 vorzeitig und ließen verkünden, dass bis zur Sommerpause keine regulären Aufführungen mehr stattfänden. Andere Häuser suchten nach Wegen, mit Hilfe von Hygieneplänen den Spielbetrieb aufrechtzuerhalten. Unter Parolen wie "Als ob es ein Morgen gäbe" (Spielzeitmotto des Stuttgarter Theaters) oder "Sonderfahrplan" (Badisches Staatstheater Karlsruhe) boten diese Theater ein in jeder Hinsicht außergewöhnliches Programm an, das beispielsweise in Karlsruhe 70 Veranstaltungen für maximal 100 Besucher umfasste. Hier, wie auch an anderen

Orten, sahen die Akteure die Krise auch als Chance. Eine Öffnung für die Gesellschaft sei möglich, wenn Proben an öffentlich zugänglichen Plätzen stattfinden oder kulturelle Stadtspaziergänge angeboten werden können, bei denen Staatsballett, Staatskapelle und Oper an verschiedenen Orten in der Stadt unter freiem Himmel auftreten. Andere Theater setzten auf digitale Formate und gingen, wie beispielsweise das Theater Freiburg, jeden Tag um 19:30 Uhr mit Hilfe eines kostenlosen Streaming-Portals auf Sendung. Während viele Häuser selbst ums finanzielle Überleben kämpften, litt auch der künstlerische Betrieb im Hintergrund erheblich (und leidet immer noch), wie die Autorin Ingeborg von Zadow, der Dramatiker Kristof Magnusson und der Regisseur Ulrich Hub in einem Gastbeitrag in der *Frankfurter Allgemeinen Zeitung* (3. 9. 2020) zu bedenken geben. Selbst nach Wiederaufnahme bleibe die Lage schwierig: "Vorstellungen, die früher ausverkauft waren, bringen uns jetzt kaum ein Fünftel der früheren Einnahmen."

Zwei Shakespeare-Inszenierungen fielen der Pandemie in dieser Spielzeit komplett zum Opfer: In Tübingen hätte ein *Hamlet* vom Landestheater Württemberg-Hohenzollern am 28. 7. 2020 seine Premiere gefeiert, und in Mainz wäre am 26. 4. 2020 *Der Widerspenstigen Zähmung* am Staatstheater zu sehen gewesen. Zu den vielbeachteten Inszenierungen, die vor der Schließung noch zur Aufführung kamen, zählen Schostakowitschs Shakespearevertonung *Lady Macbeth von Mzensk* und Rossinis *Otello*, beide an der Oper Frankfurt. Erstere Oper wurde in der Neuinszenierung von Anselm Weber, dem Geschäftsführer der Städtischen Bühnen und Intendanten des Schauspiels, und unter Leitung des Generalmusikdirektors Sebastian Weigle gespielt, letztere als Regiearbeit von Damiano Michieletto mit Sesto Quatrini am Pult. Beide Inszenierungen trugen sicherlich ihren Teil dazu bei, dass das Haus zur Oper des Jahres gekürt wurde.

Schostakowitschs Oper, die den Fokus auf Lady Macbeth verlagert und anhand dieser Figur gesellschaftliche und menschliche Abgründe beleuchtet, erzürnte Stalin bekanntlich so sehr, dass dieser bereits vor dem 4. Akt das Theater verließ. In einem Beitrag in der *Prawda* folgte das vernichtende Urteil: "Chaos statt Musik." Die beißende Satire, die sowohl im Libretto als auch in der Komposition zum Ausdruck kommt, war auf ein sowjetisches Ideal gerichtet, das eine Utopie fest im Blick behielt, dabei jedoch die Bedürfnisse und realen Verhältnisse sowohl der Kaufmannsfrau als auch des Arbeiters übersah. Es ist also keineswegs abwegig, diese Oper als Fingerzeig zu inszenieren, der auf diejenigen deutet, in deren Macht es steht, soziale Verhältnisse beim Namen zu nennen und zu verändern.

Wenngleich wir uns dem Lob der Kritiker anschließen, dass Weber "als Regisseur dort gut, ja, sogar überaus eindrucksvoll [ist], vor allem genau, wo er psychologische Motive herausarbeitet und Geschichten zu den Figuren erfindet"

(*Frankfurter Allgemeine Zeitung*, 5.11.2019), so bleibt doch die politische Dimension der Geschichte – und damit die Geschichte selbst – auf der Strecke. Im Laufe des Abends und in den folgenden Tagen stellt sich uns die Frage, was diese Inszenierung jenseits der Darstellung individueller Hilflosigkeit in den Blick rücken wollte. Diese Frage drängt sich zunächst nicht auf, denn das Ohr bekommt hier genug zu erkunden. Unter dem Dirigat von Weigle verdichten sich lyrische Tonalität und satirische Atonalität zu groteskem Pathos und ausdrucksvoller Explosivität. Bettina Boyens bescheinigt dem Generalmusikdirektor in *Musik Heute* (3.11.2019), dass er es "vorzüglich [verstand], sowohl die bedeutende Bühnenmusik der Blechbläser, die in den Beleuchtungsklappen rechts und links über dem Orchestergraben platziert waren, als auch die gewaltigen Chortableaus und die vielen satirischen Charakterstudien zu einem farbenreichen Gesamtklang zusammenzuführen". Und Judith von Sternburg konstatiert in der *Frankfurter Rundschau* (4.11.2019): "Es donnert, es gleißt, es schießt scharf, es tanzt auf dem Vulkan. Es ist irre laut. Es hört eiskalt wieder auf, irre laut zu sein. Die zentrale Heldenrolle des langen, großen Opernabends, der auch ein großes Sinfoniekonzert ist, gehört dem Orchester unter der Leitung von Generalmusikdirektor Sebastian Weigle."

Aber gerade weil die Klangwelt an diesem Abend so berauschend ist, scheint die mangelnde inszenatorische Idee deutlich auf. Jan Brachmann vermutet, dass Weber keinen richtigen Zugang zum Stück als Werkganzem gefunden hat: "Einigermaßen ratlos steht [...] Weber vor dem Stück" (*Frankfurter Allgemeine Zeitung*, 5.11.2019). Und von Sternburg gibt zu bedenken: "Während die Musik [...] aufs Ganze geht, begnügt sich die Bildwelt der Frankfurter 'Lady Macbeth' mit Einfällen, die so dahinter zurückbleiben, dass man eine Absicht – weitere Brüche – vermuten könnte" (*Frankfurter Rundschau*, 4.11.2019).

Das Bühnenbild (Kaspar Glarner) ist wenig hilfreich. Im Programmheft lesen wir, dass der halbrunde Betonrohbau und die Schutzanzüge der Arbeiter auf eine dystopische Welt nach einem Strahlenunfall verweisen. Es könnte sich auch um eine Lagerhalle oder ein Kühlhaus handeln, in das von der Decke herab das verkabelte Schlafzimmer der Lady heruntergelassen wird. Visuell schlägt sich Webers Ratlosigkeit also auch im Bühnenbild nieder. Gern sind wir geneigt, der Einschätzung zu folgen, dass "diese halbrunde Staudamm-Architektur" eventuell für die "Innenwelt der sexuell unbefriedigten Katerina Ismailowa" stehe und zugleich "Futurismus als bildungsbürgerliches Souvenir" ausstelle (*Frankfurter Allgemeine Zeitung*, 5.11.2019), aber beide Deutungsangebote laufen ins Leere; das eine engt die sozialkritische Oper psychologisierend ein, das andere bemüht ästhetische Klischees. So bleibt zu konstatieren, dass dieser Abend den Solisten gehört. "Die beiden Gegenspieler Katerina und ihr sadistischer Schwie-

Lady Macbeth von Mzensk, Oper Frankfurt, Regie: Anselm Weber
Ensemble, Dmitry Golovnin (Sergei), Anja Kampe (Katerina Ismailowa),
Dmitry Belosselski (Boris Ismailow)
Foto: Barbara Aumüller

gervater Boris waren mit der großen Sopranistin Anja Kampe und dem durchschlagenden Bassisten Dmitry Belosselsky atemberaubend besetzt", urteilt *Musik Heute* (3.11.2019). Dabei beeindrucken beide auch schauspielerisch, vor allem Kampe, "deren hochdramatische, jede Emotion unmittelbar widerspiegelnde Stimme in einem reizvollen Kontrast zu ihrem undivenhaft schlichten Auftreten passt" (*Frankfurter Rundschau*, 4.11.2019). Gelangweilt und gestraft mit einem uninteressierten und uninteressanten Ehemann (Tenor Evgeny Akimov) greift diese Katerina immer wieder zur VR-Brille, und es ist wenig mehr als diese Langeweile und ein unerfüllter Wunsch nach Liebe, die sie in Webers Inszenierung zur Mörderin werden lassen, denn, wie von Sternburg festhält, "[d]as Angebot des robusteren, sozusagen virileren Tenors Sergei, Dmitry Golovnin, beinhaltet ebenfalls so gut wie nichts" (*Frankfurter Rundschau*, 4.11.2019). Das wird auch deutlich in den 124 Takten, die die Kopulation der beiden mit einem Abwärtsglissando am Schluss ironisch kommentieren, hier nicht nur musikalisch angedeutet, sondern anschaulich verkörpert. Die Vergiftung des Schwiegervaters mit dem Pilzgericht und die Ermordung des Ehemanns lassen wenig Rückschlüsse zu, sie erscheinen als hilflose Versuche, der Langeweile zu entkommen, werden selbst aber unaufgeregt abgewickelt. Zu wenig macht Weber aus dem Klassenkonflikt, der in dieser gewalttätigen Beziehung zwischen der frustrierten und gelangweilten Kaufmannsgattin und dem lebensfrohen, amoralischen und hedonistischen Arbeiter aufscheint, wobei die Gewalt auf gespenstische Weise von Katerina ausgeht und von Sergei befeuert wird.

Vielleicht ist es Katerinas innere Leere, die Bühnenbild und karge Regie zum Ausdruck bringen möchten, doch damit entschärfen Weber und Glarner Schostakowitschs Oper. Der von den Akteuren unbehauste Rohbau bietet zu wenig Anhaltspunkte für eine soziale Verortung, die nötig ist, um Katerinas individuelle Hilflosigkeit an gesellschaftliche Bedingungen zu knüpfen. So bleibt diese Inszenierung ein Kammerspiel, für das die wesentlich im Dunkeln gehaltene Bühne zu groß erscheint. Das gilt auch für das hochdramatische Ende, wenn Katerina im Strafgefangenenlager erst die Liebhaberin Sergeis, Sonjetka (Mezzosopranistin Zanda Švēde), und dann sich selbst in den Tod stürzt. Tragisch erscheint dieses Ende nicht, vielmehr zwangslogisch. Aber die Verzweiflung Katerinas verdichtet sich nicht in diesem Akt der Befreiung. So ist der Schlussauftritt des von Tilman Michael einstudierten Chors "akustisch intensiv, szenisch verschenken die Frankfurter doch eines der erschütterndsten uns bekannten Opernenden" (*Frankfurter Rundschau*, 4. 11. 2019).

Rossinis *Otello* in Frankfurt ist eine überarbeitete Übernahme vom Theater an der Wien, wo diese Inszenierung im Jahr 2016 ihre Premiere feierte. 1816 uraufgeführt und seitdem selten gespielt, steht diese Oper im Schatten von Verdis Vertonung. Sie ist für das künstlerische Betriebsbüro allein deshalb schon eine große Herausforderung, weil sechs Rollen für Tenöre besetzt werden müssen, die jeweils ein eigenes Stimmfach und eine markante Färbung aufweisen sollten. Neben dem kraftvollem Heldentenor Otello (Enea Scala), dem höher liegenden, jugendlichen Tenor Rodrigo (Jack Swanson), dem lyrischen Tenor Jago (Theo Lebow) und dem voluminösen, im Rollstuhl sitzenden Dogen (Hans-Jürgen Lazar) steht ein fünfter strahlender Tenor auf der Bühne (Michael Petruccelli), der die Rolle des Gondolieres und des Familienarztes Lucio vereint. Historisch lässt sich diese Häufung an Tenören erklären: Anfang des neunzehnten Jahrhunderts gab es unter dem Theaterimpresario Domenico Barbaja in Neapel eine 'Tenorschwemme', und Rossini verhalf den Sängern zu Auftritten.

Die Bühne (Paolo Fantin) etabliert Ort und Zeit für diesen Wettstreit der fünf Tenöre: Wir sehen ein großbürgerliches Milieu im Hier und Jetzt und blicken in den Salon einer Villa. Von der Decke herab hängt ein imposanter Kronleuchter und die Sitzmöbel, Antiquitäten aus dem Biedermeier, dokumentieren Status und Traditionsbewusstsein. Wenn die Schiebetüren der Zwischenwand zur Seite geschoben und schließlich die ganze Wand hochgezogen wird, erweitert sich der Bühnenraum zu einem Saal, an dessen Stirnseite Gaetano Previatis "Der Tod von Paolo und Francesca" hängt. Das Liebespaar, dessen Ehebruch in Dantes *Divina Commedia* literarisch entschuldigt wird, ist hier von einem Schwert gemeinsam durchbohrt dargestellt. Das tragische Liebespaar ist allerdings nicht nur im Gemälde präsent, es tritt als Geisterduo immer wieder zwischen die Akteure. Es bringt, so Judith von Sternburg, "einen Hauch von Renaissance zwischen die ansonsten zeitgenössischen Kostüme (Business und Cocktail der oberen zehntausend) von Carla Teti" und "macht damit nicht zuletzt deutlich, wie wenig es in der Gegenwart – bei Rossini und bei Michieletto – um Liebe geht" (*Frankfurter Rundschau*, 9.9.2019). Aber um was geht es dann? Rossini hatte gemeinsam mit dem Librettisten Francesco Maria Berio Shakespeares Tragödie zu einer Familiensaga umgeschrieben. Es geht um Machterhalt und die Politik der Familienbande. Desdemona und Otello, der in dieser Inszenierung kein (nord-)afrikanischer Feldherr, sondern ein arabischer Kaufmann ist, haben heimlich geheiratet. Nun soll jedoch Desdemona mit Rodrigo den Bund der Ehe eingehen; denn Rodrigo ist der Sohn des Dogen und zugleich Cousin Jagos. Dass sich hier alles um die Logik des Familienclans dreht, der zwar nicht unbedingt mafiös, aber doch sehr auf den Zusammenhalt und nepotistische Strukturen ausgerichtet ist, macht Michieletto gleich in der Ouvertüre deutlich. Während auf den durchscheinenden Vorhang die Namen und Verwandtschaftsverhältnisse projiziert werden, reihen sich die Familienmitglieder im Hintergrund wie zu einem Gruppenportrait auf. In Michielettos Tableau sind alle miteinander verwandt, nur eben nicht Otello. Es geht auf der Handlungsebene also weniger darum, den Fremden, der als Geschäftsmann Erfolge vorweisen kann, zu integrieren und zu assimilieren, als vielmehr darum, die Clanstruktur mit dem Neuzugang zu stabilisieren.

Während sich das Scheitern dieser Vereinnahmung szenisch abzeichnet, bleiben Fragen der Integration oder gar Inklusion insgesamt vage; im Zentrum stehen vielmehr – wir sind in der Oper und es wird Rossini gespielt, nicht Verdi – Terzette, Duette und vor allem Arien mit langen Koloraturen. Und dann geht es doch auch ein wenig um Eifersucht. Jago (Theo Lebow), der bei Rossini wenig mehr ist als Rodrigos Dienstbote und Handlanger, wird unter Michielettos Regie zu dem, was er bei Shakespeare ist: ein teuflischer Drahtzieher und Manipulator, der, wie das Geisterliebespaar, um die Familienmitglieder umherschleicht und diese stets im Blick behält. "[M]it seinem hyperaktiven Auftreten und den schwarzen Lederhandschuhen", so Detlef Obens, wirkt dieser Jago "wie eine Katze auf Beutefang, die sich dabei die Krallen wetzt. Alessandro Carletti, der für das Licht verantwortlich ist, wählt für diese Szenen ein fahles graugrün" (*opernmagazin.de*, 10.9.2019). Und ganz anders als bei Shakespeare hilft Emilia (Kelsey Lauritano), hier Desdemonas jüngere Schwester, kräftig mit, Desdemona und Otello auseinanderzutreiben, auch um Rodrigos Gunst zu erhaschen. Das Familienoberhaupt, Desdemonas und Emilias Vater, der Senator Elmiro (Hans-Jürgen Lazar), herrscht mit seinem durchdringenden Bass die Töchter an und diszipliniert sie mit strengen Blicken. Elmiro ist ein Patriarch mit schwarzer Pädagogik und guten Absichten, der Otello, anders als Shakespeares Brabantio, nicht ideologisch, sondern pragmatisch begegnet. "Die Familie und der Fremde. Das ist gut gemacht, gerade weil es nicht verbissen ist", hält von Sternburg fest (*Frankfurter Rundschau*, 9.9.2019).

Eifersucht und Fremdenhass eskalieren dann aber doch bereits am Ende des ersten Aktes, wenn sich die Familienmitglieder eine Kaviarschlacht leisten. Jago greift dabei in die Silberschüssel und schmiert den Namen 'Otello' an die Wand, bewirft diesen Namen und schließlich auch Otello selbst mit Kaviar-Schlamm. Als sich der Vorhang senkt, leckt er seine verklebten Hände ab. Musikalisch und

Otello, Oper Frankfurt, Regie: Damiano Michieletto
Theo Lebow (Jago), Enea Scala (Otello), Kelsey Lauritano (Emilia),
Jack Swanson (Rodrigo), Thomas Faulkner (Elmiro) und Chor
Foto: Barbara Aumüller

szenisch wird diese Ekstase durch den umherirrenden Chor (Leitung: Tilman Michael) unterstrichen.

"Mit Geschick hält Michieletto seine Deutungen vage. Auch leuchtet keineswegs jede Idee ein. Der Regisseur macht Angebote, das ist ein Auflockern, Aufwerten, Interessanter-Machen eines sowohl konventionellen als auch etwas irrwitzigen Librettos" (*Frankfurter Rundschau*, 9.9.2019). Im dritten Akt legen Libretto und Komposition das Augenmerk auf Desdemona selbst, die nun als lyrischer Sopran ihr ganzes Leid auskosten kann. Als "engelhaft [L]eidende" ist sie "der empfindende Mensch unter Egoisten und Schurken. Die schönsten Szenen hat sie entsprechend alleine, darunter mit dem unwiderstehlichen, diesmal sehr getragenen Weidenlied [Assisa a' piè d'un salice]", urteilt von Sternburg (*Frankfurter Rundschau*, 9.9.2019). Das episodenhafte Libretto hat inzwischen die Handlung vorangetrieben: Otello hat sich mit Rodrigo duelliert, und Desdemona wurde vom Vater verstoßen. Kurz bevor Otello Desdemona auf dem Bett erschießt, weil er fälschlich glaubt, diese habe im Traum von ihrem Liebhaber gesprochen, erkennt Desdemona, dass Jago als Intrigant die Eifersucht Otellos befeuert hat. Sodann tritt Lucio auf und berichtet, dass Rodrigo Jago getötet habe, allerdings erst, nachdem dieser seine intriganten Machenschaften gestanden hatte. Im Schlussbild treten der Doge, Elmiro und Rodrigo dazu. Letzterer beteuert, dass er der Liebe zwischen Otello und Desdemona nicht im Weg stehen will, worauf Elmiro Otello die Hand seiner Tochter verspricht. Otello erkennt seinen Irrtum, gibt den Blick auf Desdemona frei und tötet sich mit der Waffe, mit der er zuvor Desdemona getötet hatte. Unter Leitung von Quatrini durchläuft Michielettos Inszenierung all diese Wirrungen an einem anregenden Abend. Das Familiendrama inklusive Ehrenmord und Suizid entfaltet sich im Spannungsfeld zwischen elegischen, lyrischen Passagen und exzentrischen, hochdramatischen Koloraturen: "Mehr Stimmungen passen in drei Stunden nicht hinein" (*Frankfurter Rundschau*, 9.9.2019).

FELIX SPRANG

Künstlerglück und Künstlerpech:
Theaterschau Österreich 2019/2020

Am 27. September 2019 hatte *Hamlet* in der Inszenierung des jungen Londoner Regisseurs Rikki Henry am Landestheater Niederösterreich in St. Pölten Premiere (Übersetzung: Angela Schanelec und Jürgen Gosch). Laut Programmheft ist das Grundkonzept der Inszenierung, dass Hamlet (Tim Breyvogel) sich in einem Traum bzw. Albtraum befindet, in dem sich bestimmte Ereignisse stets wiederholen. Obwohl er seinen Traum teilweise selbst manipulieren kann, läuft er immer Gefahr, die Kontrolle zu verlieren. Entsprechend dieser Grundidee beginnt die Inszenierung mit dem Ende des Stücks: Horatio (Bettina Kerl) hält den Prinzen im Arm, der sie darum bittet, seine Geschichte zu erzählen. Nach einem Bühnenblackout liegt Hamlet in der nächsten Szene vor dem Vorhang und erwacht wie aus einem Albtraum. Claudius (Michael Scherff) und Gertrude (Marthe Lola Deutschmann) stehen nun hinter ihm. Der König beginnt mit seiner Thronrede, und das Stück, respektive Hamlets Traum, kann seinen Lauf nehmen. Hinweise, dass die Welt und die Geschehnisse auf der Bühne des Prinzen ein Traum sind, durchziehen die Inszenierung wie ein roter Faden, besonders deutlich und spektakulär etwa vor der Pause, wenn Hamlet Claudius während seines Gebets brutal das Genick bricht. Danach setzt er sich die Krone auf, bringt noch seine Mutter um und fragt anschließend ins Publikum: "Und so bin ich gerächt?" Nach der darauffolgenden Pause wird die Handlung bis zu dem Punkt zurückgespult, an dem Hamlet hinter dem betenden Claudius steht. Eine ähnliche Horroreinlage, die eher an *Macbeth* denn an *Hamlet* denken lässt, findet sich gegen Ende des Stücks, als der totgeglaubte, blutverschmierte Polonius (Tilman Rose) plötzlich wieder aufsteht und Hamlet würgt.

Nachdem das Stück als Hamlets Traum ausgewiesen ist, steht der Protagonist in dieser Inszenierung fast noch mehr im Mittelpunkt als üblich. Tim Breyvogel ist der Herausforderung gewachsen und legt seine Rolle vielschichtig an. Er wirkt energisch und selbstbewusst, zugleich aber auch jugendlich und verletzlich, eine "Mischung aus Popstar und Psycho" (*Kurier*, 29.9.2019). Neben ihm verblassen die anderen Schauspieler. Wenn Hamlet verrückt spielt, tritt er als Exzentriker mit einer Papierkrone auf dem Kopf auf und liest in einem großen *Hamlet*-Buch seine eigene Geschichte. Sein Gesicht ist clownhaft weiß geschminkt, seine Wangen rot; er trägt einen schäbigen Mantel, silberne Strümpfe und schwarze Schuhe mit hohen Sohlen (Kostüme: Cedric Mpaka). Zu Ophelia (Laura Laufenberg) unterhält er eine leidenschaftliche Beziehung.

Das Leitmotiv des Traums wird auch durch die düstere, beatlastige Musik (Nils Strunk), das Lichtdesign (Günter Zaworka) und die Drehbühne (Max Lindner) unterstrichen, die während der gesamten Inszenierung in fast ständiger Bewegung ist. Ein Holzgerüst, dem eine riesige Krone aufgesetzt ist, teilt die Bühne in verschiedene Räume, etwa einen Thronsaal mit goldenen Wänden oder ein kleines, mit rotem Plüsch ausstaffiertes Kämmerlein, in dem Hamlet Selbstmordgedanken hegt, bevor er zum entscheidenden Duell gefordert wird.

Am Ende der Inszenierung ist Hamlet wieder am Anfang angelangt. Während der Prinz wie schlafend an der Rampe liegt, beginnt das Stück von Neuem mit dem Auftritt von Claudius und Gertrude. Anders als zuvor steht Hamlet aber nun auf und spricht den Sein-oder-Nichtsein-Monolog (den vorher schon Ophelia in ihrer Wahnsinnsszene zum Besten gegeben hatte), während das Stück im Bühnenhintergrund wie im Zeitraffer noch einmal abläuft. Wie eine Zugabe hängt Hamlet dann noch die Rede seines aus dem Jenseits zurückgekehrten Vaters an. Erst danach ist Schweigen.

Trotz dieses schwerfällig hinausgezögerten Schlusses ist Rikki Henry, der bei Peter Brook sein Handwerk gelernt hat, eine moderne, bildgewaltige und mit etwa zwei Stunden Spielzeit klug gekürzte Inszenierung gelungen, die auch von der Kritik positiv aufgenommen wurde. *Der Standard* (29.9.2019) lobte, dass an diesem *Hamlet* "kein Körnchen Staub" sei, während laut *Wiener Zeitung* die Inszenierung zeige, dass "so packend umgesetzt" *Hamlet* mehr sein könne "als nur eine Bildungsbürgerpflicht" (29.9.2019).

Martin Kusejs erste Saison als neuer Direktor des Burgtheaters stand schon vor der Corona-bedingten Schließung Mitte März unter keinem besonders glücklichen Stern. Trotz Kusejs Bemühungen, das Burgtheater künstlerisch neu auszurichten und neue Regisseure und Ensemblemitglieder zu verpflichten, war bisher keine der ohne Zweifel ambitionierten Neuinszenierungen beim Publikum und/oder der Kritik ein durchschlagender Erfolg. *This is Venice* sollte keine Ausnahme bilden (Premiere am 22.2.2020). Bei dem Stück handelt es sich um eine Bearbeitung und Neuübersetzung von *Othello* und *Der Kaufmann von Venedig* durch die Kultur- und Literaturwissenschaftlerin Elisabeth Bronfen und die Bühnenbildnerin Muriel Gerstner. Ausgangspunkt sind die zahlreichen Parallelen zwischen den beiden Dramen, vor allem die Verortung der Handlungen im kapitalistischen System der Renaissance-Metropole Venedig und der Umgang seiner rassistisch und patriarchal geprägten Gesellschaft mit Fremden und mit Frauen. In Szene gesetzt wurde das so entstandene *mash-up* durch den Schweizer Starregisseur Sebastian Nübling, der zum ersten Mal an der Burg arbeitete.

Was die Übersetzung betrifft, so modernisiert, entpoetisiert und vereinfacht *This is Venice* die Sprache der zugrundeliegenden Originale. Im Vergleich zu anderen Bearbeitungen halten sich freie Hinzufügungen und/oder Slangausdrücke jedoch in Grenzen. Eine Ausnahme stellt Brabantio (Markus Hering) dar, der sich rassistischer und rechtspopulistischer Phrasen bedient. Er ruft etwa mehrmals nach einer "Bürgerwehr", beklagt "Mischehen" und faselt vom "großen Austausch". Manchmal werden in der Inszenierung einzelne Sätze auf Englisch gesprochen oder ein deutscher Satz auf Englisch wiederholt, zum Beispiel wenn Jago (Norman Hacker) Roderigo (Dietmar König) auffordert: "Ich sage dir, mach Geld locker. Put money in thy purse." Portia, die von der schwarzen amerikanischen Schauspielerin Stacyian Jackson gespielt wird und deren Deutsch aufgrund ihres Akzents oft schwer verständlich ist, spricht hin und wieder längere Textpassagen auf Englisch. Der israelische Regisseur und Schauspieler Itay Tiran, der Shylock spielt, darf auch einige Sätze auf Hebräisch sprechen. Die Inszenierung trägt somit auch zu Martin Kusejs Vorhaben bei, das Ensemble multikultureller und die Inszenierungen mehrsprachiger werden zu lassen.

Um einer der Grundideen von *This is Venice* gerecht zu werden, wird die Handlung ausschließlich auf den Rialto in Venedig verlegt. Die Türken nähern sich nicht wie in *Othello* Zypern, sondern liegen direkt vor Venedig vor Anker. Belmont wiederum wird zu einem venezianischen Palazzo erklärt. Bühnenbildlich wird dieses Venedig durch eine fast durchgehend leere, schwarze Drehbühne repräsentiert, die im Halbrund von einem dichten Vorhang aus Silberfäden abgeschlossen wird. Zu Beginn der Inszenierung defiliert das 14-köpfige Ensemble über einen quer über die Bühne gelegten Laufsteg und präsentiert sich, angestrengt lächelnd und verbissen Zähne zeigend, dem Publikum. Die Kostüme (Pascale Martin) sind wie die Bühne überwiegend in Schwarz gehalten und zitieren unterschiedliche Zeiten und Geschlechterkonventionen. Die Protagonisten (Othello, Iago, Shylock, Antonio) tragen meistens Anzug, die anderen (auch die Männer) schwarze Röcke und unterschiedliche Oberteile. Pelzmäntel, elisabethanische Halskrausen und Schleier sind häufig präsent.

Bei der Schauspielerführung legt die Regie den Fokus auf das Ensemble als Einheit und weniger auf die Solisten. Dementsprechend befinden sich zumeist alle Schauspielerinnen und Schauspieler zugleich auf der Bühne, und die vielen Gruppenszenen sind streng durchchoreographiert (Christine Gaigg). Die Protagonisten treten bei ihren Auftritten aus der Gruppe hervor und sprechen an der Rampe oder, wie etwa Jago, in der Mitte der Bühne in ein vom Schnürboden herabhängendes Mikrofon. Während der albtraumhaften Gewaltausbrüche im Zuge des Maskenballs bzw. der Siegesfeier über die Türken tragen die Schauspielerinnen und Schauspieler zum Großteil Latexmasken und sind nicht mehr als Individuen zu erkennen. Gegen Ende der Inszenierung, vor allem in der Gerichtsszene, erstarren die Schauspielerinnen und Schauspieler immer wieder in unterschiedlichen Gruppierungen zu *tableaux vivants*, die an berühmte Renaissance-Gemälde erinnern.

Wirklich vermischt werden die Handlungsstränge von *Othello* und *Der Kaufmann von Venedig* in *This is Venice* nicht. Die meiste Zeit laufen sie abwechselnd Szene für Szene ab. Direkte Verschränkungen ergeben sich nur aufgrund des gemeinsamen Ortes, der Rolle des Dogen (Rainer Galke) und mancher Nebenfiguren, die das Geschehen kommentieren oder Botschaften weiterleiten. Die zahlreichen Doppelbesetzungen – wie etwa Dietmar König als Antonio und Roderigo oder Mehmet Atesci als Bassanio und Cassio – stiften mitunter Verwirrung. Nerissa hingegen wird gleich von vier unterschiedlichen Schauspielerinnen gespielt. Othello und Shylock sind immer wieder gemeinsam auf der Bühne, aber obwohl sie einander durchaus wahrnehmen und einmal auch längere Zeit nebeneinander sitzen, interagieren sie nicht miteinander.

Während Joachim Meyerhoff in der letzten Burgtheater-Inszenierung von *Othello* vor zehn Jahren noch schwarz angemalt war, ist Blackfacing heute nicht mehr üblich. In *This is Venice* bleibt Othellos Hautfarbe bloße Behauptung: Roland Koch wird nur ständig als "der Schwarze" tituliert. Der Starschauspieler gibt den Othello als alternden, bierbäuchigen, wenig sympathischen Prolo, der zwar selbstsicher auftritt, aber weder Jago (Norman Hacker) und seinen Intrigen noch seiner selbstbewussten jungen Frau gewachsen ist. Desdemona (Marie-Luise Stockinger) ist das Gegenteil eines willfährigen Püppchens und liefert sich mit ihrem Ehemann wilde Schreiduelle, etwa über das abhanden gekommene Taschentuch. An Othellos Kostümierung ist besonders der groteske Federkopfschmuck mit einem Stirnband aus leuchtenden Glühbirnen auffällig, mit dem er nach dem kampflosen Sieg über die Türken auftritt. Ob dieses Kleidungsstück Othellos Sinn für kauzigen Humor illustrieren soll oder als Hinweis darauf gedacht ist, dass die venezianische Gesellschaft ihn behandelt wie ein Zirkuspferd, wird nicht klar.

Die in dieser Inszenierung oft grelle Komik der Othello-Szenen lässt die tragische Shylock-Handlung in den Hintergrund geraten. Der Israeli Itay Tiran, der am Burgtheater bisher nur als Regisseur (*Die Vögel*) in Erscheinung getreten ist, spielt den jüdischen Geldverleiher mit starkem, israelischem Akzent als Geschäftsmann im teuren Anzug im Stil von Peter Zadeks berühmter Inszenierung von 1988. Sein Shylock bleibt aber im Gegensatz zu jenem von Gert Voss farblos und wenig mitreißend. Nach der Gerichtsszene wirkt er vollkommen gebrochen und muss halbnackt auf allen Vieren über die Bühne kriechen. Othello, der auch gerade auf der Bühne ist, scheint ihn als Leidensgenossen zu erkennen und zu bemitleiden. Am Ende von *This is Venice* steht ein feministischer Paukenschlag. Portia (Stacyian Jackson) erklärt nicht nur ihre Heirat mit Bassanio als hinfällig, da er ja den Ehering hergeschenkt hat, sondern sie scheint auch die Rolle des Herrschers von Venedig an sich zu reißen. Sie wiederholt – ohne Ironie – den Anfangsmonolog des Dogen über die Freiheiten, die ein Fremder in Venedig genießt, und richtet dann an das Publikum die Frage, die sie schon an Shylock am Ende der Gerichtsszene gestellt hat: "Seid ihr alle zufrieden? Are you contented all?"

This is Venice, Burgtheater Wien, Regie: Sebastian Nübling
Norman Hacker (Jago), Roland Koch (Othello)
Foto: Matthias Horn

Die Kritikerinnen und Kritiker beantworteten Portias Frage mit einem ziemlich klaren Nein. Obwohl das zugrundeliegende Konzept von *This is Venice* als überzeugend und mutig gelobt wurde, fand die dreieinhalbstündige Umsetzung wenig Anklang. *Die Presse* (24.2.2020) etwa kritisierte, dass *This is Venice* einer "Nummernrevue gleicht" und dass sich keine "faszinierende Aura entfaltet, weil dauernd die Kommunikation unterbrochen wird". Ein häufiger Kritikpunkt ist auch, dass mit *This is Venice* kein Stück aus einem Guss entstanden sei. Die *Süddeutsche Zeitung* (27.2.2020) formulierte dies folgendermaßen: "Die Kombination von zwei starken Stücken ergibt nicht etwa besonders starken Stoff, im Gegenteil, die Komponenten neutralisieren einander eher. This is Künstlerpech."

LUDWIG SCHNAUDER

Kritische Rücksprache mit Shakespeare: "Zwei wuchtig lahme Stunden" in Bern und ein "Shakespeare-Abend der Sonderklasse" in Zürich

Auch ohne die Schließung aller Kultureinrichtungen in den Frühjahrs- und Sommermonaten des vergangenen Jahres 2020 hätte es über Shakespeare-Inszenierungen an den Schweizer Theatern nicht viel mitzuteilen gegeben. Zwei Ereignisse aus dem ersten Halbjahr 2019, die an dieser Stelle noch nicht vorgestellt wurden, erregten jedoch einige Aufmerksamkeit, über die hier – ausnahmsweise aus zweiter Hand – berichtet werden soll.

Im Konzert Theater Bern setzt sich die junge deutsche Regisseurin Mizgin Bilmen mit Shakespeares früher Tragödie *Titus Andronicus* auseinander. Da aber, wie uns der Dramaturg (Michael Gmaj) im Programmheft unter Berufung auf Jan Kott verrät, Shakespeares frühe Stücke dramaturgische Schwächen haben, werden diese Probleme "umschifft", indem man die stark gekürzte Fassung Shakespeares (Übersetzung: Frank Günther) durch Passagen aus Heiner Müllers Bearbeitung *Anatomie Titus Fall of Rome: Ein Shakespearekommentar* (1984) ergänzt. Dem Programmheft sind auch die Leitgedanken zum Regiekonzept zu entnehmen. Shakespeares Rom heiße London, beide politische Machtzentren ihrer Zeit, gekennzeichnet durch "Dekadenz und Völlerei […] Gewalt und Armut" (S. 7). Wie wir ein 'dekadentes' System als Ausdruck einer Endzeit mit unserem Gefühl einer noch jungen Metropole in der frühen Phase der Neuzeit zusammendenken können, wird freilich nicht erläutert. Ohne Frage leistet Heiner Müller hier, laut Programmheft mit Blick auf den "reichen, privilegierten Westen [und dessen] entfesselten Kapitalismus" (S. 9) in den Jahren vor dem Fall des Eisernen Vorhangs, Hilfestellung, wobei wir die Frage offenlassen, ob es sich bei seiner Bearbeitung wirklich nur um eine Ost-West-Blickrichtung handelt. Interessanter sind die Ausführungen zur Psychologie der Macht und zur Manipulationsstrategie verschlagener Potentaten. Auch jüngere politische Probleme, der Zuwanderung etwa, werden aus der Attraktion dieses "dekadenten" politischen Raumes erklärt: der Reichtum "importiert" Menschen aus aller Welt, unter denen sich auch "potenziell feindliche Menschen" befinden. Die Folge: "Neue Regeln des Zusammenlebens werden definiert, neue Sicherheitsmaßnahmen etabliert, jeder büsst an Freiheit ein" (Programmheft, S. 9). Die Erklärung der Welt in zwei Stunden will umgesetzt werden.

Das karge, aus drei mehrere Meter hohen Buchstaben – "R-O-M" – bestehende Bühnenbild (Cleo Niemeyer) bekundet dieses Konzept unmissverständlich: Rom ist eine Signatur für das neue Zentrum dieser Welt, nicht nur Londons, wie man später erfährt, sondern aller Finanzmetropolen. In diese drei Buchstaben verkriechen sich die Akteure, kauern in deren Aushöhlungen oder stehen Macht gebietend auf deren Spitzen. Das ist kein schlechtes Bild: In diesem "Rom" agieren manche obenauf, andere müssen sich verkriechen – durch beeindruckende Fotos im Programmheft vermittelt.

Ansonsten aber reagierte die Kritik reserviert und sieht das im Programmheft entwickelte Konzept nicht umgesetzt. Maximilian Pahl konstatiert ernüchtert: "In zwei wuchtig lahmen Stunden bleibt [...] schleierhaft, wie man dieses Blutbad auf Zeitphänomene wie die Gelbwesten, Trump, den Populismus beziehen soll (wie das Programmheft nahelegt)" (*nachtkritik*, 22. 2. 2019). "Eine zähe Sache", stimmt Michael Feller zu, "offen bleibt, was Bilmen will" (*Berner Zeitung*, 25. 2. 2019).

Enttäuschend bleibt vor allem der durch die Einbeziehung der Texte Heiner Müllers versprochene Blick auf die Jetztzeit. Müllers Gegenlektüre von Shakespeares Aaron (Alexander Maria Schmidt), im Doppel gespielt mit der jungen Hip-Hop-Tänzerin Thamara Stampbach alias Muud, "geht unter", weil er in dieser Kurzfassung "nicht durchdacht genug" ausfällt, um derartige Themen zu verhandeln (*nachtkritik*, 22. 2. 2019), und zudem "durch unzusammenhängende szenische Gags verflacht" wird, wie Lena Rittmeyer klagt (*Der Bund*, 25. 2. 2019).

An solchen Gags mangelt es nicht. Ganz im Geist des – laut Rittmeyer längst ermatteten – Regietheaters, "das gemäss Klischee nicht ohne Blut, nackte Pimmel, übermotivierte Schauspieler und ein paar popkulturelle Referenzen auskommt" (*Der Bund*, 25. 2. 2019), werden Tamoras Söhne Chiron und Demetrius (David Brückner, David Berger) zu zwei "geile[n], knutschende[n] Brüder[n] in geschmacklosen Frauenkleidern" (Kostüme: Alexander Djurkov Hotter), wobei David Berger sein entblößtes Geschlecht zum wiederholten Male in Bern ausstellen darf, wie die Kritikerin verächtlich bemerkt. Und damit ist er nicht allein: Wenn unter waberndem Trockeneisnebel die Freiheitsstatue auf einem Rollator auf die Bühne rollt, ist sie von zwei nackten Knechten mit Ku-Klux-Klan-Hauben begleitet.

Auch das Abschlussbild steht schließlich in einem US-amerikanischen Rahmen: Titus lässt das Knochenmehl von Chiron und Demetrius nicht zu Pasteten backen, sondern serviert im Ronald-McDonald-Kostüm Hamburger-Brötchen, die "das Kaiserpaar [...] in sich hineinstopft" (Rittmeyer, *Der Bund*, 25. 2. 2019).

Dass dieser Titus von einer Frau (Chantal LeMoign) gespielt wird, scheint indes ein "Glücksgriff" (*Der Bund*, 25. 2. 2019) der Inszenierung zu sein, "Bilmens einziger Trumpf" (*nachtkritik*, 22. 2. 2019). Sie gibt einem müden, brüchigen Titus Andronicus eine beeindruckende Statur – besonnen, meditierend, ohne Pathos, "sodass ihre Monologe Lichtblicke werden" (*nachtkritik*, 22. 2. 2019). Auch Irina Wronas eiskalte Tamora und Milva Starks horrorgezeichnete Lavinia werden hervorgehoben aus einem ansonsten "auf einem Spielfeld herumsteh[enden]" Ensemble, in dem auch Marcus Andronicus (Jürg Wisbach) und Bassianus (Andreas Gaida) "engagiert, aber bleich" und Aaron (Alexander Maria Schmidt) "farblos" bleiben (*Der Bund*, 25. 2. 2019).

Dennoch erscheint dieser Ansatz grundsätzlich vielversprechend. Einen 'Klassiker' nicht durch dessen modernisierende Umschreibung zu aktualisieren und dem kanonisierten Text stillschweigend einen allein musealen "Materialwert", wie Brecht es nannte, zu unterstellen, sondern diesen Klassiker mit der Gegenlektüre eines heutigen Dramatikers zu konfrontieren, alten Text und neue Fassung auf der Bühne zu einer wechselseitigen Spiegelung zu nötigen, wird beiden Autoren gerecht und bringt womöglich etwas wirklich Neues hervor. Wenn wir das Alte nicht nur auf seine Anschlussfähigkeit, sondern auch auf seine ästhetische Leistung, die sich in einer langen Rezeptionsgeschichte behauptet hat, und auf seinen Erinnerungswert befragen, fällt die Antwort auf die Frage, welche ästhetische und intellektuelle Substanz das Neue zu bieten hat, vielleicht überzeugender aus.

Dass dieser Balanceakt der Regisseurin Mizgin Bilmen nicht gelungen ist, lag nach Meinung der Kritik nicht an der Idee, sondern an der Ausführung durch Regie und Ensemble. Vielleicht dürfen wir für 2021, in dem es am 5. Januar Dürrenmatts einhundertsten Geburtstag zu feiern gibt, einen entsprechenden Versuch mit seinem *Titus Andronicus* aus dem Jahr 1970 erwarten.

Einen "Shakespeare-Abend der Sonderklasse" erlebte hingegen das Zürcher Publikum in der Schiffbau-Box, wo Trajal Harrells (Choreographie und Inszenierung) *Juliet & Romeo* zum Jahresende 2019 eine umjubelte Premiere feierte. Und der Rezensent Daniele Muscionico für die *Neue Zürcher Zeitung* (18. 12. 2019) gibt sich mit einem Superlativ nicht zufrieden: "Wer ihn versäumt, verpasst den ersten – künstlerischen, zeitgenössischen und selbstkritischen – Höhepunkt der Intendanz von Benjamin von Blomberg und Nicolas Stemann." Allerdings war es keine Neuinszenierung, sondern eine Übernahme der Münchner Kammerspiele mit fast unverändertem Ensemble (Uraufführung: 25. 10. 2017), die Harrell mit seinem Wechsel von München auf eine feste Verpflichtung in Zürich als Visitenkarte mitbrachte. Ob das Zürcher Publikum nunmehr in Sachen Aufgeschlossenheit für "die Engführung von Tanz, Theater und bildender Kunst" Berlin "den Rang abzulaufen scheint", wie Muscionico in Anspielung auf ähnliche Bemühungen an Chris Dercons Berliner Volksbühne hofft, die Harrell enttäuscht verlassen hatte, wollen wir abwarten.

Von der Inszenierung lässt sich aus den zahl- und umfangreichen Münchner und Zürcher Presserezensionen und einem Abendzettel, den die Münchner Dramaturgin dieses Projekts (Katinka Deecke) für ein Gastspiel im Hamburger Kulturzentrum Kampnagel im Februar 2018 verfasste, ein recht guter Eindruck gewinnen.

Harrell verzichtet auf eine der Tragödienhandlung verpflichtete Nacherzählung; sie sei ja allgemein bekannt, ließ er verlauten. Seine Tragödie beginnt am Ende mit der Trauer über den Tod der Liebenden. Er setzt andere thematische Akzente, stellt um, wie schon die Namen im Titel verraten: Statt grenzenloser, leidenschaftlicher Liebe steht das Sterben im Mittelpunkt. "Mehr sterben als lieben" betitelte seinerzeit die *Süddeutsche Zeitung* ihre Münchner Besprechung (Rita Argauer, *Süddeutsche Zeitung*, 24.10.2017). Harrell erzählt den Zeitraum zwischen Tod und Versöhnung mit den großen Gefühlen des Schmerzes und der Trauer. Einige Schlüsselszenen von Shakespeares Tragödie blitzen wie tänzerisch zitierte Leitmotive auf und erinnern an den Zusammenhang. Und er spielt mit Optionen. In den Szenen zwischen Tod und Versöhnung "schickt er die Geister der Toten auf den Laufsteg. Lauter Julias oder das, was aus Julia alles hätte werden können: Verführerinnen" (Daniele Muscionico, *Neue Zürcher Zeitung*, 18.12.2019).

Im Mittelpunkt steht die Amme, getanzt und gespielt von Trajal Harrell selbst. Sie, selbst eine Liebende, beobachtet von einer Bank aus die Trauernden, umschreitet die Gräber, in wechselnden Kostümen die Haltungen und Gefühle wechselnd. Harrell lenkt und strukturiert das Geschehen, rahmt aber auch den Theaterabend, wenn er und sein Ensemble die Zuschauer beim Eintreten einzeln begrüßen und am Ende verabschieden. Er holte das Publikum in die Trauer hinein, und es ließ sich offenbar willig und betroffen auf die Einladung ein.

Acht weitere Akteure, ein Ensemble aus Tänzern und Schauspielern, spielen und tanzen die weiteren Rollen in wechselnder Besetzung und gewechselten Kostümen, jeder spielt jede, Namensschilder auf den Rücken zeigen die wechselnden Identitäten und Geschlechter an. Dabei fällt auf, dass nur Männer auf der Bühne stehen, so wie es die elisabethanische Bühne kannte. "Sie wiegen sich im Laufsteggang auf hoher, halber Spitze, springen in Chassés um die Gräber oder gehen langsam in einer Trauerparade. [...] Dazu eine Musikcollage [...], betörende und treibende Songs und Sounds, von Alessandro Scarlatti bis zu einem Beatles-Cover, Daniel Zaitchiks und Jayce Claytons 'Evil Nigger' und 'Gay Guerilla'" (Katja Schneider, *muenchner-feuilleton.de*, 18.11.2017).

Mit ihren ganz eigenen Mitteln "loten Harrell und seine Compagnie die Gefühlspalette von Trauer, Kummer, Schmerz aus" (Julia Nehmiz, *St. Gallener Tagblatt*, 18.12.2019). Diese ganz eigenen Mittel bestehen nicht zuletzt darin, dass

Harrell auch Anleihen aus der Popkultur und dem Marketing-Design in seine postmoderne Tanzästhetik integriert. Der Friedhofsweg wird zum Laufsteg, weil er das Voguing als Bewegungsmuster bevorzugt. Es "imitiert das Laufen von Models auf dem Catwalk, entstand in der schwulen New Yorker Subkultur der 1980er Jahre. Dass die postmoderne Theaterästhetik auch gesellschaftspolitisch zu lesen ist, scheint Nebensache. Harrell interessiert das menschliche, männliche Ringen um Stil, um Performance, um Haltung, Form" (Muscionico, *Neue Zürcher Zeitung*, 18.12.2019). Dass diese Schönheit auch im Dienste einer Ästhetik des Hässlichen und Politischen stehen kann, bezeugt die Kampfszene zwischen den verfeindeten Familien: "Körper ohne Worte [erzeugen] eine Atmosphäre von Aggression und schierer Gewalt [...] wirkungsmächtiger als jede ausgeführte Tat." Wenn zu Beginn die acht Akteure gemeinsam an der Rampe standen und mit Wortfetzen nach "Respekt", "Schönheit", "Musik" riefen, stehen sie am Ende dieses jeden Trost verweigernden Abends vereinzelt auf der Bühne, "jeder stößt Wünsche aus, die nach Freundschaft, Hilfe, Erinnerung rufen". Aber "[e]rfüllt werden sie nicht. [...] Der Abend endet berührend, aber ohne Trost." (Nehmiz, *St. Gallener Tagblatt*, 18.12.2019)

Dem Schmerz Form zu geben und über die Form auch eine ganz eigene 'Schönheit' zu verleihen, das ist nach allen Kritikerbezeugungen das eigentliche Faszinosum aus dieser Mischung von Shakespeare, Spiel und Tanz. Harrell versteht sich als Erfinder ritueller Vorgänge. Er bietet den "Menschen, die zwar Gott entsorgt, aber nichts an seine Stelle gesetzt haben", ein neues Vokabular für ihre Grenzsituationen an und verleiht seinen Liebes- und Todesritualen mit Anleihen aus "einem der wenigen opulenten Rituale unserer Zeit: der Fashionshow" Ausdruck und Stil (Katinka Deecke, verantwortliche Dramaturgin der Münchner Kammerspiele in einem Abendzettel für ein Gastspiel auf Kampnagel, Hamburg). Und diese Rituale werden dann doch (auch) zu einer Spielart des politischen Theaters: Indem deren Bewegungsmuster eine New Yorker Subkultur der achtziger Jahre in Erinnerung rufen, wird auch "das Anderssein selbst als Verkörperung von Schönheit in den Mittelpunkt gesetzt" (Katja Schneider, *muenchner.feuilleton.de*, 18.11.2017).

Mit der schon seit einiger Zeit zu beobachtenden Überwindung der Spartengrenzen öffnen sich dem zeitgenössischen Theater vielleicht tatsächlich neue ressourcenreiche, produktive Perspektiven, die uns zu einem neuen Sehen einladen, das das ermattet erscheinende 'Regietheater' derzeit nicht mehr recht zu lenken versteht.

Das Publikum ist offenbar bereit, wie die Haltung gegenüber dem Gewagten, Provozierenden in Bern wie in Zürich zeigt. Wenn in Zürich die Schönheit, affektive Tiefe und überzeugende ästhetische Leistung gelobt wird, dann nicht aus einer traditionellen 'kulinarischen' Rezeptionshaltung heraus, sondern aus offenkundiger Freude an der Suche eines sich als postmodernes Tanztheater verstehenden Ensembles nach neuen, zeitgemäßen Ausdrucksformen. Und ebenso ist die Ablehnung des Berner Experiments nicht konservativen Vorbehalten geschuldet, sondern der Enttäuschung darüber, dass ein Regiekonzept nicht zu erkennen war und die trotz aller Grausamkeiten freilich gar nicht mehr so provozierende Theatersprache langweilte. Ziel und Dramaturgie sind die gleichen. In Zürich gelang, was in Bern enttäuschte.

NORBERT GREINER

Verzeichnis der Shakespeare-Inszenierungen Spielzeit 2019/2020

BETTINA BOECKER UND MARIETTA WENNING

Dieses Verzeichnis enthält Angaben zu Shakespeare-Inszenierungen in Deutschland, Österreich und der Schweiz. Inszenierungen, die aus früheren Spielzeiten wieder aufgenommen wurden, wurden nur dann berücksichtigt, wenn es sich um eine stark überarbeitete Wiederaufnahme handelt. Nachdichtungen und freie Bearbeitungen, wie Opern- und Ballettaufführungen, finden sich unter dem als Vorlage dienenden Stücktitel (z. B. Porter, *Kiss Me, Kate* unter *The Taming of the Shrew*). Das Verzeichnis wurde im Oktober 2020 abgeschlossen.

Abkürzungen

B.:	Bühnenbild	R.:	Regie
Chor.:	Choreographie	Ü.:	Übersetzung
K.:	Kostüme	UA.:	Uraufführung
ML:	Musikalische Leitung		

As You Like It

Celle, Schlosstheater Celle: 13. 9. 2019, *Wie es euch gefällt*. R.: Andreas Döring, B. und K.: Sabina Moncys.

Kassel, Staatstheater Kassel (Schauspielhaus): 6. 9. 2019, *Wie es euch gefällt*. R.: Philipp Rosendahl, B.: Katharina Faltner, K.: Ulrike Obermüller.

Coriolanus

Bregenz, Vorarlberger Landestheater: 21. 9. 2019, *Cold Songs: Rom; Coriolanus* (UA.). R.: Catharina May, K.: Wicke Naujoks.

Hamlet

Baden-Baden, Theater Baden-Baden: 18. 1. 2020, *Hamlet*. R.: Harald Fuhrmann, B.: und K.: Timo Dentler und Okarina Peter.

Berlin, Maxim Gorki Theater (Container): 1. 2. 2020, *Hamlet*. Ü.: Angela Schanelec, R.: Christian Weise, B.: Julia Oschatz, K.: Paula Wellmann.

Greifswald, Theater Vorpommern (Großes Haus): 12.10.2019, *Hamlet*. Ü.: Jürgen Gosch und Andrea Schanelec, R.: Reinhard Göber, B.: Johann Jörg, K.: Kerstin Laube. (Gleiche Produktion wie in Stralsund.)
Hamburg, Thalia Theater (Großes Haus): 23.1.2020, *Hamlet*. Ü.: Frank-Patrick Steckel, R.: Jette Steckel, B.: Florian Lösche, K.: Pauline Hüners.
Köln, Bühnen der Stadt Köln – Oper (Staatenhaus): 24.11.2019, *Hamlet*. Von Brett Dean. Libretto von Matthew Jocelyn. ML: Duncan Ward, R.: Matthew Jocelyn, B.: Alain Lagarde, K.: Astrid Janson.
Rendsburg, Schleswig-Holsteinisches Landestheater (Stadttheater Rendsburg): 7.12.2019, *Hamlet*. R.: Anna-Elisabeth Frick, B. und K.: Martha-Marie Pinsker.
Rudolstadt, Theater im Stadthaus: 25.1.2020, *Hamlet*. R.: Alejandro Quintana, B. und K.: Andrea Eisensee.
Stralsund, Theater Vorpommern (Großes Haus): 30.10.2019, *Hamlet*. Ü.: Jürgen Gosch und Andrea Schanelec, R.: Reinhard Göber, B.: Johann Jörg, K.: Kerstin Laube. (Gleiche Produktion wie in Greifswald.)
St. Pölten, Landestheater Niederösterreich (Großes Haus): 27.9.2019, *Hamlet*. R.: Rikki Henry, B.: Max Lindner, K.: Cedric Mpaka.

Julius Caesar

Stuttgart, Forum-Theater: 3.10.2019, *Julius Cäsar*. R.: Dieter Nelle, B. und K.: Vesna Hiltmann.
Bregenz, Vorarlberger Landestheater: 21.9.2019, *Cold Songs: Rom; Julius Caesar* (UA.). R.: Johannes Lepper, K.: Sabine Wegmann.

King Lear

Bonn, Theater Bonn (Schauspielhaus): 28.2.2020, *König Lear*. R. und B.: Luise Voigt, B.: Stefan Bischoff, K.: Maria Strauch.
München, Münchner Kammerspiele (Kammer 1: Schauspielhaus): 28.9.2019, *König Lear*. Ü.: Thomas Melle, R.: Stefan Pucher, B.: Nina Peller, K.: Annabelle Witt.

Macbeth

Marburg, Hessisches Landestheater Marburg (Erwin-Piscator-Haus): 13.9.2019, *Macbeth*. R.: Carola Unser, B.: Fred Bielefeldt, K.: Jörn Fröhlich.

Measure for Measure

Münster, Theater Münster (Großes Haus): 16.11.2019, *Maß für Maß*. Ü.: Thomas Brasch, R.: Ronny Jakubaschk, B. und K.: David Gonter.

The Merchant of Venice

München, Münchner Volkstheater (Große Bühne): 27.10.2019, *Der Kaufmann von Venedig.* R.: Christian Stückl, B. und K.: Stefan Hageneier.

The Merry Wives of Windsor

Berlin, Staatsoper Berlin (Staatsoper Unter den Linden): 3.10.2019, *Die lustigen Weiber von Windsor.* Von Otto Nicolai. ML.: Daniel Barenboim, R.: David Bösch, B.: Patrick Bannwart, K.: Falko Herold.

A Midsummer Night's Dream

Berlin, Deutsche Oper Berlin (Großes Haus): 26.1.2020, *A Midsummer Night's Dream.* Von Benjamin Britten. Libretto von Benjamin Britten und Peter Pears. ML.: Donald Runnicles, R.: Ted Huffman, B.: Marsha Ginsberg, K.: Annemarie Woods.
Dornach, neuestheater.ch (Saal): 12.3.2020, *Ein Sommernachtstraum.* R.: Sandra Löwe.
Dortmund, Theater Dortmund (Opernhaus): 22.2.2020, *Ein Mittsommernachtstraum.* Von Mikael Karlsson. Chor., R. und B.: Alexander Ekman, K.: Bregje van Balen.
Hagen, theaterhagen (Großes Haus): 11.1.2020, *Ein Sommernachtstraum.* R.: Francis Hüsers, B.: Swen Erik Scheuerling, K.: Karina Liutaia.
Ingolstadt, Stadttheater Ingolstadt (Großes Haus): 5.10.2019, *Rose und Regen, Schwert und Wunde. Ein Sommernachtstraum nach William Shakespeare.* Von Beat Fäh. Ü.: Erich Fried, R.: Julia Mayr.
St. Gallen, Theater St. Gallen (Lokremise): 7.3.2020, *Träume einer Sommernacht nach William Shakespeare* (UA.). Von Theo Fransz. R.: Theo Fransz.
Stralsund, Theater Vorpommern (Großes Haus): 16.10.2019, *Ein Sommernachtstraum nach Shakespeare.* Aufgeführt von DIE ECKIGEN. Eine Produktion des kreisdiakonischen Werkes Stralsund e.V. in Kooperation mit dem Theater Vorpommern.
Wien, Wiener Staatsoper: 2.10.2019, *A Midsummer Night's Dream.* Von Benjamin Britten. ML.: Simone Young, R.: Irina Brook, B.: Noëlle Ginefri-Corbel, K.: Magali Castellan.

Othello

Coburg, Landestheater Coburg (Großes Haus): 8.2.2020, *Othello.* R. und K.: Konstanze Lauterbach, B.: Ariane Salzbrunn.
Darmstadt, Staatstheater Darmstadt (Kleines Haus): 14.9.2019, *Othello.* Ü.: Wolfgang Heinrich Graf Baudissin und Feridun Zaimoğlu/Günter Senkel, R.: Gustav Rueb, B.: Daniel Roskamp, K.: Dorothee Joisten.
Frankfurt am Main, Oper Frankfurt (Großes Haus): 8.9.2019, *Otello.* Von Gioachino Rossini. ML.: Sesto Quatrini, R.: Damiano Michieletto, B.: Paolo Fantin, K.: Carla Teti. (Übernahme aus Wien.)

Greifswald, Theater Vorpommern (Großes Haus): 29.2.2020, *Othello*. Von Michio Woirgardt. Chor. und R.: Ralf Dörnen, B. und K.: Klaus Hellenstein. (Gleiche Produktion wie in Stralsund.)
Hof, Theater Hof (Großes Haus): 15.2.2020, *Othello*. Ü.: Miriam Schwan, R.: Reinhardt Friese, B. und K.: Annette Mahlendorf.
München,: Theaterakademie August Everding (Akademietheater): 15.2.2020, *Othello Remix*. R.: Katja Wachter, B., Katja Wachter, K.: Barbara Mühldorfer und Christina Vogel.
Stralsund, Theater Vorpommern (Großes Haus): 1.2.2020, *Othello* (UA.). Von Michio Woirgardt. Chor. und R.: Ralf Dörnen, B. und K.: Klaus Hellenstein. (Gleiche Produktion wie in Greifswald.)

Richard III

Reutlingen, Theater Reutlingen Die Tonne (Tonnenkeller im Spitalhof): 25.1.2020, *Richard III – Great Again nach William Shakespeare* (UA.). Von Michael Miensopust. R.: Michael Miensopust.
Rostock, Volkstheater Rostock (Großes Haus): 14.9.2019, *Richard III*. Ü.: Juri Sternburg, R.: Angelika Zacek, B.: Martin Fischer, K.: Lisa-Dorothee Franke.

Romeo and Juliet

Biel, Theater Orchester Biel Solothurn (Stadttheater Solothurn): 12.3.2020, *Romeo und Julia*. Ü.: Thomas Brasch, R.: Veit Schubert, B. und K.: Stephan Fernau, Fecht-Chor.: Klaus Figge.
Bonn, Theater Bonn (Opernhaus): 15.9.2019, *West Side Story*. Von Leonard Bernstein und Stephen Sondheim. ML.: Daniel Johannes Mayr, R.: Erik Petersen.
Ingolstadt, Stadttheater Ingolstadt (Großes Haus): 18.10.2019, *Romeo und Julia*. Ü.: Sven-Eric Bechtolf und Wolfgang Wiens, R.: Mareike Mikat, B.: Simone Manthey, K.: Anna Sörensen.
Osnabrück, Städtische Bühnen Osnabrück (Theater am Domhof): 1.2.2020, *Romeo und Julia*. Ü.: Marius von Mayenburg, R.: Walter Meierjohann, B.: Steffi Wurster, K.: Hannah Petersen.
Salzburg, Salzburger Landestheater: 22.2.2020, *Romeo und Julia*. Von Sergej Prokofjew nach William Shakespeare. Chor.: Reginaldo Oliveira, B.: Sebastian Hannak, K.: Judith Adam.
Weimar, Deutsches Nationaltheater und Staatskapelle Weimar (Großes Haus): 1.2.2020, *Romeo und Julia*. R.: Jan Neumann, B.: Oliver Helf, K.: Cary Gayler.
Zürich, Schauspielhaus Zürich (Schiffbau/Box): 17.12.2019, *Juliet & Romeo*. Chor.: Trajal Harrell, B.: Erik Flatmo und Trajal Harrell, K.: Trajal Harrell.

The Taming of the Shrew

Freiburg, Theater Freiburg (Großes Haus): 13. 3. 2020, *Der Widerspenstigen Zähmung*. R.: Ewelina Marciniak, B.: Grzegorz Layer, K.: Julia Kornacka.

The Tempest

Augsburg, Staatstheater Augsburg (martini-Park): 12. 10. 2019, *Der Sturm*. R.: André Bücker, B.: Jan Steigert, K.: Suse Tobisch.
Innsbruck, Tiroler Landestheater und Orchester (Großes Haus): 2. 11. 2019, *The Tempest* (UA.). Von Enrique Gasa Valga nach William Shakespeare. Chor.: Enrique Gasa Valga, B.: Helfried Lauckner, K.: Birgit Edelbauer.

Twelfth Night

Düsseldorf, Düsseldorfer Schauspielhaus (Kleines Haus): 28. 9. 2019, *Was ihr wollt*. R.: Joanna Praml, B. und K.: Jana Denhoven und Inga Timm.
Göttingen, Deutsches Theater Göttingen (DT-1): 12. 10. 2019, *Was ihr wollt*. Ü.: Thomas Brasch, R.: Moritz Beichl, B.: Dirk Becker, K.: Astrid Klein.

The Winter's Tale

Bremen, bremer shakespeare company (Theater am Leibnizplatz): 29. 2. 2020, *Das Wintermärchen*. Ü.: Chris Alexander, R.: Patricia Benecke, B. und K.: Heike Neugebauer und Rike Schimitschek.

Weitere Stücke

Bayreuth, Studiobühne Bayreuth (Römisches Theater der Ermitage, Außenspielstätte): 18. 7. 2020, *Lockerspiele 2020 – Lustige Szenen von Shakespeare, Goethe, Molière und Karl Valentin*. R.: Birgit Franz, Werner Hildenbrand, Dominik Kern und Marieluise Müller, K.: Heike Betz und Marianne Heide.
Biel, Theater Orchester Biel Solothurn (Stadttheater Biel): 19. 1. 2020, *Romeo, Romeo, Romeo*. Chor.: Joshua Monten.
Celle, Schlosstheater Celle: 6. 12. 2019, *Sein oder Nichtsein nach Ernst Lubitsch*. Von Nick Whitby. R.: Michael Klammer.

Düsseldorf, Düsseldorfer Schauspielhaus (Großes Haus): 14.12.2019, *Henry VI. & Margaretha di Napoli nach William Shakespeare.* Von Tom Lanoye. R.: David Bösch, B.: Patrick Bannwart, K.: Falko Herold.

Eggenfelden, Theater an der Rott: 4.10.2019, *Shakespeares sämtliche Werke, leicht gekürzt.* Von Adam Long, Daniel Singer und Jess Winfield. Ü.: Dorothea Renckhoff. R.: Caroline Richards.

Frankfurt am Main, Oper Frankfurt (Großes Haus): 3.11.2019, *Lady Macbeth von Mzensk.* Von Dimitri Schostakowitsch. Libretto von Alexander G. Preis. ML.: Sebastian Weigle, R.: Anselm Weber, B. und K.: Kaspar Glaner, Chor.: Tilman Michael.

Freiberg, Mittelsächsisches Theater (Bühne Döbeln): 28.9.2019, *Sein oder Nichtsein nach Ernst Lubitsch.* Von Nick Whitby. R.: Annett Wöhlert.

Freiburg, Theater Freiburg (Großes Haus): 28.9.2019, *Falstaff.* Von Guiseppe Verdi. ML.: Fabrice Bollon, R.: Anna-Sophie Mahler, B.: Duri Bischoff, K.: Nic Tillein.

Genf, Théâtre de Carouge-Atelier de Genève (La Cuisine): 1.11.2019, *Les Sonnets.* R.: Jean Bellorini und Thierry Thieû Niang, B.: Jean Bellorini.

Greifswald, Theater Vorpommern (Rubenowsaal): 11.10.2019, *Die Hamletmaschine.* Von Heiner Müller. R.: Annett Kruschke, B. und K.: Indra Nauck. (Gleiche Produktion wie in Stralsund.)

Hamburg, Staatsoper Hamburg (Großes Haus): 19.1.2020, *Falstaff.* Von Guiseppe Verdi. ML.: Axel Kober, R.: Calixto Bieito, B.: Susanne Gschwender, K.: Anja Rabes.

Hamburg, Altonaer Theater: 27.10.2019, *Shakespeare in Love.* Von Lee Hall. Ü.: Corinna Brocher, R.: Franz-Joseph Dieken, B. und K.: Sabine Kohlstedt und Yvonne Marcour, ML.: Florian Miro.

Lübeck, Theater Lübeck (Kammerspiele): 6.9.2019, *Game of Crowns 1* (UA.). R.: Pit Holzwarth.

Osnabrück, Städtische Bühnen Osnabrück (Theater am Domhof): 28.9.2019, *Falstaff.* Von Guiseppe Verdi. Libretto von Arrigo Boito. ML.: Andreas Hotz, R.: Adriana Altaras, B.: Etienne Pluss und Sibylle Pfeiffer, K.: Nina Lepilina.

Salzburg, Salzburger Landestheater (Leopoldskroner Park, Außenspielstätte): 12.8.2020, *Elves and Errors nach William Shakespeare.* R.: Carl Philip von Maldeghem.

Salzburg, Salzburger Landestheater: 21.9.2019, *Oberon.* Von Carl Maria von Weber. Libretto von James Robinson Planché. ML.: Ido Arad, R.: Volkmar Kamm, B.: Konrad Kulke, K.: Katja Schwindowski.

St. Gallen, Theater St. Gallen (Großes Haus): 12.9.2019, *Sein oder Nichtsein nach Ernst Lubitsch.* Von Nick Whitby. R.: Barbara-David Brüesch, B.: Damian Hitz, K.: Heidi Walter.

Stralsund, Theater Vorpommern (Großes Haus): 31.10.2019, *Die Hamletmaschine.* Von Heiner Müller. R.: Annett Kruschke, B. und K.: Indra Nauck. (Gleiche Produktion wie in Greifswald.)

Wien, Burgtheater (Kasino): 17.1.2020, *Die Hamletmaschine*. Von Heiner Müller. R.: Oliver Frljić, B. und K.: Igor Pauška.

Wien, Burgtheater (Burgtheater): 22.2.2020, *This Is Venice (Othello & der Kaufmann von Venedig) nach William Shakespeare* (UA.). Von Elisabeth Bronfen und Muriel Gerstner. R.: Sebastian Nübling, B.: Muriel Gerstner, K.: Pascale Martin.

Bücherschau

Andy Amato, *The Ethical Imagination in Shakespeare and Heidegger*. London, New York: Bloomsbury, 2019. xii, 259 pp. – ISBN 978-1350083660 – £ 85.00 (hb.), ISBN 978-1350177994 – £ 28.99 (pb.).

Andy Amato's *The Ethical Imagination in Shakespeare and Heidegger* begins with the premise that though Heidegger had little to say about Shakespeare (and what he did say was far from laudatory), the two authors share modes of understanding ethics and the poetic imagination that can reciprocally inform one another. Briefly acknowledging Heidegger's "affiliation with National Socialism", Amato dismisses this potential complication for a book on ethics as "simply not the topic of this work" and offers his ruminations, instead, as a kind of "decadent exercise in aesthetic appreciation and philosophical curiosity" (p. viii). Each of the book's five chapters pairs aspects of Heideggerian philosophy with a single Shakespearean play with the overarching goal of "developing a sense of contemplative ethics and the ethical imagination" (p. viii).

Chapter 1 takes the Heideggerian notion that "the founding of truth [...] arises in the *happening of art*" and examines the ways that poetic creation opens a "rift" between the mundane and the unique dimension of human creativity, something Amato sees instantiated on stage in the conflict between Oberon and Titania in *A Midsummer Night's Dream* (p. 15). The second chapter sets *Hamlet* against Heidegger's concept of *Dasein*, or the "authentic modes and relations of a being" (p. 50). Here, the analysis takes a quasi-allegorical cast as the Ghost becomes "the Question of the Meaning of Being" (p. 41), Claudius the "Murderer of the Question" (p. 71) and Hamlet the "Retriever of the Question" (p. 57). Even so, Amato's contextualizing material yields an interesting re-interpretation of the famous "to be or not to be" soliloquy, refiguring it as a quest for recovering one's nearly lost authenticity.

Pushing against Heidegger's concept of *Gestell*, or enframing, the next chapter reads *Coriolanus* as a sympathetic exploration of what, under Heidegger, would be considered an inquiry into "the essence of modern technology" and the "possibility of a free relationship to it" (p. 119), as the protagonist, however uncanny and engine-like himself, nonetheless resists Rome's mechanizing impulses. If the physical world of the play sometimes fades too much into abstraction here – the hungry bodies of the plebeians become displaced by a more theoretically-inflected question over simply the "price" of corn (p. 98), and the "world elsewhere" of Antium (*passim*) blends effortlessly into the "elsewhere" of the "realm of art" (p. 123) – the chapter still offers an intriguing reading of *Coriolanus* as troubling the various ethical registers latent in the era's rhetoric of "efficiency" (pp. 114–116).

Drawing on Heidegger's location of the divine within the processes of creativity, Amato's fourth chapter turns to *The Tempest*, perceiving in Prospero's magic a form of poetic measurement, distinct from its scientific counterparts, that in its own way "secures the World by way of words" (p. 149). Though traversing somewhat familiar ground, the chapter nicely recalls Amato's earlier investigation of the poetic rift in *A Midsummer Night's Dream* as it has "Prospero poetically speak an insight both ancient and modern" by invoking creation as a countermeasure against "the gloom of mortality" (p. 144). The final chapter takes Heidegger's notion of language as "the house of being" (p. 187) to recover thinking as itself an efficacious form of action, something Amato traces in *The Winter's Tale*'s depiction of a kind of poetic madness which triumphs over political disorder.

The book's five chapters share an idiosyncratic style that some will find lively, others distracting. There are, for instance, multiple asides – literally, bracketed passages labelled "Aside" – that sometimes run for pages. These tend to divert from the main line of a chapter's argument even as they can contain engaging material in their own right. All told, such quirks of style fit well with the monograph's larger sensibility of presenting a free-ranging philosophical inquiry into the question of ethics and imagination.

CHRISTOPHER CROSBIE (RALEIGH)

Thomas Cartelli, *Reenacting Shakespeare in the Shakespeare Aftermath: The Intermedial Turn and Turn to Embodiment*. Reproducing Shakespeare. New York: Palgrave Macmillan, 2019. xvii, 343 pp. – ISBN 978-1-137-40481-7 – € 87.19 (hb.).

Regietheater-prone Germans are not alone in getting stumped by experimental treatments of the Bard. Partly due to imports from abroad, anglophone audiences, too, have come to leave theatres curiously confused. Here Thomas Cartelli's new book can offer guidance. Its title and introduction might seem designed to put off anyone but performance theorists, but *Reenacting Shakespeare in the Shakespeare Aftermath: The Intermedial Turn and Turn to Embodiment* actually offers reassuringly accessible analyses of some of the most radical Shakespeare productions in living memory. Though Cartelli's objects of analysis go back as far as Sven Gade and Asta Nielsen's silent film *Hamlet* (1920), most of them were produced in the last fifty years. Too numerous to list in full, they include Bond's *Lear* (1971), Müller's *Hamletmaschine* (1977), Greenaway's *Prospero's Books* (1991), al-Asadi's *Forget Hamlet* (2000), Mayer's *Anatomie Titus* (2009), van Hove's *Roman Tragedies* (2007–2018) and Dorsen's *A Piece of Work* (2013). The rationale behind their selection is partly informed by personal interest (see pp. 4–5) and not always consistent. On page 4, for example, performances which "I had not experienced myself" are flagged as unsuitable to the author's purposes, whereas on page 6 (and in the corresponding chapters) they are suddenly deemed acceptable. But then an essayistic guidebook needs to proceed neither systematically nor comprehensively. It simply needs to do justice to prominent landmarks, and Cartelli's manifest knowledge of the field makes it hard to believe that he missed any of those.

Apart from questions of intermediality and embodiment, which lend thematic coherence to the book, Cartelli also identifies a sort of formal commonality between the performances in question. He calls this the "Shakespeare aftermath", which constitutes "a discursive and performative space and condition of awareness theoretically shared by the makers, if not the receivers, of the performances or experiences on offer that all things Shakespearean are present and available for redoing and reenactment *differently*" (p. 13). Yet does this definition really distinguish his "defamiliarizing" corpus (p. 14) from more conventional productions? After all, the word *differently* (just like *redoing* and *reenactment*) leaves plenty of room for disagreement. In a sense, for example, every performance of even the most conventional enactment of a play can be seen as different from the last – especially if one regards 'works' as emerging from the interplay between texts, actors, audiences and their historical situations. Mere presence and availability, moreover, do not guarantee actual use. Would it not be easier to describe the works in question as made exclusively for veteran audiences as opposed to others that also accommodate newcomers? Not least in view of Cartelli's own reflections (cf. "audiences" [p. 13]), "first time" [p. 25] and "elite" [pp. 33–34]), this seems far less cumbersome than his "aftermath" concept. And why, in the first place, does the "space" denoted by the latter need to be elaborately differentiated from the actual works that stake it out?

I may be missing some necessary background here. Considering the present book alone, however, I cannot help being more impressed by Cartelli's critical interpretations than his theoretical framework. One might sometimes disagree with his readings as well, of course, but they are invariably well-argued and alert to competing alternatives (e.g. when he criticizes van Hove's potentially Randian politics on pp. 237–253). Furthermore, the wide-ranging contexts in which he places his chosen performances are invaluable. Acute and well-documented personal observation, sound academic scholarship, interviews, programme notes, actors' responses to direct questions by the author, and even insightful blog posts and student essays are all grist to the meaning-making mill of his discussions. I, for one, came away from them with increased understanding and feel better prepared for the next dramatic challenge.

RUDOLPH GLITZ (AMSTERDAM)

Claude Fretz, *Dreams, Sleep, and Shakespeare's Genres*. Cham: Palgrave Macmillan, 2020. 268 pp. – ISBN 978-3-030-13518-8 – € 74.89 (hb.); ISBN 978-3-030-13519-5 – € 58.84 (e-book).

A concise definition of this study's research focus is given by the author: "The aims of this book [...] are to provide historical-contextual insights into Shakespeare's use of dreams and sleep, to compare Shakespeare's representations of dreams and sleep to those in his sources and influences (including classical ones), and, crucially, to consider the dramatic effects of these devices in the context of Shakespeare's conceptions of genre" (p. 5). Claude Fretz enters upon this project using a stupendous range of classical and early modern texts that contextualize his Shakespeare readings, a great familiarity with the Shakespeare canon and a keen eye for Shakespearean textual detail.

In his first chapter, Fretz traces the dream theories current in early modern Britain from the reception of the two most important classical dream theorists: the Greek Artemidorus of Daldis distinguished between the *oneiros*, the prophetic dream of supernatural origin, and the *enhypnion*, the quasi-meaningless dream that is merely caused by all-too-present states of body and mind. The Roman Macrobius refined this binary system into a classificatory system of five dream types, three of which (*oraculum, visio* and *somnium*) correspond to the *oneiros* while the other two (*insomnium* and *visum*) are variants of the *enhypnion*. The medieval and early modern reception history of classical dream theories is anything but linear; Shakespeare wrote at a time when there was little consensus on the matter, and anybody could opine almost anything they wanted about dreams. In addition, it is unclear how many early modern dream texts – for instance by Thomas Nashe, Timothy Bright, Thomas Walkington, Nicolas Coeffeteau, Thomas Wright and Andrew Boorde – Shakespeare actually read. He was undeniably fascinated by dreams and their potential for his art, though, and he made effective use of the rich cultural palimpsest of dream theories and dream practices of his time.

The four following chapters of the book follow both a generic and a chronological order of Shakespeare plays while allowing themselves some leeway for productive excursions. Chapter 2 focuses on (early) comedy: after a dream-oriented analysis of John Lyly's *Endymion*, Fretz reads *The Taming of the Shrew* and *A Midsummer Night's Dream* with a view to their 'dreamatisations'. He concludes that in all three comedies, fictitious dreams enrich the comedic texture with darker elements that can often be traced to the religious discourses of the time, centring on fears and desires. Chapter 3 focuses on the familiar Shakespearean generic blend of histories and tragedies as it discusses *Henry VI*, *Richard III*, *Julius Caesar* and *Macbeth*. Through skilled comparisons between influential dramatic pre-texts and the Shakespearean material, Fretz brings to light changes in and complications of supernatural dreams in Shakespeare, whose plays emphasize and explore human agency without completely abolishing metaphysical frameworks of dream interpretations. Chapter 4 analyses the similarity between the hallucinatory effects of (bad) sleep and insomnia in another tragical-historical body of plays: *Antony and Cleopatra*, *2 Henry IV*, *Hamlet*, *Macbeth*, *3 Henry VI*, *Richard III*, *King Lear* and *Julius Caesar*. Four of these are also considered in the preceding chapter, but the lines of argument as well as the interpretive embeddings differ. Reading the plays against sources such as chronicles and Seneca's tragedies, sleep and sleeplessness emerge as natural phenomena and cultural practices that restlessly surround the human dimensions of Shakespeare's tragedies, often in suffering, for instance, the sleepless Macbeth, the sleeping Duncan and hallucinating characters who (may) actually see something or somebody the other characters and/or the audience do not see.

Chapter 5, entitled "'Such Stuff as Dreams Are Made On'? Shakespeare's Late Genre", applies and develops insights gained in the previous chapters and argues that in his late plays (Fretz rejects the generic label 'romance') Shakespeare uses dreams, among them the classical tragic *oneiros*, to shape the imaginaries of his dramatic fictions so that they elude the established genres of either comedy or tragedy. Placing dreams at the centre of their dramatic textures, *Pericles*, *The Winter's Tale*, *Cymbeline* and *The Tempest* – all Jacobean plays written predominantly for the Blackfriars' stage – show some things new: "like dreams and performances when their time is up, the classical protocols of genre dissolve when they are confronted with the realities of life that Shakespeare's comedies and tragedies seek to portray" (p. 193).

Perhaps the greatest strength of this study is the dialogue into which it enters with the Shakespearean texts. Certainly, Fretz speaks about the plays and their dreamscapes from a well-read historical perspective that allows him to illuminate the webs of meaning in which his primary texts are entangled. Even more importantly, though, he lets the texts speak as, in very close readings, he unravels Shakespeare's dream visions that shape and question the stage illusions they are part of. At the end of this stimulating book, its readers have gained a sense of the generic substance and significance of Shakespeare's dreams, and of his sleepers, dreamers and insomniacs. And Caliban cries to dream again.

JOACHIM FRENK (SAARBRÜCKEN)

Marta Gibińska, Małgorzata Grzegorzewska, Jacek Fabiszak and Agnieszka Żukowska eds, *This Treasure of Theatre: Shakespeare and the Arts from the Early Modern Period to the Twenty-First Century. Essays in Honour of Professor Jerzy Limon*. Gdańsk: słowo/obraz terytoria, 2020. 321 pp. – ISBN 978-83-7453-742-1 (hb.).

"So, apart from being a world-wide champion and advocate, commissioning contemporary and experimental approaches to the plays, writing innovative scholarly books that are also great everyday reading, running ground-breaking university courses, creating a world-renowned festival and building the most amazing theatre in the world, what has Jerzy Limon ever done for Shakespeare?" (p. 302) This quip is director Philip Parr's, who has adapted the famous line from Monty Python's *Life of Brian* for his *laudatio* of the man to whom this *Festschrift* is dedicated: Professor Jerzy Limon, OBE. Limon, based in Gdańsk (Poland), is indeed more than just an exceptional scholar of Shakespeare and early modern theatre; he is also a translator of William Shakespeare, Henry Chettle and Tom Stoppard, a theorist of the stage, a writer of fiction and a theatre entrepreneur, as the editors remind us in their introduction. Limon has written eleven monographs in English and Polish to date – including *Dangerous Matter: English Drama and Politics in 1623/24* (1986), *The Masque of Stuart Culture* (1990), *The Chemistry of Theatre: Performativity of Time* (2010) and *Gentlemen of a Company: The English Players in Central and Eastern Europe, 1590–1660* (1985), the first monograph to study the English actors touring continental Europe in the early seventeenth century. But he clearly stands out among Shakespeareans in combining this scholarly and literary work with a major project that began in the 1990s and was brought to fruition in 2014 with the opening of the Gdańsk Shakespeare Theatre (Gdański Teatr Szekspirowski). Designed by Renato Rizzi, this amazing building was established on the site of the Fencing School, a seventeenth-century theatre used by the English players. The Gdańsk Shakespeare Theatre is now the centre of a renowned annual international Shakespeare Festival, whose origin can be traced back to the year 1990 and the Theatrum Gedanense Foundation, in which Limon also played a central role. Praised by Michael Dobson as "one of Shakespeare's most important living disciples", Limon received the 2019 Pragnell Shakespeare Birthday Award, which "celebrates individuals who have significantly furthered our understanding, knowledge and love for The Bard's work" (Pragnell Award website).

The title of the volume – *This Treasure of Theatre* – refers to the beautiful building that is the Gdańsk Shakespeare Theatre, and which Limon himself, alluding to lines from *Richard II* (2.1.46–47), has called a "precious pearl hid in a casket of concrete walls" (p. 12). In addition, the phrase also evokes Limon's continuous engagement with the stage, over more than four decades, and the continuous inspiration that the theatre provides for his work and vice versa. The four editors – early modernists and Shakespeare scholars from Cracow (Marta Gibińska), Warsaw (Małgorzata Grzegorzewska), Poznań (Jacek Fabiszak) and Gdańsk (Agnieszka Żukowska) – have brought together an illustrious circle of writers to honour the work of Jerzy Limon. In addition to Michael Dobson's "Pragnell Address", Parr's concluding personal note in the form of a dramatic dialogue (cited above) and a complete bibliography of Limon's publications, the volume comprises fourteen contributions by renowned scholars from Europe and the US: Marvin Carlson, Nicoleta Cinpoeş, Jay L. Halio, Patrice Pavis, Manfred Pfister, Maria Shevtsova, Tadeusz Sławek, Boika Sokolova, György E. Szőnyi, Stanley Wells and the four editors. Their articles are inspired by and/or address the wide range of Limon's research interests: Shakespeare and Shakespeare festivals, the Shakespearean stage, the chemistry of theatre, drama and politics, and English plays and players in Europe (and beyond). It is impossible, in a short review, to do justice to every single article in the volume, and a mere addition of titles and topics does not provide much interesting reading. Rather than briefly summarizing the articles, I would therefore like to highlight some impressions and insights that I gained from reading this *Festschrift*.

The volume is held together by a strong interest in Shakespeare productions, translations, editions, adaptations and art installations of the last two decades. In detailed discussions of major productions up to 2019, the authors pay particular attention to the political nature of many contemporary stagings which have used Shakespeare to explore the conflicts of our times: nationalism and xenophobia, warfare and migration, and the redefinition of Europe and Britishness in the aftermath of the Brexit referendum. What I found particularly noteworthy was the inter- and transnational character of the volume. This does not merely refer to the international line-up of its contributors, but also to their engagement with a broad range of translations, productions and adaptations from Israel, Russia, Poland, Germany, France, the UK and the US. Last but not least, many individual articles develop comparative perspectives by assessing the differences, for example between European and American performance practices, by looking at translations in different contexts and cultures, and by showing an awareness of the complex travels of plays and productions, directors and troupes (not only) across Europe. In this way, the volume indirectly comments on, and offers a refreshing alternative to, the upsurge of nationalisms that can be witnessed in many parts of the world. In the twenty-first century, it seems, Shakespeare on stage is often the product of transnational collaboration: examples would be Belgian director Luk Perceval's *Macbeth* (2014), which was commissioned for the Baltic House festival in St Petersburg, or Polish director Jan Klata's *Hamlet* for Schauspielhaus Bochum (Germany), produced in 2013 with Teatr Współczesny (Wrocław, Poland). I am inclined to see these examples as modern equivalents to the travelling players of the early seventeenth century, to the many traditions from which Shakespeare and other early modern dramatists borrowed and, more generally, to the "international, multilingual, and cross-cultural" (Grzegorzewska, p. 253) character of early modernity in Europe. I hasten to add that I do not want to propose Shakespeare as the prophet of a peaceful and united Europe. Indeed, even if the articles look at the ways in which Shakespeare's plays and poetry have travelled in translation, adaptation and rewriting, they highlight, rather than smooth over, conflicts and differences. They explore the complex and contradictory ways in which "Shakespeare is used as a repository of themes, situations, and actions" (Pavis, p. 137), and in which the stage in general, and that of the Gdański Teatr Szekspirowski in particular, manages to offer its visitors and audiences a temporary "refuge from the gloom of ignorance, indifference, or [...] anguish" (p. 13). Not unlike the Gdańsk Shakespeare Theatre, the articles collected in this volume invite dia- and polylogues – between the early modern past and the contemporary present, between scholars and theatre practitioners, and across national borders as well as linguistic and media boundaries. Most importantly, they pay tribute to a scholar who has indeed done much for and with Shakespeare. I can therefore only join in the celebration and reiterate Parr's concluding words: "Cheers, Jerzy. And thanks." (p. 302)

Postscript: It was with great sadness that I heard of the passing of Jerzy Limon on the 3rd of March, 2021. My book review, which had been written to celebrate a wonderful scholar and colleague, has now turned into a final farewell.

SABINE SCHÜLTING (BERLIN)

Julián Jiménez Heffernan, *Limited Shakespeare: The Reason of Finitude*. Routledge Studies in Shakespeare. New York: Routledge, 2019. 262 pp. – ISBN 978-0367026776 – £ 120.00 (hb.).

Heffernan argues that current Shakespeare scholarship, as far as it is invested in immediacy, spontaneism, embodiment or presentism, misconstrues Shakespeare's texts. Critics attribute to them an infinite reach and a seemingly unlimited potential to fashion moralizing readings (pp. 1–2). In his introduction, Heffernan argues that such scholarship "violate[s] the basic finitude of the Shakespeare text" (p. 5) – which for him is not only concerned with exploring limits (e.g. of life, love, time or knowledge), but which also sets the limits of interpretation. In fact, it is "the only genuine limit we may stand by in the face of phenomenological subterfuge, presentist sophistry, neo-historicist confusion" (p. 3). Heffernan then advocates a scholarship that pays close attention to the texts' literariness, literary history and dramatic possibilities (pp. 9–10). His Shakespeare is a literary dramatist, but not one located in the book trade. He emerges as a (rational) "poet" (p. 191) steeped in literary tradition.

Part roadmap, part manifest, the introduction does not entirely inform the rest of the chapters. A comparative *Quellenforschung* is employed in his next chapter on Sonnet 119, where Heffernan traces the literary flow of the "siren tears" (l. 1) through European literary history. An amalgamating trope that condenses "moral-emotional features of the speaker's various female partners", the phrase is said to point to a fragmentary Homeric script in the sonnets, of "wandering, temptation, and return", with the speaker in the role of a "bedraggled Odysseus" (p. 18). The rest of the chapters (on *Romeo and Juliet*, *Hamlet*, *Othello*, *Macbeth* and *The Tempest* – the first four all read as "problem comedies" [p. 6]) are more properly concerned with philosophical discussions, specifically on historicism and teleology (*Macbeth*), a political philosophy that revisits Leo Strauss and focusses on Plato's *Republic* (*Hamlet*), epistemological questions that take their cue from Stanley Cavell (*Othello*), or a refutation of unlimited possibility by means of reading Shakespeare with Spinoza (*The Tempest*) – this last chapter incidentally also dismisses much of postcolonial criticism focussed on Caliban's agency as "gullible" (p. 206).

The loose structure of chapters, complete with some quirky subheadings, is reminiscent of Slavoj Žižek, to whom this book is also indebted (Hegel and Derrida are perhaps the most important influences). Interspersed are some productively tangential readings: Chapter 2, which takes Paul Kottman to task for failing to adequately consider the mediaeval sources of *Romeo and Juliet*, contains a deconstructive reading of how the "textual *belatedness*" of the play is somatized as "erotic *earliness*" (p. 47). In the next chapter on *Hamlet*, etymology is used as a symbolic form to think through the literal meanings of *(in)solvent* or *resolution*, flanked by a symptomatic reading to delimit the Althusserian 'problematic' of the play. 'The people' emerge as the something *rotten* in the state of Denmark, serving as a negative "rest" (p. 95) that nevertheless quilts the ideological field of the play. In a similar post-Marxist vein, Chapter 4 argues that Othello does not 'learn' but *always already knows* – a knowledge he retroactively produces and then verifies, in conjunction with Iago, by means of the handkerchief. The last chapter nicely circles back to the introduction by means of Miranda and Ferdinand's game of chess, which becomes an example of the Nietzschean-Derridean figure of *finite infinity* (p. 204), central to this book.

Heffernan's readings are challenging and sometimes hinge on certain assumptions – the weird sisters in *Macbeth* need to be unambiguously and consistently prophetic (pp. 157–158), 'the city' in *Hamlet* must be *meaningfully* absent. And while the book's philosophizing, for lack of a better word, is stimulating throughout, a few parts are shot through with so many short quotes (not all of them properly proofread) that Heffernan's style can become somewhat irritating. And just occasionally, Shakespeare's text seems to be used as a ventriloquist's prompt book, with snippets providing cues in a multi-voiced Platonic dialogue.

CHRISTIAN KRUG (ERLANGEN)

Katherine Hennessey and Margaret Litvin eds, *Shakespeare & the Arab World*. New York: Berghan, 2019. 274 pp. – ISBN 978-1-78920-259-5 – € 30.00 (pb.)

Over the last two decades, Arab translations and adaptations of Shakespeare's work have received increasing international attention. Beginning with the September 11 attacks in 2001, various political and military conflicts such as the US-led 'War on Terror', the 'Arab Spring Uprisings' of 2011 and the longstanding civil war in Syria have not only kept the Arab world in international news headlines; they have also triggered a remarkable worldwide interest in literature and theatre from this part of the globe. This development has included an increased fascination with the Arab afterlives of Shakespeare. Translations, adaptations and appropriations of his works have found new audiences and a growing number of critics have embraced the project of "putting the Arab world once and for all 'on the map' of global Shakespeare studies" (p. 1). The co-edited volume *Shakespeare*

& *the Arab World* is Katherine Hennessey and Margaret Litvin's latest contribution to this project. With each having published a monograph and several articles in this field of research, the two scholars present the first collection of articles that engages in a broadly conceived exploration of Arab Shakespeare translation, production, adaptation and criticism.

The co-edited volume contains fourteen chapters divided into two sections. The first section "Critical Approaches and Translation Studies" begins with a theoretical discussion of key concepts by Margaret Litvin. Her opening chapter addresses the limits of postcolonial appropriation theory by drawing on the example of Arab adaptations of *Hamlet*. She argues for a new approach that acknowledges the relevance of what she calls "a 'global kaleidoscope' of sources and models" (p. 15) that have influenced Arab writers and artists beyond forms of 'direct' engagement with Shakespeare's work. Without being explicitly programmatic, Litvin's contribution nevertheless prepares the conceptual ground for many of the following chapters. She emphasizes the rich nature of Arab Shakespeare traditions, highlights the functional idiosyncrasy of individual adaptations and illustrates the necessity of considering geopolitical factors and local (cultural) politics in their scholarly analysis.

The chapters following Litvin cover a wide range of topics. While the remainder of the first section largely revolves around the topic of translation, the second section, "Adaptation and Performance", engages with adaptations from countries across the Arab-speaking world and beyond. The examples range from Egyptian performances and translations of *The Taming of the Shrew* in the 1930s, over Tunisian productions of different plays between 1984 and 2007 to a 2003 Swedish-Egyptian production of *A Midsummer Night's Dream*. While most chapters focus on theatrical performance, the collection also engages with other genres and media types, including an Egyptian TV adaptation of *King Lear* and a discussion of the influence of Shakespearean tragedy on two twenty-first-century Lebanese-American novels. In addition to the more formal academic contributions, the volume also includes an interview with Moroccan playwright Nabyl Lahlou, an account of a suicide bomb attack on an amateur production of *Twelfth Night* in Qatar and a contemplation of the potential origin of the sonnet in Arabic poetry by the scholar and translator Kamal Abu-Deeb.

The thematic diversity of the volume's chapters is both the collection's greatest strength and its weakness. On the one hand, it creates a lack of cohesion that makes it difficult to connect the chapters in a systematic fashion and thus may evoke a general impression of haphazardness. On the other hand, the extraordinary range covered by the volume successfully illustrates the diverse and vibrant nature of Shakespeare's Arab afterlives and thus makes the volume a valuable contribution to the study of Shakespeare's global legacy. Moreover, it also ensures that anybody generally interested in the intersection of his work and Arab culture will find something of interest among the fourteen contributions.

MARCUS HARTNER (BIELEFELD)

Rory Loughnane and Edel Semple eds, *Staged Normality in Shakespeare's England*. Palgrave Shakespeare Studies. Basingstoke: Palgrave Macmillan, 2019. XIII, 299 pp. – ISBN 978-3-030-00892-5 – € 106.99 (hb.).

Normality is an ambiguous concept, seemingly self-evident but, in reality, hard to define. In our post-Foucauldian age, literary critics are well aware that normality is a shifting social construct which is both subject to historical conventions and a matter of subjective experience. The term has descriptive and prescriptive implications. Elizabeth Hanson explains in her contribution to the present volume that, from the seventeenth to the nineteenth centuries, "normal" implied a pattern "that *should* be followed, not one that usually is" (p. 69). As encoded in prescriptive writings, the normal seems clearly defined, but as a matter of lived experience, it was more fluid, subject to interpretation and negotiation. The present volume demonstrates that early modern theatre provides unique access to such negotiations of the normal. Theatre employs the ordinary and familiar to generate dramatic tension or satire and thus underlines its social significance. It stages the collision of individual acts and normative social expectations and it explores the dynamic between the normal and the abnormal. With its material and ritualistic aspects, 'normality' is highly performative, even beyond the world of the stage, but theatre is singularly apt to draw attention to the performativity of both everyday life and the norms or ideals against which it may be measured. As the editors of *Staged Normality* put it, "performance […] simultaneously permits the imitation of normality […] and undoes it because it is recognizably imitative of normal behavior rather than the recognized behavior itself" (p. 3).

It takes some courage to tackle such a broad idea within a single volume. Without aspiring to a comprehensive account of the topic, the present volume succeeds in assembling insightful, instructive and eminently readable essays that offer different perspectives on the complex cultural constellations and media that constitute the field of the 'normal': norms, everyday life and ordinary objects, subjective experiences and social expectations, people of different social ranks and their lives and families. The essays compiled in this volume look at various tragedies, some comedies and a few history plays, some of them by Shakespeare and others by contemporary playwrights such as Thomas Heywood and Thomas Dekker. While the individual essays cover very different aspects of normality, they have shared interests and assumptions. First, they all approach normality on stage as the effect of artifice, of a deliberate meaning-making process that draws on bodily performance, discourses and props. Second, they share a keen interest in the dynamic relation between the normal and its opposites: the "enormous" (Mazzio, p. 34), abnormal or extraordinary. Many essays deconstruct this opposition in their readings of individual plays whilst exploring the conditions in which a situation, object or demand emerges as ordinary or extraordinary.

The volume is divided into three parts: "Discourses of Normality", "Negotiating Normality in Performance" and "Staged Normality and the Domestic Space". This division combines a methodological distinction (between discourse and performance) with particular emphasis on a specific aspect: the household as the site of ordinary occurrences and everyday life. This preference may seem a little surprising. Ordinary and familiar processes can be found everywhere: in the country, the city and at court, in agriculture, commerce and craftsmanship, in school and at university. And indeed, the essays in the first and second parts of the volume address some of these areas. The emphasis on domesticity in the third part is inspired by the ground-breaking work of Frances E. Dolan, Natasha Korda, Michelle M. Dowd, Wendy Wall and others. It is thanks to their research that the household has emerged as a distinct social space that is worthy of critical attention – and not just the unremarkable backdrop to the 'real' action, be it regicide or military leadership or global exploration. Moving the household into the limelight is in line with the editors' intention to redirect critical attention towards processes and objects that appear far from extraordinary and hardly noteworthy.

In their introduction, Loughnane and Semple take care to distinguish between the early modern meaning of 'normal' and the modern sense of 'normality' that was shaped by nineteenth-century sociological positivism (p. 8) and modern statistics (see also Hanson, p. 69). This means that a quantitatively defined normality is of little use if one seeks to understand what early modern Englishmen and -women might have experienced as 'normal'. And yet, as Loughnane and Semple point out, "[n]orms, normality, and practices of normativity and normalization all existed in early modern England" (p. 12). The first part of the volume addresses this historicity: it consists of four essays which analyse historical models and discourses of normality as well as the cultural work that theatre performs in providing visibility and respectability to common people of the emerging middle class ("the middling sort", see Hanson, p. 73).

Building on Jeffrey Masten's *Queer Philologies*, Carla Mazzio introduces the square as a classical and early modern model of "moral and social ideals" (p. 34), "a space of normativity" (p. 37) that implies the regulation and gendering of behaviour but may also exemplify queering effects. While Mazzio concentrates on an intriguing historical figuration of the normal, Elizabeth Hanson discusses *The Merry Wives of Windsor* rather ingeniously as a "proleptic" play (p. 72) that anticipates a modern sense of normality: a "quantitative normal" (ibid.), an average. In her study of time, Kristine Johanson bridges the gap between then and now. She identifies the early modern "subjectivity of clock-time" and the requirement of "self-regulation" as part of "the larger history of our own time management norms" (p. 103). Julie Sanders's instructive essay on theatre's spatial proximity to tanners and shoemakers is characterized by a keen interest in material culture. Sanders approaches "everyday experience" (p. 111) through a focus on "meaning-making object[s]" (p. 114) that inscribe local economies into plays such as Thomas Heywood's *Edward IV, Part 1* and Thomas Dekker's *The Shoemaker's Holiday*.

The second part of *Staged Normality in Shakespeare's England*, "Negotiating Normality in Performance", assembles four essays which are structurally related through their interest in the dramatic juxtaposition of the ordinary and the extraordinary and in the ways in which they interact with each other. Brett Gamboa discusses the theatrical conditions of normality and draws attention to the ways in which Shakespeare's plays use stage conventions to create and disrupt mimetic illusion. Edith Semple's essay on "Transgressive Normality and Normal Transgression in *Sir Thomas More*" deconstructs the simple opposition between normality and abnormality. She explores transgression in the play as "an everyday occurrence" (p. 152). More importantly, perhaps, her lucid reading demonstrates that it is the "staging of normality" that renders More accessible and turns him into "an all too familiar victim of political exigencies" (p. 166). Michelle M. Dowd also complicates the opposition between the ordinary and the extraordinary by discussing the female heiress not just as "a challenge to the normal functioning of patrilineage" in early modern England but also as "a remarkably common figure" (p. 177), an "every-day occurrence" that Shakespeare's late romances turn "into the basis for dramatic tension" (p. 189). Her analysis focuses on the lost-child plot as a "literary 'norm'" (p. 177) that gives theatrical form to the threat that the wayward female heiress poses "to patrilineal security" (p. 178). At the same time, it offers a solution to this familiar problem. Brinda Charry's discussion of the eunuch in travel writings and plays centres on the ways in which the deviant and the normal intersect in this figure. English travel writers recognized him as "a regular feature of Ottoman society" (p. 194). Interestingly, it was not despite his aberrant body but because of it that the eunuch emerged as a particularly reliable and loyal, even ideal servant (p. 198).

The tension between the ordinary and the extraordinary is also palpable in the third part of the volume, "Staged Normality and the Domestic Space". Emily O'Brien's claim that "the tangle of normality and abnormality […] is part of the broader aesthetic and ethical project of domestic tragedy" (p. 240) is true for all essays assembled in this part. In Emma Whipday's terms, domestic tragedy demonstrates "the extent to which the domestic 'normality' prescribed by the conduct literature contains within its hierarchical structures, spatial logic, and gendered household work, the potential for extraordinary and uncanny violation" (p. 218). O'Brien's discussion centres on the role of children and their toys in the domestic context of *A Yorkshire Tragedy*, whereas Whipday's essay focuses on domestic labour and domestic objects in domestic tragedies, in which each becomes perverted, even "malign" (p. 230). Guy-Bray discusses marriage in *The Duchess of Malfi* and *Arden of Faversham*, drawing attention to the collision between a subjective impression of normality and the social norms that govern the normal. In her "Afterword", Frances E. Dolan emphasizes the role of the stage "in shaping what audiences could recognize as familiar" (p. 281). This is an important point: instead of simply exploring the ordinary or normal in relation to the extraordinary or 'enormous', theatre participates in the cultural work of constituting, affirming and renegotiating normality. This implies, on the one hand, enabling the normal to emerge not only as an ideal but as a social reality (as Elizabeth Hanson and Julie Sanders suggest) and, on the other, to explore the nature of its relation to the abnormal or extraordinary.

The essays that this volume compiles are part of a broader critical movement that combines the historicist attention to concrete discourses and practices with an interest in material culture. They attempt to reconstruct concepts from the ground – from concrete situations, objects, representational practices – rather than looking for data to support pre-existing notions. This approach is based on an acknowledgement of historical difference, but it is also inspired by the optimistic belief that early modern theatre plays a crucial role in reconstructing early modern assumptions, experiences and conflicts. In early modern England, theatre was a leading medium for making sense of social norms and expectations, for representing life and for reflecting on socio-economic transformation. Together, the essays compiled in this volume offer a rich introduction to early modern drama and the cultural work that it performs in its explorations of the normal and ordinary as objects of dramatic interest.

ANNE ENDERWITZ (BERLIN)

Eric S. Mallin, *Reading Shakespeare in the Movies: Non-Adaptations and Their Meaning*. Cham: Palgrave Macmillan, 2019. viii, 254 pp. – ISBN 978-3-030-28897-6 – £ 69.66 (hb.).

Neither an overt homage to Shakespeare, nor an explicit cinematic adaptation is what Mallin argues for in *Reading Shakespeare in the Movies*. Instead, he proposes the critical term 'non-adaptation' in order to discuss the mostly unacknowledged presence of Shakespearean themes, structures, characters and symbolic impulses in a set of films – *Memento*, *Titanic*, *Birdman*, and *The Texas Chainsaw Massacre*. He calls these "bias films" (p. 16) to foreground the oblique course his readings for their analogies to *Hamlet*, *Romeo and Juliet*, *The Tempest* and *Titus Andronicus* undertake. While these films share with the early modern plays certain thematic concerns, they repurpose these to their own ends. The production of bias films is, thus, predicated on a creative interplay between resemblance to and divergence from the source plays, bringing out new meanings in them to which more traditional adaptations cannot aspire.

If these films – or rather the screenplay writers and the directors – are themselves unaware of Shakespeare's shadow presence, this raises the question to whom the actual production of a meaningful relationship between the two should ultimately be attributed. By naming Stanley Cavell's writings on Shakespeare and film as his own critical source of inspiration, Mallin understands the conversation he proposes to be primarily an operative one. Like the American philosopher, he is the one who discovers the eclectic and unpredictable borrowings on which his readings are based. The coupling between a particular play and a film only works because the aesthetic resemblance he proposes is predicated on a pre-interpretation of both. Indeed, Cavell himself can only claim *The Winter's Tale* as the predecessor of a set of sophisticated comedies because he approaches them with a specific understanding of the reunion of Hermione and Leontes. If one does not share his conviction that there will be a meet and happy conversation between the estranged royal couple at the end of the final act, then one will not be convinced that the re-marriage these films espouse follows a similar political intuition. As Mallin self-consciously admits regarding his own project, if one takes the films he discusses to be about something other than what he suggests them to be about, then non-adaptation as a new frame of intelligibility will not be plausible.

If, however, in an act of willing suspension of critical disbelief, one follows the bias of his interpretation, the readings Mallin presents are unexpectedly illuminating. Once the obsessive desire for vengeance in both *Hamlet* and *Memento* is read as an expression of solipsistic vexation on the part of the heroes, we recognize why each of these mourners remains stuck in the very traffic of violence he initiated. Both deceive themselves about the evidence that authorizes their killing so as to block out the knowledge of their own guilt. Read through the lens of Nolan's post-modern thriller, Shakespeare's tragedy can be shown to exhibit an unease with the very revenge sensibility it performs. A similarly deconstructive gesture sustains Mallin's reading of *The Tempest* back from and through Iñárritu's *Birdman*. Once we read both as the self-reflection of an artist in the face of his own mortality, what is drawn into focus are the fractured human attachments on which solipsistic creativity is based. As Mallin insists, his hermeneutic project not only allows us to understand things about Shakespeare we might have missed. The bias film can also be understood as offering a corrective vision, neutralizing the lure of revenge, correcting the desire for romantic self-expenditure, disclosing the proximity between ignorance and ignoring, and demythologizing patriarchy's rough magic. As such, reading for non-intended connections does, indeed, bring clarity and pressing, contemporary concerns to bear on our sustained engagement with the world of Shakespeare.

ELISABETH BRONFEN (ZÜRICH)

Lindsay Ann Reid, *Shakespeare's Ovid and the Spectre of the Medieval*. Studies in Renaissance Literature. Cambridge: D. S. Brewer, 2018. xiii, 267 pp. – ISBN 978-1-84384-518-8 – £ 60.00 (hb.).

An unfortunate side-effect of New Historicism's rigorous preference for synchrony was the buttressing of timeworn, quasi-Burckhardtian ideas concerning the period divide: the 'rupturous' emergence of the Renaissance, and the concomitant construction of its pre-modern Other, the medieval. In the last couple of decades, this 'Renaissance' narrative has, of course, been frequently called into question, and the earlier polemical (medievalist) challenges have long given way to more nuanced explorations not only of the nature and history of processes of periodization, but also of important continuities between medieval and early modern English literatures. As far as Shakespeare is concerned, this has sparked a growing interest in the Bard's medievalness. Lindsay Ann Reid's *Shakespeare's Ovid and the Spectre of the Medieval* is a case in point. She is interested in the way that Shakespeare's medievalness becomes tangible precisely in those moments when Shakespeare appears to be particularly 'modern', that is, in his references to classical antiquity, in his intertextual engagement with Ovid.

Observing that scholars usually situate Shakespeare's classicism in general and his Ovidianism in particular within the contemporaneous humanist endeavour to return to the 'original', to the 'authentic' text, Reid aims to uncover "the under-acknowledged, spectral presence of the medieval" in Shakespeare's works, arguing that "ostensibly *classical* allusions" are "often simultaneously inflected by the vocabulary and heuristics – as well as hermeneutic and affective legacies – of *medieval* literature" (pp. 2–3, emphases in original), especially (but not exclusively) works by Geoffrey Chaucer and John Gower, both of whom, like Shakespeare, are habitually branded as Ovidian authors. *Shakespeare's Ovid* focuses primarily on Ovidian moments in Shakespeare's early plays and poems – *The Taming of the Shrew*, *The Two Gentlemen of Verona*, *The Rape of Lucrece*, *Romeo and Juliet* and *Twelfth Night* – at the expense of works that more obviously flag their Chaucerian and Gowerian allegiances (e.g., *A Midsummer Night's Dream*, *Troilus and Cressida*, *Pericles* and *The Two Noble Kinsmen*), whose medievalism has consequently been more often acknowledged and studied. Reid's well-argued monograph opens with a chapter that sketches her methodological and theoretical premises by way of discussing *Chaucer's Ghoast: Or, A Piece of Antiquity*, an anonymous collection of Ovidiana published in 1672. Meticulously elaborating Chaucerian and Gowerian allusions within the twelve Ovidian fables of *Chaucer's Ghoast*, Reid demonstrates how "Chaucer's and Gower's vernacular writings overlapped not only with one another's but also with Ovid's classical corpus" (p. 27). With a nod to Jacques Derrida's *Specters of Marx* (1993) and to recent studies of early modern medievalisms, Reid refers to such textual entanglements in terms of a medieval (Chaucerian, Gowerian) spectrality that defies ontological (and especially, temporal) boundaries. The subsequent four chapters are devoted to specific Ovidian intertextualities, previously discussed chiefly as references to 'classical' Ovid, whereby each chapter opens with a survey of recent work on the passages in question, followed by thorough reconstructions of medieval transformations of Ovidian analogues, structures and topoi. Thus, in her second chapter, Reid turns to *The Taming of the Shrew* in order to discuss the Ovidian overtones of the Induction, which she traces back to the structure of the medieval dream vision, especially Chaucer's *Book of the Duchess*, the most popular Chaucerian dream vision in early modern England. Reid then disentangles, in the third chapter, the Ovidian matrix of the exchange between Julia (cross-dressed as Sebastian) and Silvia at the beginning of the fourth act of *The Two Gentlemen of Verona*. Within this passage, which is usually read as an allusion to *Heroides* 10, Reid spotlights the co-presence of an alternative, medieval tradition of representing Theseus and Ariadne, characterized by a greater emphasis on Theseus's oath-breaking and the addition of

Phaedra as motivating Theseus's abandonment of Ariadne – variations that are tangible in several of Chaucer's poems, in Gower's *Confessio Amantis* and in a host of other medieval and Tudor works, including the *Ovide moralisé*, Caxton's rendering of the *Metamorphoses* and George Tuberville's translation of the *Heroides*. In the fourth chapter, Reid argues that the invocation of Philomela in the *Rape of Lucrece* is based also on the alba in *Amores* 1.13, a pairing which similarly occurs in *Romeo and Juliet* (3.5) and which is "perceptibly haunted by the interpretative legacy of *Troilus and Criseyde*" (p. 122). Reid here offers a perceptive revaluation of the alba and "inverse alba" in Books Three and Five of Chaucer's courtly romance, specifically with a view to ambivalent suggestions of rape. The chapter also comprehensively surveys the medieval transformations of the story of Philomela in *The Legend of Good Women* and Gower's *Confessio Amantis* and its redeployment – in combination with the alba tradition – in Shakespeare's *Romeo and Juliet* and *The Rape of Lucrece*. The allusions to the Narcissus (and the related Pygmalion) story in Olivia and Viola's conversation in *Twelfth Night* (1.5) are the topic of the fifth chapter. Reid emphasizes the relevance of medieval variations in the representation of a Narcissus who sees himself reflected specifically as a woman and who supposedly had a twin sister who drowned. As in the previous chapters, Reid offers a thorough and wide-raging reconstruction of the alternative medieval tradition – manifest, for instance, in Gower's *Confessio*, in *Narcisus et Dané*, in *Le Roman de la Rose* as well as in Matteo Maria Boiardo's *Orlando Innamorato* and in other early modern English works, notably Philip Sidney's *Old Arcadia* – and its surfacing in Shakespeare's comedy.

The above summary of *Shakespeare's Ovid and the Spectre of the Medieval* cannot do justice to the book's rich – and richly contextualized – reconstructions and far-reaching analyses of the textual genealogies of specific Ovidian moments in Shakespeare's poems and plays, which always offer fresh insights concerning the antecedent medieval reception and transformation of Ovid, especially, but not exclusively in works by Chaucer and Gower. Reid's impressive study will no doubt be immensely useful for scholars interested in both Shakespearean classicism and Shakespearean medievalism. Moreover, Reid's monograph prepares the way for further inquiries into the reception of antiquity in the long fifteenth century, when the engagement with Ovid often appears to refract authorial anxieties vis-à-vis Chaucer and Gower. The readings offered in *Shakespeare's Ovid* also invite reconsideration from other theoretical vantage points. I am thinking especially of recent work focused on constructions of multiple temporalities (for instance, Carolyn Dinshaw and Jonathan Gil Harris), which may provide a critical vocabulary suitable for discussions of how references to the classics become temporal signposts by way of which Shakespeare and other early modern authors (strategically) construct not one antiquity, but multiple antiquities.

WOLFRAM KELLER (BERLIN)

James Shapiro, *Shakespeare in a Divided America*. London: Faber & Faber, 2020. vii, 310 pp. – ISBN 978-0-571-33888-7 – £ 20.00 (hb.).

Den aktuellen Versuchen, Analogien zwischen Shakespeare-Dramen und der politischen Situation in den USA herzustellen, fügt der renommierte Shakespeare-Forscher James Shapiro nun eine diachrone Dimension hinzu. In acht Momentaufnahmen verfolgt er US-amerikanische Reaktionen auf Shakespeare von den 1830er Jahren bis heute, um Streitfragen bezüglich *race*, Gender, Klasse und Sexualität aufzuzeigen, welche die Nation gegenwärtig spalten. Als ideologischer Rahmen dient die detaillierte Geschichte einer *Julius Caesar*-Aufführung von 2017 im Central Park, die Shapiro beratend begleitete und deren als Trump erkennbarer Caesar republikanische Empörungsstürme auslöste. Demgegenüber basiert das historische Material auf Archivrecherchen, wie Shapiro sie schon 2014 für *Shakespeare in America* unternahm – eine Anthologie mit einem Vorwort von Bill Clinton. Auch in dem neuen Buch geht es um ein nationales Projekt. Daran lässt die laufend rhetorisch evozierte Vergemeinschaftung keinen Zweifel; sie zeigt sich etwa – wenig subtil – im Untertitel der US-amerikanischen Ausgabe: *What His Plays Tell Us about Our Past and Future*.

Einige der vignettenartigen Mikrohistorien beschwören Shakespeare als gemeinsamen nationalen Nenner herauf, indem sie auf 'bedeutende' bzw. kanonisierte und popularisierte Personen der US-Geschichte rekurrieren, die sich ihrerseits auf Shakespeare bezogen haben. So erfahren wir, wie entsetzt sich Präsident John Quincy Adams, ein Gegner der Sklaverei, über die 'Mischehe' in *Othello* äußerte. Weniger bekannt ist die Anekdote, dass Ulysses S. Grant, später ebenfalls Präsident, als junger Kadett für einen Cross-Gender-Auftritt als Desdemona vorgesehen war. Eingebettet wird der *Insider-Gossip* in veränderte Gender-Vorstellungen der Zeit. Besonders sensationell ist die Ermordung Abraham Lincolns durch den Schauspieler John Wilkes Booth, der sich rechtfertigend mit Brutus verglich. Auch Lincoln kannte Shakespeare-Texte, wie seine *Macbeth*-Referenzen zeigen. Ein (selbst)kritischer Hinweis darauf, welche Funktion die (Meta-)Zitation von Berühmtheiten durch Berühmtheiten als kulturelles Kapital im US-amerikanischen Kontext hat(te), fehlt freilich.

Nachvollziehbarer ist die historische Symptomatik des Astor Place Riot von 1849. Der gewaltsam niedergeschlagene Massenansturm gegen eine *Macbeth*-Aufführung im neuen, noblen Opera House ist zweifellos Ausdruck von Kulturwandel und Klassenkonflikten. Trotz – oder wegen – des 'politisch korrekten' Duktus der Darlegungen schleicht sich beim Lesen allerdings ein gewisses Unbehagen ein, das durch eine von Shapiro etablierte Binarität genährt wird. Er reduziert politische Haltungen auf nur zwei vermeintlich konträre Richtungen: die Liberalen und die Rechten (vgl. S. 22). Damit kein Zweifel an der 'richtigen', demokratischen Seite aufkommt, listet er etwa die Diversitäts-Errungenschaften im US-amerikanischen Theater vor Trump auf (vgl. S. 227–229).

Für das zwanzigste Jahrhundert gewährt Shapiro einen Blick hinter die Kulissen der Produktion des Musicals *Kiss Me, Kate* (1948) und des Films *Shakespeare in Love* (1998), wobei die aufmerksamkeitsheischenden Bezüge zu Monica Lewinsky und Harvey Weinstein allzu weit hergeholt erscheinen. Shakespeare ist in diesem Episodenreigen insgesamt eher Sprechanlass bzw. fungiert als "a canary in a coalmine" (S. 4). Bei einem solchen 'Ansatz' muss man in Kauf nehmen, dass der Vogel von der Stange fällt, sobald Grubengas austritt.

Das entwaffnend leicht lesbare, im Plauderton gehaltene und vielfach gelobte Buch lässt zwei Giganten aufeinandertreffen, aber der Star ist 'Amerika'. Im Wahlspektakel kann diese Shakespeare-Aneignung nur ein Bestseller werden. Sie folgt den Gesetzen des (Buch-)Marktes, der vermeintliche Grenzen zwischen Rezeption und Produktion, exklusiver Bildung und populärer Unterhaltung sowie akademischem und parteipolitischem Anliegen aufruft, nutzt und letztlich aufhebt.

DORIS FELDMANN (ERLANGEN)

Tiffany Stern ed., *Rethinking Theatrical Documents in Shakespeare's England*. London: The Arden Shakespeare, 2020. xvi, 287 pp. – ISBN 978-1-350-05134-8 – $ 90.00 (hb.).

This collection of essays documents the results of a Folger Shakespeare Library Symposium which brought together critics from the related, and yet different, fields of book history and theatre history. Its fifteen contributions pay tribute to the participating scholars' collaborative effort to understand more fully the many ways in which, as Tiffany Stern puts it in her introduction, early modern "plays, whether printed or not, intertwined performance with the text behind them" (p. 3). As becomes clear from the large variety of documents discussed in this volume, this 'text behind plays' takes different forms that can be allocated to different stages in the theatrical production process: documents before performance (such as drafts, casting lists and actors' parts); documents of performance (such as prologues, epilogues and title-boards); and documents after performance (such as playbooks, commonplace extracts and ballads). These textual categories also serve as the volume's first three sections, to which is added a fourth, on 'lost documents', which "argues [...] that an awareness of what existed at one time is itself knowledge that keeps us both wary of assumptions and disciplined in the construction of narratives unsupported by the surviving documentary record" (p. 12).

In her introduction, Tiffany Stern states that the volume is concerned with nothing less than "think[ing] anew about what even constitutes 'documents' in the first place, and as a consequence, what constitutes 'plays', what constitutes 'playbooks' and what the nature is of the relationship between events seen and heard in performance and words read on the page" (p. 2). The following thirteen chapters do her claim justice. In "Writing a Play with Robert Daborne" (Chapter 1), Lucy Munro discusses the letters the playwright wrote to Philip Henslowe in 1613–1614. Imagining Daborne "as the author of a self-help manual for the aspiring Jacobean playwright" (p. 18), Munro retraces Daborne's (financial and legal) motivation for and experience of bringing plays to the stage and, thereby, provides insight into the entangled practices of playwrights, financiers and actors which blur the boundaries between pre-performance and performance documents. In "A Sharer's Repertory" (Chapter 2), Holger Schott Syme carves out the casting practices of companies in the 1620s and 1630s from performance-related documents, thus filling the gaps left by lost repertory documents such as lists of plays, performance dates and role distributions. At the same time, Syme challenges longstanding assumptions about early modern theatre stardom. As his discussion shows, a company's "most significant member [...] would not be the one we have anachronistically identified as its 'star' [such as lead actors Richard Burbage or Edward Alleyn] but the one organizing a set of individuals into a collective" (p. 47), such as John Heminges of the King's Men, whom Syme describes as a sharer "with quasi-managerial responsibilities" (p. 46). In the next chapter, "Parts and the Playscript", James J. Marino moves the discussion to actors' parts. Focusing on the Folio and Quarto versions of *The Merry Wives of Windsor*, Marino stresses the importance of parts and cues – and the danger that changing cue-structures posed to performances. With Chapter 4, "Undocumented: Improvisation, Rehearsal, and the Clown", Richard Preiss turns to one of the unscripted parts of early modern theatre performances. Clowns relied on improvisation, "the dark matter of early modern theatre" (p. 69), which is "hidden below the surface of our [play]texts" (p. 69) and, at the same time, "proliferates into every document: commonplace books, verses, memoirs, woodcuts, shop-signs, ballads, jestbooks, drolls, printed 'themes', printed jigs, and dances" (p. 85). As Preiss shows, the clown's unscriptedness questions text-based notions of what constitutes an early modern play. Sonia Massai's and Heidi Craig's "Rethinking Prologues and Epilogues on Page and Stage" (Chapter 5) opens the volume's second section on documents of performance. Massai and Craig discuss the changing functions of prologues and epilogues as they move from performance to printed text. The next chapter, Matthew Steggle's "Title- and Scene-Boards: The Largest, Shortest Documents" is concerned with yet another "performative paratext" (p. 9). Steggle discusses the "painted signs bearing, respectively, the title of the play being acted and the location of the action" (p. 111) which were widely used on the early modern stage. Using examples from a variety of plays, Steggle argues that the boards entered into a dialogue both with each other and with the words spoken on stage. In Chapter 7, "What Is a Staged Book?", Sarah Wall-Randell shows that props could also influence the theatrical meaning-making process. Exploring the ontological status of books that appeared onstage (such as the English bible handed to Elizabeth I in Heywood's *If You Know Not Me, You Know Nobody, Part 1*), Wall-Randell delineates how books could become 'actors' as plays used their material presence on stage "to affirm, undercut or query the dialogue" (p. 147). Among the "Documents After Performance" discussed in the volume's third section are play extracts copied into commonplace books, playbook layout and typography as well as ballads. In "'Flowers for English Speaking': Play Extracts and Conversation" (Chapter 8), András Kiséry discusses "the crucial relationship between dramatic texts and colloquial interaction" (p. 157). Writing on "Shakespearean Extracts, Manuscript Cataloguing, and the Misrepresentation of the Archive" (Chapter 9), Laura Estill reads play extracts to challenge "the canon-focused biases inherent in our cataloguing and research practices" (p. 175). In "Typography *After* Performance" (Chapter 10), Claire M. L. Bourne analyses Q1 *Love's Labour's Lost* (as the play's earliest extant edition), arguing that its specific typographic strategies serve to position "readerly activity in the interstice between the idea of the play as a book and the idea of the play in performance" (p. 197). Tiffany Stern's "Shakespeare the Balladmonger?" (Chapter 11) explores the different functions of ballads *in* plays and of ballads *about* plays. Focusing on the links between ballads and plays by Shakespeare in particular, Stern makes a convincing case for seeing the playwright as using ballads as a marketing tool for his own plays, "exploiting and teaching the use of ballads as pre-play publicity, plot summaries, or/and as post-plays souvenirs" (p. 233). The volume's concluding section consists of a single chapter, Roslyn L. Knutson's and David McInnis' "Lost Documents, Absent Documents, Forged Documents". Knutson and McInnis aim to rethink the 'lostness' of non-extant plays. They encourage scholars to be open to new sources of information and to follow the archival paper trail left by the documents, both theatrical and non-theatrical, which plays generated. Taking into account repertory documents, playwrights, court documents, governmental documents and forgeries, they take the discussion of theatrical documents "outside the playhouse to consider the loss of documentation beyond that on authorial composition, players' performances, and print culture to show how much more is additionally lost (and also how much remains to be discovered)" (p. 255). For reasons which are not fully clear to me, Peter Holland begins his "Afterword: 'What's Past Is Prologue'" with quoting Hitler on the power of cultural documents to outlive the people in whose culture they originate. Holland finds the dictator's statement "unnerving [...] but [...] intriguing" (p. 260), but to me (as a German reader) its totalitarian associations sit uneasily on the preceding contributions, all of which are invested in reading texts carefully and closely and which never lose sight of the cultural and historical differences they are confronted with. Its peculiar beginning notwithstanding, Holland's afterword rounds off the volume by opening new avenues of critical enquiry (for example, into the field of ancient theatre historiography).

There is much to learn from the insightful and engaging readings of theatrical documents brought together in this collection, which succeeds in "provid[ing] new ways of understanding plays critically, interpretatively, editorially, practically and textually" (p. 12). This volume is a definite must-read for anybody interested in the collaborative practices which are at the heart of early modern English theatre.

LENA STEVEKER (LUXEMBOURG)

Berichte

Tätigkeitsbericht der Präsidentin
(Frühjahr 2020)

Das Berichtsjahr 2019/2020 sollte für die Deutsche Shakespeare-Gesellschaft unvorhersehbare Veränderungen bereithalten, die unsere Veranstaltungsplanung beeinträchtigten. Zunächst aber konnte die Gesellschaft mit ihrer Jahrestagung 2019 zum Thema "Shakespeare and Translation" ein reichhaltiges Programm zusammenstellen. International renommierte Shakespeareforscherinnen und -forscher betrachteten Übersetzungstheorien und -praktiken der Zeit Shakespeares, die wie kaum eine andere Epoche durch ihre Übersetzungstätigkeit geprägt ist. Die Tagung widmete sich weiterhin dem komplexen Zusammenspiel von Übersetzung, Literatur und Ästhetik und fragte nach Formen und Funktionen von Übersetzungen, die in einem weiten Sinne auch als Adaptionen, kreative Aneignungen, Interpretationen und Inszenierungen verstanden werden. Hier bietet das Werk Shakespeares eine enorme Vielfalt und eine bis in die Gegenwart andauernde Innovationskraft. Diese zeigt sich in Deutschland insbesondere in der äußerst produktiven Übersetzungstätigkeit herausragender Shakespeare-Übersetzerinnen und -Übersetzer, denen die Deutsche Shakespeare-Gesellschaft in vielfältiger Weise eng verbunden ist.

Die Konstellation unserer Referentinnen und Referenten aus Portugal, Italien, England, der Schweiz, Franco-Kanada und Deutschland brachte weiterführende gegenseitige Bereicherungen, insbesondere auch im Hinblick auf das Thema der Übersetzung. Der Eröffnungsvortrag Norbert Greiners, "Ein Teufelspakt mit Shakespeare?", widmete sich der Übertragung Shakespeare'scher Werkkomplexe in Thomas Manns *Doktor Faustus*. Die darauffolgenden Vorträge nahmen das Thema der Tagung unter verschiedenen Schwerpunkten in den Blick: Gabriela Schmidt (LMU München) und Alessandra Petrina (Università degli Studi di Padova) untersuchten die Rolle von Übersetzungen innerhalb der Stücke Shakespeares und verorteten diese zugleich im Kontext der frühneuzeitlichen Literaturproduktion. Neben diesen exemplarischen Untersuchungen nahmen die Beiträge Warren Boutchers (Queen Mary University of London) und Marie-Alice Belles (Université de Montréal) eine erweiterte Perspektive auf die Übersetzungspraktiken zur Zeit Shakespeares ein. Boutcher und Belle fragten auch danach, wie mithilfe des Buchdrucks und mittels Übersetzungen ein Austausch zwischen den europäischen Ländern begünstigt wurde und wie vom Standpunkt der aktuellen Forschung anhand dieser Indikatoren eine gesamteuropäische Literaturgeschichte geschrieben werden kann.

Einen kulturtheoretischen Ansatzpunkt, der sich mit präzisen Lektüren verband, verfolgte ebenso Andreas Mahler (Freie Universität Berlin), indem er mit seinem Vortrag "Translation from/into/in culture" die Mechanismen, die in den Übersetzungen Shakespeares zum Tragen kommen, im Kontext von Übersetzungsdiskursen des 16. Jahrhunderts situierte. Ebenfalls von den Dramen der Frühen Neuzeit ausgehend, erweiterte Rui Carvalho Homem (Universidade do Porto) die kulturhistorischen Ansätze der Tagung durch die Perspektive des Übersetzers. Homem, der neben den Werken Shakespeares auch die Dramen Christopher Marlowes, Seamus Heaneys und Philip Larkins aus dem Englischen ins Portugiesische übertragen hat, nahm dabei vor allem lyrische Übersetzungen und ihre interkulturellen Herausforderungen in den Blick. Den abschließenden Festvortrag hielt Elisabeth Bronfen (Universität Zürich), die sich mit Shakespeares 'Nachreife' auseinandersetzte und der Frage nachging, wie Shakespeare durch serielles Erzählen im 20. und 21. Jahrhundert in neue Medienformate übertragen und damit medial übersetzt werden kann.

Auf vielen Ebenen widmete sich die Tagung zudem den ganz praktischen Aspekten der Übersetzungsthematik. In einem lebendigen Werkstattgespräch diskutierte der Lyriker, Übersetzer und Anglist Klaus Reichert mit dem Regisseur und Intendanten des Kölner Schauspiels Stefan Bachmann. Die Regisseurin Jaq Bessell bot einen sehr nachgefragten theaterpraktischen Workshop an, und ein besonderes Augenmerk der Tagung lag auf dem Gebrauch von Übersetzungen in Schule und Universität. Diese standen im Zentrum des Forums "Shakespeare und Schule", für das der Referent Michael Mitchell zum Thema "Contemporary Fiction Meets Shakespeare" gewonnen werden konnte. Darüber hinaus bot das Shakespeare Seminar "Shakespearean Translations – Translating Shakespeare" ein anregendes Forum für NachwuchswissenschaftlerInnen.

Das die Tagung begleitende Theaterprogramm umfasste eine Inszenierung von *Macbeth*, aufgeführt vom experimentellen Jugendtheater "Die Schotte" in Erfurt, und eine szenische Darbietung von Studierenden der Ruhr-Universität Bochum; *König Lear* wurde am Puppentheater Waidspeicher in Erfurt aufgeführt sowie der *Sommernachtstraum* am DNT in Weimar.

Die Stadt Weimar feierte im Jahr 2019 eine Fülle von Jubiläen, darunter die Verabschiedung der Weimarer Reichsverfassung, 200 Jahre Goethes *West-östlicher Divan* und natürlich die Bauhaus-Gründung vor 100 Jahren. In diesem Zusammenhang war es uns eine besondere Freude, den TagungsteilnehmerInnen in Kooperation mit der Klassik Stiftung zwei Führungen durch das neu eröffnete Bauhaus-Museum ermöglichen zu können.

Über die Verbindungen zu unseren deutschen Partnerstädten hinaus intensivierten Mitglieder des Vorstands sowie des Präsidiums ihre internationalen Kontakte. Selbst konnte ich während eines Fellowships an der Universität Oxford mehrfach nach Stratford-upon-Avon reisen, um dort u. a. weitere Kooperationen mit dem Shakespeare Institute zu planen.

Aber auch in Deutschland suchten wir verstärkt die Verbindung zu Kulturinstitutionen und Ministerien. Der Vorstand erarbeitete auf Anregung der Mitglieder ein Positionspapier zur verbindlichen Verankerung Shakespeares im Schulcurriculum, in das die Dramentexte im Original Eingang finden sollten. Frau Prof. Dr. Eisenmann nahm Kontakt zum Bayerischen Bildungsministerium auf, und es ist geplant, das Papier bald an die entsprechenden Entscheidungsträger zu versenden. Unser Vizepräsident Prof. Dr. Weidle stellte die Arbeit der Deutschen Shakespeare-Gesellschaft im Ministerium für Kultur und Wissenschaft des Landes Nordrhein-Westfalen in Düsseldorf vor, und wir konnten bereits einige gemeinsame Planungen z. B. im Blick auf das Jubiläum des First Folio im Jahr 2023 skizzieren.

Äußerst erfreulich war die Intensivierung unserer Verbindung zum Bochumer Schauspielhaus und seinem Intendanten Johan Simons. So fand z. B. im Juni 2019 auf dem Campus der Ruhr-Universität Bochum eine Podiumsdiskussion zu der gefeierten und vielfach ausgezeichneten *Hamlet*-Inszenierung statt; eine weitere zu der Inszenierung von *König Lear* war für den Sommer 2020 geplant. Zudem war das Schauspielhaus bereit, unsere Frühjahrstagung 2020 mit der Premiere dieser Inszenierung zu bereichern.

Viele Gründe mag es geben, warum Tagungen in seltenen Fällen nicht stattfinden können – eine Pandemie hingegen zählte in der Geschichte unserer Gesellschaft bislang noch nicht dazu. Bis zur Verhängung des Veranstaltungsverbots im Land Nordrhein-Westfalen, dem rasch ein bundesweiter 'Lockdown' folgte, hatten wir inständig gehofft, unsere Frühjahrstagung 2020 trotz allem durchführen zu können. Die Enttäuschung und Trauer darüber, dass die im Beethoven-Jahr geplante Tagung zum Thema "Shakespeare und Tanz" schließlich ausfallen musste, war groß. Zugleich war allen Beteiligten bewusst, dass es keine Alternative zu dieser Entscheidung gab und die Dinge nicht in unserer Hand lagen. Fast eineinhalb Jahre Arbeit waren in das Programm einer Tagung eingegangen, über die sich an dieser Stelle nur im Modus eines anachronistischen 'Als-Ob' berichten lässt.

'Tanz' bei Shakespeare sollte sich in den Vorträgen, aber auch im künstlerischen Programm der Tagung aus einer Vielzahl von Perspektiven erschließen: von den historischen und kulturellen Konzeptionen des Tanzes als höfisches Phänomen, über die dramatische Ausgestaltung der Tanzszenen in Shakespeares Stücken sowie die zahlreichen, insbesondere auch zeitgenössischen Adaptionen von Werken wie *Romeo and Juliet* oder *The Winter's Tale* für das Ballett. Überdies sollte die poetische Dimension des Tanzes in Shakespeares

Sprache, ihren Rhythmen und der Bewegung ihrer Versfüße betrachtet werden, und Shakespeares Choreographien z. B. in seinen Paarbeziehungen sollten Gegenstand der Vorträge sein.

Für das Vortragsprogramm konnten viele wichtige VertreterInnen der Forschung im Bereich Shakespeare und Tanz aus Deutschland, England und den USA gewonnen werden. Susanne Scholz (Frankfurt/Main) wollte in ihrem Einführungsvortrag den Tanz im Elisabethanischen England im Hinblick auf seine Bezüge zur Geschlechterordnung bei Hofe betrachten; Richard Wilson (Kingston) wollte den mitunter prekären kulturhistorischen Verflechtungen des 20. Jahrhunderts, die im Tanz ihren Ausdruck finden, nachgehen. Die Vorträge von Emily F. Winerock (Pittsburgh) und Lynsey McCulloch (Coventry) sollten sich konkreten Aspekten des Tanzes sowie der Verwendung von Masken und Kostümen in Shakespeares Komödien und Tragödien widmen. Julia Bührle (Oxford) und Barbara Ravelhofer (Durham) sollten das weite Spektrum des Tanzes in Shakespeares Werk sowie in einzelnen Werkadaptionen betrachten.

Das Shakespeare Seminar wie auch das Forum "Shakespeare und Schule" wollten sich den vielen Verbindungen von Tanz, Theater und Text widmen. Auf dem Podium wollte die Tanz- und Theaterwissenschaftlerin Monika Woitas (Bochum) mit dem Stellvertretenden Ballettdirektor des Staatstheaters Karlsruhe Florian König sowie dem Schauspieler und Tänzer Saša Kekez diskutieren.

Auch das künstlerische Programm zur Tagung mit Beiträgen der Tänzerin Eliska Bouzkova, der Sängerin Carolanne Wright und dem Musiker Patrick Pagels sollte, neben der Ausstellung "Totentanz bei Shakespeare" im Bochumer Zentrum für Stadtgeschichte und den im Metropolis Kino gezeigten Aufführungen von *The Winter's Tale* sowie *Romeo and Juliet* des Royal Ballet, die Vielfalt und aktuelle Relevanz des Themas verdeutlichen.

In der Hoffnung auf ein Ende der gegenwärtigen Dystopie danken wir allen Beteiligten für ihr großes Verständnis und Engagement: insbesondere unseren Partnerstädten Bochum und Weimar, der Ruhr-Universität Bochum, dem Deutschen Nationaltheater Weimar, dem Schauspielhaus Bochum sowie dem Metropolis Kino für fortwährende und vielfältige Unterstützung.

Großer Dank gilt weiterhin dem Vorstand der Deutschen Shakespeare-Gesellschaft, der Leiterin der Weimarer Geschäftsstelle, Frau Rudolph, sowie Prof. Dr. Sabine Schülting für die Herausgabe des *Shakespeare Jahrbuchs*, in dem eine Auswahl der Vorträge, die in Bochum hätten gehalten werden sollen, nun veröffentlicht sind.

CLAUDIA OLK (MÜNCHEN)

"Romeo und Julia":
Online Herbsttagung, 20. – 22. November 2020

Wie in nahezu allen Bereichen des öffentlichen Lebens war das Jahr 2020 auch für die Deutsche Shakespeare-Gesellschaft von der Corona-Pandemie geprägt. Nachdem bereits die für den 24. bis 26. April in Bochum angesetzte Frühjahrstagung "Shakespeare und Tanz" komplett abgesagt wurde, musste die Herbsttagung, lange Zeit noch als hybride Veranstaltung mit Präsenzanteilen in Weimar geplant, letztendlich in rein digitaler Form stattfinden. Umso erfreulicher war es, dass als Tagungsthema in der Tradition bisheriger Herbsttagungen ein einzelnes Shakespeare-Drama gewählt wurde, welches gerade in Zeiten von *Social Distancing* wie kaum ein anderes Stück Fragen von physischer wie emotionaler Nähe und Distanz zu geliebten Mitmenschen aufwirft: *Romeo und Julia*. Eröffnet wurde die Zusammenkunft am Freitagnachmittag mit einem Grußwort des Weimarer Oberbürgermeisters Peter Kleine, der getreu Hamlets berühmter Phrase "Sein oder nicht sein" feststellte, wie sehr die gegenwärtige Situation uns die Zerbrechlichkeit des Seins vor Augen führe. Er betonte nachdrücklich die Bedeutung der Kultur für eine menschenwürdige Existenz. Die Präsidentin der Deutschen Shakespeare-Gesellschaft Claudia Olk sprach in ihrem Grußwort daraufhin zunächst dem Weimarer Oberbürgermeister Peter Kleine, Julia Miehe von der Kulturdirektion der Stadt Weimar, Angela Egli-Schmidt von der Projektförderung Kultur der Stadt Weimar, Christoph Schlierkamp vom Kulturbüro der Stadt Bochum sowie der Staatskanzlei des Freistaats Thüringen ihren Dank für die Unterstützung der Gesellschaft und der Tagung aus. Anschließend bekräftigte sie den aktuellen Zeitbezug des Tagungsthemas. *Romeo und Julia* sei nicht nur die größte Liebesgeschichte aller Zeiten, welche zugleich die tragische Unmöglichkeit von Liebe dramatisiere. Das Stück führe auch eine Gesellschaft vor, die von einer tiefen und gewalterfüllten Krise ziviler Imagination gezeichnet sei; es appelliere eindringlich daran, eben jene Krise mit allen Kräften zu überwinden – ein Appell, der im Jahr 2020 kaum relevanter sein könnte. Der Eröffnungsvortrag von Julia Bührle (Oxford), "*Romeo und Julia*: die Tragödie als Ballett", schlug eine thematische Brücke zur entfallenen Frühjahrstagung und gab einen Überblick zur breiten choreographischen Rezeption des Dramas. Bühle fokussierte sich dabei auf kanonische Adaptionen der Partitur von Sergei Prokofjew im klassischen Handlungsballett und zeigte die interpretatorische Vielfalt auf, mit welcher die wichtigsten Choreograph_innen des 20. Jahrhunderts auf den Stoff reagiert haben: von der Idealisierung junger Liebe bei John Neumeier bis hin zur Vergegenwärtigung des Todes bei Rudolf Nurejew. Musikalisch gerahmt wurde das Programm von der Sängerin Carolanne Wright und dem Gitarristen Patrick Pagels.

Die digitale Zusammenkunft wurde am Samstagmorgen von Stefan Schneckenburger (Darmstadt) mit einer botanischen Führung zu Shakespeares *Romeo und Julia* fortgeführt. Im Anschluss sprach Russell Jackson (Birmingham) zu "*Romeo and Juliet* in Performance: Energy, Pace and the Mercutio Factor". In seinem Vortrag bekräftigte er die Lesart von *Romeo und Julia* als ein zweigeteiltes Stück und stellte anhand zahlreicher Inszenierungsbeispiele, die vom 19. Jahrhundert bis ins Jahr 2016 reichten, die Bedeutung Mercutios als dramaturgisches Bindeglied zwischen den beiden Hälften heraus. Angelika Zirker (Tübingen) interpretierte das Drama in ihrem Vortrag "Die Ästhetik gemeinschaftlicher Autorschaft in *Romeo and Juliet*" als vielfältige Meta-Reflektion über gemeinschaftliche Produktionsvorgänge in der Frühen Neuzeit. Zwar sei das Stück von Shakespeare allein verfasst worden, dennoch beinhalte es zahlreiche Momente wie das Pilgersonnet oder die finale Gruftszene, aus denen sich Handlungsanweisungen für gelungene Kommunikation und auktoriale Kooperation ableiten ließen.

Nach der Mittagspause sprachen Monika Woitas (Bochum) und Julia Bührle (Oxford) in der von Anne Enderwitz (Berlin) und Felix Sprang (Siegen) moderierten Podiumsdiskussion über das Thema Shakespeare und Tanz. Sie gingen dabei vor allem der Frage nach, inwiefern sich Tanz als Adaptionsmedium für Literatur eigne und welche medienspezifischen Aspekte solche Adaptationsvorgänge beeinflussten, insbesondere hinsichtlich der verbalen Komplexität von Shakespeares Dramen. Anschließend wurde der Martin-Lehnert-Preis 2020 an Kilian Markus Schindler (Fribourg) für seine Dissertation "The Limits of Toleration: Religious Dissimulation and Early Modern Drama, c. 1590–1614" verliehen. Das Vortragsprogramm wurde von Alice Stašková (Jena) und dem Thema "'Wunderbare Umwandlungen': *Romeo und Julia* nach Schiller, A. W. Schlegel und Goethe" beschlossen. Darin zeichnete sie die Rezeption der Shakespeare'schen Liebestragödie in der deutschen Klassik nach und arbeitete heraus, dass die Frage, ob Shakespeares Werke ungekürzt gespielt werden müssten oder überarbeitet werden dürften, von zentraler Bedeutung für den deutschsprachigen Shakespeare-Diskurs gewesen sei.

Am Sonntagmorgen gab es noch zwei weitere digitale Programmpunkte, welche die Konferenz dann offiziell abrundeten: das von Vanessa Schormann (München) und Maria Eisenmann (Würzburg) moderierte Forum Shakespeare und Schule, in dem Maria Marcsek-Fuchs (Braunschweig) zu "'The measure is done, … I'll meet her online': Shakespeares *Romeo and Juliet* im kreativen Online-Unterricht" sprach, sowie das von Lukas Lammers (Berlin) und Kirsten Sandrock (Göttingen/Leipzig) moderierte Shakespeare Seminar zum Thema "Shakespeare and Dance" mit Beiträgen von Valentina Finger, Steven Ha, Marcus Hoehne, Julia Hoydis, Nancy Isenberg, Maria Marcsek-Fuchs und Marlena Tronicke.

JONAS KELLERMANN (KONSTANZ)

NACHRUFE

Zum Gedenken an den Shakespeare-Übersetzer Frank Günther (1947–2020)

Auf die Frage: Was verbindet Sie persönlich mit Shakespeare? antwortete Frank Günther im Jubiläumsjahr 2014: "eine nahezu 40-jährige intime, persönliche Bekanntschaft. Ich habe bald jedes Wort, das er zu Papier gebracht hat, ins Deutsche verwandelt und jede Rolle seiner sämtlichen Stücke am Schreibtisch gespielt. Als Ophelia bin ich unschlagbar." Und Ende 2016 schrieb er mir, erleichtert über den endlich fertiggestellten *Pericles*, den er als letztes der 37 Shakespeare-Dramen übersetzt hatte: "Nach gut 40 Jahren bin ich, wie symbolisch, durch die 40 km Marathon-Ziellinie gegangen. Nun kann der Tod kommen." Der flapsige Nachgedanke bezog sich auf den ernsten Hintergrund seiner Krebserkrankung. Am 15. Oktober 2020 ist er ihr mit 73 Jahren erlegen. Vorausgegangen war Ende Mai der Tod seiner Frau, der Malerin und Bühnenbildnerin Hille Warndorf – ein Schicksalsschlag, von dem er sich nicht erholte. Sein Verleger Norbert Treuheit konnte 2019 noch Shakespeares Verserzählungen als Band 39 der bei ars vivendi erschienenen Gesamtausgabe herausbringen – die für 2021 als Band 38 angekündigten Sonette klaffen jetzt als einzige schmerzliche Lücke.

Als ich Frank Günther kennen lernte – ein Glücksfall, den ich meiner Tätigkeit an der Münchner Shakespeare-Bibliothek verdanke –, befand er sich erst am Anfang seiner Übersetzerlaufbahn. Ich erinnere mich, dass er eines Tages vor über 45 Jahren unangekündigt in meinem Büro stand. Er war nichts weniger als raumgreifend und verfügte über einen Redefluss, der erst versiegte, als ich abends die Bibliothek zuschloss. Dann verabschiedete er sich mit der Bemerkung, dass zu Hause Arbeit auf ihn warte. Er war vor einiger Zeit aufs Land gezogen, ins oberschwäbische Rot a. d. Rot, wo er einen Einödhof bewohnte. Er müsse Pflöcke für die Einhegung der Schafe einsetzen, mit denen er sich das Mähen ersparen wollte, Böden verlegen und Heizungen einbauen. Im Laufe des kurzweilig verflogenen Nachmittags hatte er auswendig lange gereimte Passagen aus seiner *Sommernachtstraum*-Übersetzung rezitiert, die so frisch und frech, so ungewohnt heutig klangen, dass ich den Text am liebsten sofort haben wollte. Er habe auch noch *Much Ado* auf Lager, meinte er, und zwei Dramen von Middleton und Heywood, die auch nicht schlecht gelungen seien. Dann geriet er in ein Schwärmen, in das ich einstimmen konnte, über die bahnbrechende *Midsummer Night's Dream*-Inszenierung von Peter Brook. Bei seinen eigenen Regie-Arbeiten habe er diese Inszenierung stets im Hinterkopf. Zur Zeit freilich könne er Theater und Schauspieler nicht mehr aushalten, vielleicht werde er in den nächsten Jahren mehr übersetzen.

Was er hier so *en passant* erwähnte, hätte anderen zur Ausstaffierung eines halben Lebenslaufes gereicht. Schon während des Studiums (Anglistik, Germanistik, Theaterwissenschaften) war er als Dolmetscher und Assistent des amerikanischen Regisseurs Charles Marowitz ans Theater gelangt. Mit ihm hatte er sich einem der experimentierfreudigsten Vertreter seiner Zunft angeschlossen. Bei diesem Mentor sammelte Frank Günther Erfahrungen mit der englischen Schauspieler-Ausbildung, die ihm später als Dozent und Regisseur in Heidelberg, Bielefeld, Basel und Wiesbaden nützlich waren. Auch wenn er nach 1974 nur noch gelegentlich (doch keineswegs erfolglos) inszenierte, verdankt sich die besondere performative Qualität seiner Übersetzungen der intensiven Kenntnis des Theaters.

Nicht umsonst heißt es bei Shakespeare mehrfach "to hear a play"; er schrieb fürs Ohr, nicht fürs Auge. Günther gelingt es meistens, den Duktus der gesprochenen Sprache mit dem Blankvers in Einklang zu bringen, ohne Grammatik und Syntax zu vergewaltigen. Dabei dürfte ihm zugute gekommen sein, dass er als Synchronautor für über 70 Spielfilme die mundgerechte deutsche Fassung schuf. Nebenbei brachte er sich das Programmieren bei, um die Abläufe im Synchronstudio zu optimieren. Mit den von ihm besorgten 70 Folgen von *Count Duckula*, einer britischen Kultserie über eine vegetarische Vampirente, die mit großem Erfolg ab 1990 im Fernsehen ausgestrahlt wurde, schließt sich ein Kreis zu der ersten Ehrung, die dem zwölfjährigen Frank zufiel. Als Sieger eines Wettbewerbs über Donald Duck durfte er damals nach Florida reisen.

Angesichts seiner Sprachbegabung verblüfft es nur wenig, dass er auch Bühnenklassiker aus dem Spanischen, Italienischen, Französischen, sogar dem Norwegischen übersetzt hat, nebst modernen Dramatikern wie dem kompliziertbrillanten Tom Stoppard. Als Freiberufler muss man sich den Luxus, Shakespeare zu übersetzen, erst einmal leisten können, doch im Laufe der 1980er Jahre wurde Shakespeare zunehmend zu Günthers Hauptgeschäft. Es gab Auftritte bei der Shakespeare-Gesellschaft, etwa zusammen mit dem Regisseur Eike Gramms in Darmstadt 1983, wo er in freier Rede seine Übersetzungsprinzipien erläuterte, oder den wiederum frei gehaltenen *Hamlet*-Vortrag 1987 (die im Jahr darauf im *Jahrbuch* veröffentlichte Nachschrift bewahrt den improvisierten Charakter). Wie auch die alljährlichen Bühnenberichte und die Theater-Bibliographie im Shakespeare-Jahrbuch belegen, rückten seine Übersetzungen, die mittlerweile die beliebtesten Shakespeare-Dramen umfassten, zu den am häufigsten gespielten auf. Bei einem Publikumsfavoriten wie *Romeo and Juliet* war der gelegentliche Protest der lokalen Presse der Breitenwirkung durchaus förderlich. Da Günther für die Assoziationsfülle des Mehrdeutigen besonders empfänglich war und sexuelle Untertöne lustvoll ausspielte, führten die phallischen Implikationen des Dienerdialogs in 1.1 zu einem veritablen Aufschrei der Theaterkritiker. Sie mussten sich jedoch vom Übersetzer belehren lassen, dass sie ihren Shakespeare bisher nicht verstanden hatten. Denn die zunehmend obszöner werdenden Kalauer waren Schlegels Bowdlerizing zum Opfer gefallen.

In den 1990er Jahren schließlich bemerkte der Deutsche Taschenbuchverlag das Fehlen von Shakespeare in seinem Klassikerprogramm. Auf der Suche nach einem zeitgenössischen Shakespeare fand man Frank Günther. Ab 1995 erschienen in schneller Folge zunächst die bekanntesten, später auch weniger bekannte Dramen, insgesamt 21 Stücke. Das war ein gewaltiger Schritt voran in Richtung Wissenschaftlichkeit. Neu bei der zweisprachigen Taschenbuchreihe waren die Zeilenzähler für den überarbeiteten Text und historisch-stilistische Anmerkungen, die Günthers akribische philologische Feinarbeit und Vertrautheit mit Textproblemen dokumentierten. Jeder Band enthält Betrachtungen 'Aus der Übersetzerwerkstatt', die oft zentrale Themen des Stücks beleuchten und in Konkurrenz zu den ebenfalls leserfreundlich geschriebenen Essays aus der Feder von Fachwissenschaftlern treten. In einem Begleitbändchen zur Reihe findet sich der witzige Dialog eines 'Unbefangenen' und des Übersetzers, in dem letzterer seine Poetik der 'Shakespeare-Übersetzerei' darlegen kann. Seine kreative Anstrengung gilt der stilistischen Polyphonie des Sprachmanieristen Shakespeare, von der er so viel wie möglich mit heutigen Mitteln wiedergeben möchte. Dass das weitgehend gelungen sei, bescheinigten ihm die ausführlichen Rezensionen, die in der Fachpresse nach 1995 erschienen. Seit 2000 erfuhren seine Übersetzungen zudem die höheren Weihen einer bibliophilen Deluxe-Edition im bereits erwähnten ars vivendi-Verlag, der die bei dtv erschienenen Bände textgleich übernahm. Da Shakespeares Dramen heute für viele Regisseure nur noch in sehr verschlankter Form goutierbar sind, ist es tröstlich zu wissen, dass Günthers Übersetzungen in dieser schönen Reihe eine Zeitlang überleben werden.

Gerade in den Komödien, die von Wortgeplänkeln und Witzeleien strotzen, hat Günther dem Theater verloren geglaubtes Potenzial zurückerobert und Passagen des elisabethanischen Texts, die ein englischsprachiges Publikum nur noch mit Ratlosigkeit und Langeweile quittiert, zum Lacherfolg verholfen. Selbst für die verzwicktesten und verklausuliertesten Wortspiele, vor denen alle vorherigen Übersetzer kapituliert haben, hat er sich deutsche Entsprechungen einfallen lassen. Das trifft besonders auf das Stück zu, für dessen Übertragung er im Jahre 2001 mit dem Wieland-Übersetzerpreis geehrt wurde: *Verlorene Liebesmüh* (dtv, 2000). Als weitere Ehrungen kamen 2006 der Heinrich-Maria-Ledig-

Rowohlt-Preis hinzu sowie 2011 der Johann-Heinrich-Voss-Preis für Übersetzung der Deutschen Akademie für Sprache und Dichtung. Im Wintersemester 2007/2008 hatte er als erster Dozent die August-Wilhelm-von-Schlegel-Gastprofessur für Übersetzung an der Freien Universität Berlin inne.

2011 stürzte er sich mit der Besessenheit, die ihm zu eigen sein konnte, in die Kontroverse um Shakespeares Verfasserschaft. Anlass war Roland Emmerichs Hollywood-Film *Anonymous*, in dem der Earl of Oxford als Verfasser der Shakespeare-Stücke proklamiert wurde. Als Emmerich verkündete, dass sein Film auch als "eye-opener" für amerikanische Schulkinder gedacht sei, und zehn provozierend gemeinte Fragen ins Netz stellte, mit denen er die "Lügengespinste" der Stratfordianer entlarven wollte, war für Günther eine rote Linie überschritten. Wutschnaubend und triefend vor Ironie, beantwortete er diese Fragen mit so gut recherchierter Gründlichkeit, dass die Shakespeare-Gesellschaft sich seine Stellungnahme in der Kontroverse auf ihrer Website zu eigen machte.

2014, pünktlich zu Shakespeares 450. Geburtstag, erschien sein Buch *Unser Shakespeare* (dtv), das als Sachbuch gleich auf die Spiegel-Bestsellerliste kam. Hier konnte er seine mittlerweile umfassenden Kenntnisse zur Shakespeare-Biographie und zum kulturellen Kontext seiner Zeit ausbreiten und auf Verschwörungstheorien satirisch eingehen. Auch zur deutschen Shakespeare-Aneignung, zur Übersetzungsproblematik und zu einzelnen Dramen finden sich lesenswerte Kapitel. Bei den Shakespeare-Tagen in Weimar war Günther an den Feierlichkeiten beteiligt, mit einer wortgewaltigen Ansprache beim Shakespeare-Denkmal und Beiträgen beim abendlichen Bankett. Die Tische waren mit seiner zweisprachigen Zitatensammlung *Shakespeares Wortschätze* dekoriert; jeder Gast erhielt ein Freiexemplar.

Zu Shakespeares 400. Todestag (2016) überraschte er mit dem Bändchen *William Shakespeare: Die Fremden* (dtv). Was auf den ersten Blick nach einem neu entdeckten Text aussah, handelte sich um Günthers Übersetzung und literaturwissenschaftliche Einordnung jener Shakespeare zugeschriebenen Szene aus dem apokryphen Drama *The Booke of Sir Thomas Moore*, in welcher der Protagonist um Empathie mit den Flüchtlingen wirbt.

Das Jubiläumsjahr verlangte Günther eine besondere Kraftanstrengung ab. Wie andere Shakespeare-Experten war auch er ein gefragter Gesprächspartner in Radio- und Fernsehsendungen, Schulen und Universitäten. Dazu kamen 16 Auftritte mit seiner Übersetzer-Performance, einer Ein-Mann-Show, die er im Laufe der Jahre perfektioniert und stets auch um neue Kabinettstückchen bereichert hatte. Sie angemessen zu würdigen, bedürfte es einer schriftstellerischen Kunstfertigkeit, die mir fehlt. Es waren eineinhalb hochkonzentrierte Stunden mit einem Feuerwerk an Ideen und Zitaten, das jeweils mit großem Beifall belohnt wurde. Immer wieder ging es um Szenen aus dem einsamen Übersetzeralltag, um das stundenlange Ringen um einen kurzen, doch irrwitzig schwierigen Satz, den man nicht – wie es manche seiner Vorgänger getan hatten – einfach weglassen durfte. Denn wie Günther einmal sagte, sei es die größte Herausforderung für den Shakespeare-Übersetzer, nicht schreiend davon zu laufen.

Dass dieser außergewöhnliche Mensch, ein Kraftwerk an Energie und Einfallsreichtum, nun verstummt ist, ist schwer zu fassen für alle, die ihn kannten.

INGEBORG BOLTZ (MÜNCHEN)

Catherine Belsey (1940–2021)

Nur wenige Tage vor der Drucklegung des diesjährigen Jahrbuchs erreichte uns die traurige Nachricht vom Tod Catherine Belseys. Nach einem Studium in Oxford und Stationen in Warwick und Cambridge kam sie 1975 an die Cardiff University, wo sie zunächst als Lecturer, dann als Professorin (1989–2006) tätig war. Es folgten Positionen als Research Professor an der Swansea University und Visiting Professor an der University of Derby. Als Leiterin des Centre for Critical and Cultural Theory in Cardiff (1988–2003) trug sie maßgeblich zur Rezeption poststrukturalistischer Theorie nicht nur in der britischen Forschung bei. Publikationen wie *Critical Practice* (1980, 2002), *Poststructuralism: A Very Short Introduction* (2002), *Culture and the Real* (2005) und *A Future for Criticism* (2011) bieten luzide Einführungen in komplexe Theorieapparate; sie betonen vor allem aber auch den Mehrwert, ja, die Notwendigkeit von theoretischer Reflexion und ihrer Verbindung mit der Praxis des Lesens. In ihren Buchpublikationen zu Shakespeare und der Frühen Neuzeit – *The Subject of Tragedy* (1985), *John Milton: Language, Gender, Power* (1988), *Shakespeare and the Loss of Eden* (1999) und *Shakespeare in Theory and Practice* (2008) – führt sie dies in vielschichtigen Textlektüren vor, die nach Identitätskonstruktionen, Machtstrukturen und immer wieder auch Geschlechterverhältnissen fragen. *Desire: Love Stories in Western Culture* (1994) und ihr letztes Buch – *Tales of the Troubled Dead: Ghost Stories in Cultural History* (2019) – spannen weite literatur- und kulturhistorische Bögen und zeigen, wie Liebes- bzw. Gespenstergeschichten grundlegende Fragen über das Begehren, die Begegnung mit dem Anderen, das Leben und den Tod verhandeln.

Catherine Belsey war unserer Gesellschaft über viele Jahrzehnte eng verbunden; von 2006 bis 2018 war sie ein aktives Mitglied des Beirats des *Shakespeare Jahrbuchs*. Als sie mir vor drei Jahren schrieb, dass sie nun jüngeren Kolleg*innen das Feld überlassen wolle, fügte sie hinzu: "I know Anglo-German relations will survive this ludicrous Brexit". In diesem Austausch werden wir Kates Stimme und ihre scharfsinnigen Beobachtungen schmerzlich vermissen.

SABINE SCHÜLTING

Register

REGISTER · 289

Abu-Deeb, K.   257
Adams, J. Q.   266
Aebischer, P.   159
Afzal, A.   110
Akimkin, P.   143
Akimov, E.   222
al-Asadi, J.   249
Aldrian, I.   202
Alleyn, E.   268
Alonso, A.   76, 84
Amato, A.   247–248
Amini Najafi, A.   110
Anderson, L.   144
Andrade, O. de   126
Andriassen, R.-J.   94
Anglo, S.   53
Anne of Denmark, Königin
  von England, Schottland
  und Irland   38, 60
Arbeau, T.   61
Arcangeli, A.   46
Argauer, R.   235
Armfield, M.   87
Artemidoros von
  Daldis   250
Ashton, F.   167, 180, 184–185
Atesci, M.   230
Auden, W. H.   102–104, 193
Aumüller, B.   222, 225
Austen, J.   38
Awasthi, S.   127

Bachmann, S.   274
Baert, L.   18, 24, 44
Balanchine, G.   180, 185
Baldwin, P.   150
Baldwin, S.   104
Barba, E.   131
Barbaja, D.   223
Bary, L.   126
Bassell, J.   274
Bayes, H.   145
Bazinger, I.   201, 206
Bebel, A.   207
Becker, C. H.   101–102
Beckinsale, K.   55–56

Beethoven, L. van   275
Behrendt, B.   206–207
Béjart, M.   67, 83–84
Bell, A.   108
Belle, M.-A.   273
Belosselski, D.   222
Belsey, C.   286
Bendall, S.   50
Bennett, S.   34–35, 39
Beretti, F.   68, 84
Berger, D.   233
Berger, D. A.   180
Bergman, I.   153
Bergson, H.   214
Berio, F. M.   224
Berlioz, H.   84
Berns, U.   201–203
Best, E.   55
Beu, T.   215
Bharata 125
Bharucha, R.   128
Bieito, C.   202–203
Bigonzetti, M.   83–84
Billington, M.   149–150
Bilmen, M.   232–234
Birksted-Breen, N.   145
Blomberg, B. von 234
Blunden, E.   108
Boecker, B.   238–244
Boiardo, M. M.   265
Boito, A.   202
Boleyn, A.   165
Boltz, I.   281–285
Bond, E.   248
Boorde, A.   250
Booth, J. W.   266
Bösch, D.   216
Bourguignon, E.   112
Bourne, C. M. L.   269
Boutcher, W.   273
Bouzkova, E.   276
Bowd, G.   100
Boyens, B.   221
Boyes, G.   86, 91, 93, 109
Brachmann, J.   221

Bradley, A. C.   67
Bradshaw, D.   103
Brainard, I.   23–24
Bramwell, A.   86, 90, 92
Branagh, K.   55, 166, 207
Brandon, J. C.   118
Braun, B.   213–215
Braunmuller, A. R.   116
Brecht, B.   234
Breiner, B.   76, 84
Breuer, H.   94
Breyvogel, T.   227
Briest, S.   208–219
Bright, T.   250
Brissenden, A.   28, 31, 35, 40,
  43–44, 48
Bronfen, E.   164, 228, 262–
  263, 274
Brook, P.   142, 228, 281
Brooke, A.   80
Brooke, R.   92
Brown, J. R.   132, 139
Browne, E. M.   105, 108
Brückner, D.   233
Bruhn, J.   183
Bruno, E.   195
Bryant, A.   87
Buchan, J.   99
Buchanan, J.   192
Buckley, T.   124–140
Bührle, I. J.   65–84, 168–169,
  172, 276–278
Bulman, J. C.   13, 21
Burbage, R.   188, 268
Butler, F.   59
Butler, M.   36
Button, C.   99
Byrd, W.   85

Cain, J.   86
Campana, J.   163
Camus, A.   204, 218
Cappelle, L.   149
Carletti, A.   224
Carlson, M.   253
Caroso, F.   17, 29

Carpenter, S.   49, 52–54, 60–61
Cartelli, T.   248–250
Carter, A.   120–121
Castiglione, B.   62
Cavanaugh, S. T.   142
Cavell, S.   255, 262
Cavendish, D.   145
Caxton, W.   265
Celan, P.   218
Chamberlain, N.   102, 105
Chambers, E. K.   31, 49
Chapman, M. A.   51
Charry, B.   260
Chaucer, G.   264–265
Chettle, H.   252
Chevrier-Bosseau, A.   163
Cinpoeş, N.   253
Clark, M.   39
Clayton, J.   235
Clegg, R.   15, 34, 48
Clinton, B.   266
Cobb, C.   166
Cobb, C. J.   164
Coeffeteau, N.   250
Cohen, W.   104, 177
Collingridge, A.   101
Collins-Hughes, L.   157
Compasso, L.   18
Cooper, H.   165
Corrsin, S.   89
Craig, H.   269
Craine, D.   188
Crane, R.   43–44
Cranko, J.   71, 73–74, 82, 84, 169, 180, 185, 192
Crosbie, C.   247–248
Crowley, B.   181, 185–186, 188, 192
Crystal, B.   177
Crystal, D.   177
Cunneen, P.   143
Cutchins, D.   182
Cuthbertson, L.   185, 188

Daborne, R.   268
Dalcroze, É.   92
Danson, L.   166
Dante Alighieri   224
Darré, W.   107, 109
Daugherty, D.   118
Davidson, P.   61
Davies, E.   144
Daye, A.   15, 33, 36, 49, 60
Deecke, K.   235–236
Defoe, D.   218
Dekker, T.   259–260
Del Sapio Garbero, M.   165
Delaveney, E.   85
Denhoven, J.   211
Dercon, C.   234
Derrida, J.   255, 264
Dessen, A.   20, 28, 49
Deutschmann, M. L.   227
Diaghilev, S.   181
Dillon de Byington, D.   201
Dillon, J.   49, 52–53
Dinshaw, C.   265
Djurkov Hotter, A.   233
Dobson, M.   186, 252–253
Dolan, F. E.   259, 261
Donnellan, D.   141–161
Doran, G.   195
Dorsen, A.   249
Dowd, M. M.   259–260
Dowden, E.   164
Ducis, J.-F.   69
Dulac, A.-V.   148, 150–152
Dürrenmatt, F.   234
Duse, R.   70

Edward de Vere, Earl of Oxford   284
Edward III., König von England   52
Edwards, C.   55
Eggert, K.   165
Egli-Schmidt, A.   277
Eisenmann, M.   275, 278

El Guindy, H.   119
Eliot, T. S.   98, 105, 108, 117
Elizabeth I., Königin von England   16–17, 57, 61, 165, 269
Elizabeth Stuart   31
Emmerich, R.   284
Enderwitz, A.   258–261, 278
Estill, L.   269
Evans, G. B.   151

Fabiszak, J.   146, 157–158, 252–254
Fallows, D.   48
Fantin, P.   223
Faulkner, T.   225
Fayard, N.   141
Federici, S.   212
Feldmann, D.   266–267
Feller, M.   233
Finger, V.   279
Folkerth, W.   160
Forker, C.   21
Foulkes, R.   195
Fowler, D.   97
Frenk, J.   250–252
Fretz, C.   250–252
Friedrich V., Kurfürst von der Pfalz   31
Friedson, S. M.   112
Friend, R. C.   114
Frigerio, E.   73
Fuller, D.   170–171, 173, 175, 178

Gade, S.   248
Gaffoyne, J.   16
Gaida, A.   234
Gaigg, C.   229
Galke, R.   230
Gamboa, B.   260
Ganio, M.   82
Gardiner, R.   85–109
Gardner, L.   145
Garrick, D.   66
Gatiss, I.   17

George V., König des Vereinigten Königreichs von Großbritannien und Irland 105
George, Duke of Kent 104
Georgiadis, N. 73
Gerhard, G. 107
Gerstner, M. 228
Gheyn II., J. de 50–51
Gibińska, M. 252–254
Gibson, J. 143
Gielgud, J. 39
Glarner, K. 221, 223
Glitz, R. 248–250
Gmaj, M. 232
Goebbels, J. 85–86, 95–96, 101, 109
Goethe, J. W. von 99, 108, 274, 278
Golovnin, D. 222
Gonter, D. 213
Goorney, H. 108
Gosch, J. 227
Götsch, G. 95, 101, 105
Gounod, C. 76, 84
Gower, J. 264–265
Graham, M. 170, 191
Gramms, E. 282
Grant, R. 19
Grant, U. S. 266
Grawert, B. 201
Green, M. 93, 96
Greenaway, P. 39, 248
Greenblatt, S. 40, 104, 162, 177, 208, 213
Greene, R. 185, 189
Greiner, N. 232–237, 273
Greis, J. 201
Griffin, R. 103
Griffiths, R. 87, 101, 106
Grotberg, E. H. 119
Grund, S. 201
Grzegorzewska, M. 252–254
Gschwender, S. 202
Gsovsky, T. 76, 84
Günther, F. 212, 232, 281–285

Gurr, A. 22
Gutierrez, A. M. 61
Guy-Bray, S. 261

Ha, S. 279
Haberl, S. 16
Hacker, N. 229–231
Hadfield, A. 59
Halio, J. L. 253
Hall, E. 53
Hanson, E. 258–261
Harrell, T. 234–237
Harris, J. G. 265
Hartner, M. 256–258
Hassanzadeh-Javanian, M. 110–123
Heaney, S. 274
Heffernan, J. J. 255–256
Hegel, G. W. F. 255
Heidegger, M. 247–248
Hellman, J. 102
Heminges, J. 268
Hennessy, K. 256–258
Henry Frederick, Prince of Wales 17
Henry VIII., König von England 52–53, 165
Henry, R. 227–228
Henslowe, P. 268
Hering, M. 229
Herrin, J. 29, 55
Hesse, H. 90
Heydrich, R. 94
Heyl, C. 50
Heywood, T. 259–260, 269, 281
Hitler, A. 85–109, 270
Hoehne, M. 279
Höfele, A. 92
Hofmannsthal, H. von 85, 105
Holland, P. 270
Holmes, K. 61
Homem, R. Carvalho 274
Hopkins, J. B. 147–148, 155, 158

Horn, M. 231
Howard, S. 158
Hoydis, J. 279
Huang, A. 124
Huber, E. R. 116–117
Hurault, A., Sieur de Maisse 16–18
Hutcheon, L. 181–183, 197
Hutchinson, G. S. 99–100
Hytner, N. 180, 187

Ick, J. C. 130
Iñárritu, A. G. 263
Indu G. 132–133, 136–138
Ingwersen, S. 202
Innes, P. 165
Isenberg, N. 279
Ishiguro, K. 106
Ismail, H. 114, 122
Iyer, K. B. 137

Jackson, R. 278
Jackson, S. 229–230
Jakubaschk, R. 212–213
James I., König von England, Schottland und Irland 31, 38
Jefferies, M. 85, 92, 107
Jennings, L. 69–70, 186
Johanson, K. 260
Jones, I. 33, 38
Jones, S. 168
Jonson, B. 32–33, 38, 181
Jowett, J. 43–44, 59–61
Jünger, E. 99

Kampe, A. 222
Kane, E. 59
Kaplan, M. L. 165
Kashuba, I. 143
Kean, C. 195
Keith, W. J. 85
Kekez, S. 276
Keller, W. 263–266
Kellermann, J. 162–179, 277–279

Kemp, W.   48
Kennedy, D.   109
Kennedy, D.   124, 139–140
Kerl, B.   227
Kermode, F.   44
Kesting, J.   202–203
Khabari, M.   115
Kipling, R.   105–106
Kirwan, P.   142–143, 146, 149–150, 152–154
Kiséry, A.   269
Klata, J.   254
Kleine, P.   277
Klett, E.   48, 163, 168, 171, 173, 175, 178, 193
Knight, G. W.   104–105
Knowles, J.   49
Knutson, R. L.   269–270
Kober, A.   202
Kocevski, B.   204
Koch, R.   230–231
König, D.   229–230
König, F.   276
Kantorowicz, E.   215
Kooshki, M.   110
Korda, N.   259
Kott, J.   232
Kottman, P.   255
Kovalevska, M.   202
Krebs, K.   182
Kreibich, M.   201
Krockel, C.   90
Krug, C.   256
Kusej, M.   228–229
Kuttoor, R.   125
Kyle, J.   155

Laban, R.   90, 96
Lahlou, N.   257
Lamb, M. E.   164
Lambert, C.   84
Lammers, L.   203–208, 278
Lammert, N.   218
LaMothe, K.   13
Laqueur, W.   93
Larkin, P.   274

Laudenbach, P.   201, 207
Laufenberg, L.   227
Lauritano, K.   225
Lawrence, D. H.   85–90, 95–96, 99, 105
Lawrowski, L.   70, 72, 75, 77, 84
Lazar, H.-J.   223, 225
Lebow, T.   223–225
Ledger, A. J.   141
Legris, M.   71
Lei, B.-q. B.   124, 130
Leigh Foster, S.   168–169
Leitch, T.   182
LeMoign, C.   233
Lepecki, A.   33
Lerchenmüller, J.   109
Lewinsky, M.   267
Ley, R.   91
Lichtenberg, D.   146, 153–154, 158, 160
Liesau, S.   207
Limon, J.   252–254
Lincoln, A.   266
Lindley, D.   31–32, 41, 43–44
Lindner, M.   227
Littlewood, J.   108
Litvin, M.   256–258
Liu, S.   132
Long, J. H.   45
Lope de Vega   68
Lösche, F.   201
Löser, C.   205
Loudières, M.   71
Loughnane, R.   258–261
Louppe, L.   170
Low, C.   113
Lowthorp, L. K.   125, 127, 129
Luserke, M.   103
Lyly, J.   46, 251
Lyne, R.   78

Mackrell, J.   187–188
MacMillan, K.   73–74, 81–82, 84, 167, 180, 184–185, 196
Macrae, S.   56

Macrobius   250
Madhavan, A.   125
Madhu, M.   124–140
Maercker, L.   94
Maestri, A.   202
Maeyer, T. de   214
Magnusson, K.   220
Mahler, A.   273
Mallarmé, S.   181
Mallin, E. S.   262–263
Mann, T.   273
Marcsek-Fuchs, M.   174, 180–197, 278–279
Marcuse, H.   107
Mares, F. H.   27, 34
Marescalchi, L.   84
Marie, L.   69
Marino, J. J.   268
Marks, P.   145, 160
Marlowe, C.   274
Marowitz, C.   283
Marsh, C.   25
Marston, C.   39
Martin, P.   229
Martinez, M. L.   50
Mary, K.   207
Mason, D.   129
Massai, S.   269
Masten, J.   260
Matless, D.   106
Maus, K. Eisaman   104
Mayer, B. M.   249
Maynes, E. S.   93
Mazzio, C.   259–260
McCulloch, L.   15, 31–46, 48, 60, 66, 141–142, 156, 168, 185, 193, 276
McDonald, R.   171
McEachern, C.   17, 19, 25, 28
McGowan, M. M.   33
McInnis, D.   270
McJannet, L.   141–161
McManus, C.   38, 60
Mee, E. B.   132
Meftahi, I.   121
Melchiori, G.   15

Mendelssohn Bartholdy, F. 141
Mercier, L.-S. 69
Messing, S. D. 113
Meyer, B. 201
Meyerhoff, J. 230
Meyerhold, W. 214
Michael, T. 223, 226
Michieletto, D. 220, 224–226
Middleton, T. 59–60, 72, 281
Miehe, J. 277
Milton, J. 286
Mirabella, B. 61
Mirzai, B. A. 114
Mitchell, M. 274
Mohanty, S. 126
Monahin, N. 15, 33, 47, 54, 141
Montagut, B. de 48
Moore-Colyer, R. 94, 98, 102, 107
Morgese, J. 55–56
Morris, M. 70
Morris, T. 103
Morrison, S. 69, 71
Mosch, J. 208–219
Mowat, B. 48
Mpaka, C. 227
Muck-Lamberty, F. 93
Mullally, R. 20, 23
Müller, H. 201, 232–233, 248
Mulready, C. 162, 167
Munro, L. 268
Murry, J. M. 95
Muscionico, D. 234–236
Mussolini, B. 87, 100

Naeimi, H. 110
Narayanan, E. N. 135
Narayanan, M. 127
Nashe, T. 250
Natvig, R. J. 114
Negri, C. 17
Nehmiz, J. 235, 236
Neil, A. S. 92

Neill, M. 143–144, 160
Neumeier, J. 66–77, 169, 277
Nevile, J. 15, 33, 47
Neyra, J. R. 76
Nielsen, A. 248
Niemeyer, C. 232
Nijinska, B. 69, 84
Niles, R. 48
Nilsson, J. 117
Nolan, C. 263
Noverre, J.-G. 65–67, 83, 189
Nübling, S. 228–231
Nurejew, R. 71–78, 80–82, 84, 163, 277
Nye, E. 65
Nyman, M. 39

O'Brien, E. 261
O'Connell, M. 165
Obens, D. 224
Oberländer, T. 86
Olk, C. 273–277
Ong, K. S. 127
Orgel, S. 31–32, 36–37, 44
Ormerod, N. 142–143, 153–154
Oschatz, J. 106
Ostarhild, B. 89
Ostermeier, T. 203
Ovid 177, 263–266

Pagano, M. 74
Pagels, P. 276, 278
Pahl, M. 233
Palfrey, S. 162
Palucca, G. 191
Parr, P. 252–254
Parry, J. 82
Parsons, E. 185, 187
Paul, L. 96
Paulose, K. G. 129
Pauly, K. 206
Pavis, P. 126, 253–254
Payne, I. 23, 48
Penny, L. 212

Pennyman, J. 94, 98–102, 104–106
Pennyman, R. 98–101, 103–106
Perceval, L. 254
Persson, J. 146, 153, 155
Pesyani, A. 110
Petrina, A. 273
Petruccelli, M. 223
Pfister, M. 253
Phillips, L. J. 50
Piacenza, D. da 19
Piccinni, D. 69
Pitcher, J. 180
Pite, C. 163
Pitt-Rivers, M. 89
Plato 255
Playford, J. 23–24, 47
Poirée, C. 19
Polhemus, T. 121
Poshtkoohi, E. 110–123
Poston, M. 48
Pound, E. 99–100
Pourjafar, M. 115
Praml, J. 209–212
Preiss, R. 268–269
Preljocaj, A. 83–84
Prescott, P. 145, 151
Previati, G. 224
Prokofjew, S. 69–75, 77, 82, 84, 141, 277
Pronko, L. C. 118
Prynne, W. 24
Puccini, G. 156
Pugh, M. 107
Putin, V. 158

Quatrini, S. 220, 226

Rabes, A. 202
Rabsch, T. 210
Raja, K. K. 126, 134, 136
Rajewsky, I. 182
Ramsey, J. 23–24
Ravelhofer, B. 13–30, 33, 44, 48–49, 276

Reichert, K.   274
Reid, L. A.   263–266
Reinecke, R.   207
Reyher, P.   49
Richter, E.   202
Riemer, J.   212
Risen, E. L.   59
Rittmeyer, L.   233
Rizzi, R.   252
Roberts, P. B.   147–148, 155–156, 158
Robespierre, M.   213
Rodgers, A.   141
Ronzi, G.   69, 84
Rose, J.   73
Rose, T.   227
Rossini, G.   220, 223–224
Rothe, H.   92
Rourke, J.   56
Rudolph, B.   276
Runcie, C.   142

Sablon, J.   152
Sadeghi Esfahani, M.   110
Saedi, G.-H.   112
Sanders, J.   184, 260–261
Sandrock, K.   278–279
Santucci, E.   18–19
Sarhan, S.   113–114
Sathyendran, N.   129, 139
Saunders, J.   101
Saunders, V.   131
Savarese, N.   131
Savenberg, S.   201
Scala, E.   223, 225
Scarlatti, A.   235
Schanelec, A.   227
Schechner, R.   127
Scherff, M.   227
Scherzer, B.   83–84
Schiller, F.   278
Schilling, T.   83–84
Schindler, K. M.   278
Schlaeger, J.   94–96, 107
Schlegel, A. W.   278, 283
Schlierkamp, C.   277

Schlotterer, W.   212
Schmais, C.   119
Schmidt, A. M.   233–234
Schmidt, G.   273
Schnauder, L.   227–231
Schneckenburger, S.   278
Schneider, K.   235–236
Schober, R.   182–183
Scholz, S.   276
Schormann, V.   278
Schostakowitsch, D.   220, 223
Schreiber, S.   212
Schülting, S.   252–254, 286
Schwertes, H.   109
Searle, H.   77
Seidler, U.   206
Semple, E.   258–261
Shahbazi, A. S.   114
Shakespeare, W.
    All's Well that Ends Well   15
    Antony and Cleopatra   21, 251
    As You Like It   63, 143, 210
    Coriolanus   14–15, 30, 102, 247
    Cymbeline   131, 143, 164, 186, 251
    Hamlet   87–88, 96, 105, 109, 126, 201–202, 203, 206–208, 220, 227–228, 247–248, 249, 251, 254, 255–256, 257, 262, 275, 277, 282
    Henry IV   13–14, 21–22, 30, 202, 251
    Henry V   17, 22, 105–106
    Henry VI   216, 251
    Henry VIII   53–54
    Julius Caesar   251, 266
    King Lear   13, 110, 118, 208, 213–216, 248, 251, 257, 274–275
    Love's Labour's Lost   20–21, 49, 51, 53–54, 57–59, 62–64, 269, 283
    Macbeth   110–123, 124–140, 219–223, 227, 251, 254, 255–256, 266–267, 274
    Measure for Measure   141–161, 205, 208, 212–213
    The Merchant of Venice   63, 212, 228–231
    The Merry Wives of Windsor   15, 17, 63, 202–203, 260, 268
    A Midsummer Night's Dream   141–142, 158, 163, 167, 180, 184, 247–248, 251, 257, 264, 274, 281
    Much Ado About Nothing   17, 19, 23, 25–30, 34, 42, 49, 53–57, 62–64, 131, 281
    Othello   57, 110–111, 127, 165, 171, 186, 196, 205, 219–220, 223–226, 228–231, 255–256, 266
    Pericles   141–161, 164, 251, 264
    The Rape of Lucrece   264–265
    Richard II   13, 21, 253
    Richard III   22, 110, 118, 172, 203, 251
    Romeo and Juliet   53, 65–84, 105, 110, 118, 141, 163, 167, 172, 180, 184–186, 196, 203–204, 216, 234–237, 255, 262, 264, 275–276, 277–279, 282
    Sir Thomas More   260, 284
    The Sonnets   13, 255, 281

REGISTER · 295

The Taming of the Shrew 42, 110, 163, 180, 220, 251, 257, 264
The Tempest 15, 31–44, 49, 108, 143–144, 163–164, 248, 251, 255–256, 262–263
Timon of Athens 49, 53–54, 59–64
Titus Andronicus 232–234, 249, 262
Troilus and Cressida 264
Twelfth Night 19, 63, 205, 209–212, 216, 257, 264–265
The Two Gentlemen of Verona 264
The Two Noble Kinsmen 164, 264
The Winter's Tale 48, 57, 103–105, 131, 141–161, 162–179, 180–197, 248, 251, 262, 275–276
Shannon, L. 113
Shapiro, J. 266–267
Shaw, B. 15, 34, 46, 48, 60, 66, 142, 156, 168, 185
Shevtsova, M. 253
Shulman, D. 125–126
Shuttleworth, I. 149
Sidney, P. 265
Sierz, A. 142–143, 145
Simons, J. 275
Skewes, A. 50
Sławek, T. 253
Smith, B. 143
Smith, A. W. 19
Smith, J. 17
Soden, O. 97, 106
Soko, B. 113
Sokolova, B. 253
Spinoza, B. 255
Sprang, F. 219–226, 278
Springer, J. 155
Stachowiak, R. 201

Stalin, J. W. 70
Stampbach, T. 233
Stanhope, J. 16
Starks, M. 234
Stasková, A. 278
Steckel, F.-P. 201
Steckel, J. 201–202
Steggle, M. 269
Steiner, R. 90
Stemann, N. 234
Stephens, P. 90
Stern, T. 267–270
Sternburg, J. von 221–222, 224–226
Steveker, L. 267–270
Stevens, A. R. 52
Stevenson, J. 61
Stewart, I. J. 112
Stockinger, M.-L. 230
Stokes, J. 23–24
Stokowski, M. 212
Stone, D. 86, 95–96, 107
Stoppard, T. 252, 282
Stow, J. 23
Strahle, G. 19
Strauch, M. 214
Strauss, L. 255
Streatfield, G. 196
Strunk, N. 227
Stubbes, J. 24
Sullivan, B. 129, 131, 139
Švēde, Z. 223
Svolikova, M. 216
Swanson, J. 223, 225
Swarbrick, S. 174–175
Syme, H. S. 268
Szőnyi, G. E. 253

Tafreshian, A. 207
Talbot, J. 163, 168, 181, 185–188, 190
Tate, C. 56
Taylor, G. 13, 72
Tennant, D. 56
Terry, E. 195

Teti, C. 224
Thompson, A. 42
Thompson, E. 55
Thomson, L. 49
Thorp, J. 23
Thurlow, R. 100
Thurner, C. 168
Timm, I. 211
Tippett, M. 106
Tiran, I. 229–230
Toepfer, A. 93–96, 107–109
Trachternach, D. 209–210
Treneman, A. 149–150
Treuheit, N. 281
Trevien, K. 143
Tritto, G. 69
Trivedi, P. 126, 130
Tronicke, M. 279
Trump, D. 233, 266–267
Tschaikowski, P. I. 144, 168
Tuberville, G. 265
Tuckwell, S. 208–219
Twist, B. 191
Twycross, M. 49, 52–54, 60–61
Tyldesley, M. 85

Uhiara, O. 55–56
Uriot, J. 66

Valéry, P. 181
Van Breen, G. 51
van Hove, I. 249
Vaughan, A. T. 32, 38
Vaughan, V. Mason 32, 51–52
Ven-ten Bensel, E. van der 90–91, 108
Venu, G. 125, 127, 130
Verdi, G. 196, 202, 223–224
Villiers, G. 48
Voigt, L. 213–216
Voigts, E. 182, 184
Von der Aue, D. 16
Voss, G. 230

Wagner, R.   205
Walkington, T.   250
Wall, W.   259
Wallmeier, F.   206
Wallop, G.   106
Wall-Randell, S.   269
Warburton, W.   44
Ward, J.   23
Warndorf, H.   281
Watson, E.   163, 185, 187, 196
Wayne, V.   164
Weber, A.   220–223
Wehlisch, K.   204
Weidle, R.   208–219, 275
Weigle, S.   220–221
Weinstein, H.   212, 267
Weise, C.   206–208
Weise, K.   201
Weiße, C. F.   69
Wells, S.   13, 72, 79–80, 130, 186, 253
Welsford, E.   49, 93
Wenning, M.   238–244

Werstine, P.   48
West, M.   42
Wetmore, K. J.   132
Whedon, J.   55–56
Wheeldon, C.   162–179, 180–197
Whipday, E.   261
White, B.-S.   113
White, R. S.   165
Wigman, M.   92, 191
Williams, S.   55
Williamson, H.   108
Willing, J.   208–219
Willoughby, J.   23
Wilson, D. R.   23–24
Wilson, R.   85–109, 276
Winerock, E.   15, 33, 46–64, 156, 276
Winship, L.   180
Wisbach, J.   234
Woitas, M.   276–278
Wolf, W.   182
Wolfram, R.   109
Woods, G.   67, 166

Woudhuysen, H. R.   20–21
Wright, C.   276, 278
Wright, K. C.   142
Wright, L. J.   33
Wright, P.   85 107
Wright, T.   250
Wronas, I.   234

Yanowsky, Z.   188
Yeats, W. B.   181
Yong, L. L.   124, 126–127, 130, 139–140

Zadek, P.   230
Zadow, I.   von 220
Zaitchik, D.   235
Zarei, K.   115
Zaworka, G.   227
Zeffirelli, F.   81
Zimring, R.   89
Zirker, A.   278
Žižek, S.   255
Żukowska, A.   252–254
Zweiniger-Bargielowska, I. 99–100

Zu den Autor*innen der Aufsätze

Thea Buckley is a Leverhulme Early Career Fellow at Queen's University Belfast, where she is mentored by Professor Mark Burnett on her project "South Indian Shakespeares: Reimagining Art Forms and Identities". She has previously worked for the Shakespeare Institute, RSC, Shakespeare Birthplace Trust, British Library, and with the BFI while co-chairing "Indian Shakespeares on Screen", 2016. She has published essays on Shakespeare across the subcontinent in *A Year of Shakespeare* (Arden, 2013), *Shakespeare and Indian Cinemas* (Routledge, 2019), *Cahiers Élisabéthains, Multicultural Shakespeare, Shakespeare Institute Review* (co-editor) and *Birmingham Journal of Language and Literature*.

Iris Julia Bührle hat in Stuttgart, Paris und Oxford Allgemeine und Vergleichende Literaturwissenschaft, Kunstgeschichte und Internationale Beziehungen studiert. Ihre binationale Dissertation (Paris/Stuttgart) mit dem Titel *Literatur und Tanz: Die choreographische Adaptation literarischer Werke in Deutschland und Frankreich vom 18. Jahrhundert bis heute* ist 2014 bei Königshausen & Neumann erschienen. Sie arbeitet unter anderem als Tanzjournalistin und publizierte 2011 eine deutsch-englische Biographie des Tänzers Robert Tewsley. Im Anschluss an ein Leverhulme Early Career Fellowship an der Englischfakultät der Universität Oxford und ein Junior Research Fellowship am New College (2015–2018) schreibt sie derzeit die erste globale Geschichte der Ballettadaptationen von Shakespeares Werken.

Mohammadreza Hassanzadeh Javanian holds a PhD in English Language and Literature from the University of Tehran, Iran. Currently, he is a lecturer at the University of Tehran. Javanian teaches courses on literary movements, Renaissance and contemporary drama. His main research interests include drama, adaptation studies, comparative literature and media studies. Most of his publications investigate Shakespearean adaptations in the theoretical framework set by Russian philosopher and literary critic Mikhail Bakhtin. Recently, he has concentrated on Shakespeare's adaptations in Iran and their position within the country's social, cultural and political contexts.

Jonas Kellermann ist Dozent und wissenschaftlicher Mitarbeiter für Englische Literatur am Fachbereich Literatur-, Kunst- und Medienwissenschaften der Universität Konstanz. Nach seinem Bachelor- und Master-Studium an der Freien Universität Berlin und der University of Edinburgh wurde er 2020 in Konstanz mit einer Arbeit zur Darstellung von Liebe in dramatischen, musikalischen und choreographischen Adaptionen des *Romeo und Julia*-Sujets promoviert. Die Veröffentlichung der Dissertation ist aktuell in Vorbereitung. Seine Masterarbeit wurde mit dem Martin-Lehnert-Preis der Deutschen Shakespeare-Stiftung ausgezeichnet. Neben der Frühen Neuzeit befasst sich seine Forschung mit dem anglophonen Roman des 20. und 21. Jahrhunderts. Seine Essays sind unter anderem in *Cahiers Élisabéthains* erschienen.

Maria Marcsek-Fuchs ist wissenschaftliche Mitarbeiterin am Institut für Anglistik und Amerikanistik der Technischen Universität Braunschweig. Ihre Forschung konzentriert sich auf Shakespeare Adaptionen, Intermedialitäts- und Adaptionstheorien, Shakespeare und Transmedia Storytelling sowie New Writing. Ihre Publikationen umfassen die Monographie *Dance and British Literature: An Intermedial Encounter (Theory – Typology – Case Studies)* (Rodopi/Brill, 2015) sowie Aufsätze zu ihren Forschungsschwerpunkten. Durch ihre zusätzlichen Qualifikationen als Diplomchoreographin (Palucca Schule Dresden, Hochschule für Tanz) und im Fach Bühnentanz (Joffrey Ballet School, New York) sowie durch ihre Tätigkeiten als Regisseurin sind im Rahmen von Kulturprojekten am Campus (TUBS-Players, Tanz-Sport-Theater) etliche Shakespeare Produktionen entstanden. In ihrem Habilitationsprojekt beschäftigt sie sich mit *Postmodern Shakespeare(s)*.

Lynsey McCulloch is Assistant Professor of English Literature and an Associate Member of the Centre for Dance Research (C-DaRE) at Coventry University in the UK. Her research interests include memorial cultures, the reception and adaptation of Shakespeare's plays, and the relationship between dance and literature. She recently edited *The Oxford Handbook of Shakespeare and Dance* with Brandon Shaw (OUP, 2019) and is currently working on a monograph on reading dance in the works of Shakespeare and his contemporaries.

Linda McJannet is Professor of English and Media Studies (Emerita) at Bentley University, Waltham, MA, USA. She is the author of two monographs, *The Sultan Speaks: Dialogue in English Plays and Histories about the Ottoman Turks* (Palgrave Macmillan, 2006) and *The Voice of English Stage Directions: The Evolution of a Theatrical Code* (University of Delaware Press, 1998). Her articles have appeared in *Shakespeare Quarterly*, *The Huntington Library Quarterly*, *English Literary Renaissance*, *Borrowers and Lenders* and *Dance Chronicle*, among others. She has contributed chapters on physical theatre and Shakespeare to *The Oxford Handbook of Shakespeare and Dance* and *Shakespeare On Stage and Off* (both in 2019). In 2013, with Emily Winerock and Amy Rodgers, she co-founded the Shakespeare and Dance Project (www.shakespeareandance.com).

Barbara Ravelhofer is Professor in Renaissance Studies in the Department of English, Durham University. She specializes in forms of early modern literature, dance and drama, and has also published on European spectacle, editing and late medieval literature. Her book publications include an edition of the French dance treatise *Louange de la danse* (CUP, 2000) and *The Early Stuart Masque: Dance, Costume, and Music* (OUP, 2006). She is currently working on a study of seventeenth-century iconoclasm and leading a project on "Records of Early English Drama in the North East of England".

Richard Wilson is Sir Peter Hall Professor Emeritus of Shakespeare Studies at Kingston University. His books include *Worldly Shakespeare: The Theatre of Our Good Will* (Edinburgh UP, 2016), *Shakespeare and Continental Philosophy* (Edinburgh UP, 2014), *Free Will: Art and Power on Shakespeare's Stage* (Manchester UP, 2013), *Shakespeare in French Theory* (Routledge, 2007), *Secret Shakespeare: Studies in Theatre, Religion and Resistance* (Manchester UP, 2004), and *Will Power: Essays on Shakespearean authority* (Harvester Wheatsheaf, 1993). He is currently completing *Modern Friends: Shakespeare's Fascist Followers*.

Emily Winerock is a co-founder of the Shakespeare and Dance Project (https://shakespeareandance.com/) and a visiting scholar at the University of Pittsburgh. Her publications include chapters in *The Oxford Handbook of Shakespeare and Dance* (OUP, 2019), *The Oxford Handbook of Dance and Competition* (OUP, 2018), *Playthings in Early Modernity* (Medieval Institute Publications, 2017), *The Sacralization of Space and Behavior in the Early Modern World* (Ashgate, 2015) and *Worth and Repute: Valuing Gender in Late Medieval and Early Modern Europe* (Centre for Reformation and Renaissance Studies, 2011). A scholar-practitioner, she also teaches Renaissance dance workshops and choreographs for theatrical productions.

Martin-Lehnert Preis

Mit diesem Preis, den die Deutsche Shakespeare-Gesellschaft vergibt, werden Studierende bzw. junge Wissenschaftlerinnen und Wissenschaftler ausgezeichnet, die sich in herausragender Weise mit Werk und Wirkung William Shakespeares, seiner Zeitgenossen oder mit der Kultur der Shakespeare-Zeit, ihrer Rezeption und/oder Vermittlung beschäftigt haben.

Der Preis wird jährlich verliehen für eine herausragende Abschlussarbeit (Magister, Master, Staatsexamen), eine Dissertation oder ein dokumentiertes studentisches Projekt (Theaterinszenierung, Ausstellung, etc.). Das Preisgeld beträgt für eine Dissertation 2.000 €, für eine Abschlussarbeit 500 € sowie für ein studentisches Projekt 500 €. Der Preis wendet sich insbesondere an die Fachbereiche Anglistik, Germanistik und Theaterwissenschaften.

Nominiert werden können deutsch- oder englischsprachige Arbeiten, die an Hochschulen in Deutschland, Österreich oder der Schweiz verfasst bzw. eingereicht wurden. Arbeiten, die an Hochschulen im nichtdeutschsprachigen Ausland von jungen Wissenschaftler(innen) aus Deutschland, Österreich oder der Schweiz erstellt worden sind, können in der Regel ebenfalls vorgeschlagen werden. Vorschlagsberechtigt sind die wissenschaftlichen Betreuer(innen) der jeweiligen Arbeit.

Die Verleihung des Martin-Lehnert-Preises findet jeweils im Rahmen der Frühjahrstagung der Deutschen Shakespeare-Gesellschaft statt.

Vorgeschlagene Arbeiten (aus dem laufenden Jahr oder den beiden Vorjahren) können in zwei Exemplaren und unter Beifügung eines Gutachtens formlos bis zum 15. Dezember an die Deutsche Shakespeare-Gesellschaft eingereicht werden. Wir bitten um Einreichung in elektronischer Form; eine Einreichung in Papierform ist nicht nötig, aber auch möglich. Bitte senden Sie die Unterlagen an die

Deutsche Shakespeare-Gesellschaft e. V.
Frau Rudolph
Windischenstraße 4–6
99423 Weimar
office@shakespeare-gesellschaft.de

All the SONNETS of SHAKESPEARE

Edited by Paul Edmondson and Stanley Wells

'What a fresh and lovely idea! I've been speaking the sonnets for most of my life. They are such wonderful training for an actor, and the notes and paraphrases in this book are just what we all need to guide us through them.'

JUDI DENCH

September 2020 | Hardback | 9781108490399 | £12.99 | $17.95 | €15.16

www.cambridge.org /sonnets

CAMBRIDGE UNIVERSITY PRESS